Catholic and French Forever

THE PENNSYLVANIA STATE UNIVERSITY PRESS   UNIVERSITY PARK, PENNSYLVANIA

JOSEPH F. BYRNES

Catholic and French Forever

RELIGIOUS AND NATIONAL IDENTITY IN MODERN FRANCE

Library of Congress Cataloging-in-Publication Data

Byrnes, Joseph F., 1939–
    Catholic and French forever : religious and
    national identity in modern France / Joseph F.
    Byrnes.
       p.   cm.
Includes bibliographical references and index.
ISBN 0-271-02704-5 (alk. paper)
1. Church and state—France—History—19th century.
2. Church and state—Catholic Church—History—
19th century.
3. France—Church history—19th century.
4. Catholic Church—France—History—19th century.
5. Church and state—France—History—20th century.
6. Church and state—Catholic Church—History—
20th century.
7. France—Church history—20th century.
8. Catholic Church—France—History—20th century.
I. Title.

BX1530 .B97 2005
322'.1'0944—dc22
2005011290

The Pennsylvania State University Press is a member
of the Association of American University Presses.

It is the policy of The Pennsylvania State University
Press to use acid-free paper. This book is printed on
Natures Natural, containing 50% post-consumer
waste, and meets the minimum requirements of
American National Standard for Information
Sciences—Permanence of Paper for Printed Library
Materials, ANSI Z39.48–1992.

For GHISLAIN LAFONT, O.S.B.

Contents

Preface

For years now, I have been studying, pondering, puzzling about the role religion has played in French national life since the Revolution of 1789—for personal as well as intellectual reasons. As a kid, I knew that the Catholicism of my Irish-American—and I should add New England—youth was basically a French product. The formation of my parish priests was European (usually French) or their American seminary professors were Sulpician. And, of course, the missionary bishops to the New World were primarily French. Both missionary and monastic orders originated in France or French Canada. Church devotions came from French saints, too: Sacred Heart (from the vision experience of St. Marguerite-Marie Alacoque), Our Lady of LaSalette, and St. Thérèse of Lisieux. In addition, the great liturgical reform of the 1960s was the direct result of French experiments after World War II. Roman Catholic we called ourselves, but French Catholic we were. God may not have been French, but the church was.

It was as a frenchified Irish-American Catholic that I entered the seminary and was ordained in the turbulent 1960s. My religious community had been established by a eighteenth-century itinerant preacher from northwest France, Louis Grignion de Montfort, remembered for his evangelical energy and single-mindedness, his devotional style (labeled Bérullian, after the French cardinal of the 1600s who combined intense mysticism with graphic evocation of Christ's life), and the apparent lasting results of his mission to the Vendée (the region most resistant to dechristianization during the Revolution). Summers from 1962 through 1966 were spent in pursuit of a master's degree in liturgical research at the University of Notre Dame, established by another French congregation, the Holy Cross Fathers. This was my first opportunity for immersion in properly historical research and consequently in Latin texts and, often, French secondary literature on the topic. By the time annual sojourns in South Bend came to an end, I was moving about early modern Europe so to better know the Council of Trent.

Graduate work at the University of Chicago set the foundation for a career in modern European history with a predilection for the social sciences. A theme at that time was "popular religion," which we tried to isolate from formal or elitist religious thinking and practice (later deciding that "local religion" was an easier label to use). I was accordingly attracted to study the ways of pilgrimage, attended to by both historians and anthropologists, having myself visited both Paray-le-Monial, site of the Sacred Heart apparitions, and Chartres, the medieval cathedral shrine of the Blessed Virgin. In the end, I chose Chartres, wanting to do more history and less anthropology. The idea was to study the influence (I prefer the French *rayonnement*) of Chartres as a spiritual and cultural center, but I narrowed my dissertation focus to the role of Chartres cathedral in the personal and intellectual life of one man: Henry Adams of *Mont-Saint-Michel and Chartres* fame. Along the way, I arranged to spend a summer with the priests of the cathedral parish.

I may have learned as much about people, pilgrimage, and their religious ways during those long lunches and suppers with the Chartrian clergy as I did from my work in the seminary library and cathedral sacristy. I remember an old Breton priest, chaplain to one of the city's convents, who would recite with gusto the refrain of a song he remembered from his boyhood days, "Catholique et français toujours." A slight man, in poor health but of unfailing good humor, he loved to evoke those days when he and his large family were poor, quite happy together, and, well, thoroughly Catholic and thoroughly French. I have in a very *general* way traced the song to the early days of the Third Republic, with its government of moral order, and I have found only one example of such a song—in fact a pilgrimage song—in the Bibliothèque Nationale (*Cantique National,* Pèlerinage de Valfleury, 17 mai 1875 [St.-Chamond, 1875], Bibliothèque Nationale 4 YE Pièce 439). But I have worked out a series of "case studies" of the *specific* forms of the fraught relation between religious and national identity in France—across the nineteenth century and the first part of the twentieth century.

For my work I needed new and interesting archival opportunities in the French national and departmental archives as much as I needed dramatically revealing case studies. I tried to respond to both needs as I chose my topics: rebellious priests and imitation religious festivals during the Revolution, the high-profile religious and secular personalities of Chateaubriand and Destutt de Tracy across the revolutionary era and under the Napoleonic empire, pilgrimage in particular to Chartres cathedral across the nineteenth century; clerical concern for the non-French-speaking cultures of Alsace and the Roussillon during the Second Empire and early Third Republic, the face-off between priests and (often freethinking) schoolteachers in World War I, and the public influence of conciliatory historical and religious scholarship (the Sorbonne historian Émile Mâle) before and after war. As the work progressed, I began to see the contours of my three stages of development in the grass-roots church-state story: *divorce* of religion and nation, the devotional and social *defense* of an entrenched Catholicism against secularizing national governments, and *détente* between religiously enthusiastic and secularly nationalistic French citizens. The case histories may not always be the most dramatic possible, but they were among the most interesting archival challenges, and I promote them as optimally revealing dramas of religious and national identity in France.

Among my early inspirations, I signal especially the seminal works of two great contemporary historians: Eugen Weber for modern France, especially his *Peasants into Frenchmen: The Modernization of Rural France, 1870–1914,* and Natalie Zemon Davis, especially her *Society and Culture in Early Modern France: Eight Essays.* Weber ranged across a staggering number of archival sources to represent local voices and attitudes on such issues as regional languages ("A Wealth of Tongues"), town and country ("Rus in Urbe" and "Peasants and Politics"), religious practice and devotion ("Dieu est-il français" and "The Priests and the People"), and local celebrations ("The Way of All Feasts")— chapters aglow with life and color. Zemon Davis recreated the struggles across the Reformation and wars-of-religion eras by representing voices long ignored. I was impressed, too, by her pleasure in favorite French archives: she wrote, "The excitement of discovery is always associated for me with one of these settings—Mère Folle, for instance, with the beautiful eighteenth-century library at Dijon; the varied signatures of sixteenth-century artisans with the quiet reading room of the Archives du Rhône, high above the city of Lyon" (xi). On all my own research days, whether involving the excitement of discovery or not, I could take quiet pleasure in the old seminary library at Chartres, nondescript itself but overlooking the valley of the Eure River; in the archives of the wonderful departmental *chefs lieux* of Rouen, Grenoble, Perpignan, and Strasbourg (with the *Salle d'alsatiques,* then opposite the university library); in the distinguished Paris setting of the Bibliothèque de l'Institut de France, the simple plain rooms of the archives of the Archdiocese of Paris, and the library of the Centre National de Documentation Pédagogique (with those seedy cellar stocks of the century's textbooks). Then there was that rainy day on the outskirts of Rouen when I got out of my cab before the large, low, and desolate building that housed the Musée National de l'Éducation. The driver brightened everything when he looked over the whole sad scene and said, "Oh! ça fait du charme ça." He pulled away and I was ready for work. Along with all of my colleagues, I have lived through the changes across the years in the Archives Nationales and the Bibliothèque Nationale: from a new, open, and efficient researchers' hall in the Archives—closed for years now for a variety of structural maladies—to temporary locations in the BN and the Hôtel de Soubise; and from the wonderful old BN readers' room (the *Salle Labrouste*), more dysfunctional with each passing year, to the modern, mainly functional, colossus down on the Seine.

But now, hoping that readers will forgive the brief personal intrusion, I introduce my case studies of a vital people, some embracing and some dead set against the sentiments of the old song, addressed to Notre-Dame:

> *Garde au coeur des Français la foi des anciens jours*
> *Entends du haut du ciel le cri de la patrie*
> *Catholique et Français toujours*

Oklahoma City and Paris, 2005

Acknowledgments

Without the help of colleagues and friends, neither the individual case studies nor the integrated ensemble would have come to life. James Smith Allen, model teacher and scholar, and Peter J. Potter, the ever-insightful editor-in-chief of the Penn State University Press, have been my chief counselors. Weaknesses that remain in the text after such outstanding help are certainly my own.

Present and former colleagues at Oklahoma State University, especially Elizabeth Williams and Alain Saint-Saëns, were there to help me at several turning points. Bryant Reagan, Timothy Tackett, Bryan Skib, and Emmett Kennedy offered invaluable advice on matters revolutionary and festive; Thomas Kselman and Raymond Jonas, on pilgrimage in general; Pierre Bizeau and the late Joseph Lemarié, on Chartres in particular. In shaping my research in departmental archives, I obtained excellent counsel from Jean-Louis Engel and Anthony Steinhoff on Alsace, Eugène Cortade, Jean Palau, and Rosemary Wakeman on the Roussillon, and Judith Miller on Seine-Inférieure. Jean-Pierre Goehrs, that extraordinary guide to generations of Agrégé candidates, was my intellectual angel at the gates of Strasbourg. My vital debt here in matters catechetical is to Sarah Curtis and the late Joan Coffee. A chance meeting with Leonard Smith at the French army archives led to fundamental decisions on the World War I research, as well as contact with Annette Becker whose advice was crucial for my study of the clergy of that time. Crucial to my work on the *instituteurs* in that war was the advice of Alain Choppin of the Centre National de Documentation Pédagogique at Paris and Armelle Sentihles of the Musée National de l'Éducation at Mont-Saint-Aignan.

Gilberte Émile-Mâle guided me across a full range of resources on the life and work of her late father. Daniel Moulinet and Frank Thomas helped to focus and correct my interpretation; Thomas Kselman (yet again), to organize the presentation. Years ago, my old colleague and (back then) fellow *Montfortain,* Louis Pérouas made the trip to Chartres to help me sniff out some primary sources then sequestered in the cathedral sacristy. Louis has, of course, inspired two generations of archival historians to understand local religious practice and experience in France.

There is scarcely a project in this book that did not receive some financial assistance from the Oklahoma Humanities Council, directed by Anita Rasi May, known for her own studies of church, state, and education under the Second Empire. This assistance was supplemented by a travel grant from the National Endowment for the Humanities. Susan Oliver, supervising secretary of the OSU History Department, has processed every version of every chapter with competence and kindness.

Earlier versions of Chapters 2, 3, and 5 appeared in *Church History;* of Chapter 6, in *French Historical Studies;* and of Chapter 7, in *The Catholic Historical Review.* Permission to use this material is here gratefully acknowledged.

Across the years, since my departure from the University of Chicago, Martin Marty has sent along support, telling observations, and formal references that I tried to live up to rather than rest with. I thank him once again. He also introduced me to my fellow historian of France, Steven Englund, whose brilliant writing stands as a model of what the rest of us should be striving toward. The priests and staff of the Foyer St.-Jean Eudes offered me the hospitality that both enlivened and stabilized my recent Paris research trips. And Dom Ghislain Lafont, O.S.B., good Frère Ghislain, priest and theologian, is the friend and guide to whom this book is dedicated.

Introduction

Catholique et français toujours? Catholic Christianity was, indeed, the religion of France in 1789, a church-state relationship having its own dynamic, contentious, always changing history: bishops and official teachings and polity, on one hand, and dynastic or elected officials and formal laws, on the other. Here I discuss Catholicism and Frenchness as a matter of identity, even though *identity,* for all its years in the marketplace, has no simple set of agreed-upon meanings. Baby boomers went through college hearing about and studying—in psychology at least—the *identity crisis,* made famous by the Freudian revisionist Erik Erikson.[1] We can casually say that *identity* has a common meaning in modern English: the reality of somebody, true identity as against false identity. The philosopher Charles Taylor—using *The Making of the Modern Identity* as the subtitle of his study of the moral instinct—writes, "The full definition of someone's identity thus usually involves not only his stand on moral and spiritual matters but also some reference to a defining community."[2] *Identity* does, indeed, label some major attitudes and commitments of a person. Self-identity is achieved principally by moral and spiritual action in reference to a community.[3]

In *The Idea of France,* Pierre Birnbaum writes that "[France] on the one hand, has seen its soul as residing in a privileged relationship with Reason, and its deep personality expressed in an unquestioning adherence to the ideas of the Enlightenment" and "on the other hand, has conceived itself as the eldest daughter of the Church, the Catholic nation par excellence." Between the "virtuous republicans" and the "uncompromising Catholic counter-revolutionaries," there was always a struggle.[4] Although *catholique-et-français* personalities were not all of a piece, Birnbaum does see a heritage that goes from Joseph de Maistre (1754–1821), writer, diplomat, and papal absolutist, all the way through to the Vichy government. And, of course, the most ardent republicans enthusiastically traced their heritage back to the Revolution, rejecting neither Terror nor dechristianization. Liberals were caught between the proverbial hammer and anvil. Benjamin Constant, Ernest Renan, and the secular themes of the Universal Exposition of 1889 put traditional Catholics on the defensive, just as the notions of God, church, and France or church influence on education put traditional republicans on the defensive. The final battle lasted from the Dreyfus Affair, in which a Jewish French officer was accused of espionage by the heavily Catholic army administration and defended mostly by the republican left, through the official separation of church and state in 1905. The last vestiges of flexible practice on either side seemed to have disappeared; but then came the guns of August 1914.

Traveling across French terrain and back into French history, I will look at clergy and intellectuals, everyday people traveling and talking, the high drama of war, and the transmission of sophisticated learning, all to explore political and religious selves that have constituted identities in France. Gloss, for the moment, *religious identity* as "awareness and expression of one's own doctrinal, moral, and devotional (prayer) profile"; *national identity* as "awareness and expression of belonging to a country as a voter, taxpayer, and contributor to the home country's work effort" (it includes the more ideologically self-conscious nationalism). Churchgoing is the most public and visible expression of Catholic *religious identity.* Happily, for almost two hundred years local Catholicism has been monitored by French dioceses, giving us a very good idea of the number of folk who went to Sunday Mass and who made sure to partake of Communion at least once a year. It is true that we don't know what went on in the minds and hearts of these folk, and it is true that we would want some more dramatic and personal Catholic expression. But religious practice is "the support that culture furnishes to the religious life of individuals and groups."[5] As a cultural phenomenon, religion can change its meaning from one era to another and from one area to another, but there is an *identity* that endures. "Regions and social milieus maintain—across changes in the levels and meanings of their practice—an identity, a 'personality' recognizable across the years or even the centuries."[6] The form and the content of religious activity may change or may remain the same: form can persist while content changes, and content can persist while form changes. Practice may derive from vague religiosity or the beliefs and fears of earlier eras or respect for local custom or genuine devotion, but there is some genuine content.[7] In the last analysis, everyday religious practice with its elusive, changing content is preserved, elaborated, and reconfigured by religious teachers and leaders (clergy and religious primarily, in Catholicism). When people practice religion, they are part of a classic interaction between believers and authorities, local and national, contemporary and historical that is "a crossroads of shared religious vitality and individual initiative."[8] In this book, I push beyond the statistical base to reflect on unique personalities and interactions. Here, the story of religious identity features Catholic self-awareness, expression, shared vitality, and religious initiative—dark moments and shining moments in the life of a people. There is a gamut of Catholic identities involved, from loyal practicing Catholic through social or cultural Catholic, to the post-Catholic who deliberately or inadvertently searches to replace the old Catholic experience with a secular ethos.

How, then, to get to national identity? Should we talk about identification with *France* as such, or with the *nation,* or with the *Republic? France* may not mean the same thing as *nation,* and *nation* may not mean the same thing as *republic,* the predominant form of French government over the past two hundred years. The French historian-impresario Pierre Nora deliberately subdivided the series *Les Lieux de mémoire* into *La République, La Nation,* and *Les France,* and in his eloquent introductions struggled to make the *Frances* into the broadest imaginable category: the ensemble of the fighting, sharing, and passing on of the traditions and experiences that men and women acquired by simple birth and growth on the land itself. *Nation* was what the French talked about when they tried to square this belonging with everything from informal public life through formal government. And *Republic* was the solidly secular and democratic government, born in revolution and raised in an ideologically restricted world. Nora introduced these in reverse order.[9]

> Here is, first of all, the *Republic* with its symbols, monuments, pedagogy, commemorations, and examples of countermemory. Then will come *Nation,* . . . articulated around the principal themes that express its meaning: heritage from distant centuries, the great moments when historical memory was refashioned, the boundaries within which it has defined its sovereignty, and its "total being," the manner in which artists and savants have been able to decipher its lands and spaces. But here also are the places where it has best summed up its ideas of the role of the state, its greatness, its military and civil glories, its architectural and artistic patrimony, its literature and its language. In the fourth volume will appear finally *The Frances:* political, social, religious, and regional.[10]

For the Republic, Nora's essayists consider symbols, monuments, pedagogy, commemorations, and the "countermemory" or rejection; for the nation, heritage, historiography, landscapes, territory, state, patrimony, examples of monuments to national glory, and examples of preservation of a national idea. For the Frances, everything from archives, chateaux, and the French language, through cathedrals, to conversational styles and cafes are laid out tatterdemalion. Obviously, the categories are not mutually exclusive. For all of Nora's considerable efforts to justify and explain distinct categories, they remain definitively vague.[11]

No doubt but that *nation* is a protean word and defining it a conundrum.[12] Difficult to say how something called *nation* can be built out of ethnic structures and loyalties; difficult to isolate the role played by religion along the way, especially since religion may have—in a major way—constituted incipient national identity under the old regime.[13] As Philip Schlesinger writes in his essay on national identity, "national cultures are not simple repositories of shared symbols to which the entire population stands in identical fashion. Rather they are to be approached as sites of contestation in which competition over definitions takes place."[14] Anne Thiesse, in similar fashion, says that "the true birth of a nation is when a handful of individuals declares that it exists and undertakes to prove it."[15] People have at their disposal a do-it-yourself kit of nation definitions that they coordinate into a series—like language declensions—and then play out. This means that "the nation is born of a postulate and an invention, but it only lives by collective acceptance of this fiction. . . . Success here is the fruit of a sustained proselytism that teaches individuals what they are, obliges them to conform to it, and incites them to promote this collective teaching in their turn."[16] Putative ancestry and patrimony are combined with politics, economy, and society. Steven Englund has urged that the *nation* in France be seen as "a complex system, indeed a force field—of ideological discourse that gave rise in French history to several political traditions (republican, Bonapartist, constitutional monarchist) of which one (republican) gradually became so hegemonic within the country that it has successfully stifled much awareness that there were or are any alternatives."[17]

In the story as I tell it, the revolutionary government sought to divorce Catholic Christianity from national life after 1789.[18] The reaction of church people across the nineteenth century was to set up a defense against governments that did not privilege Catholicism. Government reaction was antagonism, and by the end of 1905, formal secularization. But peaceful scholarship and the trial of war brought the religious and secular French into a détente that has lasted more or less up to the present day—precariously and with interruptions.

Divorce. In 1790, the new government, in effect a constitutional monarchy, required all Catholic priests in public life to take an oath of loyalty to the newly developed constitution of the clergy. More than half of them did so, thus embarking on a new religio-political experience. Chapter 1, "Between Church and Nation: Posing, Abdicating, and Retracting Priests," traces the inner break up of the old unity, or at least compatibility, between loyalty to Catholicism and loyalty to the French nation. For many of these "constitutional" clergy, the old Catholic priestly identity became a hindrance to their image as heralds of a new political and cultural era. At first they operated within the church, but, like many a marriage of convenience, it soon led to a split, with a sizable percentage of priests abdicating their religious status, often permanently. Later, when large numbers of them sought reconciliation with the Roman Catholic Church, they renounced their earlier loyalty to the revolutionary government, in effect separating themselves from the revolution they had played along with. In any case, the old union of throne and altar was not transferred into a new union of French religious and French political identity.

Chapter 2, "National Ideals and Their Failure: Festival Celebration Under the Directory," traces, first of all, the hopes and projections of the Paris lawmakers. They would have a civil religion as part of the nation's structure, at times adopting and at times adapting the elements of the old religion. But the people would not have it, and the lawmakers' dreams of transferring the sense of the sacred from the old religion to the new nation were thwarted. Across this period, the revolutionary governments attempted to set up a system of celebrations that would replace the old Catholic festivals. Great ceremonies in central Paris and regular assemblies in town and country were planned and executed; Sacredness was to be transplanted from the old Catholic liturgies to the new government-inspired rituals. But with few exceptions the new rituals were pale imitations of the old, with ceremonies, speeches, and music that never caught on because the settings were dreary and the liturgies were consummately boring. The ritual celebration of the nation's life and meaning— its ideals—was rejected by a population that was opting for real religion or no religion, but not what to them, in its myth-and-ritual feebleness, was obviously fake religion. They collectively took one side or another in the "divorce," but a remarriage could not be forced on them.

In the end, then, traditional religion animated the minds and hearts of some, and political commitment animated the minds and hearts of others: two intellectual temperaments, two attitudes toward Catholicism's relation to the nation. Chapter 3, "Religious and Secular Extremes at the Beginning of the Nineteenth Century: Chateaubriand and Destutt de Tracy," presents two survivors of the Revolution during the reign of Napoleon: one personality shaped by commitment to traditional Catholic experience, the other shaped by science and philosophy. These men were emblematic of the now clearly separated sides. For Chateaubriand, religion defined Frenchness and for Destutt de Tracy, Frenchness—in fact, life in general—acquired nothing from religion. This was more than post-1789 political debate. The opposition was deep-seated; the ideological sides self-consciously chosen; a matter, it would appear, of vital personal experience.

For many religious leaders, religion-friendly governments were not friendly enough: not Napoleon's restoration of Catholicism in national life, not the privileging of Catholicism by the Bourbon restoration. True, the subsequent government of Louis Philippe was peopled by religiously indifferent new and old aristocrats; the brief-lived Second Republic was shot through with the old revolutionary secularism; even the Second Empire did not give church people complete authority in education; and after its initial flirtation with monarchism, the Third Republic was embodied by increasingly secular governments. Accordingly, church people developed a siege mentality among their faithful.

Defense. One great movement—perhaps *the* great movement—in defense of religion was the revival of pilgrimage during the second half of the nineteenth century. Chapter 4, "Piety Against Politics: Pilgrimage to Chartres During the Nineteenth Century" discusses the highly charged attempt to reconstruct French Catholic identity, an end run around the governments in place. Counterdemonstrations to national functions and celebrations, the pilgrimages were rallies to the church. Centers of pilgrimage became veritable fortresses of new church action. The great cathedral of Chartres, for example, embodied the religious passions and goals of France across the centuries; a traditional, religious France would be a defense against the modern secular nation, in both its imperial and republican forms. At Chartres, the clergy evoked the glories of monarchical Catholicism, presaged by French loyalty to Catholicism from the days of the Druids through the Middle Ages. The simple pastoral efforts and everyday administrative tasks of these clergy were paired with a countryside rejuvenation and conversion effort, where the piety and presence of women predominated as they had from the revolutionary era onward. The constructive spiritual energies of the women were channeled, partially at least, into the overall defensive use of pilgrimage by the official church against the government; the more secular the government, the more pointed the defense.

Defensiveness was also the principal religious reaction to the government's attempts to homogenize the French language as a means of communication and education across the hexagon. Church people in the patois-speaking and non-French-speaking regions promoted local languages to catechize the children and to safeguard against the government attempts to possess the minds and hearts of simple French peasants. Priests and nuns believed, rightly, that the defense of local languages—Breton, Flemish, Basque, Alsatian German, and Catalan—would safeguard religious practice. In Chapter 5, "Local Languages for the Defense of Religion: Alsace and the Roussillon," we find that in Alsace the support of local German helped secure a loyal church following for generations to come. Conversely, we see that the neglect of Catalan teaching in the Roussillon was one of the reasons for the decline in churchgoing. Protecting local language did not in every case serve as a genuine protection against domination by the national secular authority, but it did rally ordinary people to the defense of Catholicism.

Détente. The dramas of the Dreyfus Affair, a fight over the innocence or guilt of a French army officer accused of espionage, and the high antagonism politics of the secular revolutionary camp and the religious monarchist camp marked the decades on either side of 1900. But these quarrels paled in comparison to the worldwide catastrophe of the Great War of 1914–18, of which the French nation was a primary victim. Small wonder that the old religious and political antagonisms were put aside, suppressed, or destroyed. The two groups that represented, officially if not always in fact, religious loyalty and secular ideology, the priests and the schoolteachers (long trained to be an ideological and moral counterweight to the clergy), achieved a multiform armistice, limited though it was, in the old religion-secularism wars. This is the story in Chapter 6, "The Limits of Personal Reconciliation: Priests and *Instituteurs* in World War I."

Even before World War I, even as the church-state fights were at full tilt, an agent of reconciliation was at work: the professor and scholar Émile Mâle had published in 1898 a study of religious art in the Middle Ages that in its later editions led French secularists as well as religious believers to a new appreciation of the French Catholic medieval tradition. Beginning at the turn of the century, Mâle, eventually a professor at the Sorbonne and a member of the Académie française, integrated in his own experience and education many opposed forces in French cultural and political history: classicism and romanticism,

Catholic formation and secular education, specialized erudition and major appeal to the educated public. Many in the cultivated public accepted the central argument of his great synthesis of medieval Christian iconography; namely, that Catholicism was quintessentially French. Whereas the détente effected by the reconciliation of old antagonisms in the World War I trenches was dramatic and pragmatic, Mâle's influence, traced and analyzed in Chapter 7, "Reconciliation of Cultures in the Third Republic: The Work of Émile Mâle," was progressive, and, especially in the generation after the war, combined with a more public professional appreciation of the cultural and intellectual achievements in Catholic history.

Throughout the present book individual voices predominate, and the truth is in the individual voices. These are not the only voices that should be heard, their stories not the only stories that could be told to show how the standard-bearers of French religious identity and French national identity across the many decades first experienced divorce (Part 1), then faced off defensively (Part 2), and then entered into a longer period of détente (Part 3). Introductions to the thematic parts are full, general summaries containing subplots and voices that do not have chapters of their own. But I chose my case studies for each chapter because as a historian of modern France I found them central and representative. I trust that readers will find them more revealing of the religious and political drama of modern French history than a homogenized text on nineteenth- and twentieth-century French history.

I believe that the quandaries of revolutionary priests, the gripes of revolutionary legislators, and the particular geniuses of Chateaubriand and Destutt de Tracy show us more about the dynamics of religious and national divorce than could a generalized religious history and political outline of the revolution by itself. I believe that the writers for *La Voix de Notre-Dame de Chartres* (with their dependence upon a feminized Catholicism), the priests of Alsace, and the bishops of the Roussillon had each of them an experience of Catholicism and Frenchness, of isolation from similar threats and of rallying to the Catholic cause that speak more clearly to us today than summaries of church defensiveness and state antagonism. Certainly the suffering and dying priests and teachers of World War I saw their own standard training and experience differently, finding a new solidarity with one another in the midst of chaos. Their social détente was complemented by the intellectual détente of Emile Mâle, whose totally secular formation at the École Normale was the foundation for a new appreciation of medieval Catholic culture. These two case studies reveal inner dynamics of reconciliation that strengthened the World

War I détente between ardent Catholics and nationalists, which had its first moments in the late nineteenth century but was almost completely obscured by the polemics surrounding the separation of church and state in the first decade of the twentieth century.

In setting the stage for these dramas, we want not to trip over too many categories, but it is true that *church* and *state* are the classical pair, and that I have here set up Catholicism and Frenchness, in adjectival form *Catholique* and *Français,* as the identity categories. I propose then, to sketch the church-state setting for the chapters to come in the introductions to Parts 1, 2, and 3 and then move to the religious experience of Catholicism and the experience of France (as nation or as republic or as, simply, France) in the individual chapters. Some readers familiar with French history may see fit to omit the section introductions. Other readers may wish to read the chapters in an order based on their own interests. This is perfectly appropriate because each chapter, though part of conceptual unity, stands on its own. I would suggest, though, a reading of the appropriate part introduction when chapters are read in random order because in these introductions I explain how the chapter fits into the master plan. I need to say up front also that the history of *Catholique* (in that full gamut from loyal and practicing Catholic through post-Catholic) is fuller and more nuanced than the history of *Français.* In a history of formal politics and political theory, national identity would come into clearer focus. But these chapters present specific experiences of Catholicism in confrontation with a generalized—and often oversimplified—politics; the individuals in the book simply talk their religious identity more than their national identity, and so we let them have their way.

Part One

DIVORCE

We know now that if Louis XV (king of France, 1715–74) said, "After me, the deluge," as one tradition would have it, he was not glibly dismissing his chronic problems of unwieldy government and personal decadence. As a generally competent head of state, Louis well knew that the kingdom's resources had been depleted by the Seven Years' War in Europe, with accompanying loss of huge open territories in North America. Finances had been in a bad state since the kingdom's major New World investment, the Mississippi Company, became the "Mississippi Bubble" and self-destructed. A principal advisor, René-Nicholas de Maupeou tried to control and extract more taxes from the nobles, who then stiffened their resistance to royal authority. Earlier, even the eminently capable chief minister Cardinal André-Hercule de Fleury (third cardinal in a row to serve a Bourbon king, after Richelieu and Mazarin) was not able to fully fix the financial problems.

Cardinals were government ministers, and Catholicism was an instrument of statecraft for the royal administration, guaranteeing a functioning system of bishops and priests as well as the assurance of liturgical worship and preaching everywhere in the kingdom. Though formally united to Rome, the French church, the *Ecclesia Gallicana,* had a special set of rights and privileges dating back to the Concordat of 1516, between King Francis I and Pope Leo X. During the reign of Louis XIV, Bishop Jacques-Bénigne Bossuet, aristocrat and powerful intellectual, had made the theological case for the divine right of kings. Kingship was a religious as well as a political duty, and the king's personal religious life could be a government preoccupation. Louis XV's dynastic marriage to the plain and severe Polish princess, Marie Leczinska, resulted in a very religious family and his own extensive womanizing, with such fascinating offspring as Madame Louise, who became a very dedicated Carmelite nun and eventually a well-beloved mother superior, and an illegitimate son who became a priest (the result of both the religious family and the womanizing!).

The church in general had to be controlled as well as supported, and a complicated contest between royal administrators and the Jesuits in particular resulted in the expulsion of the Jesuits, a decision the pope was forced to accept. This was a papal surrender pure and simple rather than real complicity. The Jesuits had defended papal prerogatives in France and had many former students—aristocrats—in high places, but the pope was forced to undercut his own power in order to sustain Louis's power. Thus a throne and altar relationship existed more broadly as a church and state relationship, profoundly affecting social existence. In some cities and towns, ecclesiastical buildings and land could be more than half of the total—not all that different from earlier centuries when the church was the fundamental transnational power in Western Europe. For young men, priesthood was a principal job opportunity, and many young women found something between a vocation and a refuge in convents.

The last years of Louis XV were troubled by deaths of several possible successors—Louis's son and his oldest grandson. Fate had it that an unlikely younger grandson, underenthused and overweight (and with, as it turned out, a temporary sexual inadequacy), became Louis XVI in 1774. More fortunate in his ministers than in his natural endowments, the young king and his government trumped England in the colonial world (ensuring North American independence from England in 1781) and then turned their attention to the economic and cultural programs of the 1780s. Louis's first great move was to appoint an eminent physiocrat, Anne-Robert Turgot, to pick up where Maupeou had left off: moving quickly, Turgot challenged old, corroded government structures and private vested interests everywhere. Perhaps he moved too fast, perhaps he arrived too late, but the forces of resistance were too strong. Even Queen Marie Antoinette urged Louis to move on to someone else. The ministers who came along subsequently included—no surprise—an archbishop and then Jacques Necker, popular Protestant and father of a young woman who would become an intellectual leader in France during the Napoleonic era.

Leading intellectuals during the reigns of Louis XV and Louis XVI, in communication with one another, had the common goal of privileging Reason as the fundamental and sure way to political settlement, financial soundness, and religio-cultural balance. The corroded, clerical, Bourbon Catholic system was a problem for most of them. Voltaire would crush Catholic power while leaving it alive enough to help the simple people. Jean-Jacques Rousseau would gradually supplant it with an official sentimental deism as the state religion.

First of the Bourbon kings to be both politically accommodating and genuinely moral, Louis XVI risked losing the standard Bourbon grip on state control by the later 1780s. In 1788, the appeal was to the aristocrats in a specially called Assembly of Notables. Louis's government sought both political support and money. But there has never been a way to make an increased tax burden appealing, and whatever support the monarchy gained, it was not financial. The inevitable next step was a clear call for help to entrepreneurs and professionals. Louis and his advisors decided to reconstitute the old Estates General, a legislature of sorts, that had not met in Bourbon France for the preceding 175 years. Elections to each of the three estates—clergy, aristocracy, and commoners (those entrepreneurs and professionals)—were thus a major enterprise. The principal task of government officials was to poll the people and collect their complaints and suggestions for review by the Estates in the following May 1789. This massive project, which resulted in thousands of documents called *cahiers de doléances,* may have indicated significant dissatisfaction with society and government but contained very little criticism of the church. That would come later.

If there were three estates officially—clergy, nobles, and commoners—there were unofficially two clergies in the First Estate. The bishops of France were aristocrats (with one exception in 1789), whereas the vast majority of the priests were commoners. This clear division was not in itself insurmountable; more complex were the influences on clerical behavior of three principal movements: Gallicanism, Jansenism, and Richerism.

Gallicanism promoted a distinct French structure and style of Roman Catholicism. The Latin *Ecclesia Gallicana* was simply a problem-free label for the French church—obviously part of the Latin Western, and therefore

VUE DE LA PROCESSION DES ETATS GÉNÉRAUX, A VERSAILLES LE 4 MAI 1789.

Fig. 1.   Procession at the opening of the Estates General. At the head, the Third Estate, followed by the nobles and then the clergy; under the canopy, the Bessed Sacrament carried by the archbishop of Paris; finally the king and his entourage. This was a manifestation of the union of throne and altar that would come apart over the revolutionary decade. (Bibliothèque Nationale)

Roman, tradition. Political Gallicanism prioritized government rights over church structure and style, and an ecclesiastical Gallicanism prioritized the French bishops' rights to control their own ecclesiastical destinies within the Roman ecclesiastical system.

Jansenism was a profoundly moral reform movement that had marked French religion since the 1600s in much the same way as Puritanism had marked English religion. Distrustful of a hierarchical church structure that counted on worldly success and human righteousness, Jansenism had been condemned by Rome as antiauthority and Protestant, even though it was, in fact, a Catholic response to the values of Calvinism. Jansenists believed that they were promoting the true Catholic Christian theology transmitted by Augustine from the early church. Years of controversy, of dissembling, and, from time to time, of underground existence had given the movement a fluid shape and scattered demography that made it impossible to clearly condemn and round up: even so, the pope had condemned Jansenism in his bull *Unigenitus,* and the government of Louis XV had outlawed both public organization and expression.

Richerism (after the sixteenth- and seventeenth-century Sorbonne theologian Edmond Richer) demoted the authority of bishops to promote the authority of priests. Episcopal authority as such was not rejected, but Richer developed a theology of priestly character and rights that, he believed, came from apostolic times: Christ gave a commission to the apostles to be the first bishops, but other disciples (the seventy, according to the Gospel of Luke, chapter 10) were commissioned separately, with their own rights and duties.

Gallicanism, Jansenism, and Richerism, in spite of their differences, could overlap on some issues, theological and organizational, making it difficult to label the motivations and actions of the bishops and priests who showed up for the principal meetings of the Estates General.

The Third Estate had been already primed by the abbé Emmanuel-Joseph Sieyès, a priest from the diocese of Chartres. His triumphalist pamphlet, *Qu'est-ce que c'est le tiers état? (What Is the Third Estate?)*, answered the question with a resounding "everything." After weeks of tension, the Third Estate declared itself the final arbiter in the formation of the new government. When it appeared that they were deliberately locked out of their meeting hall, members issued their proclamation from an interior tennis court nearby—the "Tennis Court Oath"—and subsequently resisted a royal attempt to prevent the first two estates from joining them. Members of the clergy and aristocracy who were already reform-minded (looking for a constitutional monarchy or even a republican government) prevailed upon the recalcitrant majorities of both their estates to come over to the new assembly, soon afterward called the National Constituent Assembly. One immediate result was that many committees were formed to reorganize and reform every area of national life. For instance, the Committee for Public Instruction and the Ecclesiastical Committee immediately began work on reform documents, one of which, entitled *The Civil Constitution of the Clergy,* recast the old French unity of throne and altar into a new state and church relationship. Diocesan boundaries were to be redrawn in coordination with the new administrative division of France into eighty-three departments. Elections of bishops by priests and priests by parishioners were to parallel the new ways of political election. And the government, which had already taken over the physical properties of the church, was to be responsible for clergy salaries. But all this went against the ecclesiastical grain. The old-regime bishops were not ready to reorganize themselves into the new dioceses; elections seemed a scandal to many in church administration; and the rocky relationship of the old French church with papal administration in Rome was fully upset. Only the dotty Bishop Charles de Lafont de Savine was of such revolutionary enthusiasm and liturgical originality to propose the making of blue, white, and red vestments to produce a tricolor priest at Masses celebrated for the first festival of the Federation.

Out of this chaos emerged one priest in particular, the abbé Henri Grégoire, who steadfastly stood for a reformed Catholicism and a solid constitutional government. But Grégoire was just a priest; a large number of bishops were needed, and only one of the old-regime bishops was willing to consecrate new bishops: the cynical and corrupt aristocratic bishop of Autun, Charles-Maurice de Talleyrand. Week by week, the consecrations of bishops were multiplied—with Grégoire among the first—moving toward the quota of one bishop for every department. Talleyrand seems to have brought it off with seriousness and dignity; after that the new bishops carried on the task.

These were strange and shabby beginnings for a reformed French Catholic church, beginnings that the best of the new bishops and priests were never able to live down, whatever right they may have had on their side. In 1790, all pastors were required to take an oath of loyalty to the Civil Constitution of the Clergy, even as the pope—silent for many months—officially rejected it. Half of the priests who were required by law to do so took the oath; Grégoire and the other bishops began a serious campaign to show that historically and theologically the constitutional church was the legitimate Catholic authority in France.

If conflict had marked the beginning of the constitutional monarchy (from the Tennis Court Oath of May through the taking of the Bastille in July), conflict marked the spread of constitutional church authority. New bishops met major resistance from their priests, new pastors (often supplanting a priest who had refused the oath) met resistance from their parishioners; and rejection of the old corruption often mutated into rejection of the whole idea of a visible church authority. Priests and even several of the bishops married. Many constitutional priests could be far more eloquent in their praise of Enlightenment rationalism and far more committed to political reform than to religious teaching and worship. By August 1792, when the monarchy was completely dismantled, members of the constitutional church were working with advocates of political violence and dechristianization, and by 1793, former priests and even one former bishop were working on behalf of the Reign of Terror. In fact, at the very beginning of the year, some of the bishops who were members of the Convention had voted for the death of the king. Constitutional bishops and priests were on a fast train to total divorce of church and state.

In the end, these bishops and priests would have the choice between a political-revolutionary but religiously authentic Catholicism and the nationally promoted deism of Maximilien Robespierre. As long as Robespierre was the leading influence on the Convention and its principal Terror committee, Public Safety, the most revolutionary of priests and ex-priests would have a model of high priestly pretensions for their own ideological ambitions. Atheistic rationalism was another option for those who cast their lot with the state. *Chapter 1 reveals the dilemma facing constitutional priests in the chaos and confusion of revolution. In particular, it focuses on the identities they were forced to take on as the state changed and as their relation to their church changed. In the lives of these priests, probably more than anywhere else in the story of the split between Catholicism and the national government, the painful process of "divorce" became visible. These men saw themselves as workers for both church and nation, but the values of the nation trumped the values of church ministry. A large number of them jumped to the other side, promoting the joys of belonging to nation over any vestige values of church membership. And a large number of them, whatever their denial of church engagement had been, retracted that denial and, in turn, retracted their promotion of or accommodation to the revolutionary nation. The divorce took place within the lives of these men, and then across the parishes and dioceses of France. Their testimonies reveal the deterioration of a double religious and national identity, or the full identification with nation and rejection of church, or the full identification with church and rejection of revolutionary concept of nation. They reveal the inner workings of the parties to a collective divorce.*

Of course, the half of clerical France that rejected the oath was removed from office. Labeled "refractories" by revolutionary government and clergy, they, too, had to decide how to express their religious and national loyalties. Unambiguous loyalty to papal Catholicism may have been a clearer option than a national Catholicism in some kind of trouble with the pope. But no oath would equal no ministry. Tens of thousands fled the country, tens of thousands went underground, and a certain number were able with the support of faithful parishioners to carry on a normal ministry. Priests quit by the many thousands, and at least six thousand of them married.

With the clergy persecuted and in turmoil, the structures of religion itself could no longer stand. The dechristianization movement, as part of the Terror and on its own, was eminently successful. Bishop Jean-Baptiste Gobel, head of the diocese of Paris, most conspicuous among the abdicators, was subsequently thrown in prison and executed. The majority of the constitutional bishops, few of whom had ever exercised their episcopal ministry with true success out in the provinces, likewise bowed out. The majority of the old-regime bishops were in exile, along with large numbers of refractory priests. Local political administrators presided over the closing or destruction of churches or their conversion to profane use. An official government proclamation of the separation of state and church in 1795 would have been an ironic understatement if the revolutionary legislators had any sense of the catastrophic destructiveness of their politics. The fall of Robespierre and the adjournment of the Convention marked the end of the Terror, but not of the dechristianizing, nor of the suppression, nor of the marginalization. In fact, Terror-like persecution of churchmen and women would occasionally break out in the five years that followed.

The government in place after the fall of Robespierre on 9–10 thermidor (27–28 July 1794) and the remaining months of the Convention was called the Directory, a strange hybrid administration with a board of five rotating directors (hence the name) and a bicameral legislature. Wary of violence though incapable of fully ending it, the Directory politicians remained caught up in the ideological inheritance of the preceding years and, accordingly, their competition with religion. Instead of clear administrative reform and politics as compromise, the Directory continued earlier policies of reeducation by speeches, publications, and, in particular, by a commitment to public celebrations that would take the place of the old religious festivals (very frequent in Catholic France) and of Sunday. To replace the church year, earlier governments had sponsored a new calendar based on the metric system, substituting a ten-day week for a seven-day week. Not only would Christmas and Easter be gone, but Sundays would cease to exist. Every tenth day—the "décadi" as it was called—citizens would be called to assembly for speech and celebration in made-over churches; rest and leisure were assumed.

By continuing these policies, the Directory government was the agent of its own (albeit very gradual) demise. One director, Louis-Marie de La Revellière-Lépeaux, using the new calendar, attempted a wholesale replacement of Catholicism with a newly formalized deism called *Theophilanthropy*. He wanted to structure and make explicit the implicit deism of the festivals and the décadi, he wanted to take over most of the old churches, and he envisioned a new, full-blown cult. This was a particularly showy example of the attempt to get rid of everything Catholic. A famous cartoon shows the hunchbacked La Revellière-Lépeaux trying to balance himself on top of the republican calendar (styled as a wheel of fortune) in order to avoid falling to either the (far) left of the extreme Jacobins with their Robespierrest heritage or the (far) right of the monarchists with their unmitigated old-regime goals. *Chapter 2 lays open the attempt, and the failure, to transfer the old religious ways to a new festival celebration of nationhood in Paris and in the countryside. Government leaders and workers wanted the myths and rituals of Catholicism to be stripped of their Catholic exterior and made part of a spiritually enhanced nation. If the nation could appropriate the sacredness of the old religion, then the old religion would wither up and die, a useless anachronism. The story of the revolutionary festivals most clearly reveals the behavior of one party to the divorce, the national government as it tried to attract citizens to its own side of the split. But in attempting to preempt the old religious identity for a new national identity, the revolutionary government lost favor with important elements of the population. Citizens appeared to want their old Catholicism back or to be done with religion altogether. The details of this story of the attempted manufacture of an integrated national and religious identity, prepared for the citizenry to "try on," reveals also the failure of the revolutionary government to make the divorce disappear in the interest of a new unity. The festivals were an exercise in confusion and ambiguity, which highlighted the split and led to the polarization of religious and national loyalties.*

Onto this scene came the rising, shining military star, Napoleon Bonaparte, who had propped up the Directory at home and brilliantly extended its jurisdiction abroad. Born of a pious mother and an ambitious father into a threadbare Corsican aristocracy, he had attended the royal military school on the mainland and quickly distinguished himself as a young officer. Napoleon dispersed the Paris crowds that threatened to disassemble the Directory at its first convening. He led the French armies from victory to victory in northern Italy, and in the process declared to assembled clergy in the cathedral of Milan that he saw them as the backbone of society. He could be seen, then, as a defender of revolutionary government and of established religion.

No doubt in the eyes of the abbé Emmanuel-Joseph Sieyès, who had once again risen to prominence in government affairs, Napoleon was the key to a stable changeover from the Directory government to a more efficient political structure. There were touch-and-go days to this transition in 1799, when Sieyès's and Napoleon's political handlers engineered the Consulate, a new regime for France presided over by Napoleon as First Consul, Sieyès as Second Consul, and an obscure member of the Directory, Pierre-Roger Ducos, as Third Consul. But Sieyès was always a better radical writer than he was agitator or politician; whatever ideas he had of using Napoleon to his own ends were quickly dispelled by the First Consul's independence and agile power plays. As Napoleon pulled into line the Jacobin and royalist extremes that had harassed the Directory, he also worked to rebuild the destroyed relationship of religion to the nation.

Napoleon's government set up a new arrangement with church authority, the Concordat of 1801, recognizing Catholicism as "the religion of the great majority of the French people." He wanted the constitutionals reabsorbed into papal Catholicism, and a papal Catholicism pliant enough to submit to his own restructuring agenda—political and military as well as cultural. The constitutionals had to be satisfied with a retraction, forgiveness, and the integration of a few bishops into the new hierarchy. Napoleon brought Pius VII to Paris to preside at his coronation as emperor in Notre-Dame cathedral and later held him as a virtual prisoner at Savona and then at Fontainebleau. Pius had to ward off Napoleon's frequent attempts to control religious affairs, and he was in the main successful. It was not until 1814 that Napoleon sent the obstinate elderly pope back to Rome.

Napoleon's arrival on the scene put an end to the political pretensions of atheism and deism. Yet, he shared many of the ideas and ideals of the Enlightenment, as long as they did not interfere with political effectiveness. His reorganization of law, of education, and of society took a large measure of its inspiration from the writings of Montesquieu, Rousseau, and Condorcet. But he had to contend with the direct successors of these men, a second generation of intellectuals who had survived the revolutionary era and were taking advantage of the new freedoms. Napoleon's run-ins with church authority were matched by his quarrels with the new Idéologues (a label that was created at this time for these particular post-Enlightenment thinkers). He did not succeed in balancing or reconciling the ideological left and the Catholic right, but he effectively allowed enough leeway for each polarity of thought and sentiment to survive and eventually flourish. *Chapter 3 highlights the two opposed intellectual temperaments—the Catholic right and the nationalistic left—that would dominate French culture for years to come. The inner evolving dynamics of the now separate religious and national identities are nowhere more clearly revealed than in the writings and correspondence of the Catholic aristocrat François-René de Chateaubriand and the firm believer in science and secular nation Antoine-Louis-Claude Destutt de Tracy, an aristocrat who was almost executed in the Terror despite his loyalty to the Revolution. Chateaubriand developed his Catholic identity in the course of a "conversion" from the generalized religious belief of early adulthood to the full Catholic belief of his ancestors. And Tracy worked out a new science of human behavior (concomitantly with a resolutely secular approach to religion) as the foundation of his own national identity. Each was the embodiment of one side of the divorce, the clearest possible personification of what we call the two Frances as they were consolidated by the Revolution.*

Revolutionary priests, government legislators, and intellectual fashion makers—religious and secular—at the beginning of the Napoleonic era are part of a narrative that goes across the Revolution and the Empire and into the Bourbon Restoration (1814–30). The society that issued from the Revolution was an amalgam of tradition and innovation that never melded together. Church attempts at renewal on the local level were haphazard, and the loyalties of the elites were shifting. Many members of an aristocracy traumatized by revolutionary upheaval returned to authentic faith and regular churchgoing, but many members of the bourgeoisie found their intellectual and moral base in Voltaire and Rousseau. In fact, the 1790s division, with a changing cast of characters, continued for many decades.

Chapter One

BETWEEN CHURCH AND NATION: *Posing, Abdicating, and Retracting Priests*

When the Estates General, that erstwhile parliament moribund for 175 years, was called together by Louis XVI, roughly one-fourth of the delegates were clergy.[1] The so-called First Estate of the three estates was, after all, by definition the clergy estate. Arriving at Versailles in May of 1789, the delegates to this First Estate were in the main commoner priests. In their own cities and towns, they had already taken part in elections to the Estates General, worked on lists of complaints (*cahiers de doléances*) to submit to the upcoming sessions, and in a few cases formulated radical ideas, if not radical agendas, for a new political era. Even so, in the opening procession, with Robespierre (opposed to the death penalty in those days) marching in front with other members of the Third Estate, and the king marching at the end preceded by the Blessed Sacrament, the priests could have had very little revolution in mind.

Political committees of the Estates General, transformed early on into the National Constituent Assembly, worked out a series of church reforms in 1789 and 1790, activating a whole complex of religious and national passions. The priests split down the middle when obliged to take an oath of loyalty to the nation and the new Civil Constitution of the Clergy (the aristocratic bishops, with few exceptions, rejected the constitution and refused the oath). Some of the constitutional priests, or jurors, continued the old forms of priestly identity solely to promote enlightenment and revolutionary change, others abdicated priesthood, and still others retracted their oath to the revolutionary government in the interests of priestly loyalty to Rome. It was possible, of course, to have a shot at two or all three of these activities. These *poseurs, abdicataires,* and *rétractés* belong to distinct periods of the Revolution: *poseurs,* in the main from 1789 through 1794; *abdicataires,* 1793 and 1794; *rétractés,* at periodic intervals, from shortly after the oath-taking all the way through to the Concordat.[2] In highlighting their enhanced new national identity, the *poseurs* and *abdicataires* finally divorced Catholicism. The *rétractés,* of course, in re-embracing Catholicism, finally divorced their revolutionary nationalism. But in all their own testimonies we see the prejudices and, often, the process of their passage from a primarily Catholic identity to a primarily national identity—or vice versa. Other "isms," to be sure, influenced the religious and national formation and thinking of the constitutional priests. Gallicanism, Jansenism, and Richerism had, each one of them, both an ecclesiastical and a political form, with complex and overlapping influences on members of the clergy. Gallicanism determined the specific French identity of religion in national life; Jansenism, the attitudes toward morality and church hierarchy; and Richerism, the relationship of the priests and bishops to one another and their people.[3]

Curé Poseurs of *La Feuille villageoise*

One rallying point for priests using their traditional status as a power base for revolutionary thought (*poseurs*) was the popular journal, *La Feuille villageoise,* destined for the countryside—the simple people and their guides. Curés poseurs who entered into conversation with militant rationalists of *La Feuille villageoise* did not want to be curés (pastors) in the traditional sense, and eventually they did not want to be curés at all; appropriate enough, then, to call them *poseurs.*[4] *La Feuille* was a strident promoter of revolutionary ideals in the practical life of peasants in the provinces, in its own words, "addressed each week to all the villages of France, to teach them the laws, the events, and the discoveries that interest every citizen,"[5] From the beginning, the paper cultivated the favor and attention of the patriotic country curés and provided revolutionary priests with a forum for public expression. In the "avertissement" that preceded the first issue, the editors wrote: "The curés are the preceptors of religion. This task, important in every sense, will become even more important, if the teaching of civics is added to the teaching of Christianity. It would be, then, a wise thought and a good pastoral idea to assemble in their homes, in the municipal building, or in the courts of the old chateaux, or in the village church, the principal peasants, to read them, each Sunday, our review, and to explain to them the passages that need to be clarified or commented upon."[6] The founder and first editor of the *La Feuille* was himself an ex-priest, though he was never a curé.[7] Curés are the first choice for teaching the Revolution, but others such as—even—the *châtelain* or the country surgeon, may also teach Revolution.

Melvin Edelstein, in his now classic study, *La Feuille villageoise: Communication et modernisation dans les régions rurales pendant la Révolution,* could not see any direct relation between *La Feuille* and peasant action for one obvious reason: the peasants, by and large, could not read. Examining the readers, the writers, and the letters to the editor, Edelstein tried, rather, to clarify themes, goals, and controversies. The number of copies printed per issue being a matter of record, Edelstein guessed that each copy reached about twenty readers, and that the distribution of the journal was greater where the road and postal systems were most developed. He carefully quantified the letters to the editor, finding that 57% of the letters to the editor were written by priests. Of these, half were written by ten specific priests, including the following: Parent, curé of Boisisse-la-Bertrand (Seine-et-Marne) with nineteen letters, Géruzez, curé of Sacy (Marne) with eighteen, Dupuis, curé of Droyes (Haute-Marne) with ten, and Mahias, curé of Achères (Seine-et-Oise) with nine. Subjects dealt with, in order of frequency, were religion, rural economy, politics, war, the *Feuille* itself, education, patriotic activity, taxes, and national properties. As the Revolution moved to greater opposition and violence toward religion, the *Feuille* kept pace, serving as a forum for and then, finally, representing only the most radical and secularized of the revolutionary clergy.[8]

Promoting Constitutionals and Condemning Refractories

From the beginning, curés wrote often and *in extenso*. The letters were not spur-of-the-moment inspirations because they contained selections from sermons the priests delivered when they took the oath to the Civil Constitution. The editors highlighted these clerical viewpoints, thereby "correcting a certain public who believes that peasants and even pastors are quite far from the true light."[9] These pastors, for their part, were in a honeymoon period with the Revolution. One of them said to his people, "Would you be thinking that they are going to suppress a sacrament, or take away the Mass or at least vespers? Nothing of the sort. . . . The new constitution of the clergy reestablishes equality in the administration of cult . . . following the wonderful order of the primitive church. If the new regime is heretical, the apostles were major

LE CURÉ PATRIOTE.

Travaillez, mes enfans, obéissez aux loix,
Je veillerai pour vous et deffendrai vos droits.

se vend à Paris chez Desenne Imprimeur Libraire,
au Palais Royal N° 1 et 2.
Prix 10 f.

Fig. 2. *Le curé patriote* instructing his people. This idealized pastor was the model for the men who, as revolutionary priests, became poseurs, abdicators, and retractors. The image was reproduced in a number of contexts and was a frontispiece for bound volumes of *La Feuille villageoise,* published for the enlightenment of the people of the countryside and the clergy and nobles who were their guides. (Bibliothèque Nationale)

heretics."[10] The taking of the oath brought out the oratory and self-justification of the curés who conformed. "In these critical times," wrote LeGrand, curé of Aujargues (Gard), "when the enemies of the public good color their evil designs with the pretext of religion, backing up their stand by refusing to take the oath, I thought I had to forewarn my parishioners about [such] seduction."[11] He told the editors, "By sending us your *Feuille villageoise,* you have acquired the well-earned right to the esteem of all good French citizens.[12]

But the curés had many obstacles. Condemnation by oath-rejecting colleagues led to resistance and violence by parishioners. The refractories who were pushed out of their parishes by the government naturally resented their constitutional replacements, causing potential constitutional curés to hold back. But, wrote one priest, they should get rid of their scruples, which are "a remnant of aristocratic honor," "a useless commiseration," "harmful to anyone who gives in to it," "equally pernicious for religion and country," and evidence of "a wavering conscience."[13] Constitutionals should recognize refractory mischief for what it is. "Stirred up by these malevolent types, they [the people] have persecuted the new pastors, disturbed them in the exercise of their functions, insulted them even in a most outrageous manner, calling them perjurers, thieves, anti-Christs."[14]

Good Teaching for Good Parishioners

Where the people supported them, constitutional clergymen could write to the *Feuille* editors in high spirits. The curé of Septmonsel (Jura) said he was "a happy pastor of this canton, once a serf and today a free man." And he could only be grateful to the *Feuille:* "I thank you in the name of the docile inhabitants: they are like sheep as regards the law, reason, and religion. But they would be as indomitable as lions if they were to be attacked by the enemies of the fatherland."[15] Freedom for curé and people guaranteed an open learning situation. The government "watches out so that no one bothers his neighbor as he renders his own simple worship to the divinity," said Dupuis, curé of Droyes (Haute-Marne).[16] Such emphasis on freedom and openness moved him to call for the personal reconciliation of Catholics and Protestants. And he asked *La Feuille* for help in combating peasant superstition. "Gentlemen, could you find some simple way to make fun of the foolish reverence that the villagers in several regions have for relics and the statues of saints that our collectors of legends have barely heard of. The relics and images that the monks were pleased to accumulate in their convents, find refuge in parish churches, and they might receive homage that is close to idolatry."[17]

Right and reasonable teaching, then, is the principal theme, nowhere more clearly expressed than in the letters of Auguste Couet, curé of Orville (Loiret), also one of the principal clergy correspondents. He said that "the time when we could abuse the patience of the people has finally passed" and proposed that he had found a solution in preaching at the end of Mass—the people could stay or leave of their own free will.[18] Not surprisingly, he says that his reading of *La Feuille* at sermon time helped attendance. He would combine gospel and patriotic reflections and then throw in a few pages of *La Feuille* for good measure.[19]

The Reforms Needed

In the new era of freedom, priests and people turned once again to the age-old problem of priestly celibacy. It was Dupuis who broached the topic, by somewhat disingenuously posing the question: "In the new order of things, can a curé marry and keep his position?" He said that he "had read in a few news publications that priests had, in effect, gotten married, even in the capital." He said that he too would marry if his conscience so directed and, in some way, duty called: "I believe that celibacy has never helped and never will help the cause of good priests."[20] Writers returned to the subject of priestly marriage several times in subsequent months. *La Feuille* even printed a long discourse by one curé who was explaining his own marriage to his parishioners.[21] The curé of Cabrières (Hérault) made game of the hypocrisy of the priests who condemned clerical marriage at the same time they themselves engaged in sexual practices: "The majority of my confreres marry; but those of the communion of Tartuffe, instead of imitating us, cry out in loud voices, even as they defile the marriage bed of the man next door."[22]

Worship in the vernacular was of a piece with effective teaching. The curé of Salagnon (Isère) argued the party line that for religion to be authentic, people had to pray in their own language. A dead language goes completely against all reason and common sense. "If the founders of Christianity had come to tell the people to whom they were addressing themselves for the first time, 'We bring you a form of worship in which you will speak to God in a language you do not understand, and without knowing what you are saying,' . . . the apostles would have been taken for imbeciles."[23] Couet decried the Latin mumbo jumbo of his people "shouting themselves hoarse in a Latin that they did not understand, without having prayed a single prayer."[24] Without eliminating Latin completely, he went about the business of liturgical reform. No more negative and long elements of the services for the dead, no more dry sermons; he substituted instead a prayer on moral themes, civil as well as religious.[25] Parent thought that use of the vernacular would calm anxieties about religious changes. "They believe that we are going to destroy religion, but if the new missal of the former diocese of Sens, if the breviary of Paris, corrected a little and above all considerably shortened, were translated into French, the people would sense then that we have nothing against religion." And they would have the added bonus of learning more of their own language.[26]

A Republic to Replace a Decadent Monarchy

With the end of the monarchy in August of 1792, some clerical letters berated both the monarchy and a papacy they believed to be as bad as the monarchy. One curé noted that the papacy was more concerned about a king's allegiance to the papacy than a king's allegiance to his people. The "court of Rome" promoted wealth and learning, but not humility (reference is to the beggar saint, Benedict-Joseph Labré). "It is at the Vatican that one finds the source of all the superstitions of Europe. This poisoned source will dry up when the people just laugh at the thunderbolts from Rome, the briefs and (papal) bulls of the old man of the seven mountains."[27] And Dupuis substituted the great revolutionary theorists for the old religious authority. Reading Rousseau, he had the sense that he was reading scripture: "This passage [from *Émile*] contained such a clear prediction of our immortal Revolution, that the philosopher seemed to be inspired by the divinity." Rousseau seemed to know as much about the future revolution as did the major Old Testament prophets about the future of the "fanatic" Hebrew people.[28]

Across 1793 and 1794, the curés were increasingly vociferous in their defense of the Republic, with, as usual, civic and moral responsibility at the center of their message. Géruzez listed some of the mistakes of a clergy defensive of their vested interests, in contrast to Christ, who came to form good humans and not narrow believers: "Goodness, equality, and fraternity have often been forgotten in the name of a religion that preached only these virtues."[29] Parent publicly rejoiced in the marriage of a fellow curé: "Certainly I was at the wedding." Along with the other guests, he was happy to sing songs that the married curé had himself composed.[30] Refractories who condemned all this were nothing less than bad-willed and disruptive, their conduct abominable in the eyes of Christ; in the name of religion they are "tearing up the breast of your fatherland."[31] Not that an easy charity was proposed. In fact, Parent, in another context, was clearly against supporting beggars—they were parasites in society, deserving of charity, but not alms. He called beggars the "wicked poor, " saying that real charity requires they be given nothing.[32]

Morality, Personal, and Especially Political

The constitutionals did not forget about everyday moral issues. Parent was troubled by the effects of lies and obscenity on his people. He wanted to replace salacious songs with good music. "My opinion is that we *still* must get the people to sing. To that pile of lie-filled laments, superstitious hymns, to the torrent of obscene songs with which we have been flooded, especially since the Revolution, let us oppose good, reasonable, and patriotic songs."[33] Morality, economic well-being, and technical advance were vital elements of Parent's program. He said that abstinence—partial and agrarian—could help balance food consumption and thus commerce. If everyone ate the same things seasonally, the food producers would be helped.[34] He was not above giving advice on such rural basics as grinding mills, especially coffee mills.[35]

As citizens, Parent intoned, priests were part of the nation. And as salaried functionaries they had debts to the nation. "And the 1,200 pounds that the nation pays us: should it make this sacrifice only that we might conduct services? Does it not have the right to require us to serve in every way possible?"[36] Parent was making the point that priests should let people know where their real interests lay. This would fortify them against the predatory aristocrats, who were always ready to return the people to servitude. But their primary obligation would be to provide healing for the nation, to help them forget the tragedies of the Revolution. After having taken an oath in promotion of equality, will they "still have a mania for believing themselves a privileged class distinct from the rest of the citizens?"[37] Churchmen preached simplicity while they themselves were done up in sumptuous, virtually royal, vestments. The people, unfortunately, wanted to make an idol out of the priest, and did not want him "to work at . . . a profession or business like the other citizens." Parent had some suggestions here for small sums to be accorded to priests, but nothing else. Such support was not the business of government.[38] For him, even bell ringing was an ecclesiastical abuse: sounding for a baptism, wedding, or burial, the bells tie up regular life and the villagers end up "in the cabaret for the whole day."[39]

The good pastor should himself be an ideal republican; he should assume the same role in civil society that he had assumed in religious society, the two being completely amalgamated. One priest held it as his "first duty as republican, mayor, and curé" to teach hatred of royalty on the feast of the patron saint of his parish. "As pastor and as a republican I reconcile (without difficulty) the moral teaching of our religion with the principals of republicanism. By the way, all our *catholic* priests would do well to do the same."[40] He included, and the editors duly printed, a long—nine-page!—quotation from the Book of Kings, sure proof that kings were a moral evil.

Marriage in Particular

The new constitution gave confidence in the married priesthood to such as Martinet, curé of Bruys (Aisne). If his colleagues among the constitutionals had the same confidence, more of them would marry; "but they are waiting for something, they fear the counterrevolution, they do not want to lose their position or their salary with the return to the old regime."[41] He would love to have a large group of like-minded colleagues, but only a vicar of the diocese and two other priests followed him. "How happy I would be in this diocese if I could form a pleasant society of married colleagues. Vain wish! I am happy to find such agreeable society with my spouse who gives me attention and companionship."[42]

Parent, enthusiastically supporting Martinet, plunged into extensive theorizing about marriage, starting with the argument that there was nothing spiritual about celibacy. Lack of hubris was not one of Parent's problems: "In vain do many of our bishops, in vain do all the theologians of the world set up in opposition to marriage the *interior, spiritual* discipline of the church; I will prove that the element of discipline that obliges priests to celibacy is *very external, very fleshly,* and that *without need of a council,* it cannot be too quickly proscribed by a government that is a friend of morals, and consequently of the population, and consequently of marriage."[43] With the estimate (too low, we know today) that there were about 80,000 priests in France, he argued that forced celibacy impairs the effectiveness of priests and increases their potential for failure and misbehavior. Scripture supported him: *The spirit is willing but the flesh is weak,* and again, *what begins by the spirit ends by the flesh.* Worse: "In forcing them into celibacy, do you not condemn as many women to it?"[44] In sum, celibacy simply leads to debauchery and all kinds of evil.[45] Paeans of praise, then, for Father Martinet, to whom Parent would have happily rendered every pastoral service.[46]

And Health in General

It all connects up with health and sanity for Parent, who, as we have seen, was content to comment on every area of psychology and social life. His health-and-welfare remarks follow a brief discourse on game, hunting, the free use of the forest, and the vitality of nature itself. "For people of the countryside, game and the hunt are still everything; the countryside and the woods, nothing. The woods suffer from this . . . and from many other abuses."[47] Denouncing such mistreatment of nature, he turns to the problem of health, outdoor living, and exercise in general. "We are in the house too much; thus, for twenty years now we have had, all of us and city dwellers principally, a look of pleurisy and death that could frighten anyone. . . . Exercise is worth more than a branch for the fire. Instead of warming ourselves, let us warm ourselves up."[48]

Even the use of grains counted so much for Parent that he could become moralistic and exhortatory here too. His title: "Let us cease to prostitute our grains by effeminate uses."[49] And there is more of the same in the letter that follows. "Let us cease to inebriate ourselves, to play, to decorate, or rather to disfigure, ourselves with our grains; and we will have bread and peace."[50] Perhaps Parent was a spin-off physiocrat after all.

From Curés Poseurs to Men of the Revolution

The curé was necessary for education and the building of community, according to Géruzez, but not everywhere. In Paris, for example, "*sociétés populaires,* national festivals, temples dedicated to reason filled the void left by the old religion." In the countryside, though, there was no one to replace the curé. "The villagers would be sheep wandering and without a shepherd. . . . A curé patriot, then, can still be of service there." Géruzez was clearly committed to the new civil religion, especially to the replacement for Sunday (called the "décadi") in the revolutionary calendar: "With a few exhortations and some rearranging, I hope that in a short time the décadi will be the only Sunday."[51]

The hearts of these curés were in radical revolution, not in the conservation of ecclesiastical forms. When radical revolution no longer left any room for traditional religion, the curés renounced traditional religion, not only in form and expression, but in substance too. In spring 1794, Parent held forth on real religion, as over against the religion of priests, with its combination of "morality, dogmas, discipline, rituals, observances, practices, ceremonies." Priestly religion was self-serving and hypocritical. In spite of some good deeds, they are "obliged to say, *Do what we say and not what we do*. And that, in fact, was the best morality they could teach."[52] Parent continued, swinging in every direction: religion leads to fanaticism and war. "What is more absurd than their dogmas? What is more ridiculous than their disciplines? And, nevertheless, that is what they hold to most. The so-called wars of religion were not for the sake of morality, but for dogmas, practices, and observances. The morality of Calvinists and Lutherans is absolutely the same as that of Catholics. Why, then, for such a long time have they flooded Europe with blood and carnage."[53] And what was at stake in all this according to Parent? Terminology, tiny points of dogma, slight differences in moral teaching, the whole religion business that was really "no more that the tales of Bluebeard."[54] Parent wanted a religion of and for the people: "The people must be enlightened, instructed, virtuous, friends of the truth. . . . One confuses often the word *religion* with the word *worship*. We do need a religion and popular worship, or rather a religion of truth, of virtue, and of law."[55] Then the punch line, "Priestly worship; no, *we no longer have any need for priests*." His is a religion of reason, good behavior, and following the law. With a quote from two patriotic songs, he triumphantly concluded, "This is my religion. Soon without doubt it will be [the religion] of all the French and, subsequently, of the universe"—this moderated perhaps by his final words, "At least that is what I hope for and desire."[56]

Long restrained, longtime posing, the principal curé ideologues could not restrain themselves. And so Dupuis, now also ex-curé, after his long struggle to live—how shall we say it?—*side by side* with basic Catholic teachings, now attacks them as *absurdities*. "Original sin, one God in three persons, the real presence of a God in the bread one eats, unending torment in the other life. None of this could be the true religion." Catholicism has been "a work of superstition and imposture like all the others."[57] *Philosophy*, with its exploration of real causes and effects, had to be, then, the great ideology, the great savior. "It does not forget that understanding [*indulgence*] is as necessary to the philosopher as intolerance is essential to the priest."[58]

The clergy of *La Feuille villageoise* promoted the oath to the Civil Constitution, of course; it gave them their identity as revolutionary priests. They were for freedom and openness and against superstition—not much of an innovation here. When they promoted marriage and the vernacular over celibacy and Latin, they certainly went against the church polity of their day. These priests began a ministry of active engagement in the new political, social, and cultural life of the nation. But their church identity and activity was gradually swallowed up in the politics of radical revolution. With the fall of the monarchy, they attacked both monarchy and papacy while elevating Rousseau and the Republic; they attacked the worldliness of the refractories while they praised the dedication of the revolutionary clergy. They took on justification of the secular republic, secular ideology, and secular living as a moral responsibility, promoting these secularisms in the name of the gospel. Those who held out as priests the longest believed that the country people needed its priests and that a human ministry of love and tolerance justified the maintenance of the old identity. In the end, they equated standard belief with superstition and considered priesthood to be an aberration.

The clergy letter writers of *La Feuille villageoise* had decided that it would be better to publish as rationalists than perish as priests.

The *Abdicataires* of 1793–1794

The Convention had been menacing the priests for *incivisme,* in effect, any kind of behavior that displeased it. Then by a series of decrees, legislators put together a very attractive package for resigning priests. They would be immune to public suspicion and legal action against them, and they would receive a pension, *provided* they (1) removed ecclesiastical garb, (2) ceased priestly functions, (3) renounced priesthood itself, (4) and married. Within a few months, the majority of the publicly functioning clergy gave up their clerical functions, one way or another.[59]

Michel Vovelle makes the convincing case that there were between 18,500 and 20,000 *abdicataires.*[60] His statistics show that 48% of French priests had to cease functioning in 1791 and that abdications removed 57% of those who were left. As might be expected, departments that had a high percentage of constitutionals usually had a high percentage of *abdicataires:* where there was already a spirit of "giving in" to the government by taking the oath, the next step—giving in by abdication—would be the logical one. Yet such was the confusion of priests' motives and the arbitrariness of social forces around them that some departments with a high percentage of constitutionals in 1791 registered a low level of abdication of those constitutionals in 1793–94; and, conversely, departments with a low percentage of constitutionals in 1791 registered a high level of abdication. The number of priests who married—definitively abdicating in the long run—was put variously by the abbé Grégoire and Cardinal Caprara, the papal representative in France from 1801 to 1808, at 2,000 and 12,000, respectively. Vovelle puts the number closer to

3,000, which is to say, 3.5 percent of the constitutional clergy, using Caprara's own dossiers as the basis for his estimate.[61] These abdications took place across the year II (1793–94), but the second and third months, brumaire and frimaire, had far and away the greatest number, with several forces at play. Some of the *représentants en mission* excelled at the task of dechristianizing. Priests who sought reconciliation with the church years later cited fear as the principal reason for their departure.[62] Local pressures were crucial to the decisions of the rank and file: for example, the early abdications of priestly personalities of strong or high profile (such as Gobel, the bishop of Paris) and the demands of powerful officials. At times, however, the goals and attitudes of dechristianizers actually attracted constitutional priests: "in spite of the constraint and force around them, they were interiorly convinced and impregnated by a discourse they had come to practice with great familiarity." These constitutional priests appeared right at the beginning to follow the line of least resistance and only feebly contested the new system.[63] In sum, then, according to Vovelle, the two operative forces were, on one hand, the dechristianization drive and, on the other hand, the attitudes of clergy and people.[64]

Some priests resigned their parishes and the celebration of worship services. Others carefully restricted themselves to abdicating their "function" of priesthood. The formula urged on most of them required the renunciation of the "state" of being a priest, with the handing over of the documents and letters witnessing to their ordinations. Whatever formula they used, however, priests could still hedge their bets. Bernard Plongeron has said of the Paris priests that if this were not a unified action, it was at least a common way of thinking: "Let us sign our abdication, give all the evidence required to prove our patriotism, and continue with the least possible upset our pastoral work, free from continuing persecution."[65] But, in fact, an outspoken minority (developed personal expression is found only in a minority of dossiers) wanted freedom from the old religious constraints, a new status in republican society, and some kind of monetary compensation (the silent majority were not adverse to severance pay either). The bishop of Paris himself could not pass up the apparent advantages. A new feature here is the high number of religious order members who married—way out of proportion to their numbers among the clergy.[66]

The Complete Abdicataire: Father Pasquer

If there is any one document where you find a full résumé of the faults and failings considered endemic to priesthood and the writer's attempts to remedy them, it is the letter of the sixty-two-year-old Father Pasquer. Entering the seminary in his mid-teens, Pasquer remained socially insular and narrowly educated: "At sixteen, without experience of the world, never having been out of the sight of the church bell tower of my village, and having been educated only by pedants and others as untrained as myself, I was urged to cast myself into an order of fanatic friars [*mendiants*], then a standard resource for children of the lower middle class who like myself were born without means."[67] Religious education only filled his head with worse things, though after ordination he was happy to be a priest: "At the age of twenty-four, having my head stuffed with theological mumbo jumbo [*fatras théologique*] and the decisions of the casuists [*faiseurs de conscience*], I took orders with the best faith in the world, and with the satisfaction that a young priest feels when his conscience tells him that it is right to work in the vineyard of the Lord."[68]

But wider learning caused him to relativize religion: "At thirty years old, instructed by my own readings and by the trips that put me in a situation where I could study the world and above all the genius and the manners of the ministers of the principal sects which divided it, I came to recognize that all religions are only institutions invented by ambitious men to make others over into servitude, and that their dogmas are the workings of a delirious mind. Their various cults, methodical juggling acts with a seriousness and pomp that impresses the vulgar crowd; all this can briefly amuse a philosopher, who, quickly angered by the charlatanism of the priests, steps back deploring the evils produced when they [the priests] take advantage of the credulity of weak mortals."[69]

Pasquer says that twelve years earlier he was able to quietly renounce his priesthood, but that guilt for having submitted to ordination in the first place will stay with him until the end of his days, in spite of some genuine services rendered.[70] Ever since, he has taught only universal and rational moral principles and has been able to help people in ways never before possible.[71] To the earlier renunciation, he now added the public renunciation—for the following good purposes: "To hasten the yearned-for revolution in the minds of my fellow citizens, . . . and to draw the blessings of the people on the national convention, whose wisdom and courage in establishing the reign of philosophical liberty on the ruins of superstition, puts us back on the way of truth and happiness."[72] As clear proof that he was engaged in the way of enlightenment and revolution all along, he cited earlier writings: a criticism of the Book of Genesis showing "the absurdity of that novel," the necessity of the existence of the world and its eternity, a discussion of the means of bringing down tyranny, a presentation of the Canticle of Canticles by the "*érotomani-aque*" Solomon. The works themselves may not be of much value, he said, but he has "the same affection for them that an old man attaches to the children whom he has in declining years: the little creatures, however ungraced by nature, have the singular merit of bewitching the enemies of their father by creating the illusion of vigor."[73] Of the long-term value of these writings he was less sure because future generations should have "enough to be embarrassed about and enough suffering from their own error; it should not be necessary for us to take the trouble to transmit our own [errors] to them."[74]

With eloquence, originality, and a certain creative irritability, Pasquer set down the whole gamut of complaints in the abdicator repertory: resentment of formation and education, denunciation of credulity and the dishonesty of churchmen, contempt for the biblical tradition and Catholic teaching, personal satisfaction on returning to normal life where the only rule is the rule of reason.

Revolutionary Credentials

Abdicating priests flaunted what they took to be their outstanding revolutionary credentials. François Beulazet, an episcopal vicar of Strasbourg (Bas-Rhin), was a model of self-promotion: he had been "first" in everything: "First priest of the former province of Alsace to be decorated with the national cocarde and first in line for the oath; first to surrender his silver rings and pay his patriotic dues; creator of the Société populaire de Belfort; first in Strasbourg to point from the pulpit to the veil of hypocrisy which covered up superstition and fanaticism in this city."[75] Such dedication put him in real danger. Once, celebrating the liturgy at the Alsatian city of Saverne, he barely escaped assassination by men furious at his favoritism of constitutionals and his restoration of a languishing patriotic (revolutionary) society.[76] Louis Courtonne was another who considered his accomplishments eminently noteworthy, in fact, worthy of emulation. "Legislators. I want and call for revolution, my principles march on ahead of it; the revolution has only to develop these principals with greater force." Wanting an even more dramatic witness than his marriage, he "abjured publicly and voluntarily the charlatanism of a dishonest profession." He also needed government help as sequel to this public submission to the truth in order to care for his old mother, a task already of eight years standing and for which he did not really have the money.[77] Another curé played the republican game, to the point of changing his name:

"I want to be called, instead of Claude-Damas Gillard, Brutus Mucius Scaevola Gillard. Tell me, citizen legislators, when you send me the acceptance of my papers, if you accept my change of name, my zeal, and my love."[78] Dropping Christian names and picking up classical Roman names—pagan heroes instead of Christian saints—was very much the fashion by 1794.

Up front, these abdicating priests wanted everyone to know that they were not like their former colleagues. "I have always been exempt from the prejudices of my [old] state," insisted a curé from a village just by Avallon (Yonne).[79] Another curé from the Yonne wrote from prison to promise his future dedication to the cause. "My challenge is to consecrate [my liberty] to the service of the fatherland and to enroll in the Paris revolutionary army that is composed of patriotic citizens alone."[80] Likewise, a curé imprisoned in the Conciergerie, said he was waiting release with "the calm of an honest republican."[81] The abdication was called "civic baptism" by a curé from Perpignan (Pyrénées-Orientales), who bragged that secular moral and social virtues had always been part of his makeup.[82] Inasmuch as many of the priests were old and needed the financial gains of abdication, a young priest from the diocese of Pau could brag, "I am young and in my prime." After requesting money even so, he asked to be assigned to a post where he could make himself useful.[83]

Jacobin and *sans-culotte,* after the reigning revolutionary club and Paris radicals, were key self-labels. A former vicar in Saône-et-Loire vaunted his campaign against the principal rivals of the Jacobins, the Brissotins (who evolved into the Girondins), as they tried to corrupt those poor, dedicated sans-culottes.[84] He finally had to flee the town, thereby attracting the praise and notice of his fellow Jacobins. There followed a number of assignments: leading a detachment of 200 men to General Nicolas at Clermont, searching out men who had gone into hiding, such as municipal officers who had fraternized with the Lyonnais and those who had run to help the Muscadins.[85] He was, in effect, the leader on guard duty, carting away the ideologically impure or recalcitrant. A Convention deputy from the Yonne, Alexandre Paintandre, wrote, "I was the first priest chosen by the electors from the district of Tonnerre because I was known for my patriotism; and I have never given the lie to the favorable opinion that the electors formed about me."[86] And a onetime Franciscan assured the local tribunal that both he and his parents were always revolutionaries at heart. "Born poor of sans-culottes parents, but raised with their prejudices, I pronounced my vows in the order of Minims when I was seventeen." Leaving the order, he then filled the more patriotic position of military chaplain. So, they were faithful churchgoers and he became a priest, but they were all sans-culottes nevertheless.[87]

Attack on Priesthood and the Old Religion

This parading of revolutionary devotion and activity was accompanied by, sometimes simply degenerated into, attacks on the old clerical and religious ways. Paintandre wrote that he could not really admit to hypocrisy because of his lifelong aversion to it. Given the evils of clerical religion, honesty is the only salvation for a cleric. "I know that any priest who holds to the teachings of the Roman Church can only be a knave, but he who has a few philosophical notions, who checks into the eternal laws of reason and truth could not be fooled by the gross errors of this lie-filled religion."[88] And so it went for these abdicators. For one, the aristocracy was a blight on human existence, but religious fanaticism was "of all the heads of the hydra, the most deadly for the people." It could be said that religion so channels fear and distorts the conscience that healthy citizenship becomes impossible.[89] For another, ordination was a sort of original sin; he, accordingly, wanted to "obliterate the original and impure stain of my ordination, renouncing the works of the demon of fanaticism and superstition."[90] Abdication was the occasion to cover priesthood with insults: "No more priests, the public good requires it; consequently, no more priestly papers. I surrender to you my own. Holding charlatanism in horror, why would I need the papers of a charlatan?"[91] But here, abdication did not preclude the proud inclusion of a homily to celebrate the marriage of a colleague.[92] So the laws of nature are real religion, whose emissaries should give their all to the "extinction of fanaticism."[93]

Sheer nastiness suffused some texts, such as the testimony that began: "It is at the foot of the Mountain, which has hurled thunderbolts at the foul tyrant and his lascivious spouse and their vile servants, that I come before you to declare that I renounce forever the exercise of Catholic worship."[94] At times, nastiness is matched with at least minor eloquence. An Oratorian wrote the following: "I have always combated and detested priests. Do not suffer it to happen that these profoundly perverse men any longer oblige a simple and good people to prostrate themselves before a piece of bread, out of which their insolent pride would effect the creation of a god. Do not suffer it to happen that these priests, abusing the secret of confession, any longer divide families, cause blood to flow, overturn empires, and govern in any way they choose the human race."[95] At times the nastiness is simply sarcasm gone awry, as in one Benedictine's evocation of ordination day—in words reminiscent of our model *abdicataire,* Father Pasquer: "In 1772, because of my destiny, I was forced to appear before a man who was dressed as a woman. This man said a few words that I never understood and put some kind of drug on my fingers. . . . After that they told me that I was a priest." And after this ham-fisted description of vestments and anointing, he begged his witnesses not to "regard [him] as one of those Druids who have tormented our republic by their infamous maneuvers."[96]

Blame for Parents and Praise for Marriage

Not a few priests blamed their families for getting them into the foul system. A curé from the Yonne said, "I renounce my function in that state in which the foolish vanity of my parents had raised me."[97] The aforementioned ex-Benedictine did not hesitate to blame his father for his problems: "A victim of the prejudice, ambition, and callousness of a father who did not recognize my rights at all, I entered the cloister between the ages of sixteen and seventeen."[98] Sometimes the mother was to blame: "Carried from the cradle by a credulous mother to the altars of falsehood, I was not slow to see that the leaders of the papist sect destined me to be an apostle of imposture and corruption."[99]

The self-justifying mode was most prominent when one's own marriage was at issue. The foolishness of the old religion, the misbehavior of the colleagues, and the opposition of families motivated these priests to strong promotion of the married state. One priest had been married for years: "I heard the gentle voice of nature. I secretly married a girl of my age, whose virtue and charm have been my greatest happiness for twenty-two years." Betrayed by a clerical colleague with government connections, he was carried off like a criminal, held in a Franciscan convent for two years, and treated with the cruelty bred of "the Inquisition and monastic callousness."[100] Another explained the difficulties of arranging marriage in the old social context. His fiancée was still slightly underage, but more important, the father, "still attached to the old prejudices . . . could not bring himself to envisage his daughter with a priest."[101]

A priest who had worked under the constitutional bishop of Calvados, Claude Fauchet, reported with obvious satisfaction and, I do believe, a smile his move from the tradition of celibacy to the new civil celebration of marriage. "From the moment that the law allowed priests to choose a companion, I forgot about the existence of pope and councils, I heard the voice of nature, and I exchanged an old breviary for a young *Républicaine*." He had wanted to point out to colleagues in their useless state of celibacy the value of such a move. But even in the Convention several aristocrats controlled the channels of communication to the extent that the example of a good "republican priest" could not be disseminated easily.[102] Claude Fauchet himself was an obstacle according to this former associate; Fauchet who "with sacerdotal hypocrisy, spoke the language of [the pure] Joseph, but could not have been more continent than David."[103]

Praise of Reason

Positive eloquence was saved for the Revolution and Reason. A former vicar at Notre-Dame cathedral said that under the old regime he was persecuted for his views and values. If only his colleagues would abdicate also, they would contribute to this "triumph of liberty, reason, and truth."[104] Far more eloquent was a curé from Calvados, who combined an earnest prayer to Reason with a few choice labels for the old religious symbols: "Divine Reason, receive my homage. I have always offered you true worship in the secrecy of my heart, and may it today be as bright as the light. I make my offering on the altar just put in place for the people most worthy of you. Free at last, rejoicing with my whole being, I depose upon [the altar] the ridiculous baubles, the absurdities that have hung on my neck until this moment."[105] A handsomely written letter, seven pages long and bound with a decorative ribbon, made the French nation a model of this worship of reason: "Soon the altars raised in honor of the new divinity [Supreme Being] will radiate out from the center to the whole republic. Soon all foreign nations for whom the French serve as a model and guide *with good reason,* will abjure their prejudices and errors in the sanctuaries of the new temples and sing with us timeless hymns to the glory of liberty and equality."[106] Jean-Baptiste Géruzez, notable as a leading and fluent letter writer to *La Feuille villageoise,* drummed up his standard praise of philosophy. In effect he gave a little sermon to the assembly members: "Legislators, you have received of its [philosophy's] fullness, and its life-giving spirit is hovering over you." If everything these legislators do is channeled to the promotion of reason, they will be able to say, "The blind see; the deaf hear; the crippled walk; the dead come back to life; and the gospel of liberty and equality is proclaimed to the sans-culottes."[107]

All the trouble, then, comes from "fanatical, ignorant, and superstitious clergy," who have hidden God the Father behind the image of a severe judge.

It would appear that at least one abdicator kept the essence of the biblical image of God in the new dispensation: "I render homage to the worship of reason and a morality that reveals to us a good Father in the author of Nature, thereby giving us in his name the election once snatched from us, reducing us to the cruelest slavery."[108]

Uselessness of Old Careers

In the light of reason, priestly activity would have been a waste of time: "A priest at twenty-four, I was named curé of three huge parishes . . . in the department of Deux-Sèvres, where I vegetated for thirty-six years."[109] This from an episcopal vicar of the department, who at seventy-one years old (the documentation of his ordinations and other clerical dignities was surely one of the most extensive submitted) simply and calmly stated that he had always promoted the Revolution. The old life was often lived against every inclination, said another, typical of the former priests who were only too grateful to the revolutionary government, "wise and benevolent," that made it possible for those "not infatuated by fanaticism to abdicate forever both the functions of ministry and the priestly character."[110]

Constitutional priests could talk about the persecutions they had undergone in vain. A curé from Brittany professed to be "absolutely without resource, without even my own furniture, because thieves of the so-called Catholic Army have twice in a row terribly broken, pillaged, and devastated in the name of the God of peace and all justice"; they even stole his savings.[111] A former religious order member, subsequently curé of two parishes in Puy-de-Dôme, had come under life-threatening attack in one of the parishes: "My home, with its straw roof, was isolated in a mountain area. Under cover of darkness it was set on fire, my family and I nearly died in the flames, which in half an hour consumed the presbytery and all of our savings." And then he got no justice whatsoever: "The commissaires sent by the district judged our losses at 1,000, but they were much larger than that. I received 180 francs."[112]

Content to divest themselves of priestly dignity, some constitutionals still believed that they had accomplished genuine good while part of the system. A curé from the Lille region, who could not get his letters of ordination together in time for his appointed abdication date (because they were "in Paris, among my wife's papers"), said that he would use the time left as a priest to promote the Revolution. "I will profit from this little delay to explain once more to my parishioners the new republican calendar and get rid of their superstitious apprehensiveness about celebrating Sunday on the day of the décade. They are good people that anything can bother because they are for the most part devoid of learning. They are accustomed to their old routines and ways, so that everything new seems to be a violation of what they call religion."[113] In this case, we have an abdicator with some weeks or months left as a *poseur*!

Search for New Positive Roles

The printing and distribution of good literature was a rewarding task for a resident of Crépy (Oise), then in the process of setting up a reading room "for promoting the republican attitude, and the love of liberty and equality." As for the print shop, he hoped that the district would advance him a bit of money for the task.[114] Géruzez, the indefatigable ideologist also took on the worthy and high profile republican work of the printer. "Following the advice of Rousseau, I am going to do manual and independent work. I have begun as a printer. And I have embraced this work all the more willingly because it is to it [the press] that we owe the Revolution. Printing is the mother of reason; it has killed kings, nobles, and priests."[115] A former priest-teacher explored the possibilities of instruction in rhetoric and philosophy, made all the more effective in a good republican setting: "Often, at the foot of the tree of liberty that their young hands have planted, we make the air resound with our patriotic songs in celebration of French victories."[116] He is, still and all, attentive to the need to build on the decrees establishing the state system of primary education and to go on to secondary education.[117] The government has a responsibility also to the teachers themselves, those on the lower levels and the emeriti of the university of Paris "who have grown old in the honorable and difficult role of a teacher."[118]

Abdicating for a better future combined with regret at the severing of old relationships, as in this paternal message: "Circumstances do not permit me to continue my services, but as I leave you, I bring with me the satisfaction that I never preached to you anything other than a morality most genuine and right for making you better and happier people. This separation is painful for you who are close to me, and you should know that it is no less painful for me who has, for fifteen years, loved you as a father loves his children."[119] In spite of all the personal cost involved, the defense of the revolutionary goals, the religion of Reason, and the new government—all for the sake of the fatherland—make it worthwhile.[120] The author trusts that his people noticed his dedication to the "holy revolution" from the beginning and will not be scandalized by his formal renunciation of his priestly functions.[121] In contrast, an *abdicataire* could make it quite clear that handing in papers was simply handing in papers, and that such an act had nothing to do with the reality of priesthood. One municipality report read as follows: "We have received from the said citizen Petit his letters of priesthood. . . . [He] said that by the present statement and by the handing in of his letters of priesthood . . . he in no way intends to surrender his title of curé . . . abdicate, or even less renounce his quality of priest, in which he glories and will always glory even at the cost of his life's blood. But he acts only in the interest of peace."[122] In speaking out publicly, this priest may have represented the silent majority of the *abdicataires* (Plongeron, remember, thinks that this was the case in Paris). And this is the tone of voice that one hears again and again in the testimonies of the *rétractés*.

Outspoken abdicating priests—and I have highlighted the outspoken minority—made great drama of their revolutionary lives, showing how each contribution to the movement automatically gained them credentials as bona fide revolutionaries, some reaching for the Jacobin and sans-culotte labels. Many of them could not prevent themselves from attacking their old ways of life, the old-regime priestly careers and the old Catholic religion that they had come to see as decadent and damaging to its adherents: parents were to blame and marriage was the solution. Whether intellectual or not, they voiced a standardized praise of reason that was the lowest common denominator of Enlightenment philosophies. It would appear that convinced *abdicataires* wanted to remove the constraints of the priestly function and state, for the sake of a better life for themselves and, often enough, better service to others in such careers as teaching and publishing. These were angry men, and they tell us why they are angry.

Retracting the Oath—Patterns of Guilt and Justification

Large numbers of priests who had sworn that oath of loyalty to the Civil Constitution of the Clergy retracted it. And there were those who had never taken the oath but who compromised themselves by misbehavior or leaving altogether. They believed they had been seduced by revolutionary ideas and wanted to have a place—not always as members of the clergy—in the papal church. Public retractions were made across the revolutionary years: some of them published, some of them making it into government files, some only written down for the papal legation set up in Paris under the headship of Cardinal Giovanni-Baptisti Caprara upon the demand of Napoleon, whose aides saw in Caprara a conciliatory figure. The cardinal was responsible for the application of the 1801 Concordat between the Holy See and Napoleon's government. Specific forms of retraction are not limited to any one period, however, and they do run the gamut from extreme guilt to forward-looking proposals for productive secular or religious lives. We preserve intact the names of all the retracting priests in the following testimonies: their names and career highlights already figure in a printed repertoire, and so contemporary readers can explore more of the careers and contexts of these men.[123]

Haunted by Guilt

Retractions highlighting guilt and remorse abounded. Charles-François Hamart had once promoted revolutionary priesthood as a vital element of a new-era government in this profession of allegiance to the constitutional church: "I declare to you, as if I were on my deathbed, that I have no apprehension about the doctrine I am teaching you: it is that of Jesus Christ, that of the Catholic, Apostolic, and Roman Church, that of Saints Athanasius, John Chrysostom, Cyprian, Gregory, that of the clergy of France of every era; in a word, my dear children, that of a man who for twenty-five years has studied, preached, and taught this holy religion."[124] He publicly defended the oath, even published a catechism as counterweight to an anticonstitutional refractory catechism. This work he now abhorred—although seriousness, energy, and emotion had earlier gone into it—saying, "For a long time now, my dear parishioners, they have been distributing to you in great numbers a horrible catechism. It has spread a spirit of irreligion and revolt among you; broken up families; separated spouses, brothers, and friends; inspired savagery in people once most upright. In a word, I cannot portray, other than with tears of blood, all the evils it has caused among you." The formal retraction began with a confession of his major sins, straying from the Roman Catholic faith and then breaking his priestly vows by a civil marriage, "a sacrilegious union followed by the birth of two children whom death has harvested." It may be that this last sorrow had brought him to repentance, the death of the children seen as divine punishment, but he condemned and repented the theological sins of his former state, driven by guilt and renewed loyalty to the church.

Hamart's sense of sin came out of his renewed unqualified acceptance of papal authority. The oath of loyalty to the constitution was "illicit, contrary to doctrine, to the Discipline and Hierarchy of the Catholic Church," and, accordingly, his catechism was contrary to church teachings. It was absolutely necessary, then, that he retract his earlier schismatic and heretical teachings. He even urges his people to burn the catechism as well as all related writings and letters. Hamart did not expect to be accepted back into active priestly service; he simply wanted reconciliation with the church: "I live in the hope of being able to one day reenter the fold of Jesus Christ, not as minister because I recognize my unworthiness, but at least as a humble penitent resolved to undertake, carry out, suffer . . . anything to merit such a signal favor."

Louis-François Michelet was a very young man (eighteen!) when he was ordained.[125] Events disoriented him, and church authorities, including the noted constitutional bishop Claude Fauchet, failed him as spiritual guides. He would have the hearers or readers of his retraction recall those revolutionary years when everything was being swept away. God seemed to permit his servants to be tried by the surrounding depravity of the body politic. Although not totally naive, he was in no position to appreciate the holiness of the priesthood or to see through the false glamour of the role offered him. Only with time was he able to see that he had "skirted a precipice that appeared to be a meadow full of flowers and had prepared to jump over." He compared the experience to the attraction of a rose, "of which one sees only the beauty, but whose pinprick is felt when touched." His conscience came to torment him because he could see the damage done by the constitutional church, a group of "immoral" men who were responsible for many of the misfortunes suffered by France. He would renounce the oaths he had taken, knowing now that he was ordained by a schismatic bishop not in communion with the pope. After this "dead and fateful" ordination, he was not really the true pastor of those whose marriages he solemnized. All other sacraments, too, except when administered to those in danger of death, were null and void, he thought. Now with his return to the religion of the fathers, he could reflect on what he had done: "I am hateful to myself and carried away by indignation." His conclusion was a striking prayer *to* Louis XVI: "O Louis XVI, O my master. You who have gathered the palms of martyrdom and glory, you who have shared the fate of St. Louis. Have compassion on my miserable state. Please intercede for me with the great Dispenser of graces. Grant that I might, without wavering in my religion, triumph over the wicked men who will probably turn their daggers against me." Constitutional priests could admit that extremely clever politicians have used them and then thrown them away like so many worn out tools.

Guilt with Justification: Holding Back on the Oath

Without genuinely weakening the expression of guilt, retracting priests would offer some justification of their behavior. Former curés would often say that when they took the oath as constitutionals, they made public or mental reservations—limitations on the fullness of adhesion to the oath.

Michel Gibal began work as a constitutional by hedging his bets: "I took the oath with all the restrictions in favor of the Catholic religion that the circumstances could permit."[126] These restrictions he listed in his sermons and recorded in an official registry of the municipality (which did not protect him from later persecution as a constitutional). His obedience to the new system was at best begrudging, never paying a formal visit to the constitutional bishop but rather opposing him in every parish he visited. For three years, though, he did nothing about the ecclesiastical suspension that he had incurred as a constitutional. When after the coup of fructidor, the church authorities could not come to an agreement, he took the liberty on informing them that, according to the ecclesiastical brief published back in 1791, they had no right to suspend him—for the following reasons: "First, they could not say that I had taken the oath purely and simply; second, I had fulfilled the wish of the legislator and the purpose of the law had been accomplished, and they could not refuse the request for absolution I had made, even if it should be true that I had incurred some censure." But the church authorities insisted that he wait longer.

The Gibal petition, to Caprara that is, then shifted into the retracting mode with a bow to papal supremacy. He displayed theological awareness—"I know that it is only on the barque of St. Peter that one can avoid shipwreck"— admitted the validity of canon law, and assumed that he was making up for his faults as much as possible. With the conclusion, "If something is missing, I beseech your Eminence to accept new expressions of sorrow," Gibal's self-justification was near total.

Justification: Standing Fast with the Parishioners

Clear, that many of the priests had been dedicated to their parishioners (and at times to their own advancement), with the possibility of suffering and imprisonment always in the background. Genuine pastoral concern was a frequent, and I believe sincere, theme.

Jacques-René Tourteau had taken the oath and thus became eligible for a parish of twelve hundred parishioners in the nearby town of Tuffé (Sarthe), whereas he had previously been administering to a parish of two hundred communicants.[127] It would appear that he wanted to both help people and move up the clerical ladder. He told authorities that he could not submit himself to the new bishops, but they, in their turn, asked him again if he would think about working with the local constitutional bishop. His negative response lost him the pastorate at Tuffé. Then the authorities turned right around and gave him another parish, his reservations about the oath notwithstanding. In the new parish Tourteau took all the new oaths required by the new state of affairs, cavalierly noting that he would have taken whatever oaths were appropriate to a given culture and government. "I took, retook, or renewed [on the given dates] the oaths of loyalty, liberty, equality, and hatred of Royalty (as incompatible with a purely democratic state). At Rome, Naples, Madrid, St. Petersburg, and Constantinople I would have in the same sense sworn hatred of Democracy. By that time, if they have asked for a hundred oaths for and against, I would have taken them."[128] He just did not give a damn at that time.

There would be, of course, a financial advantage to a good parish appointment, and so he felt a little politicking was in order: "I secretly asked someone in the parish to ask for me there. The plan worked, and I was installed the 28 February 1793, authorized by the new bishop." So, he worked with the constitutional bishop finally; it was only the Terror that made him stop his priestly activity. He then handed over his priestly papers, certain that this would not "eclipse" his priesthood but also knowing that the people present would see it another way. There was high drama to the experience, in that the army of the Vendée almost executed him. "I was led to a nearby square and surrounded by three hundred of the soldiers, though I had [moments before] noticed only forty, and the saber was lifted over my head; they exulted in the joy (I see them still) of sacrificing a priest, while three of them stole my umbrella, wallet, and watch. Facing death, I asked for confession but was refused. Three seconds more and I would have been hacked to death. But suddenly several priests appeared. Was that their job? If I have life today, it is to one of them that I owe it." Refractory priests showed up to save him, but he suspected that they were part of the scenario. In his report on these events, he had harsh words both for revolutionaries and counterrevolutionaries. On one hand, among republican extremists, violence and hatred drove them to sacrilege. On the other hand, the counterrevolutionaries, the Chouans, hounded him, first threatening him and then, in a series of attacks and robberies, making him abandon his parish altogether.

Tourteau was, even so, willing to serve as a priest from time to time and recommended preaching to both constitutional and refractory churchmen. He even admitted his unease about the old church. "I had doubts and scruples, but I moved beyond them. . . . Because of the evil and ordeals of the era, we must bend to the ancient laws that were not democratic." He admitted that he observed and worked with genuine faith in the constitutional church: "I cannot be persuaded easily that those faithful who followed along, without wanting to separate themselves from the sovereign Pontiff . . . will be condemned to eternal damnation by the Father of Mercies."

Simple Innocence

Innocence shows through, too: the most natural thing in the world to continue in the ministry. Honestly looking for help in difficult and confusing times, it seemed right to take the oath, hand over papers, look into marriage, and work productively at some job.

Claude-Nicholas-Joseph Collignon was a Carthusian who tells a straight story of service to the constitutional church as if it were simply in the order of things.[129] "After I lived thirteen years in the Carthusian order, a law forced me to leave that state in life. I took the first oath of fidelity to the laws of the French government, and I exercised the functions of priesthood for the next eight and one-half years, until the period when they [functions] were forbidden." And he would have continued—in all innocence—had he not contracted a marriage, a fake marriage that was a strategy to save them both. The young woman had taken refuge in the home of her parents and, on the night before she was to flee the country with her family, agreed to the formal marriage in order to save him from death. She left as planned, and they never did resume contact.

Guillaume Bruzac took the oath without anxiety it would appear, but the anxieties of the persecution were more than he could bear.[130] Not knowing what to do, he consulted friends who told him that marriage was the only solution. He "had the weakness" to do this in the presence of a priest and civil official, continuing his pastoral functions for another four or five months. Then came abdication but, he emphasized, without offense to religion and without handing over the *lettres de prêtrise*. He lists simply and without comment all the actions that he is submitting to reconciliation: the oaths, the acceptance of the constitutional pension, the marriage—from which he has one daughter. All of these actions, however, are presented as the normal state of things.

Martin Bergès entered a straightforward plea of ignorance.[131] In good conscience, he swore the entire formula of the oath—with the addition of several reservations. After he had signed the written formula, he found to his chagrin that the reservations had not been added into the minutes. He protests that he never recognized the constitutional bishop. He was in contact with him but "only to send a certificate in order to obtain a dispensation from the publication of the Bans [of marriage]." He also "read a few lines of his instructions where he asked that the *Te Deum* be sung." Bergès is asking now only that an earlier reconciliation be confirmed. "I remained until the year 1795 or thereabouts, at which time I presented myself to the vicars general of my legitimate bishop, to be released from my oath."

Louis-Alexandre-Pierre Bourdon was not shy about his virtues.[132] "For twenty years . . . his conduct never ceased to merit the esteem of the natives of the canton." Those virtues were at once "the most beautiful adornments of the true pastor" and "the consolation and joy of his flock." He believed it was just natural to go on working where he had exercised his ministry, serving a parish until the height of the Terror when he went to work at the National Treasury. In fact, he could not really be classified as a constitutional priest at all.

Jean-Baptiste-Antoine Mailloc was a constitutional priest from 1791 to 1793, at which time he sent in his *lettres de prêtrise* to the Convention, getting them back after the death of Robespierre.[133] Simple innocence maybe, but as government *commissaire* he had to take down public crosses and hand over priests. He had warned them not to lead public worship and they would not cooperate. In spite of all this, he still unqualifiedly wants to remain an active priest. "All these actions went against the grain and still bother me. In the more than two years since I ceased functioning, I always wanted to ascend the altar again but dared not. I waited and hoped for a new order of things. And now it has come."

Constitutionals from the Beginning

Curés could start off as successful and fulfilled constitutional pastors, whether ordained by an old-regime bishop or a new constitutional bishop. The constitutional church was simply *their* church, taken on without soul searching or later agonies, though some do admit to errors or conniving of sorts.

Hyacinthe Doux already had a vital position in the new constitutional church when he accepted a professorial chair in the constitutional seminary

and assisted the bishop at ordinations.[134] He was a constitutional in all innocence because he had worked things out with his old-regime bishop. "I had
not at all left the parish to which I was attached, and having all the faculties
needed from the former bishop, I did not demand any from the new one."
The bishop had told him that, in the absence of communications from Rome,
he, the bishop, could effect reconciliation. Even in this letter of retraction,
Doux refers to the constitutional church as "us," as he reconciled himself to
the old-regime bishop: "After the great day of 9 thermidor, 28 July 1794, the
mourning of France was ended and the exercise of Catholic worship seemed
possible, in order to put an end to the split existing between Rome and us."

François Dusser made an especially wholesome and straightforward presentation.[135] If anyone was a born constitutional priest, he was. "He received the
four minor orders and the subdiaconate from the hands of Citizen Pouchot,
constitutional bishop of the department of the Isère on 23 April 1791, the dia-
conate on 19 June, and priesthood on 24 September of the same year 1791.
Likewise he took the oath of the Civil Constitution of the Clergy in his
capacity as vicar of Saint-Antoine, diocese of Vienne in Dauphiné, 9 October
1791." And he took all the other oaths: "Elected curé of Brépol, in the diocese of the said Vienne, by the electoral assembly of Roman, department of
the Drôme, 17 September 1792. Received canonical institution from Citizen
Marbos, constitutional bishop of the Drôme, 28 September 1792. Took the
liberté/égalité oath when taking over the pastorate of Brépol, 30 September
1792." But he finally retracted, believing now that he was an intruder and a
sort of revolutionary, and was reduced to the lay state in collusion with the
administration of the diocese of Grenoble.

Nicholas-Joseph Groult offered justification with a report of honest conniving, covering all the bases in his excuse-making.[136] He came from a family
where his parents wanted the financial advantage of having a son as a priest,
especially after his father's reversal of fortune. In his family they never talked
about any other honest ways to make a living. After several years of monastic
preparation, in accordance with custom, "he entered holy orders and was
made a priest at the beginning of the Revolution but never celebrated his first
Mass." When he says that he did not say a first Mass, one assumes he means
the home-parish celebration and not that he never said Mass. When the religious orders were suppressed in 1793, he went to Lyon and placed himself
under the republican army administration after its successful siege of the city.
From then until 1801 he was a commander in the artillery. Out of the military
after what he calls "a fairly long career," he presented himself to the Caprara

legation—subtly hedging his bets. He wanted to be released from all obligations except chastity; released, then, from the breviary and clerical dress obligations. Wanted, also, to continue in the military as a practicing Catholic, and
then, perhaps, return to the ministry one day. "By this means you will put
him in a position to reconcile with his civic life, the exercise of the Catholic
religion, for which he has always maintained a most unbreakable attachment."

Complex Innocence

Complexity could result from confused involvement in the system or an idiosyncratic religious stance. Pierre Barthélémé Barruel-Labeaume had a very
subtle way of reporting his oaths and behavior as a constitutional.[137] He
offered an elaborate and sincere justification of his constitutional apostolate.
First of all, the Civil Constitution of the Clergy of 1791 seemed quite correct,
respecting religion and the throne. His promotion of the constitution was
intellectual and not heartfelt, and even the intellectual promotion he came to
recognize as an error. Even so, for a while he tried to gather testimony and
evidence in favor of it, to help his fellow priests understand the issues. The
text was printed and promoted by the authorities under the title *Letter of a
Former Vicar General to a Curé and Friend,* but without his name attached. In
consequence he was appointed a member of the commune's municipal council. Always in contact with his old-regime bishops, Barruel-Labeaume took
the second oath, against anarchy and inequality, never thinking that he
incurred any of the censures against the constitutionals: "Having done this, he
did not think he had incurred the censures brought . . . against the *intrus* and
oath takers."

At the time he was working with the bizarre and unique Charles de Lafont
de Savine (one of the four old-regime metropolitan bishops who had taken
the oath), in a common effort to keep the peace. Still and all, those were bad
times, and he had the misfortune to be a part of them. Bishop Lafont de
Savine went along with the government while trying to embody church
authority: "the bishop of Viviers, having transferred all the feast and Sundays
to the décadi, had the impudence to claim to preach with the authority of the
church Fathers . . . and to comment on the texts for the daily and Sunday
services." Even as he made this transferal, the bishops maintained that "the
spiritual sanctification of Sundays was of apostolic tradition and should be
considered sacred." Thus Sunday kept its special status in Barruel-Labeaume's
home diocese.

Seriously ill in 1796, Barruel-Labeaume received viaticum, and of his own will made the following public statement: "I declare before God that all I have said, done, or written about the events of these times, I have done only for the good of religion and peace in the church, but recognizing now my error, I retract sincerely and with all my heart all that has been condemned and all that would subsequently be condemned by my judges concerning faith and discipline, protesting that I have submitted in mind and heart to all that is taught by the Catholic, apostolic, and Roman religion teaches. In the bosom of which I wish to live and die, and I ask pardon of God and men for the scandal that could have been given [*des scandales que je puis avoir donnés*]." This, then, was an earlier retraction and one that placed Barruel-Labeaume in the first rank of *retractés*. He did take the later oath of hatred of royalty—to continue receiving his pension—but to put everything in order, he formally requests full rehabilitation: "He casts himself at the feet of His Holiness to beg him to absolve from the censures that he could have incurred, and to reestablish him in the exercise of all the functions that he has refrained from in a spirit of penance since the church was closed, submitting himself to all it should please His Holiness to impose on him." Complex innocence.

Suffering as Ultimate Justification

Few constitutionals told as sad and bitter a story as Pierre Vistorte. He suffered at the hands of revolutionaries; his wife, at the hands of churchmen. Even so, he begged the Caprara legation that "he not be judged in the greatness of his iniquity"; instead, "he asked for forgiveness and mercy, not to appear innocent, but out of love for the truth" and declared himself ready to accept his punishment.[138] He, too, had hedged his bets on the oath, taking it with restrictions and signing nothing. A reputable clergyman and, for all practical purposes, a refractory, he was "considered a model of religious ministry, as much for his virtues as for his learning" and wanted to ensure that his own behavior did not cause his fellow priests to go astray. He was aware that his public retraction was unclear, but at least he refused to accept the mandate of the new bishop. Then, in the face of persecution, profanation, and deception, he had to take refuge. Parents were no help, "not having offered him a glass of water." A good widow, whose children he had tutored, admitted him to her aristocratic household—where he was not, in fact, safe and sound. When the political clubs set upon them, he remained calm. But for the widow it was different, "fearing for his life, safety, and liberty." Drama, then: "she suddenly fainted, and when she came to, she was unwilling to give me up. She did not see any other solution than contracting a marriage with [me]."

Although Vistorte did marry the widow, sinning thereby against church discipline, he continued to defend the true faith. Before long, he was drawn back into pastoral work. "More than once in that time of revolutionary rage and fury, when all means of finding priests in good standing with the church had been exhausted . . . he consoled the dying lest they die in despair without reception of the sacrament of penance, which he was allowed to administer in case of necessity and imminent danger of death." The only transgression was to continue on, inadvertently, to the administration of extreme unction, forbidden to unauthorized priests. But throughout all this, his conscience tormented him, and he wanted to set things straight. The "good faith" of his wife held him back, however, because she, "was ignorant of the diriment impediment that made his marriage invalid in the eyes of the church," and because he was persuaded "that a church full of tenderness for her children would, in view of the circumstances, extend its mercy to her."

Vistorte believed the opportune moment had arrived when the church made peace with the French government and appeared to be open to the reconciliation of married priests. He revealed his troubled conscience to his wife, who quite willingly agreed to the procedures necessary for reconciliation. At that point, he did not understand that the Caprara legation had full powers of dispensation. So he did not try to have the marriage validated or leave his wife, a missed opportunity all the more unfortunate in view of her final illness: "She [eventually] died as a result of breast cancer, which tormented her, and of moral suffering, which pained her even more." When she knew her illness could not be cured, she begged the curé to offer a Mass for her intentions: the grace to bear her suffering, obtain forgiveness of her sins, and die a happy death. Her request for confession was refused, even when, a second time, her condition grave, the priests refused to follow the new directives on reconciliation. "They always wanted to consider her a public concubine, and as such they required of her a full separation." Vistorte tried another tack, telling the clergy that a spouse who married innocently could be likened to the spouse of a Jew, a pagan, or an atheist. He asked them whether a spouse who behaved in a Christian manner, married her husband in accordance with all the laws and forms of his country, and then asked for the help of the church, would be refused the consolation of the church when she asked for it.

Vistorte's poor wife was begging for any kind of prayers at the end. In vain. Vistorte again argued, "You who each day pray for pagans and infidels, you refuse to recommend to the prayers of the faithful a dying woman who has great confidence in those prayers." But he finally had to admit that for his wife's well-being, even at the end, they had to part. "[He] went to the sick woman, and with great charity spoke to her thus, 'My dear spouse, you are on the threshold of eternity, the bishop is silent, the priests remain obstinate, so you must not entrust your eternal destiny to chance. . . .' With these words, the hapless couple separated, never to see one another again."

Vistorte ended his petition to the Caprara legation with a simple justification of the life he had lived subsequent to these sad events: a trusted municipal administrator, he was able to insure the safety of his fellow priests. And so he requested (1) the validation of his marriage, (2) the legitimation of his children, and perhaps even, one day "the joy of saying Mass again before dying."

A Future Apostolate

Jean-Baptiste L'Abbé quickly scampers over his constitutional career and his marriage (he separated from the woman shortly afterwards) in order to propose new apostolates in the church.[139] In his travels, he was struck by the ignorance in the countryside, and his solution would be the foundation of "two congregations, one of men and one of women, gathered in two houses with structures and rules approved by the authority of the church." Both congregations would teach the basics of reading, writing, arithmetic, and religion: the congregation of men would assure training in worship and music for the liturgical services, and the congregation of women would assure care of the churches. And both would have regular jobs! "[Members] will work with their hands to support their own needs and not be the responsibility of others; they will in a certain way bring dignity to both agriculture and the fine arts, thereby rendering themselves useful to regular society." Finally, both would have houses of education. And now, L'Abbé looks for advice: "If you believe and judge that this plan might be useful for the greater glory of God, and for the benefit of religion and society, send me a few lines in response." Either the man has lots of cheek and assumes he can distract the legation from his apostasy, or he is too much of an apostolic enthusiast to waste time on past error.

Some of the *rétractés* felt pure guilt, with abject contrition. Excuses were offered too: some took the oath with major reservations, or stayed on as constitutionals because their people needed them, or simply saw nothing wrong in the renewed church (of course, new priests never experienced anything else). But it was seldom simple: priests reported complex and confused years when they tried to work it all out. For a few, revolutionary priesthood was nothing but suffering, as much caused by the church as caused by the Revolution. Most of the testimonies we read came after the close of the revolutionary decade, but they are expressive of the inner thoughts of the men who failed to bring off an experiment that they once considered the best way to meet the political, religious, and personal challenges of the era. Retraction was the end of the line for these constitutional priests and bishops, whether in the course of the revolutionary years or at the end of the Revolution. They were responsible in no small way for the failure of the constitutional church.

In Sum

There is no doubt but that the constitutional priests of France were forced to choose between the mother church and the fatherland. They began by participating in a new national (Catholic) church and ended by jettisoning church and embracing nation: loyalty to and promotion of the nation gave them their principal identity. Formal Catholicism, their own clerical Catholicism, belonged to the Bourbon dynasty and the old-regime aristocracy. Such Catholicism came to feel superstitious, humanly constraining, and sometimes downright immoral when compared to the new, wider world of goodness and truth they experienced as members of the nation. The *poseurs* put up with the old doctrinal, moral, and devotional profile—some of them for years. *Abdicataires* felt the need to denounce explicitly and formally the old Catholicism and their identification with it. But *rétractés,* many of them perhaps never really rejecting their traditional religious profile, finally went back on their real or apparent embrace of the new political order. Seeing the divide between the national effort of the revolutionary years and Catholicism, they embraced Catholicism. They had yet to discover whether the new Rome-friendly government of Napoleon could or would engage their loyalty.

Chapter Two

NATIONAL IDEALS AND THEIR FAILURE: *Festival Celebration Under the Directory*

Divorced from Catholicism, the national government needed its own religion substitute. Festivals were planned as ritualized celebrations (speeches, tableaux, parades/processions, and music) of a revolutionary myth (new nation, elect community, pantheon of political heroes) with strong resemblance to the Christian myths and rituals celebrating creation and redemption.[1] The new myth and ritual in the case of the weekly festivals were then placed on a day set aside in the same fashion as previously Sunday had been set aside, mythologized, and ritualized. Generally successful at first, the festival celebrations went into steep decline under the Directory government, with only the commemoration of 14 July surviving the revolutionary decade. Even so, almost thirty years ago, the noted historian and philosopher Mona Ozouf argued that the experience of the sacred central to the old-regime Catholic feasts was transferred to the revolutionary festivals, and from the revolutionary festivals to the revolutionary (and postrevolutionary) government.[2] She did this by privileging the ideas of the festival planners and government legislators over the manifest, ultimately universal, unpopularity of these celebrations.

In fact, the festivals were a success on paper but a failure in public life. Legislators hoped for a beautifully functioning festival system and were sometimes heartened by the success of individual festivals. But the government files witness to the rapid deterioration of the festival system in general, to the failure of the *fêtes décadaires* as emblematic of the failure of the whole system, and to the insignificance of variations across pro- and anti-government regions of the country. Hoping and working for serious lively celebrations, the government functionaries who planned and monitored the festivals could see nothing serious or alive in them.[3] Apart from any political considerations, the festivals were fatally flawed as religious practices and could not have been occult transmitters of sacrality in any form.

Ideals of the Directory Legislators

Legislators, on 25 October 1795 (3 brumaire an IV) proclaimed a major law on public education and the organization of the festivals.[4] There were to be seven annual festivals: the Foundation of the Republic (1 vendémiaire), Youth (10 germinal), Spouses (10 floréal), Gratitude (10 prairial), Agriculture (10 messidor), Liberty (9 and 10 thermidor), and Old Age (10 fructidor). Three more festivals soon were added: Anniversary of the Death of Louis XVI on 21 January, the Fall of the Bastille, and the Fall of the Monarchy on 10 August.[5] The annual calendar was reinforced by the weekly festivals, the *fêtes décadaires*—the real foundation of the republican calendar with its ten-day week (most of the annual festivals fell on the tenth day of the week anyway). After the coup of 18 fructidor (4 September 1797 an IV) in reaction to monarchist electoral successes, the attempts to install the *fêtes décadaires* became an all-out struggle that culminated in the law of 9 September 1798 (23 fructidor an VI) making the *culte décadaire* obligatory. The Directory had decided to stake its reputation on the success of the calendar.

Educational and engaging ceremonies were advocated by many members of the Directory legislature (the Council of Five Hundred and the Council of Ancients) in official discourses, reflections, reports, opinions, and motions. Albert Mathiez divides the legislators into three camps: those who would (1) destroy Catholicism and any belief in the supernatural, (2) establish deism (belief in God and immortality of the soul) by appropriate celebrations, (3) restrict the festivals to civil and moral celebrations. Within these camps legislators ran the gamut from insistence on minimal interference in festival regulation to insistence on minute supervision of the system. Whatever their emphasis or rigor, legislators in the main promoted the dynamism of myth, ritual, and a set-aside day within the culture; and this is the important point.[6] Pierre-Claude Daunou, for example, director of the reorganized Institut de France and a former priest, focused on collective self-expression and historical commemoration in the festivals. The festivals help a people relive the triumphs and successes of the past: "they excite to great deeds when they make the great memories alive again."[7] For Daunou, remembrance would make the moral power of the past effective in the present—an essential assumption in Jewish or Christian liturgy—and he considered the only real temples to be the vast spaces of those free nations in which the festivals took place. But in the legislature there was a wide range of reflections on festival myth and ritual: emphasis was placed on engagement of mind and heart, celebration of social unity, counteraction to the bad influence of the old festivals, and promotion of the *fêtes décadaires* as the fundamental celebrations of the new culture.[8]

Engagement of Mind and Heart

The teaching function of the festivals was highlighted by the physician François-Xavier Lanthenas. "The essential and most indispensable part of this celebration ought to be the morning exercise where all the citizens . . . participate in the public discussion with the nation's representatives."[9] Durand de Maillane listed two fundamental topics for study: "the nature of our government" and the steps required "to regulate and achieve good [festival] results."[10] Jacques Bailleul went so far as to propose the establishment of *maisons d'institution,* where teachers would be "charged with the . . . preparation and celebration of the *fêtes décadaires.*"[11] But for Louis Joubert, the festivals were the foundation of the teaching system, rather than a subject to be taught: "You already have national festivals, republican ceremonies, days consecrated to the celebration of social virtue, to the memory of the great events, and the commemoration of illustrious men. Ah well! The first and biggest step has been made."[12] Joseph Echassériaux saw the festivals as a remedy for religious prejudices and fanaticism but believed that emotional experience had to be added to educational experience: "In the plan for the civic festival . . . we do not see, we do not feel enough the interest in or pleasure in the charms of equality and fraternity that brothers and assembled citizens ought to taste. We assist at [the celebration] and we leave without being moved by the spectacle of the festival; nothing strongly recalls us to it."[13]

Legislators were going beyond the didactic, then, when they required the engagement of the participants' emotions. According to Merlin de Thionville, too, the people should be more than onlookers: "It seems to me that thus far we have confused *the national festivals* with *the national spectacle:* at the spectacle the people listen or look; in the national festival they must be engaged." It is not sufficient to simply enjoy watching, "it is necessary to be a doer."[14] On the other hand, Marie-Joseph Chénier, man of letters that he was,

objected to cheap theatrical presentations. "We have also felt it to be necessary . . . at least for the moment, to renounce the dramatic presentations that
could only engage a small number of people, but which repeated to excess in
all the theaters of France, can only give theater owners the opportunity to
claim payments, the amount of which grows frighteningly every day."[15]
Marches, hymns, and a pyramid in the temple of immortality were Chénier's
examples of solid celebration: "There are the principal images that have
seemed worthy of presentation to the French people triumphant over the
tyrants of Europe, and by their conquests preparing the peace that they will
one day give to the world; the rest [of the elements of celebration] should be
left up to the genius of the people themselves."[16] In time, the festivals would
be authentic celebrations of a people.

Elements of an Authentic Celebration of Social Unity

Léonard Gay-Vernon, perhaps impelled by his earlier experiences as a curé
and constitutional bishop, would have a kind of *sacred book* central to festival
ceremonial. Philosophy and legislation ought to use "objects that elevate the
soul and make it appreciate the value of liberty." A book listing the names of
citizens who died in combat for the defense of the Republic would be a
"striking witness to their virtues and their courage."[17] According to Jean
Bosquillon, the constitution in a beautiful new edition would be both a collection of readings and a ceremonial object.[18] It could even be the center of
worship, according to Louis Dubois-Dubais, because the constitution inspires
respect, recollection, and adherence to its own stated principles.[19] Certainly it
inspired him to virtual prayer: "Homage, homage, then, to this sacred ark of
our salvation, and let perish the foolish person, if one exists, who would dare
to lay a profane and sacrilegious hand upon it."[20]

Oath taking, a proper response to any presentation of law, appeared especially appropriate for the feast of the Foundation of the Republic and the
Constitution, said Nicholas Parent-Réal: "The principal ceremony of this
solemnity will be the taking of the civic oath by the public functionaries and
all the citizens."[21] And a *fraternal meal* could be included in all festivals, said
Joseph Lequinio. After their regular days in the small family circle, people
should want to come and open their hearts to the larger family. In mutural
exchange they could "drink long drafts of the enchanting cup of good fortune, and become intoxicated by the common happiness," the meal being an
ideal means of overcoming distinctions in social status.[22]

Good order and *sensible spacing* of festivals would attract and focus attention. Portiez de l'Oise plumped for order, embodied by the national guard, "today purified of the elements of anarchism and one of the strongest supports of the national celebrations."[23] Michel Luminais admonished his colleagues to make the festivals into special occasions, in effect, highlights of the popular calendar: "The greatest harm that you could do to the republican institutions is to render them so banal that you no longer attract the attention of the people to them."[24]

Focus came from *images,* according to Pierre Mortier-Duparc, recalling with distaste and admiration those engravings popularized by the Jesuits, which "contributed singularly to nourish in the country a blind and unlimited credulity." For the new government, the image of General Marceau and other heroes would promote an equally effective, but—this time—healthy loyalty.[25]

Engaging celebrations should generate common enthusiasm, then. Antoine Français believed that the "good leaven" of contact with other people would counteract the bitterness of isolation.[26] Individuality of any sort, personal or familial, would be complemented by public festivals, according to Joseph Lequinio: "The republican, pleased to have given nine days to work and enjoyed himself peacefully in the close circle of his own family, comes into the center of the national family to pour out his feelings on the décadi . . . to bring to society his tribute of enthusiasm and joy, and to receive in exchange a reward of encouragement and example." For the citizen, celebration in union with the others would "give to his patriotism a new energy; nourish his memory with the qualities of heroism and virtue, his soul with the lessons of wisdom, his heart with pure sentiments of fraternity; and finally [give him] long drafts of the enchanting cup of happiness, to exult in shared well-being."[27] This rhetoric was echoed by François Daubermesnil, who said, "Enthusiasm must enter every pore, penetrate every sense, embrace all souls, and maintain in this unity the sentiments and opinions that, in the beautiful days of the Revolution, showed the great French family to be a fraternal people." Specifically, he would be pleased to hear the sound of martial instruments awakening the revolutionary fighting spirit for the people of even the smallest communes.[28] Louis-Marie de La Revellière-Lépaux, the most ardent promoter of the festivals among the Directory members, continued the theme of communal engagement: "We must bring together here everything that can fire the imagination, . . . inspire a love without limits for liberty, the preservation of laws, and whatever produces such a devotion that each citizen is ready to sacrifice his . . . most ardent desires for the good and glory of the Republic."[29]

Social unity, then, was the goal of ceremonial grandeur. The proposals on ceremonial—book, oath, meal, images, and good order—taken together would set up a new, formal liturgy binding citizens together.

New Celebrations to Replace the Old

The power of the old religious celebrations haunted assembly members. Joseph Débry believed that enemies of the Republic attacked the festivals to keep the Republic from taking root, "so that the rule of liberty, reduced to a few shapes and forms and driven back by the old monarchical ways, might somehow come to be an abstraction, a being of reason."[30] Pierre Audouin said that the French had lived in error for too long and now needed the remedy of new republican institutions to help them forget the monarchy.[31] According to Raymond de Barennes, the old religious festivals were successful in spite of their evil because they were spectacles. "The worst preacher was sure of having an audience, and the grossest of images had their admirers and attracted genuflections." Unfortunately, outside of Paris the republican festivals did not have similar success because people's eyes, "accustomed to copes, to chasubles, and to candles, have seen only, if I may so express myself, a sad nudity."[32] Félix Bonnaire also recalled the splendor of the old religious ceremonies and argued that now the people were entitled to something better than the off-putting republican festivals. "Has not everyone been asking that at last republican institutions be organized, that philosophical truths be proclaimed and placed within reach of the people, and that the language of reason be substituted for [the language] of passion and prejudice?"[33]

Ultimately, people's minds could be distracted from the old festivals by the reorganization of the calendar. François Sherlock wanted up-front government action to enforce it. "You should require that the eras preceding our political regeneration be no longer counted according to religious system. All the divisions of the year having been set up in France by the secular power, the right to fix the way of numbering the years that have preceded this reform belongs incontestably to it [the secular power]."[34] Martin Brothier also wanted the government to go all the way, privileging law enforcement: "Habit is the first obstacle that must be conquered if necessary changes are to be made. Reason alone will not bring about victory; recourse to authority must be joined to it."[35] Joseph Lequinio's ultimate goal was to make citizens completely forget the old religious culture, so that it would "no longer be possible for people to remember past times by date or in their former exact order."[36]

Décadi: Foundation of the New System

Held every tenth day, the *fêtes décadaires,* by replacing the Christian Sunday, could lead to definitive celebration of new religion. Collot d'Herbois listed the values of such a cult: (1) "establish [the *fêtes décadaires*] on pure foundations of the great ideas of public morality," (2) "strike at superstition," (3) "establish a rallying point for the exercise of social virtues," (4) "create periodically a home center that could nourish public emotions," and (5) "make all the citizens participate in the great events." The *fêtes décadaires* could ensure that the good to be obtained from festivals would be available in many places regularly.[37] Yes, battle lines were clear. Jean Guinau-Duprès said that the *fêtes décadaires* were supposed to be human celebrations, whereas Catholic liturgies engender obligation and mystery. Priests had to turn to condemnation, excommunication, and penal laws and to the magic of ceremonies and processions in order to oblige people to attend services. The décadi, in contrast, were a joyful combination of "open cafés, planned dances, choruses, band music, tableaux, exercises, marriages, birth congratulations, flowers cast upon the tombs of the worthy man, the virtuous woman, and the intelligent farmer."[38] A positive suggestion—one often heard—for making the décadi relevant came from Jacques Creuzé-Latouche, who wanted to illuminate the décadi celebrations by marriage ceremonies.[39]

According to wise legislators, the *fêtes décadaires* should not be made into a religious challenge or a social burden. Marie-Joseph Chénier reminded the Convention that not all practical and theoretical issues could be solved at once. The establishment and maintenance of a festival system was a major task, and it would be "ridiculously presumptuous to organize [the festivals] completely in a few hours of discussion."[40] The government would set itself up for major problems if it tried for definitive legislation of festivals and décadi, "a task that would drag us into endless discussion, without determining in a precise way the different ceremonies and the different signs that must needs distinguish the festivals from one another." Initially, only minimal legislation would be appropriate for such an immense, time-consuming task.[41]

Jean Barailon also wanted the festivals to be the fruit of "wise deliberation and the deepest meditation."[42] Joseph Terral, in particular, did not want to coerce a people long accustomed to the Christian tradition in France. "Reflect on whether you could ever destroy in the mind of twenty million French people the idea, the conviction that the day called Sunday rest (old style) is an institution of highest importance."[43] The people need the freedom

to form their own opinions and determine their own relation to the republican festivals: "Can one establish a permanent inquisition to force an individual to work or otherwise spoil his day on Sunday? *No.*"⁴⁴ Terral even
advocated tolerance of traditional Catholicism. "They say that Christianity,
Catholicism, is incompatible with republican government. That is false
because, even beyond the principles of the religion itself, the examples of
Switzerland, America, and other republics, refute the statement."⁴⁵ Such moderate views did not prevail. *Fêtes décadaires* celebrations were ever more stri-
dently proclaimed, and every effort was made to enforce their observance.
Whether the legislators were antagonistic to Catholicism or not, they were
determined to legislate annual and weekly celebrations—stories/teachings
and ceremonies.⁴⁶

The Reality of Failure

No one can deny that the festivals were successful during the first years of revolutionary government or that they enabled participants to experience elements
of the old religious sacrality with the new framework of the government festivals at least temporarily.⁴⁷ For example, the state funeral of General Hoche in
Paris, 1 October 1797 (10 vendémiaire an VI), was an outstanding example of
a successful festival—something desired but almost never achieved by the
Directory administration. From the report of the Directory president, La
Revellière-Lépaux, printed in the Paris *Rédacteur,* then, we can see what the
Directory considered to be an ideal festival.

> At eleven o'clock the Directory members get into the coaches. . . .
> Two squads of cavalry open and close the march; the cavalry and
> grenadiers of the Directory guard, a large number of line troops, and
> a detachment of the nation's veterans escort the coaches and march
> with weapons lowered. . . . In the middle of the cortege and in front
> of the Directory members, the image of General Hoche, crowned
> with the laurel of immortality is carried with pious veneration by
> four old warriors. It is placed on a stretcher, decorated with tricolor
> hanging, a trophy, and the military insignia of a general. . . . The
> cortege makes its way by the lane of poplars to the right of the
> Champ-de-Mars and makes a half turn from the amphitheater to the
> altar of the Fatherland. Before the altar a pyramid is erected, bearing

on each one of its sides an inscription that recalls the principal traits of the military life of General Hoche. [48]

As ritual expression, we see here symbols of immortality and virtue, an altar, the image of the hero; there was appropriate vesture and unified gestures.

> Forty young students from the Conservatory of Music, [are] vested in white, hair in ribbons, and carrying sashes of crepe, advance with timid step and place themselves around the mausoleum; they sing in unison, in honor of the hero, the strophe from the hymn composed by Citizen Chénier and put to music by Cherubini. . . . Citizen Daunou, member of the Institute and charged by it to extol the merits of the hero, advances at this point, holding a laurel branch in his hand; he ascends the steps of the mausoleum and pronounces the funeral eulogy of General Hoche. . . . The Directors rise and bare their heads; the whole cortege and the citizens situated on the nearby knolls also rise and bare their heads in a simultaneous movement; all waving their hats in the air and with eyes fixed on the statue of liberty, they repeat in unison the refrain: *Aux armes, citoyens!* . . . The *Chant du depart* is heard with the same avidity and arouses an almost universal enthusiasm.

The story or myth was expressed in a hymn, a recessional, and the refrain of the *Marseillaise;* a sermon/eulogy served to state and interpret. The crowds were there; they actively participated; the impression generated was of general enthusiasm. This report of the Directory president, albeit dramatic and self-promoting, was confirmed in the police records. [49]

During the later years of the Revolution, however, the attempted transfer of sacrality was completely thwarted, and the best witnesses to this festival failure were the very authorities that wanted to bring about the transfer. The files of the Directory government (1795–99) document consistently vain efforts to systematize and enforce the yearly and weekly cycles of festival celebration. An evenly divided year (twelve months of thirty days each) was organized and partially put in place in 1793; the law on education and festivals, in 1795. Subsequently the annual calendar of festivals was reinforced by the weekly festivals, the *fêtes décadaires*—the real foundation of the republican calendar with its ten-day week. After the coup of 18 fructidor (an V, 4 September 1797), the attempts to install the *fêtes décadaires* culminated in the law of 9 September 1798 (23 fructidor an VI) when the *culte décadaire* became obligatory.

Composed of an executive committee of five directors, a Council of Ancients to propose legislation, and a Council of Five Hundred to formulate and pass it, the Directory was organized to escape the heritage of the Terror.[50] In this it had a small measure of success from 26 October 1795 through the date of the coup of 18 fructidor—when three of the five directors neutralized the power of the two legislative councils and forced the overthrow of their two remaining colleagues on the Directory itself. Until this coup, political life was minimally structured and coherent, even with the polarization of Jacobin left and monarchist right.[51] Restraints were relaxed on public religious expression with the reorganization of the clergy and the reopening of the churches for Sunday services (at times in an *esprit de contrariété* against the government).[52] Unfortunately both before and after the coup of 18 fructidor, the Directory had decided to stake its reputation on the success of the calendar: the festivals were not only a failure, but their enforcement may well have brought down the Directory government. Isser Woloch has written, "the Directorial Republic was incontestably a weak and unpopular regime, overwhelmed by the forces of localism and buffeted by the prolonged settling of accounts from earlier turmoil. But in some respects it was the gratuitous agency of its own difficulties. The Republic may have needed new sources of revenue, a military draft, and 'republican institutions.' It did not need the republican calendar."[53]

The Directory bureaucracy struggled to centralize French cultural life around the festivals from September 1795, with especially desperate efforts to enforce the calendar following the coup of 18 fructidor, until the coming of the Consulate. Relevant files are found under the heading of *Esprit public* in the records of the Ministry of the Interior and the bureaus charged with festival promotion and in the papers specific to the Executive Directory.[54] In effect, the Ministry of the Interior regulated and surveyed *Esprit public* through a division of public instruction, the "Bureau of National Festivals, Theaters, and Monuments" (one of its several names in the course of periodic bureau reshuffling).

Improvements Desired

Well-kept records on *Esprit public* were, as one might expect, originally communicated from the department of the Seine in Paris.[55] The effectiveness of teaching and the mechanics of setting and action were ever-present problems. Festivals were analyzed for their success as commemorative celebrations and teaching, in other words, as myth and often they were anxiously scrutinized for details of ritual gesture and movement and physical setting. From the 10th arrondissement in the year V (1796–97) came a simple suggestion that the Festival of Old Age be improved by the presence of senior citizens and ceremonies rewarding their achievements. The departmental administration requested that the interior minister adopt an occasion "to offer a recompense to the elderly who are the objects of this festival by offering them the pleasure of the Theater where all the arts are brought together."[56] This was accompanied by a note from the Directory commissaire who said that the festivals had not heretofore been celebrated with enough solemnity, and that the Festival of Old Age would suffer the same fate "if [those responsible] do not concern themselves with it a little before the eve of the festival, which is what the department has done until now."[57] According to this official view, in the preceding year the Festival of Old Age was ceremonially inadequate.

At other times solutions to problems such as winter cold were urgently needed: "The majority of the religious buildings [*temples*] are in such a state of degradation that the cold penetrates from all sides and [people] are exposed to all winds." Since few regular citizens attended the festivals, it was the officials who suffered: "the 30 frimaire cold was so intense in the Temple of Reconnaissance (4th arrondissement) that it occasioned a large inflammation on the secretary of the administration and the serious indisposition of the commissaire of the Executive Directory."[58]

The new festivals had to be beautiful in order to compete with the old. An undated letter promoting festival music, on the stationery of the *Corps de musique* of the National Guard, was passed on by the municipal administration of the 5th arrondissement. According to the writer, "The voice that is left by the ritual of fanaticism must be replaced by the songs of liberty, and the people by their own voices [*accents*] must add to the solemnity of the festivals consecrated to the virtues that the Republic honors."[59] The new festivals also inspired artists and architects. Witness the earlier project of Monsieur Tourment who wished to offer himself and his art to the revolutionary celebration. There was a description and drawing of the project "destined for the General Peace and other festivals, to be produced on the Champs de la Réunion or other places in Paris": altar of the fatherland, obelisk, allegorical statues, pilasters, and so on placed on a high terrace with stairway access.[60]

The appurtenances and scenery of the celebration were constructed, stored, and managed by a roster of functionaries, of whom the most important in the first years of the Directory was Poisson de la Chabeaussière, author of a widely distributed *Catéchisme républicain*. The relevant Directory files are filled with lists of disbursements to carpenters, artists, sculptors, cloth and rug merchants, musicians, and every kind of food service—professionals who contributed to the physical production of the ceremonies. Always there was the challenge of logistics and finances. In one case, the actors of the Théâtre de l'Estrapade had arranged for the refinishing of the theater to make it more comfortable. They had been backed in this by M. Cardinaux, provisioner of the theater, who then wrote in desperation to the Ministry of the Police. Cardinaux says of himself and the theater, "The principal goal of this institution was to raise public opinion by the representation of comic or tragic plays to make the people feel the value of liberty and obey the government." Money promised by government officials had not come through, however, and Cardinaux found himself facing financial disaster and possible eviction from his home "on account of his devotion to the fatherland."[61] On festival days, the problems of performances and finances could swallow up all other considerations.

Problems of Participation

Broad assessments were made of personal participation in the festivals. According to one report, interest and excitement diminished as time passed. But from the beginning there was an "interior restlessness" that "caused the nuances of their execution to vary." The occasional "exaltation" felt during the year IV (1795–96) had died out: "The Minister in the course of the year V had to struggle against ill will, people coming with all kinds of pretexts to avoid the celebration of the national festivals."[62] For a while the royalists and fanatics had gotten the upper hand. The people, naturally, lost interest, and it became necessary "to create spectacles and games sufficiently interesting to attract the people to our festivals (especially those celebrated on the Camps de Mars)." After the coup of 18 fructidor hopes seemed to revive: "the execution of the funeral ceremonies of Hoche even in the most distant departments offer a satisfactory measure of the zeal of the new administration."[63]

The failure of the *fêtes décadaires* was the central issue in the Directory files by the year VI (1797–98), as well it ought to have been. The *fêtes décadaires* constituted a major change in the religious, commercial, and social week of the citizen. The ceremonial setting and atmosphere satisfied neither the organizers nor the participants. Church buildings everywhere served as a reminder of the power if not of the value of the old religion. Shared use of churches brought tensions, but use of other buildings by festival organizers only emphasized the dullness of setting and atmosphere. Without the energies

Fig. 3. Preaching to a thoroughly bored and distracted congregation at one of the revolutionary festival celebrations. The *Culte théophilanthropique,* an organized sect or cult
closely related to the *fêtes décadaires,* was conceived by ex-curés and promoted by the
Directory; it was the most serious attempt to consolidate the festivals and the festival system into a distinct, government-sponsored alternative to Catholicism. (Bibliothéque
Nationale)

provided by the old myth and ritual, the new time and the new place were
empty of vitality and meaning. Even after the coup of 18 fructidor, global discussions of the effect of the festivals and of the festival system, analyses of the
continuity of sacredness from the old festival system to the new, and interpretations of the experiences of clergy, politicians, and people, all center on failure.

Resistance of the Catholic clergy to the celebration of the décadi was
chronicled in a packet of complaints that the minister of the Interior had
received from the Directory commissaires and transmitted to one of his own
commissions. These clergy "abuse the influence they have upon credulous
minds to persuade them that whoever works on Sunday offends the divinity."[64] A commissaire from the canton of Creigny gave three reasons for laxity:

(1) religious fanaticism, (2) observation of the calendar of the old noble and sacerdotal regime, and (3) stubbornness of the Catholic clergy who do not observe the calendar of liberty.[65] Another commissaire from the Yonne reported that Sundays and feasts were celebrated with an "affected pomp" in his whole arrondissement in spite of the invitations that had been made to the Catholic clergy to "transfer their own beautiful ceremonies" to the décadi.[66] Included in the packet was a copy of an executive order from the department of the Nord threatening those who would not celebrate the décadi.

The government was asked to take firm control. From Autun came an urgent plea for the maintenance of special edifices that could be used for the *fêtes décadaires:* "The beginning of the reactionary movement was the disdain for the décadi and republican festivals; the counterrevolutionaries took it to heart to insult them and make them forgotten." Now after 18 fructidor the décadi must be celebrated in a worthy manner. Republican institutions must "subsist in a permanent and unchangeable manner and not precariously." If the Directory wanted that "temples of the fatherland consecrated to the celebration of its feasts and the holding of legal assemblies of citizens be maintained, adorned, and embellished," they should make a law to "guarantee in perpetuity the possession of these buildings to the communes, with the charge to have them maintained and repaired at their own cost."[67]

Functionaries were at a loss to control the Sunday celebrations. A magistrate from Calvados wanted to eliminate the competition between Sundays and the *fêtes décadaires.* "It is impossible for the *fêtes décadaires* to be in competition with the religious festivals: the décadi and Sundays put together will produce upheavals that will shake the political machine."[68] There were two solutions: put off the institution of the décadi to a time when the public would be a little better prepared for it, or better, forbid religious ceremonies or gatherings on all days other than the décadi. The people, concerned as they are about farming in season could not celebrate both the décadi and Sundays, so all religious gatherings must be forbidden. A resident of Paris gloomily wrote, "One barely sees in Paris a sixth of the population celebrate the décadi. It is even worse in the countryside; no inhabitant wishes to recognize them in spite of the zeal put forth by the national agents to make them observed."[69] Though not reliable as a statistic, his "sixth of the population" was a suggestive impression.

Bishop Henri Grégoire, head of the constitutional clergy, was blamed for some of these problems. The minister of the Interior, writing to the Committee on Public Instruction, said that the administration of Lot-et-Garonne "attributed the cause of this cooling [of enthusiasm for the décadi], to the Opinion put forth in the Council of Five Hundred by Citizen Grégoire. His ill will was seized upon to give the understanding that the legislative body did not want to be preoccupied with republican institutions."[70] Since it is unlikely that one intervention in the Council of Five Hundred trickled down to the population at large, Grégoire must have represented the disparaging power of the clergy in general. The priests were the most visible opponents of the décadi because they are the most ideologically involved. The Directory commissaire from Cerilly (Allier) wrote that Grégoire and his priests pretended to go along with the décadi and then preached against it (accusing the government of wanting to destroy the traditions of the ancestors and encouraging a disregard for official proclamations). Priests had to be prevented from communicating their fanaticism to youth and from assembling the public on days other than the décadi.[71] Indeed, it is clear from *Annales de la religion,* official journal of Grégoire and the constitutional clergy, that the décadi were a principal worry of the clerical hierarchy. They were especially averse to making the *fêtes décadaires* religious: "We are not ignorant of the fact that the enemies of our holy religion would like to destroy our worship and abolish the celebration of Sunday." By urging the transferal of devotional feasts to the décadi "while making a show of the preservation of Sunday," the government actually placed the décadi in competition with Sunday: "they induce the Christian people to error by making them believe that the décadi has become a religious festival, whereas it is a civil festival."[72]

Solutions were offered for the improvement of the *fêtes décadaires,* so that citizens would better understand the myth and participate in the ritual. Reports were passed across the offices of the Ministry of the Interior for definitive presentation by the Directory itself. These reports were to provide a "philosophical counterweight to superstition in order to distract the inhabitants of the countryside from their religious prejudices by giving them a new impetus and a pure nourishment for their troubled curiosity."[73] Country people needed to be taught clear thinking and the experience of social unity because local festivals distract attention from the décadi. Noting that churches are easier to get to, especially in winter when getting around is difficult, the document proposed that the Directory consider proper building construction and the substitution of cantonal village festivals for the old festivals that were sentimental, commercial, and religious. A special organization would be necessary because "the administration, distracted by affairs they regard as more urgent and more important for the public cannot give to the preparations the time and the care they would need."[74] One of the motivations for this communication may well have been a complaint from the Directory commissaire in the department of the Ardennes. (It was included in the government files with the document just quoted.) "The little success that we have comes from the methods used in the year VI to make the people of the countryside forget the patronal feasts and gives us little hope of succeeding in the year VII.[75] Simply changing the days of the festivals could not help because the old attitudes would thereby be transferred to the new festival days. The old calendar had to be obliterated from memory; the old patronal feasts made into village festivals.

Petitions to obliterate the old ways were common in these discussions of the décadi. From Autun came the view that it would be "necessary to change old habits that attach the people again to sacerdotal rust [sic] and remind them of the hideous monarchy. The old spectacle and pomp provided by the priests will be forgotten if the void caused by its disappearance is filled."[76] Much frustrated by the calendar, some inhabitants of Versailles said they were sure they needed to get rid of the "monstrosity of the two calendars that seem to dispute the domain of time, and which render the division of the year and the distribution of the days so equivocal and so confusing for citizens."[77] And Citizen Belos, président d'âge (senior president pro-tem) of the civil tribunal of the Seine, wanted the total obliteration of the old feast names and proposed a solution to scheduling problems. "Republican judges regretfully see themselves obliged to make mention in their verdicts of the terms Easter, St.-John, St.-Remy, and Christmas, used in the litigation documents. . . . They have charged me to ask the Council [of Five Hundred] at the moment when they are preparing a law on the décadi, to insert in [the law] an article to abrogate this usage and to substitute the legal terms of 1 germinal, messidor, vendémiaire, and nivôse, with a grace period [for rents due, etc.]."[78]

Compromise was sometimes suggested, though. Fisson-Joubert, a member of the committee responsible for primary schools of Cadillac (Gironde), recognized that legislators established the festivals "to inspire in each citizen a religious love of the fatherland." But since the people have obviously become completely indifferent, "it is important above all to know the causes that have altered dispositions and spirits, and then see what permits us to do what is proper in each locality." He placed the blame on royalism and not on the old religion; royalism duped people, but one could work out an arrangement with the old religion. The celebrations only facilitated love of God and "affect neither the faith nor the dogmas of the Church nor the holiness of religion; rather, they are supposed to induce love of country and peace."[79]

A document was prepared by the administration of the department of the Seine in response to the reports from the Paris arrondissements on the quality of the décadi celebrations. It noted that the minister had been informed that the celebrations offered "neither majesty nor interest nor usefulness" and then gave the causes of this failure. First, there was no initial plan; individuals should have been appointed to direct the ceremonies. In the margin of the manuscript the author noted that priests understand the value of a ceremony where every vivid gesture is determined beforehand. Secondly, the church buildings used were dirty and inappropriate. Amphitheaters should be constructed and the church buildings inspected and prepared for ceremonies. Six employees of the division office (charged with the festivals), would carry out this inspection on churches in six different arrondissements, but the ministry should appoint six more for as many other arrondissements.[80]

No faults were covered up: "You do not see anything, you do not hear anything, and this is due not only to the disposition of the locale but more to the negligence of the actors. . . . They psalm-tone the readings, they hurry the ceremonies. The touching and modest celebration of marriage . . . is often done without ceremony or interest."[81] The report suggests that the whole system was put into operation too soon. "It really was necessary before opening the décadi temples to form there types of amphitheaters where one can see and hear everything." Then those at the service "would be better able to see onto the platform where the altar of the fatherland would be placed." Viewing the *fêtes décadaires* as theater, the author of the report believed that "[festival organizers] have so to speak raised the curtain before the theater has been completely constructed and the decor completed, even before the actors have been assigned the roles they must take."[82] And that was the fate of the décadi, untimely born according to the most positive interpretations.

Provincial Variations

A comparison of four departments, two politically right (Seine-Inférieure and Hérault) and two politically left (Isère and Haute-Vienne) shows that, whatever the religious differences developing in the different regions of France, reports sent from the departmental administrations to the Ministry of the Interior vary little from department to department—undoubtedly because of uniformity of organization and guidelines for report submissions.[83] This uniformity can be seen in the complete coverage of one specific event: the oath-taking at the center of the anniversary of the death of Louis XVI—a festival

most often referred to as the "Just Punishing of the Last King." All departments sent in formal and complete descriptions of the celebration. At the center of each report was the formula of the oath itself and the list of those who
took the oath.

There are, however, some indications of the political orientations of the
departments. I believe we can illustrate these orientations by reference to only
two departments, Seine-Inférieure and the Isère.[84] Directives had been sent
out to the departments for making the décadi a day of rest as well as a day of
celebration.[85] But there appeared to be more official frustration with clerical
interference in the *fêtes décadaires* in antirepublican Seine-Inférieure. The
administrator of the canton of Creil complained dramatically, "I must not
remain silent about the near zero status of our décadi reunions; in spite of our
efforts, our assiduity, and the pomp we are trying to give them, all our methods are pure loss; and the unfeeling monuments of this church are, so to speak,
the sole witness of the décadi celebrations. We believe that the cause and
source of this is the former benefice-holder, who . . . employs the wily eloquence of imposture to calumniate and depreciate our festivals."[86] The Directory commissaire criticized the same (one assumes) clerical troublemaker: he
had one man "dragged . . . to the foot of the liberty tree to cut off his hair"
and also had "an unfortunate woman dragged one Sunday morning to Mass
without modesty or respect for her sex, and in spite of herself."[87] And by the
year VII (1798–99), this priest was able to control important members of the
local administrative system: "He has never assisted at the décadi, reunions, and
the *Juge de paix* [justice of the peace] is found there no more than he is; one
feels that this is a very bad example for the people who always have their eyes
fixed on the primary public functionaries."[88] The commissaire himself personally experienced the man's gall. "One day being near the altar of the fatherland
to converse with Citizen Dumont . . . , [he] arrives and addresses himself to
Citizen Dumont, 'go up on to the platform,' he says, 'and sell there your
snake oil.'"[89] The commissaire concluded with the suggestion that the priest
be sent back to his native Paris.

In contrast, an ardent prodécadi document was preserved by the administration of one of the districts of Seine-Inférieure: a long prospectus promoting a hymnal and written in curiously aroused language that went beyond
advertisement. "The work we propose today . . . is written with simplicity
and even with a sort of negligence. The author will easily obtain some kind of
indulgence when people learn that he has written and carved it on the walls of
his prison before giving it to the public."[90] The author was imprisoned in

Rouen during the Terror, but in spite of such punishment "the triumphs of the Republic always gave to his imagination a new energy, and his captivity only made him intensify his love for his country." On the walls of the prison "he transcribed all his dreams" and shared them with his fellow prisoners. The prospectus closed with the assurance that the humans "are all in the true republican principles and can excite the emulation of true poets who will not fail to follow after my example and who will do much better without thereby having a more praiseworthy motive or any many difficulties to conquer."[91] The poet/author himself, then, had written the prospectus, a witness to love for the Republic and its *fêtes décadaires,* even in Seine-Inférieure.

In the prorepublican Isère, also, the clergy were troublesome, although there is no record of anyone as dangerously troublesome as the curé of Creil in Seine-Inférieure. The administration president wanted the priests to join in the celebration. "The feasts instituted by the genius of liberty can only be celebrated with all the pomp desired by true patriots by requiring the ministers of religion not only to join their ceremonies to this celebration, but also to abstain from these same ceremonies on the days that prejudice and ignorance have adopted for each particular religion."[92] But the general report of the administration, saying only that the Catholic clergyman had been invited, confidently presented an otherwise successful scenario. "Today [the administration] celebrated the day of the festival by songs and by discourses pronounced in the honor of liberty; . . . the majority of the citizens came together as best they could to augment the pomp of the festival. . . . During the course of this festival we have seen shine on all faces the joy and serenity that republican virtues inspire."[93]

There was no discourse of pure confidence, even in the Isère. A report to the Central Administration of the Isère from the canton of Voiron proclaimed, "This institution [of the décadi] is one of those that will contribute not a little toward the administration of death blows to the royal and sacerdotal despotism." But help was needed: "We hope to arrive at a revival, but our efforts would be incomplete if the administration did not aid us with its authority and its enlightenment."[94] In Voiron they wanted the décadi temple to be well arranged for the celebration. The commissaire reported that "the place originally designated was not large enough for the décadi, celebrations into which must be admitted persons of every age and sex. They are using a church while waiting for the purchase and decoration of a new hall. The inhabitants of this commune in general watch with great satisfaction the repair and decoration of the celebration hall . . . near the liberty tree. . . . The news of the supposed sale of this precious place excites the general rumor that *Esprit public* is going to make great progress in this commune." There still was anxiety that momentum, perhaps we could say continuity, of *Esprit public* would be lost if the statue of liberty is "expelled from the décadi temple, the church of the Augustins" at Voiron.[95]

Clear meaning, appropriate pomp, and full celebration of the *fêtes décadaires* was partially vitiated by clerical influence in Seine-Inférieure. There was greater success in the Isère where there was less potent clerical opposition. But everywhere the priests rallied their people to reject the festivals, and officials hoped to capitalize on some successes of the *fêtes décadaires* with better rituals, ostensibly to better express the meaning or myth of the Revolution. The failure of the *fêtes décadaires* epitomized the failure of all the festivals; all were part of the same system, legislated and promoted in the same way. In government files we find frequent negative evaluations of the quality of the celebrations and discouragement expressed in the face of public neglect. The government could never do more than monitor the situation and hope for a better day.[96]

Anatomy of a Failure

Why this dismal record, this almost universal disinterest and distaste? Directory legislators had advocated educational and engaging ceremonies in their official discourses, reflections, reports, opinions, and motions. They highlighted teaching, engagement of the emotions, active communal celebration; the legislators wanted to counteract the bad influence of the old festivals and promote the *fêtes décadaires* as basic celebrations of a new culture, using ceremonial books, images, and communal meals. Their goals for the active participation of citizens can perhaps be best summed up in those words of the legislator Merlin de Thionville: "It seems to me that thus far we have confused *the national festivals* with *the national spectacle:* at the spectacle the people listen or look; in the national festival they must be engaged." Watching was not enough; Merlin believed it "necessary to be a doer."[97] The myth-and-ritual alternatives to the annual religious festivals and to Sundays were feeble in that the citizens were not engaged, not doers. The government cataloged flaws that would be fatal in any celebration: empty ceremonies, uncomfortable and inappropriate settings, dry and moralistic speeches, dullness in comparison to the old festivals. The myth system for the new festivals and *fêtes décadaires* dealt with the Republic — its origin, development, and resultant community reality; the ritual was the gathering for speeches, songs, music, and ceremonial reenactment.

But for a myth to be effective it must provide some expressed meaning of the underlying causes of human life, of all existence, of the cosmos. It should provide answers to questions about origin and meaning in a culture—with special attention to the necessities of life. In other times and cultures myths pointed or referred to supernatural events and to a foundation epoch at the beginning of history. Gods and goddesses, sacred mountains, rivers, animals, and plants were elements of this mythic imagery.[98] Superficial and didactic for the most part, the revolutionary myth system did not provide these fundamental features of myth, nor did it last long enough to transmit and represent earlier myths. For ritual to be effective it must provide gestures, movements, and a setting that makes possible individual and group experience of the myth. It must express the transcendent and the primal in concrete ceremonial. By the ritualizing of myth, individuals go through an initiation that disconnects them from their surroundings, and puts them in contact with an assumed wider social and cosmic world; men and women thereby relocate themselves within a new world order. Ritual must facilitate individual and group appropriation of the myth or other cultural expression by focusing personal energies, reinforcing the engagement of participants in the life of the culture though continuity-oriented repetition.[99] Here the festivals failed on every count.

To make matters worse, the government forced myth and ritual celebration by legislating the *fêtes décadaires* as a replacement for, or at least an alternative to, Sunday. This was a destructive attack on a long-term, central, religion-based feature of Western culture.[100] The seven-day week of Judaism was adopted in Christian and Muslim cultures, although different days of the week were set aside: Saturday for Judaism, Sunday for Christianity, and Friday for Islam. A day of rest is obviously connected to domestic and political economy, to modes of production, and, at least in some simple ways, it influences and expresses family life. The linkage of a Sunday replacement, the *fêtes décadaires,* with the annual festivals was a sure way to complicate the acceptance of a festival system. (Who would *want* a ten-day week anyway?) Such linkage compounded the problem of ineffective myth and ritual.

The idea that a transference of sacrality can be dictated is contradicted by our own understanding of any kind of psychological transference. Without taking Freud's concept of transference as a given, we must admit that in the contemporary discussion of the transference of sacrality, the Freudian gloss dominates all others.[101] If we are talking about a psychological transference of sacrality, then the process must be the direct opposite of forcing, admonishing, and even direct teaching. Our analogy is to the therapeutic setting where a patient experiences a relationship by projecting past feelings on the therapist; the sacred (even in its most diffuse forms) can only be transferred when a new setting enables people to experience the old thoughts and feelings anew.[102] No pedantic forcing of myth, no legislation of ritual can accomplish this transference. Whatever their success in separating French citizens from Catholic sacrality, legislators and officials were not able to transfer or appropriate any elements of it for the nation. By trying to express national ideals with a religion-substitute, and thereby fashion an enhanced national identity, the government only deepened the rift between religious and national identity, psychologically within each individual and socially among citizens. On either side of this divide, distinct personality types developed: loyally religious and pro-church, and resolutely secular and pro-state.

Chapter Three

RELIGIOUS AND SECULAR EXTREMES AT THE BEGINNING OF THE
NINETEENTH CENTURY: *Chateaubriand and Destutt de Tracy*

At the end of the revolutionary decade and the beginning of the Napoleonic era, François-René de Chateaubriand (1768–1848) and Antoine-Louis-Claude Destutt de Tracy (1754–1836) brilliantly promoted Catholic Christianity, on the one hand, and Enlightenment rationality, on the other. No two participants in the complex discussion of religion and secularism that took place at the highest levels of government and Parisian intellectual life at the end of the First Republic and during the Napoleonic regime better represented unconditional nostalgia for Catholicism and uncompromising intellectual pursuit of the secular scientific ideal.

It has become customary to oppose the neo-Christian intellectuals Chateaubriand, de Maistre, de Bonald, and Ballanche, to the Idéologues Destutt de Tracy, Cabanis, Maine de Biran, and others, but we can clarify this opposition by defining the extremes represented by Chateaubriand and Tracy.[1] In other words, a clear definition of the personal metaphysics—expressed thoughts and feelings—of Chateaubriand and Tracy should establish the polarities of intellectual temperament, grounded in the public intellectual life of the Napoleonic era.[2] The essential data are the publications and correspondence of each man from 1796 to 1811: we can see here the religious development of Chateaubriand in the *Essai sur les révolutions* and the *Génie du Christianisme;* and we can see Tracy's scientific idealism, expressed in his discussion of the substantial self and the role of religion in human society. Integrating these religious and secular polarities into Parisian public life of the period, we can then make the case that Chateaubriand's religious nostalgia and Tracy's scientific idealism are the clearest and most opposed examples of the two intellectual temperaments dominant during the Napoleonic era and conclude with the proposal that their temperaments were the beginning of a whole range of religious and secular polarities across the nineteenth century.

The Conversion of Chateaubriand

Born into Breton nobility, Chateaubriand received a pious upbringing, briefly directed his studies toward the priesthood at Dinan, and subsequently spent several years as an army officer. During the first years of the French Revolution he briefly visited America, but then in danger six months later because of his family connections, he was forced to flee France for exile in England.

His *Essai sur les révolutions,* written in England and representing the beginning of his ideological development, opens with the fundamental question, "Who am I?"[3] He suggests that he and his peers do not belong to their own century, that each age is like a river, and that while the republicans have had the impetuosity to master the currents to get to the other side, the others have remained somewhere in the fourteenth century. Since the problem with the republicans is that they have lost themselves in dreams and in striving for illusory perfection, Chateaubriand offers his own understanding and interpretation of individual and social life, basing it on his experience of the North American Indian, the consummately natural human being free from the constraints of society (43).

Chateaubriand interprets revolution in light of a natural human ideal and religion in relation to revolutionary activity. Although he embraces a fundamental theism/deism, he condemns the organized—that is, authoritarian—religions of history. At the beginning of his chapters on religion stands a prayer: "O Thou, whom I know not at all, . . . I do not doubt your existence. Whether you have destined me for immortality or whether I must merely pass by this way and die, I adore your decrees in silence; insect in your sight, I confess your divinity" (378). Making no attempt to clarify the nature of his theism/deism, Chateaubriand outlines the development of cult and theology: first, the innocence of the natural human being before God was lost and the perversions of superstition entered in, then religiously enterprising individuals saw the power they might possess by playing on the superstition of the masses, and clericalism was born. As he writes, "religions are born from our fears and weaknesses, grow and increase by means of fanaticism and die in indifference" (382).

Fig. 4.   François-René de Chateaubriand. Chateaubriand's portrait by Girodet-Trioson shows him meditating on the ruins of Rome. His nostalgia for medieval (Christian) ruins was in total contrast to the rational agnosticism of Destutt de Tracy. (Bibliothèque Nationale)

Although he places great value on the sublime Jewish idea of God and the actuality of the love symbolized by Jesus' life story, Chateaubriand decries the hierarchical structuring of Christianity that began with the Constantinian church. He believes that the Crusades and the Reformation represented deformations of Christianity, which were surpassed in fanaticism by the revocation of the Edict of Nantes by Louis XIV. With hatred and self-interest as its heritage, Christianity in France achieved terminal decadence, justifying philosophical attacks on both the substance and the historicity of Christianity. Chateaubriand himself strongly criticizes the hierarchical organization of the church, the form of its liturgies (in spite of their sometime grandeur), and especially the monarchies that support authoritarian, egotistical hierarchies. The question finally becomes, "What will be the religion that replaces Christianity [in Europe]?" (428) and, alas, to this final question he has no answer. All he knows is that "religion is necessary or society perishes" (429).

In the years between the completion of the *Essai sur les révolutions* and serious work on the *Génie du Christianisme,* the faith of his ancestors was idealized
as the embodiment of the divinity that he praised in the *Essai.* In his own
poetic account of his conversion, he describes his emotions on receiving a letter from his sister, Mme de Farcy, announcing the death of their mother; he
describes, too, the sad turn of events whereby his sister had died before the
letter reached him. In the fateful letter his sister reproaches him for the pain
he caused their mother because of his renunciation of the traditional faith. In
the *Mémoires d'outre-tombe* he writes, "The two voices that came out of the
tomb, the one death serving as the interpreter of the other, struck home. I did
not give up. I acknowledged their message, to great supernatural lights. A firm
interior conviction was produced; I wept and I believed."[4] But Chateaubriand
had arranged events to dramatic effect, because his sister did not die (26 July
1799) until more than a year after his mother (31 May 1798). It is evident that
he had begun working on *Génie* before his sister's death, because he wrote to
the publisher Baudus de Villenove on 5 April 1799, "I have a little manuscript
on *The Christian Religion, Morality and Poetry,*" adding that the manuscript will
be about forty-eight pages long.[5]

Since he was dealing with a publisher at this time, one might wonder if his
self-interest as a writer was a more important motive for the writing of *Génie
du Christianisme* than his remorse over the suffering he caused his mother and
sister. He goes on to say in his letter to Baudus, "This work is *very Christian,*
quite relevant to the present moment, and can scarcely miss having the success
of all relevant works."[6] A month later he attributed its relevance to a revival of
concern for religion in some important circles in France and said that the
work was begun at the instigation of his friend, Louis de Fontanes.[7] And a
mere four months after that he was telling Fontanes of a volume of around 430
pages in octavo, to be entitled *De la religion chrétienne par rapport à la morale et
aux beaux-arts.* It is evident from this letter of 19 August 1799 and another letter, also to Fontanes, on the following day that by mid-August 1799 he had a
well-worked-out sketch of the book that was published in 1802 under the
title *Le Génie du Christianisme, ou Les beautés de la religion chrétienne.*[8] If
Chateaubriand's letters of April, May, and August 1799 referred to work that
went from a projected 48 pages to 430 pages in that time period, it should be
safe to assume that about the time of his mother's death he had been elaborating his ideas for a full study. The evidence does point to mixed motivation
and a *gradual* "conversion," but there is no substantive reason to doubt that
his chagrin over his mother's last sad days and death were, in fact, a genuine

motivation for his writing of *Génie du Christianisme*. We can, in fact, establish the components of a gradually unfolding religious experience, even though Paul Christophorov had proven that a precise chronology is impossible. Henri Guillemin, in *L'Homme des "Mémoires d'outre-tombe,"* notes that Chateaubriand knew of his mother's death by 29 June 1798 (less that a month afterward). Chateaubriand's uncle Bedée had mentioned in his own correspondence a letter from his nephew dated 29 June mourning the death of Madame de Chateaubriand. Guillemin argues that Chateaubriand knew of the death of his mother long before he began the first "sketch" of *Génie du Christianisme*. But even though Guillemin demonstrates that Chateaubriand's regrets were not the sole motivation for his first efforts on *Génie,* we can still make the case that his mother's death was a major influence on the ensuing book-length study.[9]

The *Génie du Christianisme* was a broad poetic presentation of Christianity that, on one hand, represented the state of Chateaubriand's thought and emotions and, on the other, was a highly contrived history written for dramatic effect. Chateaubriand was as interested in carving a niche for himself as an author at the same time as he was in carrying out a religious mission to rehabilitate Catholic Christianity in France. The book was divided into four parts: "Dogmes et doctrines," "Poétique de Christianisme," "Beaux-arts et littérature," and "Culte." Naturally one searches for the originality of the work in the predominance of themes that came to be standard in the newly developing French romantic movement. Or perhaps we should say "movements"; in any case, I prefer to use a rostrum of theoreticians and practitioners as the basis for discussion, following D. G. Charlton who entitled his study *The French Romantics*. The first phase of the movement was marked by the nationalist and nature orientation (inspired by August Wilhelm and Friedrich Schlegel) of Madame de Staël and Benjamin Constant: a new favoritism of the medieval and Christian world over the ancient world, the northern European world in contrast to the Mediterranean world, as well as the opposition of the nationalist and modern to classicist doctrines.[10]

In the section on dogmas and doctrine, Chateaubriand explores the marvels of nature and human sentiment as evidence for the existence of God and the immortality of the soul. In the other three sections Chateaubriand makes his own case for Christianity: it is true because it is beautiful. In the "Poétique de Christianisme" he shows that Greco-Roman and Western Christian poetry reveal the meaning of the personality, its emotions, and its relation to the supernatural. In "Beaux-arts et littérature" he also considers philosophy, historiography, oratory, and something that he calls "Harmonies of the Christian religion with scenes of nature and the passion of the human heart." And in "Culte" he praises churches, their architecture, prayers and festal celebrations, tombs, the clergy and knighthood, and the human services provided by Christian charitable organizations across the centuries.

In his "Harmonies," there are lavish descriptions of architectural ruins from the Middle Ages, even a long poem on the Chartreuse of Paris. For Chateaubriand, "everyone has a secret attraction for ruins," and he explains it this way: "This sentiment comes from the fragility of our nature, a secret conformity between destroyed monuments and the swift passage of our existence. To this you can add an idea that consoles us in our smallness when we see that whole peoples and once famous men could not live much beyond the days assigned to our obscure existence. Ruins represent a moral effort in the middle of scenes of nature; when they are placed in a painting, one's eyes can scarcely leave them" (881). But the sentiment that lies behind this love of ruins is principally religious. Leaving the ruins of the Chartreuse, Chateaubriand wanders into the night and hears the singing of Psalm 150, "Laudate Dominum, omnes gentes." He imagines a voice from heaven saying, "Christians without faith, why do you lose hope? Do you believe that I change my plans as men do—that I abandon because I punish? Do not question my decrees but imitate these faithful servants, who bless the stroke of my hand, even from under the ruins where they have been struck down" (883). Elsewhere in this same "Harmonies" section he paints an entire scene around the ruins of a church in Scotland (886), and in "Tombes" he resurrects the churchmen and kings of medieval France (935), making the abbey church of Saint Denis a symbol of the grandeur of France and assuming that visitors would see it and depart thinking the words of St. Gregory, "This kingdom is truly the greatest among the nations" (937).

Depending upon how you look, you can see a break or continuity between the *Essai* and *Le Génie,* and there is an extensive contemporary literature on the subject.[11] For Emmanuelle Rebardy, who made a quantitative study of themes and issues, the maternal symbols and traditional social order in Chateaubriand's life come together as the *Mère-Patrie;* and Chateaubriand's France was cut off from the *Mère-Patrie* by the Enlightenment and the Revolution. Bertrand Aureau believes in Chateaubriand's analysis that revolutionary fervor at first replaced religious fervor, the continuity being energy that comes from God. Rupture came, Chateaubriand later decided, when revolutionary fervor was replaced by revolutionary rage. For Jean Dagen, Chateaubriand, when he wrote the *Mémoires d'outre-tombe,* came to see more of a continuity in the two earlier works than a rupture.

Returning to the circumstances surrounding the *Essai* and *Le Génie,* we should probably argue that Chateaubriand's literary works were the natural, step-wise result of his nostalgia and pragmatism. Faith was a form of liberation from the tragedy that had befallen his Breton Catholic culture, the hierarchical society once dominated by aristocratic families such as his own, and the most beloved members of that family. After his selfless approval of the Revolution, he withdrew from the chaotic political and religious culture of the day to his own meditative and poetic world of old-regime religious images. Nostalgic memory engendered a religious experience that appears to be a combination of the joys, sorrows, and memories of youth and family and ethnic tradition projected on the monuments symbolic of the grander days of that tradition. We may well suppose a fundamental stage of simple nostalgia when he first responded with emotion to the memories of the past. In a less idealistic, reflexive stage, represented by the *Essai sur les révolutions,* Chateaubriand clearly described the political and religious deficiencies of the old regime while retaining belief in an objective divinity whom he addressed in a personal way. Finally, in the highly organized nostalgia that we see in the *Génie du Christianisme* he promoted Catholicism not only because it had supported the most beloved members of his family but also because it enhanced his self-image, serving as a balance for feelings of guilt. He wanted to be admired by a reading audience, and so he knowingly used his own nostalgia to create similarly personal and pleasing sentiments in others. If we are to attribute authenticity to the work, then we must admit that his desires for self-enhancement and career advancement were absorbed into the raw experience of yearning for past family setting, state structures, and religious customs.[12]

The First Secular Ideology

Destutt de Tracy, born into Bourbonnais nobility, received a university education at Strasbourg and entered the army. In 1789 he served as a deputy to the Estates General and was an enthusiastic supporter of the Revolution until its turn to violence in 1792. As an adolescent he made a journey to Voltaire's Ferney, although at first he did not openly rebel against the family religion around him, and later he did not object to the Catholic practices of some friends and family members (at the same time as he was portraying religion as a social and personal liability).[13] The basic intellectual goal of his mature years was to study "the existence of the human race in his own country, its difference from the same existence at other times and other places, the development of society, the multiplicity and variety of concerns, affections, affairs, relations, knowledge, opinions, and occupations which unite, divide, separate, differentiate individuals living on the same soil."[14] The ideas that were published in *Élémens d'idéologie,* his major study, developed from his reading of Condillac while in the prison of Carmes during the Terror. Tracy did not have the opportunity to develop a dialogue with Condorcet, who died in prison by his own hand, but facing the possibility of execution, he immersed himself in an Enlightenment philosophical texts, building on his youthful devotion to Voltaire. The *Élémens* was published in five separate parts from 1801 through 1815 in Paris; a unified five-volume edition was published in 1824–26. His first developed presentation of "ideology" was in a speculative memoir read before the Class of Moral and Political Sciences of the Institut de France in five installments—between 21 April 1796 and 15 February 1798, according to Emmet Kennedy.[15]

Tracy's "ideology" was a social science of the origin, nature, and operation of ideas. He tried to systematize the study of the communication of ideas and the logical combination of these ideas in order to discover truth and regulate human passions. The origin of the French expression "*la science sociale*" has been the subject of careful inquiries by Keith Baker and Brian Head. Condorcet made the term his own in his *Esquisse d'un tableau historique des progrès de l'esprit humain,* where, according to Baker, the term had several meanings: (1) "rational principles of social organization derived from the nature of man by the method of the analysis of sensations and ideas"; (2) "a comprehensive statistical science of man in society that would subject the fact of human existence to empirical analysis through mathematical calculation"; and (3) a relational social art that would continuously revolutionize the conditions of human existence." Obviously, it was the first meaning that was developed by Tracy, who said that the term applied to some extent to his own ideology. Brian Head more fully examines the emergence of the term in the light of the eighteenth-century use of "science," and the Physiocrats' use of "*l'art social.*" He comes to the conclusion that "empiricism was wielded as an ideological weapon against the religious doctrines and political philosophy which had been associated with the irrational and oppressive past."[16]

Tracy wanted to expunge from his own work all metaphysical concepts found in Condillac—especially the concept of soul or its equivalent. Unequivocally, ideology was to be the science of sensations, perceptions, feelings, and ideas. Furthermore, still within the framework of rigorous science, it was to be the basis of grammar, of logic, of the combination of these two,

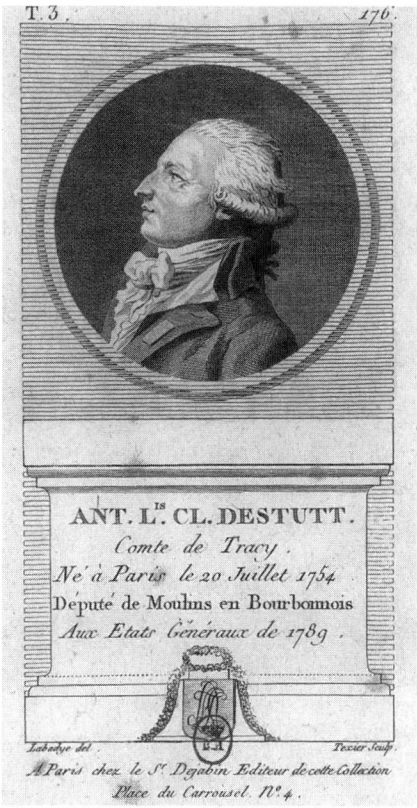

Fig. 5. Antoine-Louis-Claude Destutt de Tracy, shown here in a contemporary engraving published at the beginning of the Revolution. (Bibliothèque Nationale)

leading to the full reformation of education and personal and public morality. Working his way across both Condillac and Berkeley, Tracy privileged the concrete, the material, in his quest for scientific objectivity. Following Condillac, he started with *touch* and *resistance:* here was the beginning of knowledge. Following d'Holbach, he added *movement* as another central feature of the idea formation process, because when movement encounters resistance the beginning of sensation occurs. Unwilling to posit a central controlling self (a notion very close to "soul"), Tracy decided that the will had to be the controlling and unifying faculty and thereby opened himself up to a number of problems, not least of which, of course, was the problem of freedom of the will. Notably excluded from Tracy's system were religious sciences because he held that theology "either . . . comes from God, in which case it is above human reason, or else [it comes] from human dreaming, in which case it is below [human] reason."[17] Tracy was adamantly opposed to the notion of soul; more than anyone else, he single-mindedly tried to remove all spiritualist concepts, believing that his empirical ideology had no need of them.

Tracy's principal challenges came from the nascent spiritualism of his admiring colleagues, especially the protopsychologist Maine de Biran. In response, Tracy worked on formulations that merged sensation and will, but Maine de Biran pointed out the contradictions evident in the merging of the two—sensation being passive and will being active. For Maine de Biran there must exist some sentiment of self-awareness, even some sort of internal world. In letters responding to Maine de Biran, Tracy chides the psychologist for introducing a species of "substratum" into the explanation of personal functioning. Tracy believed that this substratum was a theoretical parasite in the scientific explanation and offered further defenses of his own means of unifying passive and active faculties (sensation and willing):

> I admit to you that I do not understand and I do not perceive this *sentiment,* this living force, that I call our sensibility. When it experiences an impression, it *feels, passively* if you will. When it feels a willing, a desire, it still feels, *actively* if you will, but it is always feeling, and feeling such and such a determined thing. The first manner of feeling only leads it to sense itself, to know the "I." The second, when it consists in willing this movement, leads it to know beings *other* than itself, *other* than the "I," and consequently to know better this "I" itself, distinguishing it, circumscribing it, joining to itself the parts that belong to it because of certain specific rapports (such as the organs). In my view, it [the "I"] becomes all the *affections* or impressions that it experiences successively, but without ceasing to be those things that it has experienced and which it recalls, thanks to the memory. . . . But I repeat, I do not see a *substratum.* . . . This substratum, I must say, appears to me a parasitic being that you introduced there without proof.[18]

Tracy was unremitting in his opposition to spirituality, and a fortiori to any specifically religious discourse. In fact, in *Quels sonts les moyens de fonder la morale chez un peuple?* a work written six years before his letter to Maine de Biran, he takes Voltaire himself to task. Since Voltaire had said that morality was divine, that it came from the hand of the Great Being, and that for this reason moral principles are the same everywhere, Tracy complains that "the proof that he [Voltaire] gives for this false assertion is that everywhere assassination and rape have been placed in the rank of crimes, and that everywhere violence and treachery have been condemned."[19] Although Tracy would have tolerated the word "nature" instead of "Great Being" in Voltaire's writing, his own explanation would have been in accord with rules of moral and social behavior that, in his view, are objective. He says, "Without doubt two men could not live together without feeling that if one of them killed or wounded the other, he would destroy the advantages of their society."[20]

Tracy believed that Christianity, in contrast to his objectively grounded ideology, incorporated "the most recent superstitions," and that "Christ, too, was only an imaginary being, one of the thousand metamorphoses of the Sun-God."[21] Such an attitude was naturally accompanied by anticlericalism; accordingly, when Tracy was given authority within the committees established to reform the school system, he was most concerned to keep education out of the hands of the clergy. The religious revival facilitated by Napoleon's political use of religion was a disaster for him, not only because the emperor was showing increasing contempt for his ideas, but also because the new religious atmosphere provided a very receptive setting for the spiritualization of ideology. He reacted by issuing a revision of his long analysis of Charles Dupuis's study of religion, *Origines de tous les cultes*. The work appeared, first, in a journal,[22] and then it was published in booklet form in 1799 and again in the 1804 edition that is used here. Charles Dupuis, himself a former priest, was a member of the Institut at its beginnings, along with Tracy. In his earlier years he had been a professor of rhetoric, but after establishing the beginnings of a literary reputation, he returned in a way to his first love, mathematics, following the course of a leading astronomer of the day, Lalande. He developed his ideas on the relation between ancient myths and astronomy between 1778 and 1794 when he published *Origines de tous les cultes*. At the same time, a political career had developed out of his academic career, and he was elected first to the Legislative Assembly and then to the Council of Five Hundred under the Directory. The *Abrégé* that Tracy analyzed was published in 1798.

For Tracy, Dupuis's work was the dawning of the light of truth in an area that had known mostly darkness, the theology and the philosophy of religion. Dupuis was able to reduce Christianity and all religions originating in the ancient Near East to worship of the sun, its planets, and the other stars. He posited a period of primordial cosmological science before the degradations of theology and priestcraft, when people knew they were dealing with solar and stellar realities and did not disguise them in foolish mythologies. According to Dupuis, as reported by Tracy, the personalities and activities of divinity figures and heroes were creatively imagined by ancient peoples in the names and the images attached to the constellations of stars in the sky. Nature was the only God in the beginning, and hence the constellations and planets were an extension of God, personifications of his powers and attributes. Then allegories of the movements of the universe, mythological fables, were concocted; the sun, the moon, the planets, the constellations of the zodiac, and individual stars were personified, and stories were told about them. Sun religion was embodied in the myths of Hercules, Osiris, Attis, Adonis, Mithra, Jason, Theseus, and of course Christ. The imagery of the Apocalypse should be considered the most acceptable representation of the Christ myth because its mythic solar status is clear from the beginning. Whereas the gospel writers degraded the solar myth to a literal history of Jesus (who never existed at all according to Dupuis and Tracy), the author of the Apocalypse created a basic interpretation of the sun out of Egyptian, Persian, Jewish, and Greek sources.

In the end, Tracy can find nothing good to say about Christianity or any other theism. The process by which people come to attribute divinity to nature is, he says, no different from reactions of children who personify the rocks that injure or resist them: they strike out at an inanimate rock as if it were animated. He poses a question very much like the question Chateaubriand posed at the end of his *Essai sur les révolutions:* "If you destroy religion, what do you put in its place?" For Tracy the answer was easy: "In place of a bad moral system based on a defective reasoning that spoils the mind and on suppositions that lead it astray, usage will posit a good [system] dictated by a reason that it will perfect by its own exercise, and which is founded on the observation of the intellectual faculties of man." He approves Dupuis's just pride in his deciphering of early science and its gradual mythologization: myths "composed by men who, having lost the thread of meaning of ancient ideas, merely conserved the names of fantastic beings, which were no longer connected to the physical order of the world."[23] At the end of this *Analyse raisonnée de "l'Origine de tous les cultes,"* Tracy's understanding of the importance of religion is far different from Chateaubriand's disappointed conclusion expressed at the end of the *Essai sur les révolutions,* that religion, though often a damaging and dangerous phenomenon, cannot easily be replaced.

In sum, instead of looking back to family history, national tradition, and related religious symbols, Tracy looked only to the future and the quasi-scientific perfection of life that some of the Enlightenment philosophers had promised. No "conversion" to religion took place because the youthful and family experiences he remembered included his idealization of Enlightenment thought and his family's toleration of this idealization. In his search for truth and for certainty about the ways truth is known, Tracy was an unrelenting advocate of a rational, analytic ideal—he placed total confidence in the discernibility of objective reality. And here I follow one line of personality interpretation attributing personal qualities to the analytical scientist that are different from other types: "conceptual theorist," "conceptual humanist," and "particular humanist." The analytical scientist is likely to be disinterested, unbiased, impersonal, precise, expert, specialist, skeptical, exact, and methodological. Although Tracy could not have forgotten his early admiration of Voltaire and other Enlightenment thinkers, nostalgia was not dynamically operative in his personal and intellectual development.[24] We do not know whether the stability of Tracy's formation and education, and the strength he developed to meet the challenge of the revolutionary crisis, nourished his desire to attain the scientific ideal in his intellectual work, or whether the scientific ideal nourished his personal stability. But certainly, across the contrasting years of violent republicanism and religious restoration, he developed and lived by an ideology composed of radical agnosticism, political and educational theories about the perfectibility of human nature, and a belief in the objective truth of social science.

Polar Opposites

Chateaubriand and Destutt de Tracy were both highly placed in public intellectual life in Paris, or in close touch with Paris, during the years reviewed here; looking for polarities, we are dealing with a limited and definable society. The journals they wrote for had a calculable circulation, and the literary salons they frequented were made up of small handfuls of people who possessed genuinely visible leadership and influence. The two men knew one another and, as one would expect of philosophical and emotional opposites, thoroughly disapproved of one another. Chateaubriand's ideas were promoted by the *Mercure de France* and developed in intellectual circles of which he himself was at times the center, while Tracy and his circle of associates, called the *Idéologues,* were influential in the *Décade philosophique* and in a variety of moderate republican contexts.[25] There was not so much active opposition as negative evaluation of one another during their more productive years. Chateaubriand admitted that a refutation of ideology was implicit in his *Génie du Christianisme;* of course, Tracy allowed for no redeeming value to religion in his formal writing.[26]

The *Mercure de France* between 1800 and 1810 was the purveyor of monarchist and Catholic thought and sentiment. More than 150 years old, it had ceased publication in the republican form it had taken during the earliest years of the Revolution.[27] Louis de Fontanes, Chateaubriand's mentor and friend, who took control of the journal in 1800, immediately wrote a negative and lengthy review of Madame de Staël's *De la littérature* and suggested in its place a work that "chance has caused to fall into our hands . . . , which is not yet published and which has for its title, *Des Beautés morales et poétiques de la Religion Chrétienne.*"[28] Chateaubriand was a presence, then, at the conception of the new *Mercure* and soon began to write for the journal himself.

In contrast, the *Décade philosophique,* having begun during the Terror as a non-Jacobin republican journal, developed as a vehicle for Tracy and his associates. Joanna Kitchin argues that although the journal was supposedly a forum for the presentation of the great Enlightenment philosophers— Voltaire, Montesquieu, Rousseau, Diderot, Helvétius, d'Holbach, Condorcet— "it hardly went into their thought in depth. The editors contented themselves with banal and partial presentations."[29] The *Décade* was, rather, the organ of the Idéologues; not, to be sure, the ideology of Tracy only, but of the full range of those members of the Institut de France who were in dialogue (though not always in agreement) with Tracy.[30] With the reorganized *Mercure* as its formidable adversary, the *Décade* entered into religious polemics, decrying the renewal of religious sentiment with its convenient forgetfulness of the evils of church history.[31] In full support of Dupuis's *Origines de tous les cultes,* the editor, Pierre-Louis Ginguené, wrote three articles in criticism of *Le Génie du Christianisme.* Although he admitted that Chateaubriand presented some important instances of beauty, poetry, and service to society in Christian history, Ginguené insisted on the antisocial and counterrevolutionary character of Christianity—on balance, more harmful than helpful.[32]

Chateaubriand and Tracy were drawn into greater proximity to one another with each passing year. As Napoleon attempted to resolve conflicts in his empire, he forced opposing groups and individuals to work together, and this included the writers for the journals *Mercure de France* and *Décade philosophique.* By 1808, Napoleon insisted on the amalgamation of the monarchist and Catholic *Mercure* with the republican and anti-Christian *Décade.*

Staffs of both journals looked to their own recent issues to see what might have been the cause of the emperor's displeasure but could not be sure of the reason. Perhaps he intended to weaken the two at the same time. In any case, the upshot of the combination was that the name of the *Mercure* was retained, and because Chateaubriand and his colleagues refused to cooperate, the intellectual ideology of the *Décade*, though weakened, predominated.

Tracy had been a member of the Institut de France since 1795. Although the Institut had been formed during the Revolution to replace the royal academies, Napoleon restructured the Institut to include a class that corresponded to the old Académie française, suppressing the Class of Moral and Political Sciences, from which the Idéologues had dominated the Institut. It was in his interest to propose the conservative Chateaubriand as a counterbalance in an Institut still influenced by Idéologues. Chateaubriand was in fact elected in 1810 to fill the chair left vacant by the death of Marie-Joseph Chénier, but he was never allowed to deliver his official discourse to the Institut because he refused Napoleon's modifications of his criticism of Chénier.[33] He would not be officially received into the Institut until the Restoration. Napoleon also wanted a prize to be granted every ten years for two outstanding books of the decade. Both Tracy's *Élémens d'idéologie* and Chateaubriand's *Génie du Christianisme* were proposed, one in the general scholarly category and the other in literature. A commission set up for the purpose—and from which Tracy, a member, naturally absented himself—awarded the prize to neither work. Though no one pursued the issue on behalf of Tracy, Napoleon himself wanted to know why Chateaubriand's book did not even receive mention. A specially appointed, religiously diverse jury prepared extensive evaluations of Chateaubriand's work praising its rhetoric but criticizing its substance.[34] Given this tension and Chateaubriand's wild scheme to criticize his own predecessor in the reception discourse prepared for the Institut, Tracy wrote to his colleague Fauriel, "Pinel [the insanity specialist] himself will not treat . . . the brilliant Chateaubriand.[35]

Living and working within the two generally opposed factions of the Institut de France—represented by the journals for which they wrote—Chateaubriand and Tracy were opposites of thought and feeling in every aspect of their professional and personal lives.[36] To be sure, there were other writers who, for their own reasons, were as proreligious as Chateaubriand or as prosecular as Tracy. More radically propapal than Chateaubriand, Joseph de Maistre argued that society needed an infallible interpreter of undoubtable truth, and Louis de Bonald argued for the truth of Catholicism as an absolute against which error had no rights, but neither of these two men argued on behalf of the total religious culture of earlier ages. In fact, de Maistre was not part of the Paris intellectual life—a Savoyard, he spent his productive years in the diplomatic employ of the king of Piedmont—and de Bonald, though older than Chateaubriand, did not rise to intellectual prominence until some years after the Chateaubriand-Tracy encounter, when he entered into a similar controversy with Benjamin Constant. The figure closest to the Chateaubriand of the *Génie du Christianisme* was Pierre Ballanche, whose own ruminations on the cultural values of Christianity preceded Chateaubriand's study, but Ballanche believed that a compromise should be reached with the doctrines of Rousseau and Condorcet. And as regards Tracy, it should be clear by now that the precise issues on which he disagreed with the Idéologues closest to him concerned the spirituality of the soul and the social role values to assign to religion in history. If Charles Dupuis, Tracy's mentor in the matter of history of religions and a fellow member of the Institut, was likewise a champion of secularity, his prominence and influence were by no means as great: Dupuis's publications were mostly confined to astronomy and mathematics, whereas Tracy took the lead in promoting a secularizing ideology.[37]

The personal animosity between Chateaubriand and Tracy would diminish as the years went on because of a common concern for freedom of the press and, indeed, for personal freedom in the matter of religion, but in Paris for more than ten years their intellectual temperaments as expressed in their publications were the polarities of religion and secularism. I suggest that these temperaments were, in a basic way, the origins of two types of experience in nineteenth-century France. In the footsteps of Chateaubriand followed romantic novelists and poets (such as Victor Hugo and Alphonse Lamartine), medieval revivalists, and the enthusiastically loyal clergy of the nineteenth century. In the footsteps of Tracy followed Stendahl, playing human freedom against religious constraint, the Semitics scholar Ernest Renan, the lexicographer Émile Littré, and the anticlericals of the second and third decades of the Third Republic. Such a division is based on the existential experiences of those engaged in a variety of intellectual and political conflicts and depends on a demonstration of the similarity and continuity of each temperament. Direct and to the point, then, are the following stories of the *defenses* set up to keep separate a sensitive and fragile Catholicism, sustained by nostalgia and protected by clergy. Easier to be Catholic and French if one could avoid everything national—secular and scientific.

Part Two

DEFENSE

·

For fifteen years Napoleon ruled France (1799–1814/15), and for fifteen years Louis XVIII (1814/15–1824) and Charles X (1824–30), brothers of the executed Louis XVI, refashioned as best they could the old Bourbon regime. During this time Napoleon tried to make the church an ally in his pacification of monarchists and revolutionaries, and the Bourbons attempted a new union of throne and altar. Can we not say, then, that government and church were reconciled and the divorce ended, in spite of polarities of sentiment and thought? No, not really. The problem was that the divorce not only existed between the formal structures of church and throne/state, but it also cut across culture and society. Church leaders and faithful, so many of them, were traumatized by the destructiveness of the Revolution, the manipulations of Napoleon, and the Bourbons' campaign for royal privilege. And all the while the revolutionary elements of French society maintained an underground existence in opposition to the Restoration.

It took decades to consolidate a defense on the Catholic side, however. Resisting both Napoleon and the pope, a small group of bishops and faithful formed the *Petite Église,* believing that neither imperial nor papal authority had the right to demand the resignations of the French bishops in order to forge the Concordat of church and state. Then, intransigent aristocrats formed special units in a new federation of religious confraternities. In the *Chevaliers de la foi*, aristocratic social and political interests trumped any purely devotional reforms of the broader *Congrégation* (a pious confraternity of young laymen founded under the Empire and reshaped with the help of a Jesuit). The very Gallican comte François-Dominique de Montlosier made a name for himself by an attack on imagined subversion of government and church. He demonized the clergy, the Jesuits in particular, and in so doing became a model of self-destructiveness. By attacking other forms of monarchical conservatism he undermined his own.

High level self-destructiveness within monarchical France was not the unique possession of Montlosier. King Louis XVIII, taking his role literally and seriously, was ready to work with a representative legislature. But conservative aristocrats, appropriately labeled *ultras,* so dominated the legislature that the other European governments urged Louis to control them. When church interests coincided with aristocratic interests, church interests were advanced, as in the old regime. But now the religious life of the church—cultivation of sacramental life, prayer, and works of charity—was a lesser concern. Royal incompetence ruined everything. After the death of the morbidly obese Louis in 1824, his *ultra* brother, Charles X, a libertine who became a *dévot* as he grew older, was the unwitting and witless cause of the fall of the monarchy and the further degradation of the image of the church. Charles was crowned according to medieval ritual at Reims cathedral and dedicated his rule to the restoration of an imagined medieval union of throne and altar. Along with his eccentric and incompetent minister Comte Jules Armand de Polignac, he worked to restore noble properties and legislate respect for the church. And here the prize for lunatic legislation must go to the law requiring the death penalty for anyone who would destroy or profane the consecrated bread and wine, the person's sacrilegious hand to be severed prior to execution. Damage control by a more enlightened chief minister was insufficient to prevent the overthrow of the Bourbon regime in 1830. At the same time as Charles was driven out of the country, Parisian mobs sacked the archbishop's residence at Notre-Dame in a signal gesture of contempt for Catholic hierarchical submission to the Bourbon agenda.

In this era, the 1820s, French bishops began to assess the levels of religious practice and to support teams of preachers for those areas where faith appeared to be failing. One educated guess, coming from 1826, put the percentage of the population with minimal knowledge of the faith at one-half, and the number of churchgoers in Paris at one-eighth, the great majority of them women. These figures would turn out to be optimistic after individual dioceses made organized efforts to tabulate Mass attendance and reception of communion. Preachers highlighted divine anger and punishment for sin, turning their invective from the sins of the nation to sins of the individual. The bishops looked less to the government for religious restoration and more to the developing resources within the church. Even the powerful prelate in charge of national education, Bishop Denys Frayssinous, quickly became a minor player in church life.

The social tectonic shift here, though, was the feminization of French religion. Beginning a generation earlier, women were the consistent champions of Catholic practice in the face of the male generated political and religious confusions of the Revolution. Now, with more careful assessments of religious practice attracting the attention of churchmen, the French church awoke socially and found itself feminine. In most regions the level of churchgoing and participation in the sacraments was higher for women than for men; much higher in regions that had been effectively dechristianized during the Revolution. Women were more receptive to sermons and the moral demands of the clergy. The clergy counted on women for the animation of parish life and the support of church teaching in the home. Husbands could be jealous of the curé's influence in their wives' daily lives and suspicious (sometimes with good reason) of their wives' attraction to the wifeless, and so available curé.

Catholic leaders at the end of the Restoration and during the reign of Louis-Philippe (king of France, 1830–48) developed in a distinctly defensive mode, and at their best they could even mount a certain offensive against governments unresponsive to their demands. If the official Catholicism of the Bourbon government had not brought revival and reform to the church, why count on the religiously casual and indifferent Louis-Philippe, a virtual Voltairian who attended Mass?

This king had the potential, in politics at least, to establish a durable modern monarchy. The House of Orléans, cousins of the direct Bourbon line, had maintained an egalitarian attitude across the revolutionary, Napoleonic, and Restoration years. Louis-Philippe's father, *dit* Philippe Egalité during the Revolution, was a republican, and Louis-Philippe himself, across the 1820s, maintained his house in Paris as a center of liberal political and intellectual life. He lived without ceremonial, from his simple swearing in as king in the presence of the legislature through his years of handling his own dress and grooming.

He carefully attended to the advancement of business and industry and the direction of an elite representative government. In this he was assisted by François Guizot, an authoritarian Protestant dedicated to an orderly, rational, and even religious society. "The bourgeois monarchy" was an appropriate label for the whole operation.

The first years of Louis-Philippe's reign, however, were far from tranquil. Factionalism was fueled by the presence Charles X's daughter-in-law, who had given birth to the legitimist pretender to the throne several months after the assassination of her husband, and by Napoleon's nephew, the dreamer and adventurer who would later become Emperor Napoleon III. Worker discontent led to insurrections, violently suppressed, in Lyon and Paris. A pen-and-ink sketch by Honoré Daumier of a massacred family dead on the floor of their bedroom, the father in nightgown lying on top of the baby, has immortalized this event. It was after these dramas that Louis-Philippe came to rely on the rigorous, Calvinistic François Guizot (who had much in common, then, with the leftover Jansenists and the traditionally religious old aristocracy). Some of the most famous caricatures of the period were of Louis-Philippe, his head pictured in a sequence of changes from bejowled heaviness to juicy pear, and of Guizot, his sharp and pointed nose poised high in the air, ready to strike and labeled "Guizotine."

Powerful and mesmerizing writers substituted a new vision of humanity for the old theology. Their most appealing portrayals of churchmen highlight human goodness rather than spirituality. Put here the dynamic country curés of Honoré de Balzac; Victor Hugo's humble bishop, who allows a desperate Jean Valjean to steal from him and then saves him from the police in Les Misérables; and Alexandre Dumas's prisoner priest in Le Comte de Monte Christo, who trains Edmond Dantès in persevering escape strategies and for the pursuit of hidden treasure. More often, clerical avarice and psychological control of the people were the staples of French fiction during the reign of Louis-Philippe. Other ideological alternatives to Christianity included Saint-Simon's campaign to alleviate the misery of the poor and Auguste Comte's scientific study of human social life (positivism). Leading Paris intellectuals, Victor Cousin in philosophy and Hippolyte Taine in literature, saw their work as studies of natural religion and as scientific metaphysics. Churchmen worried about these influences more than the occult attraction of the Swedish mystic Emmanuel Swedenborg or the syncretism of the Rosicrucians, a post-Renaissance attempt to recover the mysteries of ancient religions.

Under Louis-Philippe, church leaders wanted to manage their own interests and programs with a minimum of interference from the government.

Félicité de Lamennais was a dynamic priest-intellectual who took the lead here. Instinctively he saw that the more the French church recognized or augmented the pope's spiritual and disciplinary powers, the more the French church would control its own destiny relative to the state; and so began the long development of nineteenth-century *ultramontanism,* an old label for the attitudes and movements that maximize the prerogatives of the pope, "beyond the mountains," i.e., the Alps. But in earlier *Essai sur l'indifférence* (1817) and then in his journal *L'Avenir,* Lamennais highlighted philosophical and historical arguments in support of Christianity, as against conservative theological arguments. The pope and his aides believed that Lamennais's powerful, independent mind was more a hindrance than a help to the Catholic cause and condemned his efforts. A shocked Lamennais could do no more than mumble his submission and harden his heart, becoming the opposite of a papal maximalist: a thoroughgoing secularist forever unreconciled to both church and state.

Leading French Catholics and onetime allies of Lamennais, among them the preacher Father Henri Lacordaire, the intellectual and historian Count Charles de Montalembert, and the founder of the St. Vincent de Paul Society, Frédéric Ozanam, each in his own way made peace with the ultramontanism they had helped to revive. Dom Prosper Guéranger's newly resurrected Benedictine community at Solesmes further reinforced the authority of the pope by revising traditional liturgical books to conform to the Roman liturgy. And many church leaders in France supported a conservative Catholic offensive mounted by the layman journalist Louis Veuillot and Veuillot's coterie of ultramontanist campaigners, of whom Bishop Edouard Pie was the rising star. Moderates and liberals, some of them bishops (Félix Dupanloup of Orléans was their leader), were the preferred targets of these new, purely Catholic *ultras,* who were never satisfied by government reconciliation or favor, no matter how generous. *Across the religious confusion, the pilgrimage movement, here presented in Chapter 4, brought together the forces and sentiments of both clergy and people in opposition to religious indifference on the national level: devotion to the Sacred Heart of Jesus, an image dating to the seventeenth-century vision of Christ to a French nun in the Burgundian town of Paray-le-Monial and politicized during the Revolution, and devotion to Notre-Dame in her royal role as Virgin Mother of God at Chartres cathedral or in her luminous kindness as an apparition at Lourdes. The story of Chartres is highlighted here because it reveals the economics and the politics, the social benefits and the devotional coloring of defensive religious identity in the middle and late decades of the nineteenth century. If the cathedral clergy dominated, female imagery predominated, both in the public evocations of Notre-Dame as Virgin and Mother, and in*

the private devotions of pilgrims, the women in particular. Women had been the
strength of local Catholicism almost everywhere since the days of the Revolution and
were now the substantial force used by the priest coordinators of pilgrimage. As they
integrated themselves into the clerical defense of Catholicism, they could often set the
agenda.

When Louis-Philippe was forced to abdicate in February of 1848, after
eighteen years of sponsoring capitalism and intellectual freedom (if not cynicism and indifference), the French church had a brief opportunity to make its
peace with the revolutionary tradition—newly revived in the Second French
Republic (1848–52). Archbishop Denys-Augustin Affre of Paris and many of
his fellow bishops supported the new Republic. Catholic liberals, such as
Lacordaire, and conservatives, such as Veuillot, protested their loyalty also.
But when Parisian workers elevated barricades against government troops in
July and Archbishop Affre was killed while trying to mediate, the earlier
openness quickly faded away.

The new president, Louis-Napoleon Bonaparte, a man driven by opposing
instincts, revolutionary and imperial, permissive and dominating, saw the
church as a force for order and promoted it to this end. The antichurch group
fell into line so that, even among the old secularists, it was no longer chic to
bad-mouth the clergy or mock the religion of the simple. In the second year
of Louis-Napoleon's presidency, a new law on religious rights in secondary
education was worked out by Viscount Alfred de Falloux, minister of education. Unwilling to take "yes" for an answer, old Veuillot and his cronies
damned a national government that would not cede full control of education
to the clerical and ultramontane parties. Louis-Napoleon could never satisfy
them, but as Emperor Napoleon III he strove at the behest of his pious spouse,
the Empress Eugénie, to support French Catholicism as a primary spiritual
and cultural strength of the Empire. This Second Empire (1852–70) was
praised and damned by some churchmen, but the majority of them remained
wary of the still vital scientific and philosophical ideas that dated back to the
Revolution and the Enlightenment. The efforts of clergy to defend their people against secular culture occasionally, and easily, turned into opposition.

Pius IX (pope from 1846 to 1878) displayed some vestige liberalism in his
early years of office at the end of the bourgeois monarchy, but his whole pon-
tificate was a systematic promotion of authoritarian Catholicism, submissive
only to political expediency—if then. The political turmoil surrounding him,
the dissolution of the Papal States, and the formation of a united secular Italy

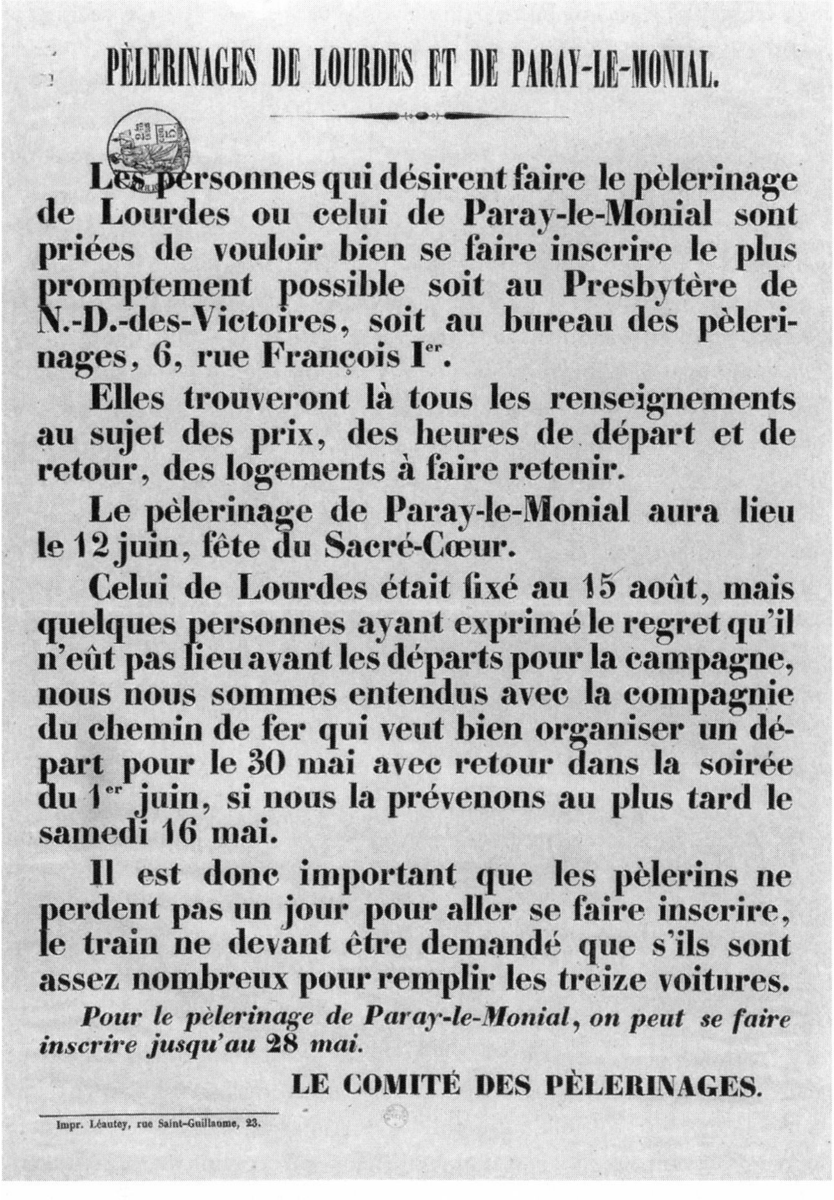

PÈLERINAGES DE LOURDES ET DE PARAY-LE-MONIAL.

Les personnes qui désirent faire le pèlerinage de Lourdes ou celui de Paray-le-Monial sont priées de vouloir bien se faire inscrire le plus promptement possible soit au Presbytère de N.-D.-des-Victoires, soit au bureau des pèlerinages, 6, rue François Iᵉʳ.

Elles trouveront là tous les renseignements au sujet des prix, des heures de départ et de retour, des logements à faire retenir.

Le pèlerinage de Paray-le-Monial aura lieu le 12 juin, fête du Sacré-Cœur.

Celui de Lourdes était fixé au 15 août, mais quelques personnes ayant exprimé le regret qu'il n'eût pas lieu avant les départs pour la campagne, nous nous sommes entendus avec la compagnie du chemin de fer qui veut bien organiser un départ pour le 30 mai avec retour dans la soirée du 1ᵉʳ juin, si nous la prévenons au plus tard le samedi 16 mai.

Il est donc important que les pèlerins ne perdent pas un jour pour aller se faire inscrire, le train ne devant être demandé que s'ils sont assez nombreux pour remplir les treize voitures.

Pour le pèlerinage de Paray-le-Monial, on peut se faire inscrire jusqu'au 28 mai.

LE COMITÉ DES PÈLERINAGES.

Impr. Léautey, rue Saint-Guillaume, 23.

Fig. 6. A poster advertising pilgrimages to Lourdes and Paray-le-Monial from Paris. Both clergy and religious order members advocated pilgrimages to shrines old and new in order to focus French loyalties on religion and away from the state. (Bibliothèque Nationale)

aggravated his siege mentality. He was only too happy to have the aid of Napoleon III in maintaining his civil authority in Rome. In fact, French troops kept Rome a papal city until called to duty in the Franco-Prussian War of 1870. But by then Pius IX had convened the First Vatican Council. Subsequently, he assured the declaration of papal infallibility just as the troops of the Italian Republic were entering Rome to take away his temporal authority.

The Franco-Prussian War quickly ended in disaster for Napoleon III, who was captured by German forces at Sedan. Archbishop Georges Darboy, who opposed the declaration of infallibility as inopportune, headed back to a Paris besieged by the Germans and subsequently ruled by a radical commune government in open rebellion against the new national French government. In its final and worst days, a desperate commune took to executing hostages, seventy-four of them, including poor Archbishop Darboy and twenty-four priests. This was a small number compared to the 20,000 *communards* who were slaughtered when national government troops chased down all suspected resisters, trapping and slaughtering final hold-outs in the old Paris cemetery of Père Lachaise.

Even during the preceding decade, as Napoleon III was permitting more freedom of expression and a loyal opposition in the legislature, Pius had systematically closed off every avenue of dialogue between Catholicism and the political and religious thought of the era. The ultramontane church in France rejoiced in this intransigence, and the moderates just had to live with it. The pope targeted democracy, liberty of conscience, and such fluid religious attitudes and movements as "modernism" and "americanism" in his pronouncements to the church at large, especially in his encyclical *Quanta Cura* with its "Syllabus of Errors." In France, Veuillot was vindicated and Dupanloup was not, the latter trying desperately to put an acceptable spin on the pope's scattered condemnations of sincere intellectual movements in society and the church.

It had been a losing political battle, then, for the authoritarian bishops and clergy across the manipulative First Empire, the Bourbon Restoration, the secular bourgeois monarchy, the politically confused Second Republic, and the morally permissive Second Empire. They needed to find alternate ways to influence public life. The number of priests had been increasing since the end of the Restoration period, but with more and more of them coming from the lower classes, the maintenance of a clerical united front was a challenge. Opposition to the government was one source of unity. Another was the catechism: apart from adaptations made in support of the authority of successive political regimes, catechisms had changed little since the old regime itself! For the diocesan clergy, the catechizing of children in their own idiom was of consummate importance, and attempts to monitor and homogenize religious education were viewed with fear and suspicion. *With the catechism itself a valued defense against presumed or real antichurch forces, clergy drew a line of defense around the non-French-speaking regions of France from the 1860s through the rule of Napoleon III and into the first decades of the Third Republic. In Chapter 5, German-speaking Alsace stands in for the other high-level churchgoing regions—where Flemish, Breton, and Basque were spoken. Alsace contrasts strikingly with the Catalan-speaking Roussillon in the far south of France, the only non-French-speaking region where the percentage level of churchgoers was low. The Roussillon being the only case of a low-practice non-French-speaking region, Alsace was the inevitable choice to be paired with it: they both became part of France during the same era and had been handled administratively in similar ways since the days of Louis XIV. The story here emphasizes the clergy's defense of German in Alsace, in the 1860s in particular when Alsace was part of France, the lasting effects of this across the decades, and the contrasting clerical neglect of Catalan from 1860 through 1890.*

The Third French Republic was headed by the old constitutional monarchist Adolphe Thiers until he was tricked into resigning in favor of the Franco-Prussian War general, Patrice MacMahon. This so-called moral order government was an encouragement to conservative churchmen, who had a horror for the forces of republican liberalism led by Léon Gambetta. The latter's "*Clericalisme, voilà l'ennemi* " (clericalism, there's the enemy) coming from his 1877 election campaign, was not totally paranoid. At that time, there were approximately 130,000 sisters and 56,000 secular priests in France. Ultramontane reverence for Pope Pius IX had reached the level of personality cult. The popular piety that energized pilgrimages was flourishing in local parishes, where ordinary people appreciated the emotional warmth of devotions to the Sacred Heart and Eucharistic presence of Christ, and to the Virgin Mary, and to the saints. Missionary ardor and domestic combativeness, too, had served the rejuvenation of the French church.

Attacks on Christian belief by scholars of the preceding decades—the historian Jules Michelet, the social scientist Auguste Comte, and the Semitics scholar Ernest Renan are major figures here—had been countered by churchmen who questioned their honesty and demonized their motives. Conservative Catholics put their hopes in President MacMahon and a pretender to the monarchy, the comte de Chambord, grandson of Charles X and the last great hope for a Catholic France. If clericalism was not the enemy of the government, conservative Catholicism certainly was. In a daring symbolic gesture, as political as it was religious, Catholic lay and clerical leaders conceived and promoted the building of an enormous church, the basilica of the Sacré Coeur, which would loom over the city of Paris from the heights of Montmartre. Dedicated legislative assembly members even obtained official government support for the project, obviously believing that a strong offense would be the best defense.

Chapter Four

PIETY AGAINST POLITICS: *Pilgrimage to Chartres During the Nineteenth Century*

Local pilgrimages, supported by the piety and personal needs of the faithful, regained something of their prerevolutionary popularity under the Restoration. Subsequently, the reputation of the humble curé of Ars, Jean-Marie Vianney, brought pilgrims to his village from 1830 until his death in 1859—when they were averaging 70,000 a year.[1] In midcentury, devotion to the Sacred Heart was given dramatic impetus by the pilgrimage apostolate of the Jesuit Victor Drevon. This devotion had already been extended to a cultural elite during the reign of Louis XIV when, at Paray-le-Monial in Burgundy, the Visitandine nun Marguerite-Marie Alacoque experienced a series of visions of Christ with a flaming heart in his breast. During the Revolution the image of the Sacred Heart was worn by the Chouans, and during the Restoration the story was circulated that Louis XVI linked the saving of the monarchy to the Sacred Heart. In 1856, Pius IX dramatically consecrated the world to the Sacred Heart as a defense against liberal, often antireligious politics, and he beatified Marguerite-Marie Alacoque in 1864.

Promoting the Paray-le-Monial shrine from the 1840s on, Victor Drevon proposed in 1872 to the bishop of Autun a Sacred Heart pilgrimage in conjunction with the pilgrimages to LaSalette and Lourdes. The Drevon circular, a pastoral letter from the bishop, and special indulgences promised by Pius IX brought sizeable crowds during the month of June (of the following year). The Jesuit had also obtained hundreds of promises from members of the National Assembly to come on pilgrimage, although only fifty of the two hundred he had expected finally came. Gabriel Belcastel, the legitimist assembly member from Haute-Garonne, consecrated France to the Sacred Heart,

speaking for his colleagues in the National Assembly—so he proclaimed—
and for all of France.[2]

Above all it was the era of the Madonnas. Reports of visions of the Blessed
Virgin exerted a special attraction in the central years of political crisis, when
European Catholicism was opposed by the new revolutionary liberalism. The
mountain village of La Salette in the Isère became a new center, in spite of the
uninspiring personalities of the young children who reported a vision of a
weeping Virgin. The image and the promise of miracles carried the children's
message through to episcopal approval and a La Salette confraternity membership of 18,000 members. Four years after the proclamation of the dogma of
the Immaculate Conception in 1854, Bernadette Soubirous reported eighteen
conversations with the Virgin between 11 February and 4 March. The local
bishop presided at services there in 1864 and the railroad arrived in 1866.[3]
There is no doubt that the construction of the great European railroad system
in the years following 1848 contributed to the nationalizing and internation-
alizing of the most attractive and best promoted pilgrimage centers. The
Franco-Prussian War in 1870 further intensified both the Sacred Heart and
Marian pilgrimage efforts.[4]

It became clear to the religious orders that pilgrimages could be an effective
way of regaining some of the old influence of religion on public life. Immediately after the war, the Maison de la Bonne Presse was established as an important part of the apostolate of the Augustinians of the Assumption, newly
founded by Emmanuel d'Alzon and François Picard. The Assumptionist Vincent de Paul Bailly engineered the establishment in 1872 of a Conseil Général
de Pèlerinages and the official bulletin of the Conseil, Le Pèlerin.[5] The first
issue of Le Pèlerin, published in 1873, begins, "The thought of pilgrimage is
born of our sorrows and the persecutions to which the common Father of the
faithful [the pope] has been submitted, as if God wanted to teach us never to
despair."[6] In the same issue, the Assumptionist Father Tilloy pointed out that
the pilgrimage movement had a solid theological foundation: "God has placed
at intervals along the way these stations of faith where his grace works with
greater efficacy."[7] And grace would bring people to repentance: "For us
Christians, who know that public and national crimes can be expiated only by
public and national reparation, there is no doubt that among the ways offered
us to appease the justice of God and to ward off the lighting of his anger, a
most efficacious and opportune way is public prayer, national reparation, such
as it is widely practiced in our day by pilgrimages."[8] The Assumptionists were
the most influential religious-order sponsors of the pilgrimage movement,
orchestrating pilgrimages to La Salette and Lourdes in particular.

CHARTRES
Portail Méridional.

Dess. d'ap.nat.lith.par Deroy.

Imp.Lemercier,Paris.

Fig. 7.   Lithograph by Deroy of the south portal of Chartres Cathedral, published in 1853, shortly before the pilgrimage journal *La Voix de Notre-Dame de Chartres* began publication to promote the cathedral as the historic center of French Catholic life. (Bibliothèque Nationale)

In 1873, 40,000 pilgrims journeyed to Lourdes and 40,000 journeyed to Chartres. Lourdes came to attract international attention in the late nineteenth—and twentieth—centuries, whereas Chartres remained mostly French. In fact, religious and political expression at Chartres were so clearly in the long-term interests of a very Catholic France that the cathedral-shrine of Chartres merits special attention. Whereas devotion to the Sacred Heart dated from the old regime, Chartrian devotion to Mary dated from the early Middle Ages, with even earlier antecedents. Whereas apparition shrines attracted popular religious expression subsequently appropriated by the clergy, the clergy in nineteenth-century Chartres were the initiators. Each French—or European—shrine was the setting for its own special blend of religious expression and political maneuvering, and none offered greater variety than Chartres: mystical, devotional, and philosophical religious expression *and* hard-core political maneuvering. Even if Chartres did not produce the widest variety of religious expression and political maneuvering, it was the most minutely described by the organizing clergy, in a journal published for locals and visitors, *La Voix de Notre-Dame de Chartres*.[9] Here we see Chartres pilgrimage from the viewpoint of a clergy who promoted their own religious, political, and economic goals, who remained aware of both elite and simple needs and, yes, depended on women's fervor even as they channeled it to their own purposes. But the evidence in the following pages does not fully justify the anticlerical stereotype of pilgrimages, with its "images of theocratic clerics, reactionary aristocrats, and society ladies battling passionately against republican emancipation," as Ruth Harris aptly styled it all.[10]

Financial Foundations

Fifteen years before the founding of *Le Pèlerin, La Voix de Notre-Dame de Chartres* had been founded, in intimate connection, as we will see, with the revival of pilgrimage. The abbé André Goussard (1835–1913), editor of the review for more than fifty years, wrote that this was a new kind of publication in France, preceded only by some small parish bulletins. But it was later imitated by a large number of diocesan newspapers and reviews of pious works, such as the *Semaines religieuses* and *Échos des pèlerinages*.[11] A statement of purpose, in high devotional tones, was placed inside the front cover. "*La Voix de Notre-Dame de Chartres* has for its main purpose: first, to aid in the restoration of our ancient and illustrious church and in the material repairs of one of the most famous shrines of Mary, in renewing the faith and devotion of peoples toward the Virgin of Chartres, once so venerated throughout Christendom; second, to show that Mary is now, as formerly, the Virgin who must become a mother; that children, especially today, must be born to grace by her and become her little apostles for the salvation of society. Consequently, the worship rendered to the Virgin of Chartres, the Virgin about to give birth, is most opportune and ought to be more fruitful than ever" (1857, 2, front cover).[12] Alexander Clerval (1859–1918), a priest and superior of Chartres and later professor of church history at the Institut Catholique of Paris, described those years of revival, during which the cathedral chapels and venerable statues of the Virgin were restored in connection with the revival of the choir school. The connecting link was another priest of Chartres, Cyril Ychard (1822–96), who was probably more concerned than his colleagues by the importance of an all-encompassing Catholic formation.[13] The choir school that he founded, the Maîtrise, was his passion and the motive behind own promotion of Chartres pilgrimage.[14] In effect, he founded La Voix in order to (1) restore a shrine, (2) encourage pilgrimage, and so (3) foster a nursery for clerical vocations.[15] A similar, but more culturally broad set of expectations are found in the very first article of La Voix, where priest-historian Adrien-Chrysostome Hénault (b. 1828) listed lovers of art and lovers of history, as well as the religiously devout: "Some, lovers of beauty, enthusiastic admirers of form, will eagerly look at all the marvels that man has been able to create with his compass, his chisel and his brush. . . . Others, not endowed with a feeling for beauty, but impassioned researchers of all the old adventures, of all the simple naive tales, of all the notable facts buried in the mystery of the past . . . will search through an edifice for scattered legends and ancient traditions. . . . There is one group, and it is the largest, for whom the sacred temple has no other charm than that of piety, no other voice than that of religion. . . . For them, the Gothic cathedral is a venerated shrine, it is a haven of repose, offered to the tired pilgrim here below" (1857, 1, 5–6). Hénault feels that La Voix should thus appeal to all the tastes which the great cathedral itself appeals to, but he assumes that even artists and historians will appreciate the cathedral on a religious, spiritual level. At Chartres, he believed, "filial respect for our forefathers intertwines with a touching veneration for her whom the nations call Blessed" (1857, 1, 6).

During the first year, the editors developed an arrangement of material that was to continue for many decades: religious news, chronicles of pious practices, statements of the hierarchy. The historical-archeological articles featured the

history of Chartres, a story of druids that was accepted with most of its myth-
ical baggage even by clergy and believers who had some training in history.
Hénault sounded the keynote of this story, calling Chartres "the most ancient
sanctuary where the mother of Jesus was honored before her birth, the first
center to which the people's devotion was directed, the most ancient city
where God to honor his mother worked wonders in her name, the first place
in Gaul where the light of truth drove out the darkness of paganism" (1857, 3,
44). There was, from 1857 on, a constant emphasis on the continuity of faith
with the old tradition which stated that, on the very site of the cathedral, the
druidic priests of ancient Gaul once worshiped a *virgo paritura,* a virgin about
to give birth. This was an old notion, dating back to the Renaissance, that
devotion to the Virgin Mary had been prefigured in pagan worship. The first
historian of the modern era to write a study of the cathedral, Sébastien Rouil-
lard, assumed the validity of the legend about the altar to the *virgo paritura.* In
fact, a conflation of stories about druidic worship and early Christian local
history (fourth century) was probably processed into the medieval cult of the
Virgin.[16] Church historians also had to correct the belief that the actual Gothic
cathedral was built under Fulbert (960–1028), the renowned bishop of
Chartres in the eleventh century. Marcel-Joseph Bulteau (d. 1882) was the
first priest of Chartres to affirm that Fulbert's Romanesque edifice was
destroyed, and that there was no substance to the then-current legend that the
existing cathedral was built by Fulbert.[17]

Even though the cathedral abounds in images of the Virgin—done in
sculpture, painting, and stained glass—two of them were singled out in the
devotional life of the pilgrims and visitors to Chartres over past centuries. At
the center of restoration of devotion to the Virgin of Chartres was a statue, a
reproduction of the druidic *virgo paritura,* dating from the Middle Ages and
destroyed during the Revolution. Located in the crypt, and so appropriately
called *Notre-Dame de Sous-Terre,* this statue of the Virgin and child had been
the object of a Marian devotion for over seven centuries. The new statue
replaced the original one (1389), which was burnt in a fire set by revolutionaries in 1793. On the main level of the cathedral, another statue with its own
chapel, *Notre-Dame du Pilier,* had been an object of popular devotion since
early in the sixteenth century.[18] The purpose of the dedication of the new
Notre-Dame de Sous-Terre was to bring the reproduction into continuity with
the original. The influential Cardinal Louis-Edouard Pie (1815–80), a former
priest of the diocese of Chartres, said in his dedication sermon that the new
statue was as "real" as the original: "No, this statue is not the same as the old

one, but it was reproduced in accordance with the tradition of Chartres: I affirm this evening that the new statue, which is going to be placed where the old one once was, will inherit all its power." And, of course, the cardinal would highlight the ceremonial transformation of the inanimate wood by the ceremonial blessing with holy water. Why worry about historical authenticity when blessing and consecration are what really make the statue a prayer-worthy representation of the Virgin (1857, 10, 230)?

For all the Marian imagery, the renewal of pilgrimage at Chartres cannot be attributed directly to the proportionately greater presence of women in parish congregations and their continuing faithfulness to Catholic practice and devotions as revealed by nineteenth-century surveys.[19] Women did not have a correspondingly greater influence on the way these devotions were presented. Nor did female response to the images of Mary as Virgin and Mother lead to radically new expressions of virtue and sacrifice in this highly clerical-ized French setting. A modern feminist scholar notes that "in nineteenth-century Catholicism . . . a female model for sacramental and public leadership roles seemed inconceivable. Any official and public version of the apparitions would have to suit a celibate priesthood's sense of fitness. Mary the pure and passive vessel was an important part of the inherited interpretation."[20] At Chartres, as at all places of pilgrimage, priests and bishops felt obliged to chan-nel and control as best they could women's religious expression.[21]

The clerical *La Voix* carefully monitored pilgrimage revival, extolled Roman authority, and attacked any real or apparent departures from the true faith. Special venom was reserved for the Orientalist and philosopher Ernest Renan (1823–92), whose *Vie de Jésus* (1863) denied the existence of a tran-scendent, incarnate God. By 1864, all Ychard's educational goals were real-ized: the abbé Goussard, who had taken over as editor after Ychard, in that succulent ultramontane language of the era, wrote, "The common Father of the faithful, the Vicar of Jesus Christ, the Supreme Pontiff, on the demand of our beloved Bishop, has just solemnly approved the *Oeuvre des Clercs de Notre-Dame* for the recruitment of ecclesiastical vocations among poor boys, grant-ing indulgences for all those who will aid in its extension by their alms and prayers. This is an absolute approval which gives, as the sun's rays do for nature, light, warmth, and life for a pious association" (1864, 3, 33). *La Voix* from then on could concentrate on the importance of pilgrimage in general and national religious renewal in particular. The basic operational structure at Chartres itself had been established. Finally, in March of 1864, all the aposto-lates at Chartres were tied together by a decree giving official Roman approval to a pious association that, by means of prayers and contributions, supported shrine restoration, pilgrimage, and the Maîtrise. Clearly, Chartres pilgrimages were not structured to lead to any sociopolitical reform any more than apparition-shrine pilgrimage led to sociopolitical reform: "they [visions] never carried a message of social transformation or suggested that the realm of Mary or the coming of Christ meant the overcoming of exploitation or oppression."[22] Hardly revolutionary, pilgrimage organizers had their implicit agendas for holding republican nationalism at bay and highlighting the historical heritage.

Chartres: Historic Center of French Catholic Patriotism

The pilgrimages of 1873 were a great show of religious patriotism and antirationalism. The January issue of *La Voix* began with a résumé of the accomplishments of the review itself, but it immediately turned to the larger struggle at hand. The number of subscribers had continued to grow, whereas other reviews had ceased publication due to the Franco-Prussian War: the editors were happy about their own survival but warned that war was being waged against God by the members of the National Assembly itself. "Courage is necessary to put up with the sight of a society overturned by the Revolution and saturated with deadly principles . . . to resist the invasion of error and falsehood which prepared the way for an attack of satanic brutality." This was the era of the conservative Republic, on the verge of returning to monarchy, with radical republicans, Gambetta in the lead, working behind the scenes. More vigilance was required: "Let us speak without ceasing of a Religion that is outraged, of rights unrecognized, of a real program of demagoguery which uses the pen to lie or to trick the poor people" (1873, 1, 3–4). Not only the government but also the press controlled by the Freemasons was a source of evil propaganda. *La Voix* wished to oppose these forces with publications that would be "healthy, moral and true" (1873, 1, 4); in this it was allied to the movement of the Assumptionist priests and the efforts of Father Vincent de Paul Bailly to found a center for Catholic publications. Bailly led the staff of popular Assumptionist publication *Le Pèlerin* in attacks on the government, the Jews, and the Freemasons; he was displeased with the earliest issues of that journal because they contained only pious reflections on pilgrimage.[23]

In 1873, the great pilgrimage year in France, *La Voix* separated its news reports into national, local, and pilgrimage news, all pretty much connected with the clerical defense of French Catholicism. In one issue a pious story,

"The General and the Curé," showed that military and political figures were most patriotic when they were most Catholic. The report on the *Croisade des Enfants* was followed, two issues later, by a letter from the bishop of Chartres, Louis-Eugène Regnault (1800–1889), on Christian teaching: "Antireligious men said simply to themselves: we take no account of the traditions of the past . . . we do not want the name of Jesus Christ to be whispered any longer by the children" (1873, 2, 44). The enemy was always the secular politicians and teachers, and the trouble they caused was often reported in *La Voix*. Conversely, the staff was happy to report news of faithful Catholics and flourishing Catholicism. In Rome on the Feast of the Immaculate Conception, a group of French pilgrims presented the pope with 70,000 francs and a book containing 70,000 signatures: "the first names were those of the count of Chambord, the king of Naples, the duke of Modena and Parma, the grand duchess of Tuscany" (1873, 1, 16). There were plenty of well-known people in France and elsewhere standing up for the Church of Rome. Furthermore, the Catholic schools were doing quite well: when the municipal council voted for free, obligatory public schooling, 10 percent of the students were taken out and put in Catholic schools by their parents (1873, 1, 16). And, finally, the apparition shrines were thriving, including Pontmain. There, on the evening of 17 January 1871, the Virgin appeared in a star-filled sky, visible to many of the children of this small village. Though none of the adults saw the vision, they readily believed the children.[24] In the preceding year, the Pontmain shrine was witness to 2,000 Masses said and 90,000 people on pilgrimage (1873, 1, 17).

In that year of pilgrimage 1873, a general review of pilgrimage statistics for Chartres was in order. For the years 1867–72, *La Voix* gave the number of vigil lights requested as 6,481; children consecrated, 1,972; individual pilgrims to the *Sous-Terre* shrine, 44,119 (not including major pilgrimage groups); Masses said in the crypt, 17,271; and visitors to the bell towers, 21,715 (1873, 1, 18). *La Voix* published an enthusiastic letter from the abbé Bulteau, who was the first successful clerical historian of Chartres and who had done his major work about twenty-five years before. This was followed by a pastoral letter by Bishop Regnault on the great pilgrimage planned for 27–28 May, which would begin to repair the damage and indifference of the past century: "This is why, under the auspices of this lovable mother and to acquiesce to the requests addressed to us by Catholics from different regions, we have resolved to authorize in our city of Chartres a solemn pilgrimage; we have formed there a committee composed of ecclesiastics and persons well known for their religious sentiment. This committee has formed a program for the feast days, and it will take the necessary means to direct the crowds properly and to conduct the ceremonies in perfect order" (1873, 4, 75). Not only were the ceremonies to be in perfect order, but the pilgrimage committee wanted the arrivals to be in perfect order. *La Voix* published an extensive list of train arrangements and bargain prices for the major train routes. (1873, 5, 100ff.).

The first pilgrim train on 27 May 1873 came from Versailles. When the train stopped in the station, the clergy of the cathedral were gathered there in choir habit, and the bands were playing. Next came two groups from Orléans—two processions moved toward the cathedral singing: a total of 10 churchmen, 1,500 people, and, according to *La Voix,* there were 900 communions. People came from Le Mans, la Flèche, la Ferté-Bernard, Mamers, Connerré, Alençon, Argentan, Séez, Mortagne, Nogent-le-Rotrou, and Condé. Six hundred pilgrims from Angers and Sablé had to be brought by a special train. From Mayenne, there were 580. On regular train runs, pilgrims and churchmen came from Quimper, Saint-Brieuc, Nantes, Rennes. From the diocese of Le Mans, they came with banners and special songs. Nearby Dreux and Evreux were well represented because a new train line had just been inaugurated; *La Voix* asks, "Was not this sacred voyage a benediction for the train?" (1873, 6, 148).

Then came the pilgrims from Cambrai, Lille, Arras. The groups from Paris set foot on the "holy" ground, banners floating, ex-votos gleaming. More trains arrived from Le Mans, Paris, Blois, as well as groups from Tours, Vendôme, Montoire. Always, there was the triumphal march with clergy and music to the cathedral, where a special Mass was celebrated for each group somewhere in the church, and there were many communions: "Communion is the act par excellence of the true pilgrim, for it bears the seal of sacrifice and is a proof of love" (1873, 6, 148). The author of the report tries to evoke the drama of the occasion, a show of religious force impressing the faithful and filling to the brim the cup of clergy satisfaction. For the finale: "The bishops raise their hands and pronounce the solemn prayer. We catch some of their words, we understand their gestures and we pray. Then, enthusiastic shouts follow the final Amen: shouts from all sides: Vive Pius IX! Vive La France! Vive Notre-Dame de Chartres! 'My God, you will save France!' said a pilgrim priest, 'O Mary, you will exalt the Church.' For the shouts have rung out to the heavens—coming from the very heart of France" (1873, 6, 150).

Thus, the reigning concept and the rallying cry of the decade of Chartrian pilgrimages, and especially of 1873, was patriotic reparation for the Revolution and the nineteenth-century violence that followed it, by loyalty to the "oldest" specifically Catholic French religious symbol. *La Voix* made a special point of describing the delegations of the Chamber of Deputies and the army generals. The editor, the abbé Goussard, did complain that local officials, lacking piety, would not permit exterior decorations, which would have enhanced the celebration, but that was not particularly important. Rather, "Chartres has found again the brilliance of its past because the way to its temple has been taken up again by the pilgrims: *Laus Deo et Mariae!*" (1873, 6, 158). Numbers were important all along, and Goussard cannot resist making some rough estimates. Although statistical accuracy is impossible and the newspaper estimates vary quite a bit, the editor of *La Voix* figures the numbers of pilgrims to have easily reached fifty to sixty thousand (1873, 6, 159).

Three years later there was another major pilgrimage, the thousandth anniversary of the presentation of the veil of the Virgin to the church of Chartres by Charles the Bald in 876.[25] Clergy at Chartres were motivated by the success of the 1873 pilgrimages with their emphasis on the *Sous-Terre* shrine. *La Voix* reports that back in 1873, the bishop of Chartres resolved to repeat the performance, "for the glory of Chartres is not solely the splendid cathedral," but "unquestionably the most precious treasure is . . . none other than the Holy Tunic or the very veil which was wrapped about the Mother of God" (1876, 4, 73). A decade earlier *La Voix* had called attention to this primary relic of Chartres, the veil of the Virgin, otherwise referred to as a tunic (*tunique*) or undergarment (*chemise*). The bearing of *chemisettes,* small replicas of the veil or "chemise" of the virgin, had been a medieval custom which, in the antirationalist and promiraculous context of the nineteenth century, could help the Chartres devotion: "The reviving devotion to the *chemisettes* will soon be, without doubt, the occasion of other stories of the protection given to the sick and to those who invoke our Mother for diverse needs" (1867, 11, 168). In giving a brief history of the *chemisettes,* the author says that the faithful have used these objects of devotion for more than six hundred years; that a cloth replica has been a source of protection and cure for women in labor, for those in grave peril, and for the sick; that various types of gold replicas have also been used with devotion (1867, 11, 168–69).

This 1876 celebration was shaped to serve a number of purposes, some of them new, some of them an extension of previous practices and celebrations. It seems that in 1873 the clergy sensed the beginnings of victory over secularism, and they were determined to push it further, to the end, to the point where they could demand unconditional surrender from the secularists. Goussard's report on the upcoming pilgrimage contained a potshot at the

Revolution of 1789 and the forthcoming anniversary of two key figures who inspired it: Voltaire and Rousseau. He wrote that the secularists planned "to celebrate in 1878 the hundredth anniversary of the two monsters of impiety and immorality, the two fiends whom the Revolution followed so well and whose maxims were applied, the two audacious writers whose books, condemned by the church, still soil too many libraries" (1876, 8, 169). No room for political compromise here! Reports on pilgrimages, although straightforward and without political commentary, focused on the large crowds and the grandeur of the pilgrimages. Such head-counting as there was never offered any helpful gender statistics, though we might assume some parallels to the church-going statistics for the dioceses and parishes that the pilgrims came from.[26]

Chartres and Lourdes

With the increasing attention given to Lourdes, it is small wonder that by 1872 one writer for *La Voix*, Clementine de Chabannes, felt compelled to acknowledge the success of the shrine at Lourdes and to interpret the role of Chartres in relation to that success. De Chabannes was experienced in the devotional ways of Chartres and a unique female voice in this clerical setting.[27]

> I will tell you first of all that I brought to Lourdes, with all the pilgrims of *Notre-Dame de Chartres,* a feeling of the incomparable dignity with which we were invested in representing the most ancient sanctuary of the VIRGIN MARY at the later shrine which so soon after its beginning attracted to it great crowds of worshipers. The metal image of the *holy tunic* or the *chemisette* of Mary, hung from our necks on a blue ribbon, was our rallying sign, and we marched behind a magnificent banner, with a lively joy and a noble pride. This banner, white and bordered with gold, bore on top the design of the holy tunic or veil of Mary:
>
> On the left, the image of *NOTRE-DAME DE SOUS-TERRE* with the inscription *Virgini pariturae;*
>
> On the right, the *Black Virgin,* with the inscription *NOTRE-DAME DU PILIER.*
>
> A large inscription underneath: *To Notre-Dame de Lourdes, from the Children of Notre-Dame de Chartres.*
>
> On the bottom, the arms of the Holy Father and the arms of the bishop of Chartres. (1872, 11, 247–48)

> Pilgrims of Notre-Dame de Chartres, let us return to the mysterious crypt, many times profaned, to continue the sacred hymn begun at the feet of Notre-Dame de Lourdes, and may these cherished titles [as they are being sung], which recall so many marvels to us, be forever engraved in our memories and in our hearts. (1872, 11, 249–50)

All the images associated with Chartres are brought to Lourdes: the banner bearing images of the two ancient statues of Mary in the cathedral; little replicas of the Virgin's veil—historically the prime relic at Chartres; and that mysterious inscription, "To Notre-Dame de Lourdes, from the children of Notre-Dame de Chartres." The pilgrim of Notre-Dame de Chartres was not fully at home but was trying; the hymns, the prayer themes of Lourdes could be adopted (and perhaps adapted); memory and sentiment could go to work on the experience to ensure that Lourdes and Chartres would be but two aspects of the same spiritual relation between the pilgrim and Notre-Dame.

This pilgrim, then, was the devout and literary countess de Chabannes. One finds the following entry on this aristocratic lady in the *Dictionnaire de biographie française:* "Chabannes (Clementine de la Morre, Mme Armand de). Born in 1813, died 15 October 1901 at Chartres where she had resided since 1856, she published a considerable number of edifying novels (*romans moraux*): . . . books of piety and lives of the saints. From 1895 to 1898, she edited *La Voix de Notre-Dame de Chartres.*"[28] Further information can be found in the *Procès-verbaux de la Société archéologique d'Eure-et-Loir,* where it is stated that she wrote "under the pseudonyms *A humble servant of Mary* or *A Franciscan tertiary* or under her initials, C. de C. (Clementine de Chabannes)."[29] Daughter of a very Catholic aristocrat and mother of a Jesuit, the countess de Chabannes was not the editor-in-chief, but she was more than an occasional contributer. Father Goussard, director of *La Voix* for more than fifty years, praised her work in a long history of the family published in one of the weekly supplements to *La Voix.* In 1901, at the time of her death, he wrote, "The ever so fruitful and persevering collaboration in the editing of *La Voix* is one of the clearest testimonies to her extraordinary devotion to Notre-Dame de Chartres and one of her good deeds on behalf of the *Oeuvre des clercs,* of which *La Voix* is the official publication.[30]

Back in the 1870s, Father Goussard followed the example of de Chabannes in assigning devotional tasks to the two Marian shrines and to Paray-le-Monial. At Chartres, there were grandiose ceremonies; at Lourdes, miracles. At Chartres, the Virgin about to bring forth; at Lourdes, the Immaculate Virgin appearing to the poor little peasant. At Paray the focus is on a different heavenly personality, the victim of Calvary. But here the reference is more political in that "France," finally, "after two hundred years" is beginning to turn toward and respond to the Sacred Heart (1873, 7, 196). Even if the ceremonies at Paray were not as impressive as those of Chartres, Paray was in the vanguard of the Catholic effort to repossess France.[31] Several years later Goussard was still concerned about modalities of the presence of Mary. At Lourdes, the apparition; at Chartres, the relic: "If she is not there in person, as she was seen at La Salette and at Lourdes, at least the precious relic that clung to her virginal body passes through our ranks as a pledge [*gage*] of the blessings that Mary bestows upon us from the heights of heaven" (1876, 10, 225–26).

The countess de Chabannes meditated the relation between the Lourdes and Chartres images of Mary again in 1881. For her the disappointment on taking leave of Lourdes was compensated by the prospect of further completion, that is, "the prospect of seeing the termination and fulfillment of our pilgrimage at the feet of *Notre-Dame de Sous-Terre*." She wrote, "At Lourdes, the MIRACLE surrounds you and seizes complete hold of you, it appears to you in sensible and moving ways; but the miracle—that divine exception to the natural order—produces its full effect on the soul only in quiet contemplation. And this is precisely what happens in the old grotto of the Druids. Lourdes and Chartres make a wonderful combination: two sisters, the elder of whom seems to cede to the younger that power which through the centuries attracted princes and kings, in the blessed sanctuary, all the time preserving her mysterious charms and her marvelous fruitfulness. *Farewell* then, O Notre-Dame de Lourdes! But greetings to you, O Virgin of Chartres; you will be forever united in my heart, and nothing can erase your dear names from my grateful memory" (1881, 10, 226).

So the elder shrine, Chartres, has been the preferred place of pilgrimage across French history for kings and princes. Countess de Chabannes made no references to national, republican, or imperial governments because public authorities made no significant journeys to Chartres in these eras. Her version of the Chartrian Virgin and Mother, regardless of her aristocratic background and clerical context, is a long step away from the feminized religion of stereotypical nineteenth-century Catholicism. Not a passionless Virgin but a virgin of "mysterious charms," and not a unidimensional dutiful mother but a mother of "marvelous fruitfulness." These were experiences, she said, that could be fully appreciated only in quiet contemplation. De Chabannes covered just about the same topics as did Father Goussard, but her devotional concerns and female sensitivities gave her work wider focus. She had to reconcile the different mental images and emotional experiences of Chartres and Lourdes. Chartres was her home territory; the dignified historical cathedral, a spiritual counterpart of her aristocratic ancestry. Goussard had only to coordinate the historical contrasts of Chartres and Lourdes and the political implications of the Sacred Heart, showing the technical and theological differences between the two Marian apparitions in particular. It is possible to see here differences of gender expression that seldom reveal themselves in the masculine, clericalized testimonies of *La Voix*. The writing of Clementine de Chabannes is valuable evidence of what might have been if the clericalized institutional defense of Catholicism had been conditioned by the agendas of women, even women who were themselves aristocratic defenders of conservative Catholic values.

Religious Patriotism

With the death of Cardinal Edouard Pie in 1880 an era came to an end. Pie had begun his illustrious career as vicar general for the old Gallican bishop of Chartres, Hippolyte Clausel de Montals, who had suffered through the Revolution as secret seminarian and spent his later years fighting its effects. Pie had done his early ecclesiastical schooling at Chartres, so he was, for all practical purposes, trained to fight the effects of the Revolution with Chartrian piety. He returned to preach at all the revivals thus far mentioned. It was Pie's nostalgia and his expression of it that served as the rallying cry for Ychard and Goussard when they attempted to revive *Sous-Terre* as an expression of their own nostalgia and for the satisfaction of the financial needs of their educational apostolate. As bishop of Poitiers (1849–80), Cardinal Pie became the most renowned French ultramontanist of his time and, unlike his old mentor Clausel de Montals, he put historic-patriotic devotions at the service of papal centralization. This combination created a Catholic absolutism that opposed secular forces, with many pious memories of the good old Catholic monarchy on one side and the glorious Revolution on the other.[32]

In July 1880, *La Voix* published the funeral oration for Cardinal Pie, which evoked Pie's alignment of Chartres and French history. Immediately following in the review was an article by the abbé Goussard, which summed up, though at length, the history of pilgrimage from 1855, when Pie had preached at the rededication of the statue of *Notre-Dame du Pilier* and predicted that Chartres would once again become the great center of religion in France. Indeed, only two years later, in 1857, the rededication of *Sous-Terre*, the revival of pilgrimage, and the publication of *La Voix* itself took place. The abbé Goussard begins, however, with 1855: "We love to think back on this great event of contemporary religious history, the crowning of Our Lady of Chartres (31 May 1855). . . . This discourse [of Cardinal Pie] retraced the homage rendered by past centuries to Mary in our thousand-year-old basilica; then raising himself to prophecy, he saluted the future of this same church as resplendent in glory and fruitful in works which would develop marvelously the cult of Notre-Dame de Chartres" (1880, 7, 150).

There had been continuing progress, then, since 1855, and the staff of *La Voix* was pleased to report on the major manifestations. Even with incomplete statistics the editors were pleased by the number of associates all over France (1880, 7, 151). Everywhere members were being recruited for the Archconfraternity of Notre-Dame de Chartres by special volunteers: Lille and Dunkerque to the north; Perpignan to the south; Finistère and Brest in Brittany; Strasbourg, Metz, and Nancy to the east.[33] Pilgrims continued to come from Le Mans, Cambrai, Arras, Versailles, Blois, and Orléans. They came, too, from some of the better-known churches in France: Notre-Dame de Fouvières, Notre-Dame de la Garde. Chartres was commemorated by a window at La Salette; *La Voix* was sold at Pontmain; Chartrian banners flew at Lourdes, Paray-le-Monial, and Mont-Saint-Michel. Furthermore, the editors could cite instances of devotion to Notre-Dame de Chartres in Spain, England, Belgium, and Germany. In the great cities of America and Africa, everywhere that the Sisters of Saint-Paul of Chartres and the Sisters of Sainte-Croix had gone, from the Gulf of Tonkin to the state of Indiana, Chartres was known, as the abbé Goussard's closing words testify—citing Cardinal Pie at the end of his talk, as he had at the beginning. "We certainly have given enough indication of the fame that the cult of Notre-Dame de Chartres has attained, a fame constantly increasing since 30 and 31 May 1855, since the forever memorable days when the altar of sacrifice was placed in the holy grotto, when the statue was crowned in the upper church, where these words—which we never tire of repeating—were pronounced by the preacher [Cardinal Pie], the most illustrious of Mary's children: 'I dare to predict: Chartres will become more than ever the center of devotion in the West; they will come in great crowds, from many parts of the world as in former days'" (1880, 7, 153).

Over the next decade, the pilgrim business calmed down to a steady stream of people, including one dramatically large pilgrimage in 1891 (6,000 came by train). There was an attempt, at one and the same time, to build up diocesan pilgrimage and to promote notable connections from outside. *La Voix* was happy to report on the especially enthusiastic words of the prime minister of Canada, whose speech was published in a separate pamphlet. He declared that Canadians, "French by origin and sentiment," place great value on "the unity of national and religious sentiment." He cited in evidence a great monument in Quebec to Jacques Cartier and Jean de Brébeuf—"the secular explorer and the Catholic missionary" (1891, 7, 145). *La Voix* could rejoice in the continued, perhaps even increased, success of diocesan and outside pilgrimage, but it remained highly sensitive to anticlerical activity.

The intensity of the Catholic-republican fight in the government was reflected on the pages of other Catholic publications, such as *Le Pèlerin* and the daily *La Croix*. Pope Leo XIII had urged reconciliation of the French church with the Republic, but publications like *La Voix* retained traces of the old monarchist ideology through the last decade of the nineteenth century and into the first decade of the twentieth. The Freemasons had long been a specific target; Jews and Protestants, particularly the Jews, were castigated from time to time. Nasty citations were carted over from the pages of *La Croix*:[34] "Jews in France—an anomaly—In France, the position of the Jews, who are only 60 thousand out of 38 million inhabitants, is, no less than in Italy, a prodigious insult to the vast majority of the nation" (1891,1, 22). According to the statistics at hand, Jews possess 80 billion francs of the total capital in France, estimated at 200 billion francs; the capital of the average Jew is between 800,000 and 1 million francs; and there are 21 Jews in the National Assembly. If Christians were represented proportionately in the Assembly, they would have 40,000 deputies. Or again, more explicitly and viciously, "To the Jew Naquet we owe the law of divorce; to the Jew Saloman, the cremation of the dead; to the Jew Camille Sée, the girls' lycees. . . . Such are the gifts bestowed upon us by the Jews. But the Jew, as is just, does not give anything for nothing. As payment for his good services, he rolls around in billions of our francs" (1892, 11, 167).

Similar cynicism was directed at Protestants (here Anglicans), even as they moved in the direction of "Catholic" reform, with the restoration of religious orders: "The Protestant bishop of Marlborough has placed himself at the head of the movement and has collected the necessary amount of money (Protestants always start that way). The future community will be called the Congregation of Saint Paul. But we have found the core of the problem; the new monks are *one* in number. We might ask how the vow of obedience will be expressed" (1891, 6, 144).

In 1892, the potpourri of reports on life in general included the following: readers were told that Louis XVI was, unhappily, the victim of the Masons;

they were also told that the basilica of the Sacré-Cœur, after being given official support by the National Assembly, was dedicated in triumph; on the local
front there was a major problem in keeping the cathedral heated. Nor was
cathedral heating or shrine upkeep unimportant if *La Voix*'s statistics about
the number of pilgrims in circulation are correct. In 1896, the staff reported
the results of calculations of an indeterminate nature: 28 million French people at the 1,200 shrines of Mary each year. This, of course, would have been a
substantial portion of the population were it not for the fact that some individuals set out on the road eleven or twelve times and, thereby, somewhat
complicated the effect of these remarkable figures (1896, 11, 263).

On the artistic level, the staff was disturbed by a seeming affront made, in
all innocence, by a convert, who, in the eyes of the staff of *La Voix*, was not
converted enough: Joris-Karl Huysmans (1848–1907), the novelist, essayist,
and art critic. According to the reviewer, "*La Cathédrale* [has the tendency] to
accuse the church of prudery in its painting and in its asceticism. Huysmans
consecrates several pages to taking her to task on this subject; he would like
her to have less fear of the proper word, that is to say, the dirty word; less fear
of nude pictures and raw details, and, instead of recommending innocence
and flight when it comes to delicate temptations, that she accustom souls to
meet the flesh and its appetites head-on; in a word, for her own good he
would have her less prim and proper" (1898, 3, 59–60). This could be enough
to get the work on the index of forbidden books, a pity according to the
reviewer, because Huysmans meant well and produced "good insights" now
and then. Still, the book is tasteless and boring; Chartres cathedral deserves
better for its "first novelist" than this recent convert, with insufficient knowledge, overly liberal moral judgment, and little tact (1898, 3, 63). Thus, at the
end of the last decade of the nineteenth century, *La Voix* denounced a book
about Chartres that was to become renowned, reaching an audience far
beyond the circle of pious devotees. But a few years earlier, a small booklet
about Chartres targeted those pious devotees so successfully that reprints were
necessary right up to 1918.

Diffusion of Religious Patriotism: The Official Booklet

The booklet, *Notre-Dame de Chartres*, written for the use of Chartres pilgrims,
represented a summation—if not the culmination—of nineteenth-century
Chartrian piety. It was a simple popular history of the cathedral as a shrine,

but in an article in *La Voix,* a writer expressed confidence in quickly selling out two batches of 6,000 copies each (1891, 9, 197). It was a distillation of the attitudes and emphases of the staff of *La Voix,* designed for families and schools, not only for Chartres and France, but even "the most distant lands" (i.e., where there are subscribers of *La Voix,* so a fairly homogeneous readership even so) (1891, 9, 198). Written by Father Emile Legué (1848–1910) of the staff of the Maîtrise, probably with the helping hand of Alexander Clerval, the booklet devotes equal time to explanations of *Notre-Dame de Sous-Terre,* the veil of the Virgin, and *Notre-Dame du Pilier.* From there it moves on to the interior and exterior of the cathedral, a fundamentalist presentation of miracles, and a history of pilgrimage with special attention to the nineteenth century. The illustrations are small but dramatic pen-and-ink sketches.

On the first page, there is a sketch of the cathedral of Chartres towering dramatically above the town; one reads the words of Cardinal Pie: "From whatever distance you see [the cathedral], imitate the piety of your fathers and fall to your knees to greet Notre-Dame. This name is the name of the edifice, as it is the name of her to whom the edifice belongs" (*Notre-Dame,* 1).[35] Unsurprisingly, the text opens with this quasi-historical pious sentiment of Edouard Pie and moves to his praise of *Sous-Terre.* This tradition, it is noted in the booklet, goes as far back as the kings of France; this, presumably, refers to Clovis and others. Once again, Cardinal Pie: "*La Nostre-Dame de Soubs-Terre,* from the first days of Christianity, has been the celebrated European sanctuary of Mary: miracles without number have been seen there; a long line of kings, popes, saints, bishops, Christians of every age, sex and condition. An ancient author has given the reason for it: the principal devotion of all the churches built here has been to this altar" (*Notre-Dame,* 5). The modern author calls on another powerful clerical witness, Father Jean-Jacques Olier (1608–57), founder of the Sulpicians and a great devotee of Chartres. His priests trained generations of French clergy, and the parish of St.-Sulpice in Paris sent a sizeable pilgrimage to Chartres every year following the renewal of pilgrimage begun in 1850s. According to Olier, Chartres was "the world's first center of devotion in its antiquity, erected by prophetic insight" (*Notre-Dame,* 3). So, the author does not so much marshal historical evidence behind the tradition of the *Sous-Terre* statue as pass on the clerical interpretations of Pie and Olier.

The story of the veil of the Virgin is apparently as much military history as anything else. First of all, the veil put Rollo and the Normans to flight, then it attracted them back to baptism, and "they became at the same time Christians and French" (*Notre-Dame,* 7). Indeed, it had such power that, in those chivalrous

days, the knights who wore reproductions of it were obliged by a sense of justice to warn those they were dueling against that they were protected by
supernatural power (*Notre-Dame,* 7). Charles the Bald gave the relic to
Chartres. A third cathedral shrine, to *Notre-Dame du Pilier,* was especially dear
to the Chartrians themselves: mothers in particular would bring their babies
and toddlers to the miraculous statue, as priests on duty every day from seven
a.m. to seven p.m. well know (*Notre-Dame,* 11).

The history of Chartres is a history of miraculous intervention in simple
ways. A list was made from a medieval text entitled *Miracles de Notre-Dame de
Chartres.* During a great epidemic, the Virgin Mary cooled the feverish lips of
Bishop Fulbert with a few drops of maternal milk ("according to a charming
tradition," says the author). When the sick visited her statue in the crypt they
were cured in nine days. Pregnant mothers who wore an image of the holy
tunic were given a successful delivery. And there were also the supermiracles:
restoring the torn-out tongue of a child, curing the cancer of an elderly lady,
and returning four dead children to life (*Notre-Dame,* 19).

The Virgin of Chartres intervened in the great moments of French history,
from Rollo through Louis XIV, averting at one time a pagan and at another a
Protestant ascendency. She saved "France" in 911 by the conversion of Rollo
the Viking. She saved France and Chartres from English rule, "and consequently from the Anglican heresy," in 1363 by bringing a mighty storm on
Edward III and thereby convincing him to sign the Treaty of Brétigny. She
saved France from Protestantism in 1568 when she stopped the duke de
Condé, who, a Huguenot iconoclast, was planning to feed his horse at the
main altar. Battle victories abounded thanks to Notre-Dame de Chartres:
Philip the Fair at Mons-en-Ruelle and Philip of Valois at Cassel ("the two of
them came to hang their armor on the pillars of the basilica"); Prince Louis de
Bourbon, forerunner of the royal dynasty, saved from prison, Baron de Breuil
at Milan (saved by wearing the *chemisette*); Louis XIII from childlessness by the
birth of the future Louis XIV (*Notre-Dame,* 19–21). In sum, as Cardinal Pie
had put it, "All the great lines of the history of France end at *Notre-Dame de
Chartres;* it is the historical and national pilgrimage par excellence" (*Notre-
Dame,* 23).

By way of a brief description of the great pilgrimages, the author returns to
the *Oeuvre des Clercs de Notre-Dame de Chartres,* that is, the Maîtrise, which
Cyril Ychard founded. One might well wonder if, in the minds of the staff, all
the great lines of history led to Notre-Dame de Chartres or to the Maîtrise.
Which was the stronger motivation to success through the years: Ychard's

Maîtrise or Pie's nostalgia? Certainly, on these pages they are intertwined. The booklet, which began with the words of Cardinal Pie, ends with a description of the *Oeuvre des Clercs,* which "has no other resource than Providence itself, which by a daily miracle has sustained it for more than thirty years and has through it given more than 150 priests to the church. It is fitting to terminate this brochure by recommending to the sympathy of pilgrims this interesting *Oeuvre,* so dear to the heart of Notre-Dame. May Notre-Dame bless also its author and all the devout pilgrims" (*Notre-Dame,* 32).

Breakdown of the Clerical Defense: A Postscript

At first, clerical defense and cultural openness moved on parallel tracks. In 1912, the comte de Souancé compiled an index of the persons and places presented in the first fifty years of *La Voix*'s publication, *Table alphabétique des noms de personnel et de lieux contenus dans les cinquante premières années de "La Voix de Notre-Dame de Chartres" (1857–1906),* with an acknowledged emphasis on clerical history. "I have followed the following plan: to introduce in this table, (1) scrupulously, the names of all ecclesiastics, parishes, works, communities of the diocese; (2) faithfully . . . the names of ecclesiastics, religious, persons of every walk of life, who were involved in the religious history of the diocese: (3) fully, the names of those useful to know for a general history of the church." Undoubtedly, this index was worked out with the approval of the aged abbé Goussard; he had edited *La Voix* practically since its beginning and died the year following the publication of the index. Father Ernest Métra (1872–1949), professor at the Maîtrise, took over, but only briefly; he was soon followed, in 1914, by Father Henri Planchette (1869–1927) superior of the Maîtrise. Planchette edited *La Voix* during the World War I years. It was the clerical church that presided here.

With the coming of World War I, even that powerful Catholic family magazine *Le Pèlerin* ceased its harassment of the government.[36] *La Voix* noted that Frenchmen had at last put aside their differences and, in many cases, had gone back to church. "Yesterday France was sadly divided, the poor hated the rich, the worker threatened his employer; today all fraternize with one another under the same flag." At the churches of the Sacré Coeur and Notre-Dame des Victoires in Paris, and certainly at Chartres itself, great numbers of people returned to active churchgoing, such that there are not enough priests to minister to them (1914, 9, 199). The hierarchy of France planned a national pilgrimage to Lourdes as soon as hostilities ceased. The French bishops' letter, cited in the November 1916 issue, was a response to numerous demands for an expression of "national faith," in effect a prayer for victory and the establishment of peace. The letter cites the apparitions and other manifestations of Our Lady in France: the Miraculous Medal apparition to Catherine Labouré, 1830; Notre-Dame des Victoires, 1836; La Salette, 1846; Pontmain, 1871. But there is a contrapuntal theme running through the letter: if France is to conquer Germany, it will have to be a victory of French Catholicism over German barbarism (1916, 10, 47).

Throughout 1917, *La Voix* continued to reinforce the image of a patriotic Catholic France with observations and articles on Notre-Dame, of course, but also Joan of Arc and, most interestingly, Louis XVI, the most illustrious of the Revolution's victims. "Almost from the day following his execution, he was called the king-martyr and, in the Consistory which followed soon after the fatal event, the pope, Pius VI, eulogized the noble victim in a way which could be interpreted as the preface of a future canonization." In monarchist circles, the hope for Louis XVI's canonization was kept alive across the nineteenth century until 1892, when a formal petition was sent to the pope proposing the canonization (1917, 12, 175–76). No doubt! Victory over Germany and the canonization of Louis XVI would not only make French Catholicism the strongest power in Europe, but also, since Germany had defeated France—enfeebled by the Revolution—in 1871, the defeat of Germany would definitively reverse the Revolution and would reestablish France, Catholic forever.

Pilgrimage to Chartres did take on a new look, however. There are hints that the staff of *La Voix* was concerned with some species of accuracy in theology and purity in spirituality during the war years. When Father Planchette took over in 1914, he echoed the perennial complaint about exaggerated devotionalism but seemed afraid to go against the popular current. For the staff, an exaggerated devotion was little to complain about in the face of both secularism and anticlericalism. Local devotees *were* ordinary folk, and even across the anticlerical years, there seemed to be no fall off in "singularly confident" devotions. In his hours on duty in the cathedral, Planchette saw people arriving the throughout the day to fervently kiss the statue of *Notre-Dame du Pilier,* and this was enough of a guarantee of orthodoxy for him. "One could groan about the inconsistency of a piety which forgets God and only invokes the saints; but one should rejoice above all that the deluge of indifference has not swallowed up everyone. . . . When people remain attached to the Mother, they certainly have not broken off relations with the Son (1914, 5, 50). He reports that all the old works are continuing, including the confraternity and the "correspondence," a sort of letters-to-the-editor page with extracts from letters describing petitions granted; these continued to express the concerns and gratitude of the correspondents: children kept safe by their mothers' prayers, sick who are healed, and sinners who are converted (1914, 5, 50).

If one compares the correspondence across the years, one does notice a trend away from the miraculous, even though the "miraculous" at Chartres was never terribly sensational in comparison with the apparition shrines. Each issue of 1873, for example, contained a list of nine or ten favors granted, including some striking recoveries; next to each short paragraph were the initials of the correspondent and the diocese where he or she lived. By 1906, the lines were shorter; there were references only to "favors" and "benefits," statements about enclosed money offerings. The original letters were not preserved, so there are no other details—one knows only that this level of pious expression was catered to by *La Voix*.

Certainly *La Voix* favored the local populace over the elite from afar, as presented by Planchette. But if staff willingly put up with the indiscretions of pious believers who were not theologically sophisticated, there was less tolerance for divergence from the Chartrian tradition on the part of historians and theologians. In February 1918, the staff took to task the Benedictine scholar Dom Henri Leclercq (1869–1945) and the *Dictionnaire d'archéologie chrétienne et de liturgie (DACL)*. Quoting from a letter sent by a priest-historian of Sens who complained about the doubts *DACL* cast upon the preaching of the early Chartrian saints, Potentian and Savinian, the staff said that the article in *DACL* reduced the liturgical books to works "of imagination, anecdote and jest" (1918, 2, 29). The bishop of Chartres, Henri-Louis Bouquet (1829–1926), denounced this work to the Holy See, and the Holy Father requested the Congregation of Religious to "inflict both on Dom Leclercq, author of the article thus accused, and Dom Cabrol, who tolerated the publication of it, a serious warning because of that unfortunate work's destructive and terrible contempt toward such venerable tradition, a work to which they applied themselves, much to the scandal of the faithful and to the detriment of peace within dioceses and in the Church itself" (1918, 2, 29). [37]

And yet, there was a new and open attitude: young intellectuals from Paris, under the leadership of the intellectual Father Antonin Sertillanges (1863–1948) and inspired by the poetry of Charles Péguy (1873–1914), were renewing the concept of Chartres pilgrimage. After the 1918 pilgrimage, their magazine, the *Revue des Jeunes,* ran a full series of articles about Chartres, which included some history, some experiences, and a homily preached on the occasion of the pilgrimage; *La Voix* simply reproduced several of those *Revue des Jeunes* articles. Perhaps for the first time on the pages of *La Voix,* there appeared a vision that was not clerical; one might describe it as some sort of intellectual but highly romantic interpretation of French Catholic history—orthodoxy united with poetic vision. Was this perhaps what *La Voix* had lacked all these years? Was the staff happy to note that the vision of the late and lamented poet Charles Péguy was the force behind this movement? Was this direction more like what Planchette, then editor for four years, had in mind when he complained about the coarseness of local Catholicism? The staff of *La Voix* had accepted onto its pages a new expression of Catholic belief and piety, one not motivated and designed to fight off secularism by militant devotion, but motivated instead by the vision of a poet and designed by young intellectuals, who laid their plans even as they contemplated the sculptures of the Old and New Testament figures. Recalling that Charles Péguy made his own pilgrimage to Chartres in the spirit of the great medieval pilgrimages, the new generation also wanted "to repudiate the chaos of ideologies and willfulness, once again entering into the reality of France," and they "know how to build up this reality and live within it." The resolve was to return in great numbers in the spring and thereafter, to the glory of "Notre-Dame, Queen of Heaven, Queen of France" (1918, 7, 35).

There is traditional Catholicism here; indeed, there is patriotism. But it is new and different, following after World War I and influenced by Charles Péguy. To distinguish more clearly between this view and the earlier patriotic reparation view, one has only to read the sermon of Father Sertillanges, preached at the Vespers service for the Feast of the Ascension on the occasion of the *Revue des Jeunes* pilgrimage. He announced to the bishop and the congregation that this group of writers, teachers, and Catholic actionists had come as brothers and sisters "in Jesus Christ, Notre-Dame, and France" (1918, 7, 75). The faith is patriotic in the sense that it is part of the collective memory of a people: "Chartres especially attracts the faithful of the tradition because its origins make of it one of the roots of French culture. We have other memories, but those of Chartres run across all the centuries of our history and are buried in the prehistory of France" (1918, 7, 77). Chartres does not function solely as a cause of interior faith; the historical existence of the cathedral and its schools signifies an active faith, a manifested faith.

Sertillanges lists the virtues signified by Chartres, "daughter of the church and the liturgy," and of the great guilds, and he recalls the brilliance and Europe-wide renown of the medieval school of Chartres (i.e., the theological and philosophical tradition) (1918, 7, 79). The young pilgrims are also attracted by the sheer beauty of cathedral, although Art here is a servant of God, leading directly to him (1918, 7, 80). "We refuse to see nature on one hand, supernature on the other; humanity left to itself, organizing itself in pagan fashion, with religion living apart, solemn and empty." The great separation must end: "science, art, scattered truths, beauty abandoned to capricious or perverse influences; faith and mysticism taking refuge in the secrecy of our hearts" (1918, 7, 83). The activities of these pilgrims—artists and intellectuals as they are—comprise a renewal of the great spiritual synthesis of the Middle Ages. The detailed rostrum of group members includes painters, architects, decorators, poets, playwrights, and even actors and publishers. The goal of restoring true Christianity, and the dispersed elements of beauty and truth, and the scattered sheep, is especially appropriate to Chartres (1918, 7, 83–84). The focal point of this believing Christian humanism, which manifests itself now at Chartres, is Notre-Dame. In the accents of Sertillanges: to draw strength from the Spirit, to be apostles and renew the face of the earth in beauty, one journeys to the land where she herself is manifested. "We are not simply writers, I tell you, nor simply aesthetes, still less pagan traditionalists: we are apostles. For remembering that the Queen of Apostles loved the land here, that she chose it, and made this edifice flourish with her smile" (1918, 7, 84).[38]

This was a détente between pilgrims with their leaders and the broader society. World War I and the years of intellectual change that preceded it had weakened the force and the need for the old clerical defense. Détente is one principal part of the history, but in chapters yet to come. In this chapter on "piety against politics," the story of the reduction and gradual elimination of the old antagonism, has been appropriately labeled a "postscript." If we return to the nineteenth century, when the pilgrimage apostolate was at its height of defensiveness, and especially if we look to those regions of France isolated by culture and language, we find another successful defense of Catholicism in the form of the clerical protection of local languages.

Chapter Five

LOCAL LANGUAGES FOR THE DEFENSE OF RELIGION: *Alsace and the Roussillon*

Citizens who spoke a language other than French had always been a problem for the central government. The revolutionary and legislator Bertrand Barrère in his *Sur les idiomes étrangers et l'enseignement de la langue française* had written, "Federalism and superstition speak Breton; emigration and hatred of the Republic speak German; the counterrevolution speaks Italian, and fanaticism speaks Basque."[1] For Barrère, regional languages were intertwined with religion ("superstition," "fanaticism") and the other antigovernment forces. Almost from the beginning of the Revolution, the French language was considered a means of unity and a sign of loyalty to the Paris regime. True, some revolutionaries believed that the nation of free and independent citizens would naturally embrace the multitude of dialects. But they were in the minority.[2] In fact, France was linguistically divided across the many centuries. The language of the north—the *langue d'Oïl*—prevailed, whereas the language of the south—the *langue d'Oc*—has survived only in places. But the *langue d'Oïl* of the north was bounded by three regional languages: a German dialect in Alsace-Lorraine, Flemish in the department of the Nord, and Celtic in Brittany, with each of the three spoken in identical or related forms in Germany (a confederation and then an empire), the Netherlands, and areas of the British Isles. And the *langue d'Oc* of the south was bounded by two regional languages—Basque and Catalan—spoken also in Spain.[3] Surveys made in the last century indicate that of those regions where a language other than French was spoken (German in Alsace-Lorraine, Flemish in the department of the Nord, Gaelic in Brittany, Basque in the southwest, and Catalan in the Roussillon), all save the Roussillon had statistically high levels of religious practice.[4] To be sure, social surveys of the past two decades reveal other correlations: Hervé Le Bras and Emmanuel Todd report that religious practice positively correlates with an authoritarian family structure, where children obey, marry late, and preserve family tradition. Religious practice, finally, according to Hervé Le Bras, correlates positively with regional political autonomy, whether accompanied by a distinctive regional language or not.[5] But in the main, the revolutionary Bertrand Barrère was right.

A comparison of the high-practice region of Alsace and the low-practice region of the Roussillon in the last half of the nineteenth century reveals how linguistic cultures could be appropriated for the defense of religion. These linguistic cultures, or milieux,[6] of the non-French-speaking regions were originally shaped by the politics of Louis XIV. Studies of the period make a special point of juxtaposing Alsace and the Roussillon to explain the king's approach to the language problem.[7] According to David Bell, "[royal edicts] were directed exclusively at newly conquered areas (Flanders, Alsace, Roussillon), where elites as well as common people spoke a 'foreign' tongue. Even here, moreover, coercive measures were almost nonexistent, and the issuing of edicts ceased within a generation or two of annexation—the time it took for the elites of the new provinces to become bilingual."[8] Furthermore, the much earlier edict of Villers-Cotterêts requiring that all documents be written "en langage maternel françois et non autrement" really referred to any vernacular spoken in France; only Latin was excluded.[9] By the nineteenth century, the linguistic politics of the French government had changed completely and church people in the two former conquered provinces responded in opposite ways, protecting the German dialect in Alsace and neglecting Catalan in the Roussillon.[10] Nor should the French loss of Alsace in 1870 distract from a comparison of the religion and language dynamics of the two regions. The clergy attracted the religious loyalty of German-speaking Alsatians under French rule, and the loyalty of French-speaking Alsatians under German rule. In the broken French of one down-to-earth citizen, "Français ne peux, allemand ne veux, alsacien suis." Loyalty was local, with French citizenship favored: "Can't be French, don't want to be German, I'm just Alsatian," a quote backed by other evidence that Catholic faith was compatible with French citizenship.[11] In Alsace, the loyalty to Catholicism was clear and loyalty to France was made possible by the efforts of church people to neutralize governmental promotion of French in the 1860s.

I will focus on events and statistics in Alsace and the Roussillon from the 1860s through the 1890s: from the attempts after 1863 of Victor Duruy,

Napoleon III's minister of education, to guarantee a French education in all the non-French-speaking regions, through the beginnings of the German rule of Alsace following the Franco-Prussian War of 1870 and the later legislation of the anticlerical Third Republic in the Roussillon. To compare Alsace (here, Catholic Alsace) and the Roussillon, I used diocesan surveys of religious practice from 1883 and 1887: comparable statistics exist for "Easter duty" (fulfilling the Catholic obligation to receive Communion during the Easter period and confess, if necessary, beforehand).[12] In effect, then, I worked with education statistics in the 1860s and with other relevant data between 1860 and 1890. Until modern times in France, significant changes in the linguistic map and in the map of religious practice did not take place within any thirty-year period. Regions of high and low practice are remarkably consistent over a century or even several centuries, apart from the cataclysms of the revocation of Huguenot Protestant freedoms under Louis XIV and the Revolution itself. The closer we get to our own era, with increased mobility and the rapid development of regional economies, the more sudden and dramatic cultural and religious changes become.[13] In the nineteenth century, however, change came slowly.

By 1883 most of the Alsatians in the northern half of the region, the department of Bas-Rhin, made their Easter duty. Very few cantons showed results of less than 90 percent, and all of these were above 80 percent with one outstanding exception: the town of Schiltigheim just to the north of Strasbourg (and now part of the city). Here the percentage was an astonishingly low 46.5 percent. Schiltigheim was a center of brewing and manufacturing and had a railway depot that employed a large number of non-Alsatians. The normal relations of the Alsatian clergy with their people were thrown off-kilter, which may in itself account for the low level of churchgoing. One indication in the departmental archives that all was not right in the city parish and that non-Alsatians were the problem comes from 1874, after the German takeover. There had been complaints about the curé: his attitude toward the restoration of the altar, his liberties with prayers, and his lack of interest in the liturgy. The official diocesan inquiry, consisting of interviews, was aptly recorded: "Question: Does he hear confessions [regularly]? Answer: Yes, but here I must reproach M. le Curé. You perhaps know that he welcomes outsiders [étrangers]. This year it happened that on the last Sunday of the Easter season there were many people waiting to go to confession, and among them were a number of outsiders. He was not able to hear everyone, and a dozen of his parishioners were not able to make their Easter duty. He should not have admitted the outsiders." We cannot be sure that the man was complaining about non-Alsatians, but given the railroad depot atmosphere of Schiltigheim, it is likely. Perhaps they were less dependable or prodigal children whom the fatherly priest worked overtime to reconcile.[14]

Statistics for the Roussillon in approximately the same period show that in the years 1887–89, the percentage of the population making their Easter duty held at 34.6 percent with individual cantons varying widely from the average, from 13.9 percent to 41 percent—and beyond at times. The highest levels of practice were found in the cantons of Mount-Louis, with 60.7 percent, and Saillagouse, with 59.5 percent. Two other cantons had figures over 41 percent, with neither of them reaching the 50-percent level.[15] This means that most of the Roussillon had Easter duty figures considerably lower than the lowest level—the wildly negative exception of Schiltigheim—in Alsace. High levels of religious practice were not simply the result of Protestant-Catholic competition in Alsace: such levels characterized the other foreign-language regions of France, none of which had a Protestant presence. In Alsace itself, Catholic practice was not higher or lower in the uniformly Catholic, uniformly Protestant, or mixed towns.[16]

Differences in the histories of Alsace and Roussillon could complicate comparisons between the two regions. First of all, the dechristianization campaign of 1793–94 had a greater effect on churchgoing in the Roussillon (though in both regions the vast majority of priests refused to swear allegiance to the revolutionary government). And second, in 1870, Alsace, coming under German rule, was protected from the secular goals of the public school reform of Jules Ferry. After the Revolution, Roussillon had a strong religious spirit and faithful clergy: there had to be another reason for the falloff in practice. And, while it is true that Alsace and the Roussillon had different political destinies after 1870, the cultures appeared to follow their own set of dynamics. The passage of Alsace from French rule to German rule and the stepped-up campaign to secularize the schools in the Roussillon during the ministry of Jules Ferry did not significantly modify the high level of practice in Alsace or the low level of practice in the Roussillon. Practice levels in Alsace-Lorraine were high both before and after the takeover. In the Roussillon, the reforms of Ferry were just beginning to have effect in the 1880s.

The Mediating Role of Education

The preoccupation of the church with language culture was most visible in the schools—religious education, of course, being basic. Historian of religious instruction Pierre Zind has dramatically evoked the close relation of language and religious instruction. "Language speaks to the heart and makes itself heard by the heart; it forms the soul by definitively programming the brain through mysterious harmonies that bring words and ideas together in a manner proper to the genius of each linguistic group. . . . To reach the depths of a person, religious instruction must use the channel of the maternal dialects; to avoid being removed from everyday life along with school language, it must tie its destiny to that of the maternal dialects."[17] Linguistic historian Paul Lévy believed that the psychological power of a mother tongue virtually guaranteed its broad importance. "The memories that make us cherish the locales of the emotional experiences of our childhood and bring us back to them as often as possible, make us return also to the language of our youth. It is these more or less instinctive sentiments that explain the preference and fidelity that people of all times and places bestow upon their own way of speaking." Lévy does note that during the period 1850–70, "for the great mass of Alsatians and inhabitants of the Lorraine . . . the language question was a matter of indifference." But they were indifferent in the sense that they went their way speaking the German dialect without caring what the authorities did to enforce French. Lévy believed that the signing of petitions (in favor of the maintenance of German) was not a political manifesto because people often signed to please the local curé. And yet, when absolutely necessary, Alsatians would defend their German-speaking rights. In his *Psychanalyse de l'Alsace,* Frédéric Moffet writes, "The Catholic populations [masses] remained as attached as Protestant populations to the German language and their regional traditions. When in 1924 the French government threatened to introduce the separation laws [*lois laïques*] in Alsace and suppress the teaching of German at the same time, Catholics rose up as much against the bill as the Protestants."[18]

The data on language comes from the 1860s, the period of educational reform under Victor Duruy, who was trying to offset the influence of the religious congregations in the public schools. Beginning in 1860, the French government had allowed the church considerable say in the running of the school system.[19] Duruy himself ordered a survey of schoolchildren throughout France, and so determined that barely half of them spoke French.[20] Sandra Horvath-Peterson sums up Duruy's goals: "For him, therefore, it was sufficient to encourage Frenchmen who did not know French to become bilingual—which he did indirectly by way of the letters he sent to bishops and prefects—and to rely on schoolteachers, libraries, and adult education courses to encourage the learning of French."[21] In 1864 he solicited a report on the use of language in the primary schools of France, which summarized the state of affairs in 1863. Later he asked the departmental prefects for more detailed information on the use of patois and dialect. He wanted them to suggest ways and means for promoting French without "doing injury to the customs, habits and local predilections."[22]

The 1864 survey reveals significant differences between Alsace and the Roussillon regarding the linguistic role of the church in general education. In Alsace, on one hand (again, in the northern half, Bas-Rhin), 513 out of 614 schools used the German dialect (and an additional 45 used *only* the dialect). In the Roussillon, on the other hand, not a single school used Catalan as the language of instruction. And almost half of these schools were taught by sisters and brothers.[23] It would appear that in Alsace, church people not only fought for the catechism in the maternal dialect, not only worked to preserve the old Alsatian culture, but they also ensured the preservation of linguistic culture in the schools. In the Roussillon, church people fought for the catechism and encouraged the preservation of the Catalan culture, but the cultural and religious priorities inherited or established by the priests, sisters, and brothers of the Roussillon did not include the maintenance of Catalan in the schools.

The Catholic clergy across the nineteenth century did not defend the vernacular in all places and at all times. During the reign of Napoleon and the Bourbon Restoration, political and cultural forces for centralization were also operative in ecclesiastical structures. Churchmen in general were only too happy to oblige their imperial and royal governments in return for support. This tendency was reinforced by the assignment of bishops to dioceses other than those they came from and originally served.[24] With recruitment of more rural and lower-middle-class priests, regional awareness and with it defense of regional languages increased. At the same time, some members of the nobility, and even of the upper bourgeoisie, discovered advantages in regional distinctiveness. In Alsace, for example, the French-speaking local elites were quite content to preserve the German dialects of the masses because their own authority would thereby remain uncontested. Here the business class was less concerned than the ideologically committed, that is, teachers and clergy.[25] After 1870, scholarly priests were involved in studies of local culture, though there were always clergy who wanted education in French to supplant education in any other idiom as rapidly as possible. In the end, anticlericalism moved even the pro-French clergy to pull back: the centralizing education and language goals of Paris would weaken Catholic influence. Gérard Cholvy distinguishes three types of clergy: (1) those who simply promoted French;

(2) those who catered to the linguistic needs of the faithful whether the latter be the dominant group, a minority, or migrants; and (3) those who were actively involved in regional language movements.[26] In sum, the clergy's promotion of regional languages was neither consistent nor uniform—except when it came to teaching catechism in the primary grades. There, the vast majority wavered not. Encounter with God's truth could only come in the language of the home, the regional language. Attitudes and methods varied, depending upon the history and structures of the regional culture.

Fundamental questions about language, religion, and the mediating role of education have been pondered in two great doctoral dissertations: Alfred Wahl's study of voting in Alsace (and Baden) and Gérard Cholvy's study of religion in the Hérault. In *Confession et comportement dans les campagnes d'Alsace et de Bade,* Wahl examines the cultural role of religion in Alsace after it was incorporated into the German Reich;[27] in *Géographie religieuse de l'Hérault contemporain,* Cholvy studies the area adjacent to the Roussillon in the present century.[28] For Wahl, cultural milieu determined loyalties, taking precedence even over economic interests in Alsace: "the mentality of the cultural group takes precedence over individual conscience and material interest.[29] Wahl had gathered evidence that "rural people did not . . . separate clearly the material from the spiritual: the religious world and the profane world remained closely overlapping in their minds."[30] The ensemble of symbols and sensibilities, formal politics and popular celebrations produced a milieu effect. Religious practice and language were made to support one another as part of the ensemble. For Cholvy, language isolation may have preserved religious tradition in the Hérault. But his evidence shows that when language came to be considered a sign of ignorance or poverty, people wanted to get away from it. The level of churchgoing was higher where the church provided good education, francophone though it was.[31] In other words, Wahl found that cultural *tradition* took priority in Alsace, whereas Cholvy found that cultural *transformation* took priority in the Hérault. In either case, the church maintained its influence by responding, through its educational system, to the cultural priorities of the populace.

In the following profiles of Alsace and the Roussillon I will explore the role of the church in linguistic education, first by a brief study of the attitudes of public school teachers to church and language, and second, by the study of local church efforts to promote the mother tongue—all of this set in appropriate cultural history.

The Culture of Alsace: Language, Religion, and Education

The competing cultures in Alsace in early modern times were Protestant and Catholic. They could not be national, obviously: there was no unified German identity when Alsace, albeit German-speaking, was part of the very loosely confederated Holy Roman Empire, and France was a dynastic state. In the years following the Revolution, the attempts to promote French in Alsace found success only in the cities, where an urban elite gradually formed. Writing of the 1820s and 1830s, Paul Leuillot says that "German remained almost the only language of school teaching. At Strasbourg without doubt, they made children speak the two languages together, but not without difficulties."[32] At that time, "in many communes where the population was partly French, they hardly ever preached in French, in a few communes *never*. . . . In fact, religious literature properly speaking was in the German language.[33]

Clear witness to the clergy's role in education comes from the 1860 essays of primary schoolteachers in Bas-Rhin, submitted in a nationwide contest set up during the education ministry of Gustave Rouland and brought to conclusion during the education ministry of Victor Duruy.[34] From the commune of Otterstat, a teacher wrote that he originally thought too much time was given over to German and catechism but had come to see them as fundamental exercises. A teacher from the canton of Petite-Pierre commented, perhaps even complained, that class could not begin at eight o'clock because the children were forced to go to Mass at that time, with the teacher often serving as sacristan. A more optimistic view came from Lauterbourg: "The parish priest teaching the catechism will explain it in French and the children will respond in French. Following this method from chapter to chapter to the end of the catechism, the students will then have a ready tongue. Then the priest will preach alternately from the pulpit in French and German, and will continue this experience for several years. To your satisfaction you will see a young French generation grow up." This meant that the priest might be counted on to resolve the language problem. One should keep in mind, however, that education was not obligatory, although school systems in Alsace were probably the most developed in France, in part because Protestants required schooling for confirmation.[35]

Schools and religion go together as far as the rural people are concerned, said a teacher from the canton of Bouxwiller: they "would not hesitate to support the church in its efforts to kill the schools regarded [by the church] as a dangerous poison for the souls of the faithful and for its own existence." From the canton of Benfeld, a teacher reported that the schools would have good students if only they came regularly; the problem was that the priests who prepared students for First Communion took not only those of the appropriate ages (thirteen for girls and fourteen for boys) but everyone. The author of this essay certainly believed that religious instruction dominated school life. Another teacher from the canton of Benfeld noted the church's prerogatives and listed appropriate ways of teaching the recitation and literal interpretation of the diocesan catechism, sacred history, and the Sunday Gospel. Yet the author maintained the value of French: "The national language tightens more and more the line that exists between the different inhabitants of France, draws them together in common attraction, and facilitates communication. It is the language of the history of the state, that of the courts and administrations; it should be in common circulation."[36] Few of the teachers pointed to explicit defense and teaching of German by church people. But the teachers' compositions pointed to the clergy's ability to manipulate the educational system for their own ecclesiastical needs.

Church people were intimately involved in the preservation of Alsatian linguistic culture in the 1860s, first and foremost the great Germanizing bishop, André Raess. A native of Alsace, he was trained in Germany and was the superior of a German seminary (at Mainz) before he was made the bishop of Strasbourg in 1842, a position he held for forty-five years. Raess not only sought to protect German among his people for their own good but was himself most at home in the language and the culture. He was ordained the year after the fall of Napoleon and spent his clerical career in seminary education and administration. Although not the favorite of the bishop of Strasbourg, Raess was made the coadjutor of the diocese because the local prefect favored him (and, in accordance with the Concordat, had considerable influence). As spiritual leader, he pressed home the importance of papal authority. Devotion to the Immaculate Conception after 1854 and submission to papal authority after 1870 were key goals of his administration.[37] Though accused of unmitigated opportunism, he defended church (especially clerical) interests across the regimes of Louis-Philippe, the Second Republic, Napoleon III, and, finally, the kaiser. But certainly he made as little trouble as possible for these governments: clergy who did not like him complained that he tyrannized them even as he accommodated government officials. From the beginning of German rule, but especially under the German Catholic governor, Edwin Manteuffel, Raess worked to conciliate his diocese to German rule and to its language policy. In this, he displeased some of his clergy but pleased the majority of the people.[38]

CHEMINS DE FER DE L'EST

STRASBOURG
Vue prise des Ponts couverts

Fig. 8.   View of the city of Strasbourg (Bas-Rhin) assuming a French-speaking reader and published by the French rail company that connected Paris and Strasbourg. Church people defended Alsatian German against the supposition that French should be the language of the region. (Bibliothèque Nationale)

During Raess's pre-1870 episcopacy, the Paris government received from Strasbourg a copy of the report made by an inspector at the Academy of Strasbourg to the rector of the academy on the extent of the use of German in Alsace. The inspector wrote, "If the [local] authority publishes its decrees in German, it does so in the end because it wants to, and in deference to local ways that it does not want to offend. In Alsace, they do not speak good German, but a vulgar patois with German roots." Mayors of communes could not be counted upon: "I have had frequent occasion to respond to mayors of rural communes who have just conversed with me in German about school affairs, 'If you do not know French, which is the language of law and business, go learn it, and I will listen to you then.'" Even teachers could not be completely counted upon: "At one time we in effect awarded diplomas to teachers who didn't know a word of French; there still are eight of that group in the

Department." But the heart of the problem, said the inspector, was prayer: "So that French may pass completely into popular usage, it is above all necessary that the language of prayer be in French. None of it is now, neither in Catholic nor Protestant worship." Here he admitted that the young curés were willing to teach French in the schools. The old clergy were, the inspector reported, still mouthing clichés about French as the language of Voltaire and the Revolution. They also liked to keep the Alsatian girls away from the French soldiers. By and large, for both Catholic and Protestant clergy, "French . . . is the language of the Revolution, the language of conquest, the language of new ways hostile to their authority." What was to be done? "I believe that a formal prohibition coming from Your Excellency and *completely* forbidding foreign languages and patois . . . would have a good effect."[39]

The clergy were clearly an obstacle to the spread of French. For example, M. Boucault, an officer of the academy—and so, a government bureaucrat likely to be biased—said of the Guebwiller population, "You have asked me to indicate the cause preventing the French language from being adopted by the people of Alsace; I have the honor to respond that it resides in that the clergy do not want to give religious instruction in French in order to better dominate the faithful; the child is obliged to know how to read and write German at fourteen years of age and subsequently to become attached to that language."[40] In fact, members of the clergy could be quite clear about their goals, purely religious goals in their belief. The priests of Souffelsweyersheim, for example, insisted that language and moral guidance were closely allied in Alsace: "Religious teaching must be disseminated in the native language, which is the German language, because one is apt to practice only what one understands well. The relationships of man with God and with his neighbor are of such importance that they should be interpreted in the form most accessible to the intellect." The results otherwise are doubts and indifference, leading to rejection of religion. The priests had tried to experiment with the catechism in French several times and it never worked, "because the mind and the heart, lacking understanding could not engage."[41]

In contrast to the above measured language, clerical hubris, if not nastiness, permeates the letter of the abbé Bretz, chaplain of the Château Impérial de Strasbourg. To begin with, Bretz protested the abuse suffered by priests and religious who taught in German, noting that the government of Napoleon III had no intention whatsoever of suppressing German. Bretz unqualifiedly connected the survival of the faith to the survival of the native language, German. "Today, for fairly disreputable reasons, you hunt down the German language in those who have the sacred duty to teach it; you know full well that, after its suppression, religious faith will disappear from our province." Rehearsing the worst of the moral liabilities of French culture, he insisted that all solid morality would ultimately be destroyed: "It should be noticed that with the disappearance of the German language the seriousness of our Alsatian character will disappear and will be replaced by the reprehensible superficiality of the French character." He showed how language destruction would lead to the destruction of religion: "One is likely to practice only what one understands well; the relations of man with God are of such importance that they ought to be interpreted in the form most accessible to the intellect, because tone and words [*accents*] insufficiently understood engender skepticism, indifference, and negation. Understanding the German language is serious; it is the language of the soul, of the heart, whereas the French language is the speech [*parole*] of reason, of conversation, of correspondence, about any light subject."[42]

Not all the clergy of Alsace (or Lorraine) went to the extremes of Bretz. Officials in Lorraine could cite the behavior and attitudes of the Alsatian clergy as examples of a spirit of compromise not shown by the clergy of Lorraine.[43] Both Alsace and Lorraine are surveyed in *La Langue française dans les départements de l'Est,* by J. Wirth, who says that when Alsatian children have learned enough French in school the clergy do not hesitate to teach the catechism in French. They believe in the gradual introduction of the national language, carefully avoiding any challenges to the deep-seated customs of the people.[44] Such pedagogical compromise could be found in Lorraine also. From an École normale of the same department came a lesson plan for the teaching of French through the Lord's Prayer: "I enclose here a page in manuscript containing a sample copy of the method for learning the Lord's Prayer that I propose to make our children follow. . . . [The German explanations] serve as a point of departure for teaching; the teacher can abandon the German words and phrases, making use of the French words and phrases to the extent that the children assimilate them." This method obviously makes prayer instruction—in effect, one element of catechetical instruction—the principal means across the language divide. Did the author deliberately seek to bring together the clergy (who wanted to ensure that the children experienced religion in the psychologically congenial way of the maternal language), and the government officials, teachers, and others (who sought to ensure linguistic, and therefore political, loyalty to the French government)? Here the union of linguistic and religious instruction is especially intimate—beyond the use of religious examples in general schoolwork.[45]

More formal clerical defenses of German (and the Alsatian dialect) can be found in (1) the pamphlet authored by a prominent Strasbourg priest Louis Cazeaux; and (2) the response of Father Ignace Waltzer, writing in *Revue catholique d'Alsace,* to an attack on the clergy's linguistic behavior by the editor of the *Journal de Belfort.* Cazeaux was a pastor in Strasbourg for years, and the *Revue* was founded by two priests assigned to the minor seminary of Strasbourg: Pantaléon Mury, professor of rhetoric and history from 1843 to 1866, and Alexandre Straub, professor of history from 1850 to 1867. Straub was also an "inspector" for the Société française d'archéologie for Bas-Rhin and president of the Société des monuments historiques. The *Revue* was essentially edited by priests for priests and included among its writers both Louis Cazeaux and Ignace Waltzer.[46]

For Father Cazeaux generally, the knowledge of German "provides social pleasures of more than one sort, protects interests as numerous as they are serious, and gives to our province a certain superiority over the other parts of France."[47] Of course, the "influence of the German language on religion and mores in Alsace" concerned Cazeaux the most. His axiom was that religion and morality had proved themselves in history to be the only solid foundation of individual, family, and national happiness. Cazeaux began his defense of the religious importance of German with the citation of a document sent to the rector of the Académie de Strasbourg, Laurent Delcasso, from the Cantonal Committee of Bischwiller, whose membership included Catholics, Protestants, and Jews. "The religious education of Alsatian youth seems to require that, in our schools, a larger place be given to the study of the German language."[48] If this should not happen, the rector went on to say, "Their minds will grow rusty [*s'enrouillera*] at the same time as their hearts will contract a certain moral insensitivity." Then, unable to really hear the Word of God, they will gradually lose their understanding of it, their religious faith, and, consequently, their souls.[49] Negligence of German would result in a "state of semi-knowledge and semi-ignorance of the two languages."[50] The sources of piety, readings, and sermons would no longer speak to the people, and prayer would lose its power. Then "our dear Alsace will be despoiled of its most beautiful ornament, of its reputation as a religious land, which, up to the present, it has enjoyed throughout France."[51]

For Cazeaux, introducing French would not be a problem if German did not suffer thereby. The language problems "flow naturally, and contrary to the intent of everyone, from the exclusive and precipitate way in which the system of teaching, good in itself, is applied."[52] Though he exalted the cultural value of German in itself throughout his pamphlet, Cazeaux admitted that standard German must be taught to his dialect-speaking Alsatians. But he believed that less time would be necessary "to teach Alsatians to speak well and write in a grammatically proper way two languages than would be necessary to popularize French at the expense of German."[53]

With the preservation of German, Cazeaux could assign a political role to Alsace: mediation between France and Germany. "Does not France have a certain advantage in possessing a faithful province that, within the broad expanse of its territory, speaks the language of peoples who have already been its enemies and who could become such again?"[54] Cazeaux and many other Alsatians felt the pressure of Bismarck's expansion and unification policies. Germany "could" be an enemy, but it did not have to be such if Alsace could serve as "a magnificent hyphen [*trait d'union*] between our beautiful fatherland and the greater Germany."[55] This goal, of course, turned out to be unrealizable.

Before Cazeaux, leading Alsatian clergy had fought the language battle with public authorities. In their role as teachers of Catholicism, the clergy sought to ensure comprehension and appreciation of the church's teaching. In the chronicle section of the *Revue catholique d'Alsace,* one of its editors, Pantaléon Mury, reported that the editor of the *Journal de Belfort,* who served as spokesman for the public council of the arrondissement of Sarrebourg, had said, "The language of Racine and Voltaire is generally little spoken in our rural communes." Mury responded, "First of all, if the language of Voltaire is neither spoken or understood here, so much the better."[56] Learning French could compromise the faith of young Alsatians, in Mury's view.

The most developed argument against the *Journal* editor, Monsieur Clerc, was published in the same volume of the *Revue* by Father Ignace Waltzer, a colleague of Father Mury.[57] In "La langue allemande en Alsace," Waltzer declared, "If we use the German language to teach religion to the children, it is because we are determined to be understood."[58] He went on to say that as soon as the children understood French sufficiently, French would be used as the medium of instruction. Such was already the case in Strasbourg, Colmar, Mulhouse, Saverne, Sélestat, and Hagenau. But the anti-German-language decision of the council of the arrondissement of Sarrebourg "could only *interfere with religion.*"[59] Waltzer used language instruction itself as the example of fundamental teaching procedures. To teach other languages one should start with the language that the students themselves speak and understand. The mystery language—the object hidden in darkness that must be illuminated— for Alsatian children would be French: "The light for them is the language they learned on the knees of their mothers."[60]

The arguments of Waltzer were more nuanced than the brief remarks of Mury. Waltzer made it clear that he did not want to protect the children from French simply because of Voltaire: "Those of us who love French love it as the language of Bossuet, Fénelon, and also Racine; thus, far from fearing it, we want to introduce it."[61] The clergy had a problem with French because many of the rural children did not receive any effective schooling in French, coming to school only in the winter. "Will we amuse them, to say nothing about fatiguing them, by making them hear for a few months, during one or two winters, French words they will not retain and which in any case they will not understand?"[62]

After 1870, the tables turned and local administrations received requests for the wider use of French in both the "French" and "German" areas. By 1882, 435 communes freely permitted French in the schools, alongside the 1,250 communes that permitted only German. But where Francophones were in the majority, German had to be taught also; where Germanophones were in the majority, French did not have to be learned at all. Ecclesiastics then took on the defense of French—though records of this defense are somewhat scarce. For this period, we must search the records of the diocese of Strasbourg. The *Revue catholique d'Alsace* had been suspended and not yet replaced by a German-language publication. Little evidence can be found in the minutes of the meetings of the bishop's council, though this is not surprising.[63] There are references to language only in the period after 1870 in the correspondence to the prefect of Haut-Rhin. In one letter, the vicar general of the diocese of Strasbourg wrote to the prefect of Haut-Rhin, "with the very simple observation that in the manual of statistics for Alsace-Lorraine, beginning 1 January 1884, the community of Willern is numbered among those communities dispensed from the requirement of German. Should this dispensation be rescinded after 1 January 1884, I would then request notification of this fact."[64] In addition, there was a general promise that one of the church organizations would make use of German as the legally required language of commerce.[65] And in Lorraine, Bishop Louis Fleck of Metz, though initially criticized by the *Républicain lorrain* for being a Germanophile, carefully defended the rights of the Francophones to receive religious guidance and training in French. In an 1887 report to the pope, he explained the linguistic situation in his diocese: both before and after the war, in spite of change in the territorial size of the diocese, two-fifths of the parishes in his jurisdiction were French-speaking and three-fifths, German; religious ministry was exercised accordingly.[66] Stephen Harp, in his recent study of primary schooling and nation-building in Alsace and Lorraine, reports on the continuing vigilance exercised by Catholic clergy in the decades following the German takeover. In fact, with Bismarck's *Kulturkampf* to restrict Catholic clerical influence on German schools in full operation, clergy had even more motivation to maintain their traditional control of schooling in Alsace.[67]

The Culture of the Roussillon: Language, Religion, and Education

From the beginning, efforts to press French education on the general population were more extensive in the Roussillon than in Alsace.[68] Yet officials were lenient. During the rule of Louis XV one of them wrote, "It is not by being violent toward the inhabitants of a country far removed from the center of the kingdom, who hold on to the mores, customs, and prejudices transmitted by their fathers, that we will succeed in having them adopt the tastes, customs, and methods which can be accepted in the rest of France."[69] The Frenchifying of the population began with the upper classes and moved to the middle classes.[70]

Local, or popular, religion was little affected by old-regime ecclesiastical policies and administrative attempts at acculturation of the region: prayer books, plays, and hymns were printed in Catalan; pilgrimages, rosary confraternities, women's religious societies had enduring strength.[71] According to Peter Sahlins, to the extent that "the continuing strength of Catalan cults and confraternities expressed a popular religious sentiment tied to a distinctive local culture, the French crown failed to reshape those indigenous beliefs."[72] There is no indication of widespread alienation of the population from the church in the eighteenth century.

The Roussillon resisted the Revolution, and its priests strongly resisted the Civil Constitution of the Clergy. In fact, their resistance resembled the resistance of the Alsatian clergy and the clergy of those other foreign-language regions of France that maintained high practice across the nineteenth century.[73] Peter McPhee records the motivation of the minority who welcomed the revolutionary government. "There was some relief for them, for it was they who had to buy salt, essential for their livestock, at high prices, perform the *corvée* and pay the church tithe, which could be as high as 14 percent in the Vallespir [region]."[74] But McPhee focuses on a petition, with its evocation of the centrality of tradition and religion, that came from the town of Saint-Laurent: "In particular, the petition of 24 April explained Saint-Laurent's hostility to the Revolution as stemming from the fidelity of its ancestors to the monarchy, its horror at Louis XVI's death, and above all, its attachment to its *premiers et légitimes pasteurs*." In light of "wider evidence," McPhee believes that "insofar as the document placed priority on community outrage at the Civil Constitution of the Clergy, it went to the heart of the matter."[75] One cause of this resistance to the Revolution was the Spanish ecclesiastical connection and moderating influence.[76] Yet this was compatible with resistance to clericalism. During the constitutional-refractory clergy controversy, the people of Saint-Laurent insisted on their right to choose their clergy. McPhee refers to a "populist, authoritarian religiosity" and suggests that "communal solidarity was reimposed from below."[77] This combination of factors would explain why the people insisted on their religious rights during the Revolution but did not, in the long term, maintain equally strong sentiments in favor of official (highly clericalized) religious practices. In sum, room to maneuver was a fundamental need.[78] While resisting strong clerical control, the people opted for a traditional clergy over a state-imposed clergy. While resisting Spanish influence and French revolutionary nationalism, they did not insist on a totally separate Catalan identity. One day this insistence on their right to maneuver would lead some to reject religion in favor of a secular ideology and lead others to favor vestige local religion over official church practice.

Local religion lost its social and religious strength during the years of revolutionary persecution and the dispersal of religious and clerical strength, according to Michael Brunet. He explains the falloff in religious practice after the Revolution as a failure of local religion in a very specific sense. Popular practices did not have staying power when religion was forced into hiding: "Theatricality and conviviality played a role in traditional piety that could not be adapted to clandestine existence. The faith of the Roussillonnais accommodated itself badly to the catacombs."[79] Furthermore, following the revolutionary and Napoleonic eras, the antagonisms among clergy, between clergy and people, and between Catalans of Spanish and those of French orientation diminished the vitality of Roussillonnais religion. In fact, Brunet believes that the unity of the population never recovered after the antagonisms of the revolutionary era: "The covert civil war in connection with emigration and the return of the émigrés, the pillaging, and the sale of the *biens nationaux* had broken the fundamental social pact."[80] Instead the clergy were "arrogant and cold functionaries of a vindictive state." And theological problems coalesced into regionwide problems: "The crumbling of the parish had to accompany the crumbling of the *universitas* itself, and this decline of base communities announced the triumph of the state.[81]

Teaching in Catalan was not promoted in the schools, even though many of the schools were in the hands of nuns and teaching brothers during the Second Empire. Writing to the Ministry of Education, the rector of the Academy of Montpellier noted that the clergy at least used Catalan in preaching and catechizing: "This state of things obliges the clergy to provide teaching in a language that the people understand; several members of the clergy, themselves children of the region, find it easier perhaps to express themselves in this language." But he also reported that no special language instruction was given to Catalan-speaking children who did not understand French. The implication was that something had to be done: "In Pyrénées-Orientales Catalan is the language of the people. This language is spoken on the two sides of the Pyrenees, Spanish and French, in a uniform manner; it has, besides, its monuments, its grammar, its lexicon. If then, in primary school, the child is forbidden to speak one single word of Catalan, as soon as he is on the playground with his friends or away [from school] with his parents, he gets back to the mother tongue and forgets that which he had not the time and often the good will to understand well."[82] This was, however, a single document in the ministry's papers on language, standing in stark contrast to all the documentation sent from the Academy of Strasbourg to the Ministry of Education.

The 1860 essays of primary schoolteachers indicate that church people had genuine social influence and that language was a problem for the educational system. Religious influence was not parleyed into promotion of the language, however. Even those Roussillonais schoolteachers from the two cantons with the highest level of churchgoing, Mont-Louis and Saillagouse, did not cite any instance of the promotion of Catalan. A teacher from Mont-Louis, as might be expected from a relatively high-practice region, had good words for the curé after a diatribe against the other local authorities and their ignorance of the people's needs. "His influence at school, properly handled, could produce the most happy effects; he lacks neither training nor spare time as does the mayor." Another made the church a model of seriousness and long-lasting influence: "But there exists in each commune, even the most forgotten, a revered place, which is the church. Would it not be possible to give to the school something of this religious seriousness that, striking the imagination of the child, would leave him with such an impression that he would only speak with veneration of the place where he received his first education." This writer promoted the independent—equal and complementary—roles of mayor, teacher, and curé: "Everyone functions according to his own specialty. Both the religious and secular aspects [of community life] would be equally fulfilled and would compete without admixture or confusion in the great task of moralization and the training." The attitude here was nonconfrontational. Unlike Alsace, the clergy did not seem to have a polarizing influence on education.

From the other high-practice canton of Saillagouse came a composition that dealt with the language problem. It would appear that the teacher simply taught in French, using words over and over until the students understood them: "The children of the countryside hear spoken in class only a language that they do not understand, even as regards the simplest terms. Should the teacher try to explain a word, he must use a certain number of other terms which are scarcely more understandable for the student." And the teacher recognized also the power of the clergy. Religious order teachers "impose conditions as regards locale and materiel; [lay teachers] can only formulate wishes that are too seldom accepted."[83] In both Mont-Louis and Saillagouse, then, some clerical authority was recognized, but no connection was made between religion and language.

The clearest essay on language came from neither Mont-Louis nor Saillagouse. A composition by Pierre Imbert, reprinted in a recent collection of documentation published by the departmental archives of Pyrénées–Orientales, is an enormous ribbon-bound manuscript, larger and more ornate than anything else in the collection of essays from the Roussillon (or Bas-Rhin). More important, this is an exceptional essay in its honesty and openness. "In a region such as the Roussillon where the mother tongue is not French, the trials and difficulties are insurmountable for the teacher of young people." The children speak a language that little resembles French and varies considerably from one region to another. Since they do not understand the national language, the teacher must explain things all the time in the local language. "For it is otherwise impossible to inculcate those little bits of knowledge that are needed to nourish their minds and show them the way to rational, nonmechanical learning." It is not that they so much resist French language instruction, but at play they hang around with others who do not go to the school, and at home they are with parents who are non-French-speaking, and who are, for the most part illiterate, "and so the fruit of lessons taught earlier at school is lost in a moment. We always have to begin again.[84] Clearly, major efforts toward effective language instruction were needed in the Roussillon of the 1860s.

The bishops, in fact, appeared more concerned with ecclesiastical prerogatives than with Catalan culture. Bishop Ramadié, bishop from 1856 to 1876 during the last years of the Second Empire and the beginning of the Third Republic, was an active agent of Frenchification, although this fact did not help him reconcile the ardent republicans in his diocese. In 1872 he wrote to the prefect and the mayor of Perpignan complaining that a crowd gathered in the Place de l'Église had shouted insults against "religion, the army, authority" right after one of the May evening services in honor of Mary.[85] Bishop Goussail (bishop, 1886–89), "closer to the sensitivities of the region,"[86] did publish a catechism in French and Catalan. But in his government file, one finds a description sent by the prefect of the department to the government in Paris: the bishop, it was said, had great influence on the clergy, but "his influence on the population is just about nil." The prefect added that "even in the reactionary communes, the influence of the clergy is feeble, the inhabitants do not like their clergy to become involved in local affairs."[87]

Reviewing the bishops' pastoral letters over the thirty-year period being considered here, I found no discussion of language, teaching, and apostolate in contexts where it would be natural to draw the issues together. In 1865, Bishop Ramadié, reviewing the history of his predecessors, placed high value on elite erudition: "[Bishop Gerbet] came to you crowned with the laurels of glory that had already given him entry to the precincts of that great institution of learning, the Sorbonne."[88] Even when promoting a new catechism, he made no reference to the language needs of the Catalans. Addressing teachers, he said, "Insert and keep this sacred manual of knowledge and good morals in your classes in the distinguished place it deserves. Without it you would not succeed in training a single French citizen, for without it you would make neither a man nor a Christian."[89] Nor did he mention Catalan when exhorting his priests to offer gentleness and encouragement to the simplest of parishioners: "Let us distribute in abundance the bread of the divine word to our ignorant peoples, and we will avoid addressing to them humiliating reproaches, invectives that are too severe, ironies or satires in bad taste."[90]

Bishop Goussail himself, addressing artisans and farmers on ancestral traditions and priestly vocations, said nothing about ancestral language: "And you, working families of artisans and cultivators who have preserved the pious traditions of the faith of our ancestors, make the generous sacrifice to God of your children when he gives you the honor of signing them with the august sign of a priestly vocation. Cultivate with great religious care this grain of mustard seed in the home, and then bring this young plant to the salutary nursery known as the seminary; there it will become a tree of life under the salutary influence of the waters of grace and of the sweet radiating of faith and divine love."[91] And there does not appear to be any reference to Catalan in the diocesan news, *La Semaine religieuse,* in the years following 1869.

The bishop and his clergy, however, did want the people to be preached to and taught catechism in Catalan to the extent necessary for minimal comprehension and learning. Goussail eventually supported publication of a catechism in Catalan, introducing it formally in 1898: "Enough people will perhaps try to teach them [Catalan-speaking Catholics] a more polite language, and we ourselves will not neglect at the proper time to promote the legitimate progress of civilization among them through knowledge of our dear and noble French language; but for us this need is secondary."[92]

Only Bishop Jules Carsalade du Pont (bishop, 1899–1932), the religious figure who dominated the Roussillon in the first decades of the twentieth century (as André Raess had dominated Alsace in the middle decades of the nineteenth century), came to believe that where Catalan failed, religion failed: "Experience has proved to us that the abandonment of the Catalan language in the teaching of catechism was, without any doubt, one of the principal causes of the religious ignorance we so painfully suffer, and, in consequence, of the diminishment of faith among our peoples."[93] By the Carsalade era, priest-writers and priest-poets were strong promoters of the preservation of Catalan in the Roussillon. Clerical scholarship, however, focused on the coming of Christianity and the medieval period and less on the modern era (to be sure, Father Phillipe Torreilles focused on the Revolution). Joseph Bonafont, curé of l'Ile-sur-Têt and a poet, was one of the founders of the *Revue historique et littéraire du diocèse de Perpignan,* a review that appeared from 1921 to 1933.[94] Efforts on behalf of Catalan were individual and isolated.

Neither school nor church, then, helped to centralize Catalan culture, nor did they appear to want to do so.[95] Just before the turn of the century, Henri Baudrillard noted that "the Catalan language has remained the ordinary language of the Roussillon countryside . . . landowners are forced to use the Catalan language: the peasants, even if they understand French, impose it upon them. By speaking in Catalan, they try to keep their distance, and they feel humiliated in hearing orders given in an idiom which they do not see as their own. A certain moral isolation results from this difference of idioms."[96] As Jean Sagnes sums it up, material considerations rather than cultural considerations predominated here. Only in those regions that lay outside areas of major economic change could higher levels of religious practice be found. Submission to, or nostalgia for, the old order also influenced practice. In Salanques, an old Catholic nobility was still esteemed and, accordingly, positively

NOTRE-DAME DE FONT-ROMEU
(Pyrénées Orientales)

NOSTRA-SENYORA DE FONT-ROMEU | NUESTRA-SEÑORA DE FONT-ROMEU

Perpignan. H. St MARTORI

Fig. 9.   View of the Roussillon shrine of Notre-Dame de Font Renou in three languages (French, Catalan, and Spanish). A population base of Catalan-speaking devotees never received support for their language from church people in their own towns and villages. (Bibliothèque Nationale)

influenced churchgoing in the region. This was in contrast to the market-oriented cantons (vine growing, truck gardening, fruit growing, trade, and crafts), with their lower level of churchgoing. Lastly, the presence of industrial workers adversely affected religious practice. Influence of economic factors meant that the population on the coastal plain was the most feeble in practice—the closer to the plain, the more feeble the practice. With the arrival of immigrants to the plain, the clergy could not keep up with the population increase there: "Pastoral duties down on the plain were double what they were in the mountains."[97]

Catalan identity probably was associated with religion, but more with local religion (itself enfeebled at the beginning of the nineteenth century) than with churchgoing. The church may have served as a refuge, but it was not a unifying force in the maintenance of cultural identity. As usual, blame for the diminution of Catholic influence in the schools is placed at the feet of Jules Ferry. But even before Ferry, Catalan was failing as a practical social and economic force, in other words, as a vital means of communication. Sagnes quotes Albert Saisset to the effect that Catalan was not an effective vehicle for the arts and sciences, with their varieties of speculation and abstraction. Rather was it apt for image and metaphor.[98] In any case, it could not regain the cultural ground lost to the economic changes—literary revival and pedagogical theory being no help here.

Religious Practice and Linguistic Culture

Look at the general picture. Even before the 1789 Revolution, the clergy dominated cultural life in Alsace. In the Roussillon, the people preserved their independence and maneuverability, even though the clergy maintained an effective presence. In Alsace, the Revolution did not diminish the force of local religion, whereas in the Roussillon, local religion became weak in its clandestine existence. In the nineteenth century, most cultural forces supported regional language in Alsace; in the Roussillon there was only isolated support for local language. Alsatian elites coordinated and promoted the study of German; Roussillonnais elites were totally Frenchified and separated from the Catalan speakers. In Alsace, there was a far greater community of spiritual and material interests than in the Roussillon, where diversity predominated.

Specifically, 1863 statistics indicated that in northern Alsace, 513 out of 614 schools used the German dialect, and another 45 schools used it exclusively.

In the Roussillon at the exact same time, Catalan was totally absent from the primary schools, half of them taught by sisters and brothers.[99] These statistics and my other evidence on the ecclesiastical promotion of language should explain why Alsace had a practice level of more than 90 percent, whereas the Roussillon attained an average of about 35 percent.

In Alsace, church people not only fought for the catechism in the maternal dialect, not only worked to preserve the old Alsatian culture, they also helped to ensure the preservation of linguistic culture in the schools. Alsatian school-teachers in the 1860s witnessed both clerical influence in the schools and the importance of German. Children were expected to speak German and be eased into French with care. Influential priests in the diocese of Strasbourg defended—by the pamphlet, the journal article, and a variety of public pronouncements—Alsatian linguistic culture. Education administrators on the local and national level had no doubt that clergy were a primary obstacle to the advancement of French. Under German rule, Alsatian clergy defended the mother tongue of Francophones.

In the Roussillon, schoolteachers referred to the Catalan problem and to the potential influence of the clergy without suggesting that the clergy had anything special to do with linguistic culture. The clergy did not even privilege Catalan—or barely privileged Catalan—for the teaching of the catechism. Government officials did not fault church people for linguistic policies, only for antirepublican attitudes. The cultural and religious priorities inherited or established by the priests, sisters, and brothers of the Roussillon did not include the maintenance of Catalan in the schools.

But in the Roussillon, there might have been one other possibility, *pace* Bishop Carsalade du Pont. The case might be made that people are loyal to organized religion when it offers them a vital channel or means to basic material (and personal) satisfaction. We have already noted that in the southern department of the Hérault, where Catholic education helped advance the social and economic status of the population, the people went to church in greater numbers.[100] In high-practice western France, the church was a major support in the search for employment, charity, education, land, and social activities. In Mediterranean France, the church was not such a resource, and material considerations did, in fact, predominate in the Roussillon.[101]

In sum, then, support of local language helped church people maintain their religious influence when language concerns were central to the culture because they could transmute linguistic loyalty into religious loyalty. Otherwise they had to create linguistic loyalty or choose other cultural options. In

Alsace, the church could take advantage of an existing strong linguistic culture and consolidate its own privileged place within that culture. In the Roussillon, the church chose, or defaulted into, a strategy of laissez-faire that genuinely impaired its influence. To maintain its ascendancy, the church had a fundamental choice: support cultural tradition or cultural transformation, one or the other. In the Roussillon, it supported neither.

Part Three

DÉTENTE

Détente in the Third Republic was a long time in coming. *It took a cataclysm to bring the marginalized Catholic political and social leaders back into national public life. But cataclysm there was: the unprecedented horror of World War I, the dramatic setting for the realization of the détente between the Catholic and secular forces within France, and the subject of Chapter 6. Men from all walks of French society were thrown together in a last stand against the invading armies of August 1914. The secular republican government was forced to accept the services of Catholic generals, and the Catholic hierarchy was forced to place moral authority at the service of the government. Among the great stories of reconciliation and continuing suspicion (sometimes with mutual recrimination), none more clearly embodies the reality of the détente than positive interaction of the key representatives of religious teaching—priests—and the key representatives of government education—schoolteachers—in the trenches of the Western Front.*

Back in 1890, French clergy and people were not at all primed for a diplomatically dramatic move by Pope Leo XIII. But Leo wanted the French church reconciled to the government and deputed the archbishop of Algiers, Cardinal Charles Lavigerie, a strong administrator and religious order

Lavigerie

Le Cardinal Lavigerie promoteur de la République catholique chez le Pape

21ᵉ ANNÉE. — N° 1.037

FRANCE : 15 CENTIMES

Paris 22 février 1891.

22 Février 1891.

BUREAUX
5, cité Bergère, 5
PARIS

ABONNEMENTS
FRANCE
UN AN......... 8 fr.
SIX MOIS...... 4
TROIS MOIS.... 2
15 c. le numéro

PARAIT LE DIMANCHE
—
ADRESSER
Lettres et Mandats à E. J. MADRE
Directeur-Gérant

BUREAUX
5, cité Bergère, 5
PARIS

ABONNEMENTS
ÉTRANGER
UN AN........ 10 fr.
SIX MOIS...... 5
TROIS MOIS.... 2 50
20 c. le numéro.

PARAIT LE DIMANCHE
—
PUBLICITÉ
Les annonces sont reçues
aux bureaux du journal

LE GRELOT

Tout abonné à un journal Parisien peut recevoir gratuitement le GRELOT (Voir en tête de la 2ᵉ page)

L'EXTRA-LUCIDE DU VATICAN

Fig. 10. A cartoon of Cardinal Charles Lavigerie (fifth from left) in a group of social, political, and religious clients and the pope (center) as fortune-teller in the satirical magazine *Le Grelot*. Lavigerie tried to fulfill the hopes of Pope Leo XIII for a French church reconciled to the republican government when he formally proposed the idea at a formal dinner for French officers in his see city of Algiers. The agents of reconciliation eventually won the day. (Roger-Viollet/ Getty Images)

founder, to kick off the campaign (called the *Ralliement)* to accomplish this. Lavigerie chose as his moment a formal dinner, heavily attended by regional French military leaders. Standing to deliver a toast, he declared to an unresponsive, even stunned audience: "When the will of a people is clearly affirmed, and the form of government is no way contrary—as Leo XIII recently put it—to the principles that vivify Christian and civilized nations; and when support without afterthought of this government is necessary to rescue the country from the abysses that threaten it, the time comes to declare the contest over and put an end to our discussions and sacrifice all that conscience and honor permit." At least a third of the French bishops were hostile to this subsequently notorious "Toast of Algiers." For their part, the anticlerical politicians who had come to dominate the government of the Third Republic were highly suspicious of anything coming from Rome.

The political opposition to the church, famously championed in the 1870s by Léon Gambetta, was managed from 1880 on by the considerably calmer and perhaps more serious heads of government. First as minister of education, and later as premier, Jules Ferry wanted a clean republican sweep of education at a time when about half the school children were taught by sisters, brothers, and priests. Kantian philosophy and the social science of Auguste Comte were his intellectual foundations, but his civilized philosophical style had been unsettled by Pius IX's condemnation of contemporary freethinking and democracy in the "Syllabus of Errors." Prodded by former Premier Jules Simon, Ferry promoted legislation to eliminate religious teachers from higher education, using decades-old legal precedents that regulated the public functioning and teaching rights of religious congregations. Subsequently he worked to remove religious teaching and teachers from secondary and primary education. However, in strongly supporting the expansion of the French colonial empire, he assumed that Catholic missionaries and teachers could serve as agents of civilization. Limited compromise may have been possible, but extremists in both church and government saw plots and chicanery everywhere among the opposition. In particular, the bribery at the center of French government involvement in the building of the Panama Canal contributed to chronic public suspicion of hidden forces at work in the government.

Tensions were augmented one hundredfold by a chance occurrence of minor espionage in the French army, which was twisted and turned into a national drama simply known as *L'Affaire*—the Dreyfus Affair. A loyal, financially well-off officer, Captain Alfred Dreyfus, Alsatian and Jewish, was accused of passing classified information to the German army. Evidence was a

memorandum, apparently in Dreyfus's handwriting, "found" in a wastebas-
ket. Although an army court found him guilty, suspicions that he had been
framed remained. Some in the government believed that the army administration, a favored venue for aristocratic Catholic families, was covering up evidence. Within the army itself, one leading investigator, Colonel Georges
Picquart, discovered that secret information was still being passed to Germany
and that the likely culprit was a Major Walsin Esterhazy, but Picquart was
silenced and assigned overseas. There were trials and retrials, in the course of
which Dreyfus was sent to Devil's Island, brought back, and granted an
amnesty that did not fully settle the question of his guilt or innocence.

Legal confusion in the Dreyfus Affair caused men and women to take impassioned stands on the basis of their political and religious orientations: Catholics
favored the army and at the same time suspected government republicans of
Masonic or Jewish intrigue. In this they were primed by the anti-Semitic writings of small-time journalist Edouard Drumont, who revived the old cliché
about a broad Jewish political and financial conspiracy. (Several French officials
indicted in the Panama Canal scandal were Jewish.) Republicans favored Dreyfus and suspected the army, the conservative minority in government, and above
all Catholic hierarchical intrigue. Rare, indeed, were independent thinkers of
the temper of Charles de Gaulle's father, who was politically a constitutional
monarchist, religiously a pious Catholic professor in a Jesuit secondary school,
and pro-Dreyfus! It was twelve years, from 1894 to 1906, before Dreyfus was
completely exonerated and restored to his rank in the army.

The high antagonism politics of the secular revolutionary camp and the
religious monarchist camp marked the decades on either side of 1900. There
were more wildly varying skirmishes between church and state in these
twenty years than in any other epoch since the Revolution. Defensive clerical
anger against the de-Catholicizing of France, fueled by the Dreyfus Affair,
reactivated the Catholic verbal and social attacks on the Republic. Some priests
and bishops insisted that opposition to a government perverted by non-Catholics
was a Catholic duty. Across the years of the Dreyfus Affair, self-consciously
Catholic individuals and organizations generated more than their fair share of
hateful words, scurrilous articles, and vicious condemnations. Several religious congregations, the Assumptionists in particular (a latter day variant of
Martin Luther's old order, the Augustinians), were notorious for their antagonism to the republican government, the Freemasons, and the Jews. The
Assumptionist-run Catholic daily *La Croix* not only published inflammatory
articles, but it accompanied them by cartoons caricaturing Jews in particular.

As Dreyfus and his republican supporters were being vindicated, leading government officials fought back against the church by removing the last legal supports for any Catholic activity in the schools. A new government of radical republicans was elected in 1899, headed by René Waldeck-Rousseau and animated by an ex-seminarian and anticlerical, Émile Combes. Waldeck-Rousseau was a genuine politician who, in response to the Dreyfus scandal, wanted radical republican control of conservative army officers and of troublesome religious congregations. Inasmuch as the old Napoleonic Concordat favored the diocesan church organization and said very little about the rights and duties of religious orders, and inasmuch as the Ferry laws had given a completely secular cast to French education, he had useful legal precedents to work from. Accordingly, he developed a set of strict limits to the teaching and publishing of the priests, brothers, and sisters. Assumptionists and Jesuits were primary targets because of Assumptionist violence and Jesuit influence. The fundamental explanation for new controls was simple: the state has the right to regulate all aspects of public life and so the behavior of all groups and institutions in the country. Religious groups and institutions, therefore, should be subject to state regulations and limits. Assurances were given to the pope that the new, apparently restrictive laws would be applied with the utmost liberality, but, in fact, French bishops who condemned or severely criticized the government were fined and reprimanded. It came as no surprise that the campaigns for national and local elections turned into heated debates between the most ideologically tuned Catholics and republicans.

When the ever-earnest Émile Combes took over from Waldeck-Rousseau, he wanted more than control of the congregations and more than their simple disenfranchisement in education; he wanted them disbanded. This was an extreme position to take at the beginning of the century, with the Revolution long gone and the population at least nominally Catholic. Still, the government, as manipulated by Combes and his allies, managed to expel religious teachers and monks, whole monasteries and convents at a time in fact. Perhaps the most infamous event was the seizure of the great Carthusian monastery in the mountains beyond Grenoble. Loyal Catholics had gathered all along the roads into the mountains, torches flaming in the night, to witness the arrival of the police at three in the morning. Officials hacked their way through the entrance to arrest the monks at their night office. One would say that the days of the Terror, or of the post-Reformation wars of religion, had returned—although this time the monks were not harmed. This was an application of the Law against the Congregations of 1901, and whatever loopholes were left at that time, they were complemented by further legislation in 1904. From all parts of France, religious groups left for other European countries and America, making a major contribution to Catholic education in those areas. This departure was in complement to the continuing apostolate of French foreign missionaries, whether members of the teaching congregations or other purely missionary groups.

Combes was an early-twentieth-century version of the destructive ex-priests of the Revolution (though he was kept short of ordination as a young man) in that his antireligious mission was a mutated form of his earlier religious mission. Combes's final efforts went toward the repudiation of the Concordat and the final separation of church and state. Unlike the Law against the Congregations, the projected repeal of the Concordat was not in itself anti-Catholic or antireligious. Catholic voices could be heard in favor of this separation, which would give the church complete independence from the state. Legislators, even some authentic radical Republicans were growing weary of the anticlerical, Combesian religion obsession and of the church-state discussions in the Assembly. But in 1905, by a vote of 341 to 233, more than two hundred years after the Napoleonic Concordat with the Catholic Church, the French government legally declared the separation of church and state.

For generations, the Concordat had really been what the radical politician Georges Clemenceau called a "discordat," an especially apt label for the period after the death of Pope Leo XIII in 1903. Leo's successor, Pius X, refused all negotiations with the French government, whether in matters of education and the Law against the Congregations, or in matters of church-state relations and the Law of Separation of Church and State. In fact, Pius was also disturbed by the spirit of research and intellectual freedom then developing in the French church. In the domain of scripture studies, Marie-Joseph Lagrange, a Dominican father, worked out a program of Old Testament research based solely on authentic archeological and historical evidence, thereby eliminating some of the standard scriptural "proofs" for theological teachings. And Father Alfred Loisy, a specialist in Semitic languages like Renan before him, worked to purify the formulations of church doctrines and teachings on the basis of this new historical evidence. Papal antagonism to Loisy in particular was then extended to historically rigorous and theologically liberal research and teaching, all of it together labeled "modernism." The end result was an official papal condemnation of a collective theological effort that was in the main French.

Conservative Catholicism was also abetted by a new type of political organization, called the *Action française*. The founder of the movement, Charles

Maurras, was not a practicing Catholic believer, but he promoted the tradition in the service of his idiosyncratic royalist nationalism and his own ideal of French cultural purity. Antirepublicans of every stripe supported the *Action française,* including a significant number of loyal Catholics. But the political goals and rhetoric of the movement were too limited to be paired with the broad religious conservatism that otherwise would have appealed to the pope. A condemnation was planned by Pius X, but he deferred its publication, as did his successor, Benedict XV. By the time Pius XI decided to publicly condemn this abuse of Catholicism in the service of French nationalism, Catholic members could more easily renounce, it would appear, their membership in the movement. The *Action française* was not the only neonationalism that found a use for French Catholicism. There had been a brief shining moment in 1889 when General Georges Boulanger's supporters hoped for a return to the regime security of Napoleon's days. But after his flight from politics (and suicide at the grave of his lover), conservative nationalists honestly made do with the Republic, though with an emphasis on regional origins. Loyalty to the government had to be tailored to loyalty to the land.

Politically marginalized, Catholic social activity found expression in the charitable works and organizations geared to the needs of youth and workers. Here also, Catholic activists of a theologically liberal, more socialist style would be seriously scrutinized. Marc Sangnier, in particular, and his movement and publication, *Le Sillon,* was the subject of Roman inquest and final condemnation. Although Sangnier was a man of the people, his promotion of Catholic action and popular education led to amorphous and dubious projects that did not fit the restrained and orderly domestic mission of French Catholicism, at least as it was envisioned by the pope. Rome and some of the French hierarchy feared that Marxist socialism, rather than Christianity, might rule the hearts of the Catholic social actionists. Even the openness of the great socialist leader of the turn of the century, Jean Jaurès, was no consolation.

Helpful mediation certainly did not come from the high profile converts to Catholicism. Joris-Karl Huysmans, Paul Claudel, Léon Bloy, and Jacques and Raïssa Maritain were authors and intellectuals who eventually gained an international audience. But it was the creativity of their individual experiences of Catholicism that gained attention, and in that creativity there was little compromise with the surrounding culture, republican or otherwise. In fact, outstanding spiritual voices spoke for a world apart: Thérèse of Lisieux and Dom Chautard from the cloister, and Charles de Foucauld from his hermitage in the North African desert. The one embodiment of opposites in all of this was the poet and Latin Quarter intellectual, Charles Péguy, socialist and Catholic,

Drefusard and pilgrimage promoter. Yet all of these men and women were influential witnesses to the wisdom and energy of the Catholic tradition and so prepared the way for later cultural rapprochements.

Beginning at the turn of the century and across the years, Émile Mâle, religious art historian and eventually professor at the Sorbonne, was clarifying the original meaning of medieval French art and architecture and its importance in French history. In the 1880s and 1890s, as revivals of medieval philosophy were being attempted, and in the first decades of the twentieth century when the noted converts and spiritual voices of French Catholicism were making themselves heard, Mâle was leading French secularists as well as religious believers to a new appreciation of medieval culture as Catholic and French. Chapter 7 reveals how Mâle embodied in himself, perhaps more than the others, the reconciliation of Catholicism and a specifically national identity. As a young scholar at the École Normale, he chose as his doctoral thesis the art of the great thirteenth-century cathedrals. The École, France's most prestigious institute of higher learning, had been dutifully offering a secular education perfectly compatible with the most rigorous republicanism for decades. Mâle had absorbed the school's emphasis on humanistic, independent learning, but he came to believe that the religious Middle Ages were a high point in the development of such learning, a belief he supported by exacting research and the publication of four powerful syntheses of religious art history.

So the détente desired by Pope Leo XIII, and the more clairvoyant of the national-level politicians who opposed the antichurch legislation, finally came to be. If it was not the orderly, clear political détente they had hoped for, it was a personal and social détente in the trenches of World War I, and it was a cultural détente promoted eventually in universities and schools across the nation.

Chapter Six

THE LIMITS OF PERSONAL RECONCILIATION: *Priests and* Instituteurs *in World War I*

In 1914 the president of France, Raymond Poincaré, introduced the expression *union sacrée* to label and encourage the natural alliance of French peoples threatened by the invading German armies.[1] But no one idealized the union more than the novelist and nationalist politician Maurice Barrès. In *Les Diverses Familles spirituelles de la France,* he argued that Catholics, Protestants, Jews, socialists, and traditionalists came together in a "profound unanimity" with the beginning of World War I: "We have seen, for the benefit of the public good, all the moral forces enter the campaign, whether born in religion, philosophy, or education. All show themselves to be excellent for nourishing the soul. And this army, filled with maddening contradictions, has shown itself to the Germans united and striking in its spiritual beauty."[2] Barrès in his nationalism was characterized by Eugen Weber as "republican, traditionalistic, respectful of the established order even when he disapproved of it," with his writings an echo of the nationalism of the 1880s when General Georges Boulanger was successfully touting his combination of revolutionary politics and aristocratic order. This was not the nationalism of Charles Maurras and the *Action française,* damned by Weber as "rebellious nationalism, antirepublican, whose assertive traditionalism rejected a whole century of French tradition, revolutionary because royalist, and chauvinistic by reaction against the foreign elements that it felt were swamping French life and culture."[3] As his prime examples of reconciliation, Barrès offered the priest and the *instituteur* (schoolteacher). Each would say, "Could I have been mistaken each time

that I had misgivings about those who failed to appreciate me?" Barrès saw
the flaming candles and the eager crowds in the churches. And he saw the
socialists, once pacifist in orientation (and well represented among the *instituteurs*), enlist in the service of France. Now his socialists would say, "All the
prophets who want to lift their hands to heaven during the battle: we are
ready to support their arms." At the end of the book, Barrès quoted an army
captain, a "freethinker and freemason" who wanted to keep faith with a slain
priest and fellow officer: "The death of Millon pains me greatly. If I had fallen
first, he would have said a Mass for me. I am not a believer, but one never
knows! If the soul is immortal, Millon will be happy that I am thinking of
him. Do you want us to go and ask the priest for a service in his memory?"
Called on to speak at the end of the service for his priest friend, the captain
said, "the France of tomorrow needs the close collaboration of the priest, the
[army] officer, and the teacher."[4] These are the last words of the book. Take
out the ideologically ambivalent figure of the officer and one finds a call for
reconciliation, based on war experience, of the priest and the *instituteur*.

Both priests and *instituteurs* were thoroughly rooted in national life, and
both purported to educate the population to a fuller personal life. Yet the
"party line" of French and international Catholicism and that of the French
national education system were set up in mutual antagonism, based on
uncompromisingly sacred and secular orientations.[5] To be sure, neither priests
nor teachers were a solid bloc before the war: not all priests were antagonistic
to the government, and far from all of the teachers were anticlerical (in fact, a
third of them considered themselves Catholic). Old differences were put aside
at the beginning of the war. Georges Clemenceau wrote in the anticlerical
publication *Homme libre* and was happily quoted in the Catholic daily *La
Croix:* "Germans! Send your parliamentarians. They will see our most timid
socialists claim their proper place in combat. . . . Monks are there, too. Yes,
the monks we have chased away, as they themselves say, not without exaggeration."[6] Yet in the long run, according to Jean-Jacques Becker, doyen of
World War I research in France, "If the French were in agreement in facing
what they considered to be aggression, if they agreed to limit the violence of
their former antagonisms, no one . . . had the intention of abandoning his
deep convictions for the sake of those others."[7] Jacques Fontana, studying
specifically religious and secular orientations, sees both antagonism and reconciliation. On one hand, he describes the growth of an increasingly bitter
strain of anticlericalism; on the other, he claims that "in the main there was
much more respect for the convictions of the other person."[8]

The *union sacrée* was really, then, a pragmatic, partial, and evolving unity, which, according to Becker, lost its power as a "national sentiment" (that is, a continuing feeling of unity and belonging) to the extent that the old "political ideologies" (a specialized set of social, cultural, and political assumptions about the homeland) reemerged.[9] Scholars who participated in the 1989 conference on French nationalism at Cambridge University promoted this distinction between sentiment and ideologies. They agreed that sentiment "was compatible with a wide range of social, political and intellectual positions, from royalist to socialist." Ideological nationalists, they claimed, "promoted the values and interests of the nation to a position of primacy, subordinating or even excluding from consideration other loyalties or beliefs."[10] The evidence suggests that national sentiment dominated initially because the pure ideologists were in the minority. When Becker studied the nationalist enthusiasms of youth, writers, the bourgeoisie, the church, and the army, he found that youth were by and large uninterested, writers were utterly diverse, the middle class valued political stability as the key to economic stability and progress, the clergy often took their cues from rightist republicanism, and the soldiers, hardened by the crushing experience of war, felt little more than the basic components of national sentiment.[11] By studying the trench newspapers, Stéphane Audouin-Rouzeau isolated these basic components as "a sense of defending the land and the community, hostility towards the enemy, the concept of duty, and confidence in victory,"[12] all of which could be found across the ideological spectrum.

Here, then, is one example, a primary example according to Barrès, of reconciliation: a profile of priests and *instituteurs* together, with attention to common sentiment and diverse ideologies: first a look at the expressed national sentiment and religious ideology of the priests, using the clergy review *Prêtre aux armées* and a selection of commemorative biographies collected at the Bibliothèque de documentation internationale et contemporaine,[13] then a look at the expressed national sentiment and religious ideology of the teachers, using the periodical *La Revue pédagogique* and a small selection of teachers' memoirs.[14]

Priest Combatants

According to Jacques Fontana, more than 32,500 members of the clergy were mobilized for the war effort.[15] This count presumably includes all seminarians who were of combat age, who will figure in this study to the extent that their experiences clarify the general profile. The exact percentage of priests who were true combatants is not known; those ordained before the 1905 Law of Separation of Church and State were allowed to serve as stretcher-bearers and medics. Joseph Brugerette thinks that about 12,000 were on the front with guns in their hands, with an equal number serving as stretcher-bearers and medics.[16] But a sampling of *La Preuve du sang: Livre d'or du clergé et des congréga-tions* would indicate that this percentage of gun-toting priests is exaggerated.[17] In any case, the majority did provide priestly services to their fellow soldiers, whatever military function they fulfilled. Only a tiny minority were officially appointed chaplains. All priests, apart from the official chaplains, were in a compromising situation. Catholic Church law forbade them to "shed blood," hence, to make war.[18]

During and after the war, priests received high praise for capturing enemy positions, bombing German-held cities and towns, and encouraging soldiers to the attack. In his introduction to *La Preuve du sang,* Henry Bordeaux summa-rizes the exploits of the priest combatants that are presented in brief encyclope-dic entries across the two volumes. The abbés Amiot of Angers and Mirabail of the Collège de Saint-Caprais figure among Bordeaux's striking examples. Amiot had "forced his way across the Aisne under enemy fire and penetrated into the village of Balhan, where he played a large part in the capture of the whole garrison." Mirabail was an aviator who "shot down Fokkers [and] bombed Metz-les-Sablons and Karlsruhe. When he was returning from this last exposure [to danger] . . . engine trouble forced him to land, and he had the presence of mind, before his descent, to jettison his machine gun and destroy his card and papers."[19] These were certainly warrior priests: one led the attack, and the other dropped bombs. Although *La Preuve du sang* is an invaluable source of fundamental information about the types of priests in military service, and the specifically military activities that gained them recognition in the army, we need to go beyond it to understand better how the priests combined national sentiment and religious ideology—how they interpreted their role in the *union sacrée*—by turning to publications by and about these priests and examining side by side expressions of national sentiment and religious ideology.

Prêtre aux armées

The review *Prêtre aux armées,* one of several published for priests in the armed services, first appeared in February 1915. In subsequent months (and years), clerical readers received a wide range of spiritual direction and practical advice. A citation from a letter about Joan of Arc encouraged priest soldiers to heroism: "The voice of your conscience, after you have examined before God where your duty lies, pushes you like Joan of Arc and says to you, *Son of God, go forth!* Because the church suspends, if not the censure, at least the effects of censure, and permits you to follow the call of the fatherland. Son of France, go! Go and show that the minister of God and of peace knows how to be a hero and martyr."[20] A young priest of Kremlin-Bicêtre, who perished leading his men in a charge, wrote in his last letter, "I believe that with the help of God I will be strong enough to lead my men well, and so arrange their lives with the sovereign power as to give them, if they fall, a better life."[21] But the journal's foremost concern was the spiritual life of the priest, including such paradoxical juxtapositions of values as childlikeness in the acceptance of death ("as a little child ought to accept everything smilingly from his beloved father") and sacrifice of one's youthful body as a priestly sacrifice.[22]

Discussions of pure sacrifice and spiritual growth did not mask the huge spiritual risk inherent in the chaos of war. Priests sometimes set a bad example: "A soldier from my region remarked that several priests took care to avoid their duty and to leave it to others."[23] Always lurking in the background was the problem of shedding the blood of others. A clarification was necessary: "His Eminence Cardinal Sevin, in the well-known consultation granted *Prêtre aux armées,* has responded that because of the seriousness of the defense situation and because of superior motives, the priest can obey . . . but *he cannot take the initiative in offering himself for the task of taking life.*"[24] It is one thing to be forced to tote guns, another to offer oneself to the task. Nevertheless, the priest could still be a moral watchdog. One priest corporal, decrying obscenities in soldiers' songs, had written "The Song on the Front" with a promise to provide more lyrics free of scurrility.[25] Here the priest soldier had opportunities that the chaplains did not have: the soldiers knew that the priest soldiers "share[d] their life."[26]

The Biographies

During and after the war, biographies of priests proliferated, sometimes written as hagiographies, sometimes with substantial quotes from war letters. Peering through the occasional cloud of the hagiographer's incense, readers can still see the honest self-expression of the soldier priest.

For example, a middle-aged Franciscan, Father Edouard de Massat, expressed simple patriotism and belief in the saving power of the priesthood.

De Massat had been in Canada for ten years following his expulsion from France. He was a perfect example of Clemenceau's monks, who returned "after we chased them away." Fifty-four years old when he came back to fight, de Massat went racing into battle beside the soldiers, carrying the sacred host and wearing his habit. There is a photo in the de Massat biography with a quote from one of his letters: "Cross in hand, I made the attack with my Zouaves." The photo has a strange posed look about it, however. Explaining his motivation to his sister, de Massat wrote, "I have made the sacrifice of my life to God for my dear and beloved country." When receiving the Croix de guerre, he concluded his remarks with "and long live France the immortal." He was there to use his sacramental powers to bring God to his fellows, and it was clear that he did it for the sake of France: "During this time, I was just about everywhere to give absolution and care to those who were falling around me. My habit, my haversack, everything up to my crucifix were red with blood. . . . During the attack, I carried the sacred host with me, and it is to the presence of God that I attribute our success, which cost us relatively few losses." He was even able to make the language of violence his own. Describing a church service, de Massat concluded, "Our last words and our farewell were, 'We will have our revenge.'"[27]

Seminarians without sacramental powers seemed more anxious about their vocation and less secure about what they could offer the fatherland. Jean Audouin, a major seminarian and combatant, saw his sacrifice as a Mass. Writing to his family, he begged them to "pray for our poor France. She is not lost, but will make up for her sins by much bloodshed. . . . I will have fulfilled my role as victim and priest; I will have followed my mentor. Let us abandon ourselves to the will of God."[28] The nineteen-year-old seminarian Manuel Baillet of the Cordeliers seemed a figure of goodness, simple piety, and sensitivity. He thought about family and friends while in the field. But there is little or nothing about France in the published selections from his letters, preoccupied as he was with his own vocation: "The first shells that reach me could also end my vocation by a canonical irregularity, or even by death, which is always possible." Surrounded by temptations, he was worried about genuinely losing his vocation.[29]

But some priests could integrate their apostolate with combat. Writing fifty years later, Father Grivelet remembered that he took his fighting techniques seriously: "I draw my saber remembering my fencing lessons, and pull out my revolver. Suddenly, a few hundred meters from us, we see a sortie of I do not know how many enemy soldiers in columns of four, coming toward

Fig. 11.   A Mass celebrated for French soldiers near the front in World War I. The majority of priests of military age fought alongside anticlericals and the religiously indifferent. Men of opposed ideological orientations came to accept their differences. (Roger-Viollet/Getty Images)

us." Wounded in the arms and legs by bullets and shrapnel, he was resting at a medical station when he heard someone call out for a priest. He then gave the man absolution with his good arm—priestly ministry counted above all. Naturally, he attributed a subsequent narrow escape from the destruction of his medical station to divine providence.[30]

Father Joseph Arlet also went about his soldiering earnestly. His bishop describes approvingly how Arlet died, still firing his revolver: "Suddenly, there he was, face to face with the enemy. Directed to surrender, he responded by pistol shots. Then grenades and other explosives were thrown at his feet. From this whirlwind of destruction he was carried off to eternity." Arlet, feeling no hesitation in associating *le bon Dieu* with bloodshed, had already said, "our good God wants us to win out over these unjust aggressors, and to inflict on them the most bloody defeats." Wanting to be useful to France and the church, he was buoyed up by the opportunity to bring spiritual consolation to the soldiers.[31]

One killed people, of course, in defending France. Marie-Bernard Lavergue, well into his major seminary years, was proud to be a soldier. He was both a combatant and a cleric. To his mother he wrote that he was happy to bear arms and knew how to use them against the Germans. "You should know that I 'brought down' three Prussians. That will be three who will not fire on us again." Not bloodthirstiness—on the contrary, this was understood as a just war ethic. At any rate, it would seem that Lavergue envisioned his own sacrificial death more than the death of others: "To die for the fatherland . . . is an enviable fate for those who dream of the priesthood, because in the sacrifice of one's life, offered in youth for a good cause, there are many elements of priestly immolation." He understood that redemption could occur in the midst of the fighting. "A brutish life, then? No. A tough life, if you will, in its context; a beautiful life, in sum, because it is a life of total abandonment, of perfect submission to the will of God, sole master of tomorrow." He believed that in the midst of chaos of reason, sense, and imagination, a mysterious personal transformation was taking place. "If this is accomplished, what else matters?"[32]

The Jesuit priest Pierre Durouchoux was a genuine soldier who suffered from being such. A veteran and officer, he was likely to be in the thick of the fighting, which was deeply disturbing to him: "Physical suffering is nothing; the moral suffering of the priest, who is forced to fight and to strike his neighbor, even though the enemy of his country, is frightful. The victory is costly. But let us pray that the Virgin of the Rosary will at length grant it to us." His mission, as he described it to his mother, was religious and national: "The war has brought God out of the churches to receive public and national worship! Dear *Maman,* I am happy and proud to be associated with this religious renewal of our French men, and, in my own small way, to be an agent of it."[33]

The Jesuit novice René de la Perraudière, though fascinated by military progress, was not at home—therefore effective—with the ordinary soldiers. And he was not sure whether his motivation came from social pride or the reasonable certainty that he would simply have more influence on his own social level, that is, among the officers. He was less guarded about his expression of French patriotism and his specifically French spiritual ministry: "I will help to save the world and France by working actively, in taking to heart more my obligations as a sergeant." In his dark moments, he was still able to say that he was delighted to defend the fatherland. And he seemed positively excited about an important military advance: "How I would love to be with the French who enter Metz, and this is something I can perhaps hope for now." A slight wound evokes the most patriotic sentiments: "Yesterday a shell falling nearby caused some drops of my blood to be shed for France by scraping my cheek with stone fragments."[34] A contrast to the social discomforts of de la Perraudière was the experience of André de la Barre de Carroy, a priest from an aristocratic family with generations in the military, who complained that his appointment as army chaplain isolated him from his men.[35]

In some stories, fighting and killing were muffled to mere background noise. Take the biography of Father Jean-Louis Dabo, *Une Fleur de saint abandon*. The title suggests a book to edify the pious. Even though Dabo commanded the artillery, there is no reference to specific battles: "I succeeded [my captain] as commander of the battery, which involves a sizable fight, above all in the fracas that we are passing through now."[36] Examples of profound Christian spirituality, by contrast, abounded. For Father Pierre Babouard, the death of soldiers for France was an introduction to the mystery of Christ's death for the world: "That was a frightful death: the skull shattered, the bones crushed; machine-gun bullets plowing into the chest, exposing the intestines, carving up the limbs with horrible wounds. But was the death of Christ more gentle? His head also was torn, his limbs pierced; his poor lacerated body appeared to onlookers and executioners as one great wound."[37] Perhaps the happy balance of fighting and ministry was best articulated by Father Georges Sevin. Clear that religious vocation, or any role assigned by Providence, has to do with the salvation of France, he affirmed that "our daily tasks . . . cannot keep our thoughts from turning constantly toward France, our own people and loved ones. . . . Each one of us has a place marked out by Providence to contribute to *the salvation of France* during this horrible war." In this same letter to his mother, Sevin described the military camps at Salonika, devastating as they were for the moral well-being of numerous priests. His criticism of Greece and the allies indicates his worldly and military preoccupations: "It seems to me and everyone else that we have let ourselves be *betrayed by Greece* too long." As far as he was concerned, the Allies had been betrayed by a recalcitrant Greece, and those officials resisting the Allies should be overthrown.[38]

There is no indication thus far in the religious historiography of World War I that priests from different religious orders and congregations varied among themselves in their basic reaction to the war. Naturally, median age of members, social background, and education would have bearing on the extent to which a priest or seminarian was "prepared" for military life. The Jesuits, because of the long years of seminary training, were more likely to have young men primed for apostolate and action—even as soldiers.[39] In fact, of all the personalities examined, it was a Jesuit, the novice Lucien Chabord, who, by his apostolic concern and his fighting spirit, seemed to embody to the fullest extent both minister of religion (though not yet a priest) and soldier. Chabord combined the intense devotion of the seminarian and novice with the responsibility and patriotism of an officer: "Our riflemen were happy with the results . . . with regrets, however, that they were not able to redden their bayonets! You may find this to be an awful detail, but war, as a German ambassador has been saying these days, 'is not five-o'clock tea.'" But he was a devotional warrior: "We were attacking at noon, and before that there was intense artillery and infantry fire. . . . I was reading *The Imitation of Christ* with a priest sergeant major when I heard myself called. 'Chabord!' 'Yes, Captain.' 'Advance with your section.'"[40]

Unlike some of his clerical colleagues, Chabord had a theology of the guiltless enemy soldier: "That we have come so to deal with one another, O God, have pity on us! O Jesus, God of peace, you who have shed your blood for all men, grant, I beseech you, that people may offer a kiss of peace to one another and that you might be glorified by all the earth." Like many of his clerical colleagues, the foundation of his patriotism was the home territory—in his case, the Savoy. "Here I am," he wrote to his confreres in the novitiate, "in my dear Savoy, with my parents whom I so often thought I would never see again, at the base of mountains that I am now trying to hold within myself, so that I can carry their image with me more surely onto tomorrow's battlefields."[41]

Reflecting on a freethinker (an *instituteur,* perhaps?) he met, Chabord was a combination of understanding and argument. The man was not aware of reality. On one hand, the illusion of future material happiness presented real solutions to life's problems; on the other hand, he sometimes appeared to experience "the profound melancholy of a soul that ignores what it is." At least the man resisted pseudo-solutions to life's problems "because of that unrest known by [John Henry] Newman while he was searching for ten years, in prayer, study, and tears, the way of life." As a theologian, Chabord distinguished between dying for France and dying to attain heaven: "And the riflemen have responded to this call [to surrender] with their last rounds of fire. They died, hit standing up, crying, 'Vive la France!' Is that not beautiful? And yet, *illi ut corruptibilem coronam accipiant, nos autem*" [1 Cor. 9:25].[42]

Problems of ministry and secular ideology were also topics of reflection for the Jesuit seminarian Jean Nourisson. Nourisson pointed to the lack of spiritual transformation, observing that the men were brave at the front but nothing special when they were brought back—swearing, threatening one another:

"Will this be the renewal of France by the young? It could be something great, but in any case, we have much work to do if we want this harvest to ripen." His patriotism was also a theologically conscious act, in the good company of Thomas Aquinas: "Is it in no way permitted to cast a look at the great sorrow of the land of France? It appears that Saint Thomas exalts the love of the fatherland." Religious ideals were in complete contrast to secular ideals: "The church is very much hierarchized, but its doctrine is complete humility, whereas the foundation of the egalitarian spirit is pride." The situation was doubly objectionable because the secular government attributed to itself messianic accomplishments. People were told that "humanity made progress and civilization finally came into the world, thanks to the Revolution and the Third Republic; and they believed it." These types criticized anything from past tradition; the secularists found nothing of value in the old Catholic tradition: "'Before.' That was the old regime, Catholicism, all the retrograde institutions. One should not 'return to the past,' to the time when there was no happiness for the worker, when Jules Ferry had not invented the public school, when one burned alive the founders of unions and those who did not bow before processions." Nourisson criticized also the socialist priests. Prayer, mortification, gospel living were all more important than social action of the clergy: "Do you not think that there has been a debasing of priestly consciousness among the 'socialist' clergy?"[43]

Clergy could not forget the damage done by secularism. A biography of the Jesuit intellectual Paul Doncoeur includes his report on ministry to a deserter. The young soldier had never known his mother, was beaten by his father, and had never been raised in any religion. Doncoeur had less than an hour to instruct the lad but did so in such a way as to get him to confess and to receive Communion. The soldier embraced Doncoeur before the brief Mass and Communion; taken out of the church, he embraced the priest a second time and was shot. "I felt types of anger rise within me that I had never experienced before in my life." Doncoeur cited "those who, having refused this little French lad any kind of religion, forbade him any kind of discipline, faith, and hope.... On what heroic course would he have been placed, if such young men had not been willfully thrown headlong into anarchy." Here secular education was seen as archly destructive.[44]

Father Pierre Lelièvre was a chaplain, not a combatant, but his wartime witness, *Le Fléau de Dieu*,[45] was commended as "the most solid, the most sincere of the war books by ecclesiastics" by Jean Norton Cru in his *Témoins*, a massive catalog and analysis of war writings.[46] Lelièvre gave special attention to the military action in and about the city of Reims. In his interpretation of the cannonading of the cathedral (where the church crowned the kings of France), Lelièvre gave voice to the French Catholic commonplace that the cathedral was an incarnation of France: "The baptism of Clovis by Saint Remi [took place here] after [the battle of] Tolbiac. The cathedral was [also] where Charles VII was crowned under the victorious standard of Joan, the Maid [of Orléans]. Two unforgettable dates in the history of a France that stubbornly wants to forget in these latter times all of our formal history. Without the victory of Clovis over the Germans, the Île-de-France would not have become the gentle cradle of our race; and without Clotilde and Remi, the church would not have leaned over this cradle, so like a region of violence. Without Joan the Maid finally, what would have become of French unity, saved at that time by a daughter of the people, incarnating the fatherland and inclining her king before God." Of course, the worshippers inside counted the most; the cathedral served them by giving them a liturgy to live by; and this liturgy animated their souls: "Yes, this people once had a soul, and they lived out of the eternal." The liturgy was of a piece with the art and architecture; the symbolism, naturally, pointed beyond itself to the mystical life: "How much I would like to linger . . . to study the marvels and the symbolism of each detail and of the whole: the figures of the apostles and those of the Virtues around the Virgin! How much I would like to reexamine my education and my religious faith, so positivistic and dry in comparison to the faith so mystical and loving of those former ages."[47]

When the cathedral was shelled, people cursed the barbarity that ended in the cannonading of one of the masterpieces of world architecture. Lelièvre, however, did not share their surprise: "I expected it at each hour, so logical and inevitable did the disaster appear to me." Such a breakdown in humanity was not to be blamed solely on Germany. As he lamented the war as a breakdown of civilization, he lamented his fellow citizens' loss of true identity: "Nothing is more French in France than our cathedrals, and the cathedral of Reims most of all. But we did not understand this. We had become so strange to our national religion and history that we needed a German Baedeker to explain the cathedral of Reims, the purest masterpiece of the French soul."[48] Even so, Lelièvre was more appreciative than many clerics of the simple, powerful human forces at work in the war; his humanity was broader than that of the self-interested priests who peddled religion with the enthusiasm and the attitudes of salespeople. He saw himself as part of a rich national and religious tradition as well as a flawed national and religious existence.

The testimonies by and about the priests are a mixture of national sentiment and religious ideology: fighting for France could be done within the context of a priestly vocation.[49] Saintly figures (such as Joan of Arc) and childlike virtue were the types to imitate. The priest could not choose to take life but could be forced to do so by war; even so, he must ever remain the moral guide. From God came life, and one should be willing to surrender it. But it would be perfectly appropriate to do so for the sake of France—to safeguard the integrity of French soil and to share in the blood sacrifice of fellow French men and women. De Massat believed that his sacramental powers were his greatest contribution to the war effort, but he still felt that he was ready to give his life for the nation. Seminarians Audouin and Baillet were more concerned about their potential for sacramental service than they were about France. Grivelet put his powers as a priest at the service of his fellow soldiers and his training as a soldier at the service of the nation. Arlet died firing his revolver, a French soldier with a Christian mission. Lavergue was happy to shoot Germans, believing that to put his own life on the line was in the spiritual tradition of self-abandonment. Durouchoux, however, was among the clearest in expressing his horror at killing the German, his "neighbor." The Jesuit novice de la Perraudière clearly saw his specific career as a soldier in the context of his mission to serve the world. Dabo was portrayed as a priest who just happened to be an artillery captain. Babouard was more graphic than most in likening the torn and crushed body of the soldier to the body of Christ. But Sevin clearly categorized the priest's Christian mission in the context of the war as a mission for the salvation of France. The Jesuit novice Chabord had worked out a more systematic set of reflections on his work as a soldier and as a religious leader. Killing in war was a job, so one could be pleased to do it well. Religious love of all people was paired with a special, personal love for family and homeland. One should love enemies and understand fellow citizens with truncated and secular values, especially if they are trying to find the truth. Another Jesuit novice, Nourisson, was clear that the love of the homeland was specifically provided for in Catholic theology by Aquinas. More than his fellow Jesuit Chabord, Nourisson was clear that secularism and socialism were still destructive. Jesuit clerics most clearly meditated their roles as mystics and moral guides, neatly distinguishing their double striving: for the Kingdom of God and for France. They, more than others, felt called on to refute the secularism that gripped France and blamed it all on the educational system. Although fighting for Christian civilization, one was fighting also to preserve a patrimony that went back to the coronation of

Clovis at Reims. According to Lelièvre, the cathedral was the expression of a soul that was both Christian and French.

Instituteur Combatants

The number of *instituteurs* called up is given by Becker as thirty thousand, roughly the same number as clergy. Becker also writes that "antiwar sentiments were apparently not shared by more than a small proportion of even the unionised teachers."[50] Most of the information we have about teachers during the war concerns the endeavors of those at home to promote the war effort.[51] However, a survey of retired *instituteurs* made from 1961 to 1963 by the historian Jacques Ozouf indicated that the antagonism of *instituteurs* to religion and clergy was balanced and somewhat moderated even before the war. For one thing, a substantial number of them were Catholic: 35 percent of them, as against 41 percent freethinkers (among the *institutrices,* the figure was 56 percent Catholic and 24 percent freethinkers).[52] The survey questionnaire provided for nuanced responses, with some Catholics indicating their belonging as cultural or pragmatic and some freethinkers believing their position quite compatible with religious tendencies. Numerous *instituteurs* had been married in the Catholic church. And those *instituteurs* whose fathers had also been *instituteurs* showed an even greater tendency to declare themselves Catholic.[53] The war experience did not figure much in the survey because the questions concerned teaching and personal experiences before 1915. Some who were already in the process of rejecting religious faith lost it completely because of the war. One former infantry sergeant, Marcel Comyn of the Nord, was completely changed in the matter of religion by the war. To the religion question he answered, "I would have replied before the war, 'practicing Catholic' or rather 'deist.' In the war, in the face of all that I saw, I lost my faith completely." A former lieutenant, Ferdinand Morineau of the Vendée, did not say whether the war had anything to do with a return to the faith. "I had lost the faith and ceased all religious practice. Having found it subsequently, I had a church marriage (1923) and the children baptized."[54]

The most striking feature of this survey of teachers is that the majority did not wish to turn their students against religion, nor even turn them into political anticlericals.[55] Yet some of them described personal or family experiences that turned them against priest and church, including ferocious clerical antagonism to the public school system and the fights over the removal of religious objects from the classrooms. Overall, however, a calm, resolute secularism predominated in the official expressions of the profession.

La Revue pédagogique

On the pages of the principal French journal for teachers, *La Revue péda-gogique*, there was no lack of confidence in the civilizing and unifying mission of the *instituteur*. In the early days of the war, the French army pushed across Alsace, assuming that a return to French control would fill the inhabitants with joy. One of the first things the soldier *instituteur* set himself to was the teaching of the French language: "The soldier was in peacetime an *instituteur*. They [the Alsatians] guessed it. But they understood above all that the honor of teaching them the elements of French belonged to those who, at the risk of their own lives, were the first to come to them." The essential part of this experience was the reintegration of Alsace into the French nation, most appreciated by some elder Alsatians who arrived to learn French with the kids: "It added to their emotion to see in the back of the room, on the benches that normally remained empty, men from the village, old men, ready to read and to listen. These were the ones who had attended the last French classes in March 1871 and who had returned to continue their interrupted studies." A lycée professor voiced the basic nationalism of the soldier teacher as he thought of his classroom and students back home: "Tell them that those on the lines are thinking of them." All that the soldiers endure—danger, suffering, and fatigue—they endure willingly, "and with a holy joy" they think of France and its future generations. They are grateful for both the educational system and their own teachers. A young teacher wrote to one of his former mentors: "Please believe that at those times [in the midst of battle] mental images of you often took form before me; they took on their freshness above all in the hours when one feels that one will have to leave all attachments behind." He hoped that the war would lead to a new moral sense. The joy of the cultivated life came to mind "when the letters arrived from a master under whose tutelage we had known the intense joys of intellectual development." He added that "this awakening of the memory of the best years brings with it some bitterness about the present circumstances," which, even so, did not totally interfere with his scholarly drives: after subscribing to the *Revue de métaphysique et de morale*, he could hardly wait to get his hands on it.[56]

Not only durability but the ability to endure underlined this profound statement of the *instituteur*'s mission, which was to guide both minds and hearts: "I believe that the simple public school must draw strength from its essential mission, as from a more clear and alive conscience, in these tragic circumstances. It must form wills, energetic souls capable of accepting the cruelest sufferings and making the ultimate sacrifices to produce the triumph of the great human causes."[57]

Some writers felt a need for the dramatic description of battle; in this they may have differed from the priests. The issues of *La Revue pédagogique* for the first half of 1915 had the war on almost every page—quite different from the last years of the war, when war features were few and far between. In 1915, the patriotic and pedagogical discourses of Paul Lapié and Ferdinand Buisson were highlighted in the midst of a variety of lesser testimonies. Lapié's "The *Instituteur* and the War" was an organized national education ideology with useful statistics: "On the whole, the primary school has supplied the army with more than thirty thousand men." Soldiers who had a reputation for pacifism were able to turn this very virtue into endurance in battle: "Even under enemy fire, they do not forget that they are *instituteurs*. And who knows but there might exist a connection between their military valor and their belonging to a profession that is doubtless pacific but that also requires self-denial." They attended to damaged schools, lent a hand to colleagues in the same region, and wrote to students. Some were aware that their wounds could give them a new authority: "A crutch is not unbecoming a schoolmaster."[58] This document, along with several others, was published in Paul Lapié's book of the same title. The final section contains a letter from an *instituteur* who was not at the front. "Without teaching them hatred of Germany or any other people, I sought to inculcate in them love of the fatherland. I exalted the wonders accomplished by our heroes of past ages. . . . [François] Bara, [Joseph] Viala had each his turn. I insisted that the French do not want war, but if anyone attacks them they will defend themselves with extraordinary bravery." This sort of teacher does not demonize; humanity remains; military virtue is exalted.[59]

According to Ferdinand Buisson, the secular schoolteachers and those with contrasting ideologies would be brought together by the war that is now fashioning them into "a single soul, that of France." "After the war, public and private schoolteachers, believers or freethinkers, of one party or another, will have only to remember and to allow their hearts to speak." The *union sacrée* will continue to exist everywhere in France, across institutions and occupations, and especially in the educational system. Duty unites all, including, among others, the priest and the *instituteur*, whether in the guise of the freethinker or the revolutionary: "The Jew and the Christian, the priest and the freethinker, the royalist [*camelot du roi*] and the revolutionary syndicalist have not only shed their blood together, they have made common cause in heroism, or simply in duty. Whatever happens, they will never again forget."[60]

Teacher combatants wounded at the front could be used as moral guides to great effect. Stories and symbols were suggested as part of a program for instruction in moral and military virtues. One teacher at home recounted the effect on the students of a soldier recovering from battle wounds. The man simply told his battle stories, and the teacher told the students that by honoring the soldiers they were honoring a wounded fatherland. "My audience was quiet and moved, and when the wounded man crossed the outside grill, a cry rose out of the children's breasts: hurrah for our wounded soldiers! *Vive la France!* The next morning I had no difficulty in getting responses to my moral lesson. They all wanted to answer at once. I no longer recognized my class." The list of stories contained a number of letters and accounts that had achieved some notoriety in the popular press (such as a letter from a peasant woman of Lorraine to her soldier husband, heroic sacrifice of an English officer for a wounded German, a brave little Breton). Brief suggestions were offered for lessons on the flag, conferences at The Hague, soldiers at the front, charity and kindness during time of duress. Defense of the fatherland colored the basic moral lessons; one of the principal themes of the discussion of the fatherland was still the *union sacrée*.[61]

The "letters from the front" printed in *La Revue pédagogique* underscored the role of the school in preparing one for duty. "My three years of schooling have above all given me a strong morale, so necessary today." One teacher observed, "When a *normalien* leaves the school, he is equipped for real life; he has had little experience, but he has been taught to think." Another confessed, "I will not hide from you that at the beginning the severe regimental discipline, so different from the very paternal discipline of the École normale, frightened me."[62]

The *union sacrée* of diverse forces was still an invigorating experience. An École normale professor praised the *union sacrée* as the negations of antagonisms due to politics, religious beliefs, family interests, professional interests, and differences in milieu. Less frequently than the clergy, teachers here refer to the France of ages past. Nobles, knights, and those later heroes of the Revolution provide the examples: "And above all do not forget to tell and repeat to your students that their papas, brothers, friends, and all the soldiers at the front are as brave as [Pierre du Terrail] Bayard, as determined and patient as

[Bertrand] Du Guesclin, as valiant as the paladins, and indeed worthy of our great forebears of the First Republic."⁶³

Extensive reflections on "the idea of sacrifice" were printed up from the papers turned in by candidates from the École normale at Fontenay-aux-Roses. These reflections clearly paralleled the identification, on the religious side, of soldiers' suffering with the suffering of Christ. The offering of oneself to God was paralleled by sacrifice of oneself for the fatherland, itself hyposta-sized as immortal: "The soldiers who have died for France have given of themselves so that the fatherland might live, that ideal Being in whose soul are incarnated their best collective aspirations, that immortal Being who lived before them and who will live on after them. They die and expect nothing in return." There then followed a list of themes: "The obligation of sacrifice, the sacrifices of women, hidden sacrifices, the lessons of sacrifice, sacrifice and optimism, the drunkenness of sacrifice, the contagion of sacrifice." No reli-gious references informed the long text, apart from one mention of Pascal. Sacrifice would be, then, "somewhat comparable to the order of charity spo-ken about by Pascal."⁶⁴

An occasional expression of appreciation of the cultural heritage included the religious patrimony: "Poor Senlis! Poor northern and eastern France. The heart bleeds when we think of all the ruins and all the profanations; I hope more than ever for our final revenge." In a slightly different genre of narra-tive, "Tales of Captivity," there is a clear indication that ideological differ-ences are well remembered but suppressed in the presence of the enemy. In a town captured by the Germans, the mayor, the curé, and the *instituteur* were marched around together. A German soldier had been fired on; consequently, the three village leaders were threatened with execution. During their forced march, the teacher said nothing about his relationship to the mayor and the curé.⁶⁵

In the second half of 1917, *La Revue pédagogique* presented ample quotes from Maurice Masson's *Lettres de guerre.*⁶⁶ Masson was a graduate of the École normale and a professor at the University of Fribourg-en-Suisse. He wrote of death and religion at the same time, perhaps not surprising in one who had obtained a post at a Catholic university: "The thought of the possibility of death is one of my fundamental thoughts, and I begin each day with a renewal, which I try to make as generous and Christian as possible, of the great sacrifice that might be demanded of me." But here he downplayed the theme of sacri-fice, so touted by the religious and the nonreligious alike: "One could reproach oneself for exaggerating the greatness of the sacrifice, and one comes to see in death no more than one of the realities of daily life."[67] This was certainly more simple than Ferdinand Buisson's "The Religious Foundation of Secular Morality," an ideological lecture in which the war was not discussed. Maintaining a contrast between laity and Christianity, Buisson nevertheless continued his earlier emphasis on reconciliation, an affirmation of the overlapping of values, by quoting Raoul Allier: "The more secular the morality, the more religious it is, and the more religious, the more secular it is."[68]

The war was providing lessons that teachers presumably could communicate to their students. In "What a Class Ought to Be," the author gave the basic sources for teaching the meaning of France: "The word, the landscape, the historical account, and the hero get to the child in the most direct way possible." In fact, the war "will be one of the most effective lessons for making future generations understand that France wants law and justice, not only for herself but for all." It is in the direct line of other French civilizing achievements, such as the Crusades, the erection of communes, and the American and French revolutions. The secular school system was touted as the great moral educator, training cells for those who renew and perpetuate French civilization.[69]

In the last year of the war, articles such as "The War and Teaching After the War" and "A Look at the Postwar School" dominated. In "The Ruins," a secular sense of the religious patrimony was maintained, in spite of explicit appreciative reference to Émile Mâle, who taught generations of French professors and students to appreciate the specifically religious qualities of the patrimony, and whose influence is the subject of Chapter 7: "Will not the light and airy cathedral of Soissons weigh heavy on our souls, with the heaviness of its stone blocks leveled by the fall of their primitive reality? Will we even be able to recover the knowledge enclosed in the admirable cathedral of Amiens, which [John] Ruskin taught us to read as a familiar book of hours?"[70] The writer, moreover, wants the love of these ruins to bring the French together: "Let us try then to understand what went together to make up France, to analyze the disjointed elements, to search for the texture of their cement, to perceive the place and role assigned to them by the architect in the general economy of the work."[71] This view of the religious patrimony was at least complementary to the positive appreciation of the clergy. A variation of this complementarity appeared earlier in the year when ruined religious and republican monuments were both nostalgically mourned. "Approaching [the village of Chauny], you see the vault of the collapsed nave; one must climb across the rubble to see the ravaged choir and the looted chapels, although in one of them the statue of the Sacred Heart remained intact, as did the bust of the Republic in a room on the first floor of the city hall."[72]

Memoirs

Individual *instituteurs* were quite conscious of their secularism. In his *Mémoires d'un instituteur,* Joseph Pascal told how he recuperated from his wounds under the watchful eye of a zealous nursing sister and how he was, apparently, hustled along for being irreligious: "We also received homilies from the mother superior of the Sisters of Saint Vincent de Paul, the head nurse, who, little concerned with neutrality, imposed on us an evening prayer in unison, in which I was the only one who remained silent. She had spotted my admission card at [the hospital], on which I had written: Profession? *Instituteur.* Religion? None. . . . At the end of five days, she proposed that I leave for the convalescent hospital, the Hôpital Parmentier, from which I am writing you while I help out with the latest arrivals." The new hospital he was moved to was run by the Congrégation des frères des écoles chrétiennes. Here he does not fail to notice that the hospital was the "lavish country house of the congregation."[73]

Nevertheless, an *instituteur* could show his openness to both the secular and the religious elements of Western culture. Paul Cazin began his *L'Humaniste à la guerre* with epigraphs from the *Odyssey* and the Book of Psalms, finding consolation in both: "Masters of the sacred and profane lyre, I brought you along in my knapsack between my handkerchiefs and biscuits, or kept you in a corner of my cartridge pouch. You have helped me out of a real fix, enabling me to suffer this trial with dignity." He thanked, praised, and loved the texts—but nonetheless labeled them "grandiose fictions." In this same spirit of love (presumably without belief), he addressed himself at the end of his book both to Zeus and to God the Father. More eloquently, and at greater length, however, he addressed himself to the fatherland: "O France, you who have taught me to speak this ancient tongue. You whose soil has been made from the dust of my forefathers, Fatherland, I love you. . . . I love you because I feel myself to be your child, and because you were the first to smile on my desire for beauty. I love you because I have seen the dragonflies play in the salty wind of the Camargue under the sun, the sun of Provence; because I have seen the light shine and go down in the windows of Chartres; because I have seen Mont-Saint-Michel, great Madonna to whom the winds have made cling a veil of stones, while at her feet trails off into the infinite the humid train of sandy shores." Evoking his love for the monuments of Catholic

France, Cazin would not want to have lived in the Middle Ages: "Perhaps I would not have gotten on with the preaching friars. I am and want to be a Frenchman of the year 1906, who makes his living where he can, but who can only live near to you. And though my spirit is filled with curiosity about the changing horizons of this world and the different customs of its peoples, [my spirit] longs for familiar beauties and can only take its rest in them."[74] For *instituteurs* such as Cazin, then, Catholic patrimony, yes; Catholic theology, no.

The literature on and by the *instituteurs* puts the work of the soldier within the vocation of a teacher, just as the literature on and by the priests puts the work of the soldier within the vocation of a priest. *La Revue pédagogique* sees the soldier in a teaching situation even as he defends the fatherland. *Instituteurs* do all that they do for the sake of the freedom and education of the children; at times they can teach formal classes (such as French to Alsatians) in the midst of war. And they are supported in their suffering by the memory of their own education. Their character formed by instruction in duty and morality, they can now transmit this learning experience to the next generation. In official publications, the virtue of *instituteurs* was not attributed directly to religion. It arose rather out of the secular ideology that the school system represented. While maintaining this distinction, educators were anxious to put the old fights behind them. Religious and secular values were considered complementary, justifying the *union sacrée,* which must never be terminated. Eternity, immortality, and spirituality are found in the life, in the reality, of France. And the war for justice and truth is part of a mission to teach the world. Secularism, often positive on religion, was secularism nevertheless. Joseph Pascal was well aware that his lack of religious practice was objectionable to true believers; Paul Cazin made it clear that appreciation of the Catholic artistic and intellectual traditions did not commit him formally to Catholic beliefs and practices.

Reconciled and Wary

Instead of coding and quantifying the experiences of priest and *instituteur* combatants, I have sketched a profile based on a gamut of experiences described in representative reviews and collections of memoirs.[75] In the publications by and about priests, national sentiment revealed itself in the references to the identity of the priest as warrior, giving his life for the fatherland.

He is to defeat—even kill—the enemy or die trying. Even as soldier, it would be appropriate to take on any position of leadership assigned to him as officer. There was ultimate national value here because the nation he was defending went back to Clovis. Religious ideology revealed itself in evocations of the warrior image of Joan of Arc. Blood would be shed with reluctance, of course. Sacrifice of life was noble, but a living priestly ministry would be better. Death would be participation in the death of Christ and submission to God's will. Leading men in battle was secondary to leading them morally and spiritually. The ideal of striving for the French nation was subsumed into the ideal of striving for the kingdom of God. In contrast, in the publications by and about *instituteurs,* national sentiment revealed itself in the emphasis on personal strength, leading to supreme endurance for the fatherland. Suffering would prove loyalty to the war effort, and all were willing to suffer for land and patrimony. Secular ideology revealed itself in the role assigned to public education: the creation of strength and moral consciousness. And sacrifice was a principal means of educating and inspiring to virtue. One placed optimal value on the intellectual and artistic heritage of France for its own sake. In fact, the cultural and artistic heritage of all Christendom could be appreciated without any formal commitment to a faith.

Certainly the national sentiment expressed by priests and teachers included the four elements found in the trench newspapers: defending the land and its people, condemning the enemy, doing one's duty, and striving for victory. But for priests and teachers there was more: feeling for the land was nuanced by love of art and architecture. Condemnation of the enemy was relativized by a sense of history. Duty was seen as a moral imperative. And, finally, victory was a means of establishing justice and truth. Priests and *instituters* maintained parallel ideologies: suffering in imitation of Christ, expressed awareness of the presence of God, and defense of eternal law, on the one hand, and suffering in the name of duty, expressed awareness of the evolution of civilization, and defense of human freedom, on the other.

Although the primarily religious national self-identity of priests and the primarily secular one of *instituteurs* did not have to negate one another, they were not completely compatible. Ideology could still be a partial obstacle, as the following two examples indicate—one a book about teachers by a priest, the other a final selection of teacher-survey responses on the subject of religion and the clergy. On the clerical side, we have an example of expectations and lack of resolution of ideological differences. Father Albert Bessières wrote *Âmes nouvelles-instituteurs-soldats* as, according to its subtitle, a "promotion of hope." Although his theme is reconciliation, he insists that *instituteurs* must come around to full appreciation of the church: "The *instituteur* will ask the priest to help him put a little order in the philosophical chaos created in his thought; he will ask him for an understanding of life and a rational justification of the faith of which the priest is the minister. And this appeal will not be without benefit for the priest; it will force him, should it be necessary, to shape and broaden his knowledge and to correct his hastily formed opinions." On the face of it, Bessières presents us with a teacher who needed only to put a little philosophical precision into his faith and a priest who needed a broader scholarly and educational background and more restrained judgment. He decries the continuing opposition of the secularists to the freedom to teach religion in the schools. Bessières ended his book with a portrayal of his expulsion from France in 1901 and his return to take part in the war. "Vivent les religieux," shouted the crowd. He wondered, in effect, why the holdouts among the teachers could not be as welcoming.[76] Neither in Bessières nor in the priest biographies was there any tolerance of the rejection of all religion in the schools. Here antagonism remained.

The teachers were still wary of any clericalism. In that famous 1961–63 survey made by Jacques Ozouf, references to the faith of the *Vicaire savoyard* and the need for a completely secular religion showed that the ghost of Rousseau still haunted the *instituteurs'* imagination. "The ideal would be the rapid creation of a simple, rationalist religion, acceptable to all, without a transcendental, unprovable God and sectarian priests."[77] Just as Bessières's proposals for an ideal teacher would have been unacceptable to a secular teacher, this "rationalist religion" would have been unacceptable to the priest.

One of the Nord *instituteurs* wrote at length about his resentment of the clergy but distinguished the admirable priest from the mediocre one: "We *instituteurs* were considered by the Right and the clergy as antipatriots and antimilitarists, but the 1914 war happened, and it was the *instituteurs,* not the priests or the rich, who risked their skin. I remember that a newspaper during the war—I believe it was the *Dépêche de Toulouse*—offered a million [francs] to anyone who could give the name of a rich man or a priest on the front line. It was not completely wrong, because when I was evacuated from the front lines in January 1915 for typhoid fever, I came to the hospital of Uzerche (Corrèze); the orderly was a priest of my age, but what a strapping fellow. It would have been a shame to destroy such a handsome and strong man. . . . When I returned a second time to the front, I arrived at my company alone. I replaced a curé sent to the rear, a clumsy man who could not handle it."[78]

Another *instituteur* from the Nord, who spent most of the war as a prisoner, laconically described the relationship of priests and people in this officially Catholic region of France: "Secularization was accomplished in the region without incident, because in the Valenciennais priests in general are sufficiently self-effacing, and the majority of people, although Catholic, do not practice much."[79]

In fact, the *instituteurs* from some of the Catholic regions may well have been more offended by, because more confronted with, clericalism. Those from the Vendée answered questions on laicization at length and with intensity. One of them described himself as "anticlerical . . . for the church caused and still causes a lot of trouble in the Vendée."[80] Another described himself as a nonpracticing Catholic before 1914, explaining that "it is the influence of the Vendéen clerical milieu that makes all the anticlericals into friends of mine."[81] Still another had been put off by a despotic curé.[82]

Religion itself need not be opposed or constrained. A former government official of Douai, president of the Commission sénatoriale de l'éducation nationale and veteran from the department of the Nord, recalled that religious belief and practice should be judged in the light of a general humanism: "It seemed to me then [1914–18], and I am very close to thinking now, that society ought to be secular; it being understood that to be secular does not signify opposition to one or another of the existing churches, one or another of the [existing] philosophies, when these churches, these religions, these philosophies are not obstacles to liberty nor a constraint on the flourishing of the sacred rights of man and his dignity."[83]

These, then, were the limits to reconciliation. Father Bessières and others like him would not forget that intolerant secularism remained a danger. And *instituteurs* such as those from the churchgoing departments of the Vendée and Nord would not forget that oppressive clericalism remained a danger. But the *union sacrée,* a morally refined and educated sharing of national sentiment, dominated the self-expression of priests and *instituteurs* even as ideological differences remained. Both priests and *instituteurs* clearly wanted to minimize these differences and effect a meeting of faith and secularism in the realm of cultural values. A détente was put in place: priests would more freely embrace the nation, and *instituteurs,* guardians of secularism, would more easily accept Catholicism as a way of being French. Détente developed into full reconciliation only when, ideology aside, the historian and public intellectual, Émile Mâle brought his highly secularized fellow citizens face to face with their French Catholic heritage.

Chapter Seven

RECONCILIATION OF CULTURES IN THE THIRD REPUBLIC: *The Work of Émile Mâle*

When Émile Mâle (1862–1956) deciphered the art programs of the French medieval cathedrals, and, in fact, a complex repertoire of Western religious art from the twelfth to the eighteenth centuries, he rediscovered a culture—clerical, artistic, and popular—that had been expressed in the art.[1] Over a period of thirty-four years, Mâle published four great syntheses of religious art history. Each synthesis was effected in a different manner, depending upon the sources used to explain the subject matter and the media employed by the artists. For *L'Art religieux du XIIIe siècle en France* (1898; Religious Art of the Thirteenth Century in France), his source was the *Speculum Majus,* the encyclopedia of religious thought by Vincent of Beauvais. In *L'Art religieux de la fin du moyen âge en France* (1908; Religious Art of the End of the Middle Ages in France), it was the Franciscan theologians of deep religious sentiment; in *L'Art religieux du XIIe siècle en France* (1922; Religious Art of the Twelfth Century in France), it was St. Bernard, Suger, and the great abbots of Cluny; and in *L'Art religieux après le concile de Trente* (1932; Religious Art after the Council of Trent), it was the theologians of the Counter-Reformation.[2] To put it another way, the unity, the synthesizing principle of the epoch and of Mâle's own work, was *thought* for the thirteenth century, *sentiment* at the end of the Middle Ages, the *monastic impulse* (powerful monastic foundations produced and patronized both religious activity and artistic expression) for the twelfth century, and *church authority,* organized for defensive—and offensive—action, in the period after the Council of Trent.

Thought, sentiment, movement, and institution exist in cultures: elite clerics, artists, and religiously active people from various levels of the social hierarchy—from princes to poor intellectuals and, yes, even some of the farmers and small merchants—transmuted their experiences into a common religious culture.[3] In Mâle's hands, iconography, generally understood to be the classification and interpretation of images, became a study of the ideas and methods that produced the images and of the culture that produced the ideas and methods. The subtitle of his first book, "A Study of Medieval Iconography and Its Sources of Inspiration," makes it clear that iconography is, in its primary sense, the actual artistic expression of ideas; secondarily, it is the study of this artistic expression.[4] His achievement was uniquely different from the cataloguing, conservation, and restoration of medieval monuments effected by Ludovic Vitet, Prosper Mérimée, and Eugène Viollet-le-Duc; uniquely different, also, from the deciphering efforts of Adolphe-Napoléon Didron, and the clerical team of Charles Cahier and Arthur Martin.[5] The religious art of the Middle Ages was not simply an element of the national patrimony, to be preserved and reverenced, a *lieu de mémoire* or place where one could meditate on France as nation and republic.[6]

Mâle confronted his colleagues and readers with a French way of life from another age. It was that culture, as signified in the art and reconstituted in his prose, that became the *lieu de mémoire*. We can demonstrate how Mâle's accomplishments derive from his powers to place his own culture, the intellectuals and educated readers of the Third Republic, in contact with medieval Catholic culture. He thereby gained broad acceptance of this culture as an element of the French national patrimony. This is not to discount earlier efforts to salvage and rehabilitate medieval monuments, nor the revivals of medieval philosophy in the decades across the turn of the century. Even though Mâle was directly responsible for the training of a generation of art historians, medieval historical studies in France across the first half of the twentieth century had diverse masters. The philosophers Jacques Maritain and Etienne Gilson presented medieval philosophy as corrective to, and an enhancement of, modern thought. The research of Marc Bloch (in his youth a lycée student of Mâle's) served to deepen modern understanding of feudal society. Their work, which also rehabilitated medieval thought and society in educated circles, was an accompaniment and a complement to the profound and pervasive reconciliation brought on by Mâle's influence. Actually, Maritain and those other high-profile converts to Catholicism, Joris-Karl Huysmans, Paul Claudel, and Léon Bloy, were utterly uncompromising with the secularism about them, and the secular medievalists had little social mediation in mind; but their efforts had the long-term effect of making the medieval Catholic heritage more intellectually respectable.[7] Mâle was a signal figure, but he was not alone.

Here I will follow Mâle's accomplishments across the years, with some departures from a year-to-year chronology, first attending to his entry in the École Normale Supérieure and, with the end of his course work, to his initial historical research. Then I double back to his earlier home life and lycée days, along with the teaching activities that paralleled advanced dissertation research. At center is his particular use of church-historical and iconographical sources to put together his presentation of medieval Catholic France. Viewing his distinguished career, we can assess his high profile love of France and low profile political expression. Finally, I trace his influence on scholars, the well-educated readers (the French expression is *le public cultivé*), and the general public.

Republican and Catholic Formation

The Third Republic was born in turmoil, political and religious. In 1871, the Paris Commune, inspired by an exaggerated revolutionary republicanism, was accompanied by an anticlerical violence that culminated in the execution of the archbishop of Paris, Georges Darboy. In reaction, the new National Assembly, led by monarchists, voted for public prayers of reparation, a vote reinforced by the activities of mayors, magistrates, and army officers. Early rivalry of the leading republicans, the moderate Adolphe Thiers and the opportunist Léon Gambetta, gave way before the electoral success of the monarchist general Patrice MacMahon and his government of "moral order." For six years MacMahon presided over attempts to restore conservative (even aristocratic) political and religious control of France. When he was finally forced to resign, the republican government sought to control religious orders: teaching congregations were required to ask for state authorization; monasteries were closed; many priests and religious were expelled. Control of the schools was the fundamental goal. Jules Ferry, alternately minister of public instruction and prime minister, established the fully secularized public education system by law. Laws voted into place between 1882 and 1886 in particular concretized Ferry's program.[8] When Émile Mâle entered the École Normale in 1883, the Ferry ministry had just appointed as its head Georges

Perrot, a sincere republican. Mâle was loyal to this intellectual tradition even as he searched for the religious and cultural meaning of a tradition of living and thinking that the Revolution, the republican tradition, had renounced.[9] In fact, knowing the varieties of national sentiment embodied in the political language and culture of the predominant intellectuals and politicians of the Third Republic, he fashioned the history of medieval religious art in the form of a communication to his own times. In other words, by representing the alien medieval religious culture in the intellectual "native language" of his day, he served as the bridge across the divide that separated secular intellectual life in the Third Republic from the Catholic religious experiences and expressions of medieval France.

Recalling that he had never worked more ardently than he did for admission to the École Normale, he wrote, "If I succeeded, it was because I had the lively desire to succeed that without doubt came to me from my father."[10] He was admitted on 19 August 1883, along with Lucien Herr, later librarian of the École Normale, and a significant intellectual influence there for many years; Stéphane Gsell, the historian of North Africa; and Joseph Bédier, specialist in French medieval literature, and Joseph Texte, specialist in comparative literature. Though not ranked among the highest after the entrance examinations because he had missed a question in history, his exceptional abilities were quickly recognized. After his first major presentation—on the Egyptian gods—Ernest Desjardins, his history and geography professor, stood up and said, "In the twenty-five years that I have been a professor at the École Normale I have never seen a debut as remarkable as this one."[11]

To Mâle, the École Normale offered an advanced education and a personal experience of national community: "This common life, this daily companionship will certainly develop all sorts of qualities that one would look for in vain in the faculties. Fraternity, that is the great strength of the École Normale. I understood that from the first day."[12] His notebooks preserved from the period, written in tiny, tight script, are the evidence for his intense work habits—though his work did not blind him to his old family values.[13] He wrote to his parents, "I have not seen much, but I have read much, and books often supply for experience.—Well, do believe that nothing, nothing in the world inspires as much respect in me as the simplicity and honesty of your life. Ancient wisdom said that parents find in their children their punishment and their reward: be happy—you have all my love and all my respect."[14]

Without disparaging education, Mâle stated that plain and simple people had a spirit and a wisdom that could not be inculcated by anything as superficial as

Fig. 12.   Photo of 1883 entry class in arts and letters at the leading Paris institution of higher learning, the École Normale. Shown here are Émile Mâle (first row, third from right), the historian of medieval Christian art, and his good friend Lucien Herr (third row, second from left), mentor of Jean Jaurès and other leading French socialists. Also in this photo are Joseph Bédier (second row, first on left), specialist in medieval literature; Stéphane Gsell (second row, second on left), historian of North Africa; Ernest Lebègue (first row, third from left), a cousin of Mâle's; and Joseph Texte (first row, first on right), specialist in comparative literature. Mâle's rapport with his colleagues engendered acceptance for his scholarly appreciation of medieval Catholicism. (École Normale Supérieure)

a teaching method. His grandfather Mâle was for him, as he said in his later years, "the peasant of pure race, . . . the peasant of a thousand years ago and of two thousand years ago."[15] In one of his earliest publications, a speech delivered to the lycéens of Toulouse in 1891, he extolled the merits of the ordinary people who knew enough to appreciate the beauty and monuments of France. Savants from the days of Fénelon and Voltaire down to his École Normale teachers and classmates, who were taken with Roman history and Italy, did not have such an appreciation. Rather, said Mâle, "The people alone, at a time when the savants no longer understood, knew how to love beautiful things with a profound instinct."[16] He praised the stone cutters and the carpenters and ordinary French visitors who alone knew how to love the arena of Arles, the portals at Chartres, and the great nave at Amiens. In modern times, he said, Michelet and the other great historians have learned to feel and think like the people. Because their solidarity with popular sentiment was lost, these intellectuals now had to know much in order to love much.

Encounter with the work of Ernest Renan helped Mâle to define his own Catholic sentiments. He had attended some of Renan's lectures at the Collège de France and had read *L'Histoire des origines du christianisme* in 1885 when he brought the book home with him during a grip epidemic—all the *normaliens* were sent home during this period. He said that those few weeks passed at Monthieux counted for much in his intellectual formation. He knew then that Renan could never be for him "a master of thought, but only a master of style."[17] Mâle could not understand how one could explain away the miracles of Christ and the spread of Christianity as purely natural history. He realized the strength of his "Catholic" sentiments: across the years his father had attended Mass each week, and his mother was quite devout. Although Mâle's mother's family, of Bourbonnais origins, had been living in Charolles, the city next to Paray-le-Monial (site of the Sacred Heart apparitions), there is no record of them entering into the religious controversies of the epoch. In fact, Mâle could recall his father reading aloud to the family from Victor Hugo's *Notre-Dame de Paris* (Hugo's works had been placed on the Catholic Index of Forbidden Books). The religious turbulence of Paris did not reach their home, with the exception of the Commune uprising, when there was such danger to the management class everywhere that Gilbert Mâle decided to keep a revolver close to his bed at night.[18]

After having lapsed from active religious practice in the secular atmosphere of the École Normale, Émile returned to active church life when he became deeply involved in his study of the Middle Ages.[19] He finished first in the *agrégation des lettres* from the École Normale. As such he was entitled to go to the École Française at Athens, where he would have a chance to pursue his passion for Greek art and thought. But a profound intellectual and emotional experience in Florence focused his attention on the rationality and beauty of medieval art. While traveling in Provence and northern Italy with his cousin Gustave Debrière during September 1886, he came to Florence and the Church of Santa Maria Novella. Standing in the Spanish Chapel of the Florence church, he studied the fourteenth-century frescoes of Andrea da Firenze, "The Triumph of St. Thomas Aquinas" and "The Church Militant and Triumphant."

"I was struck by the grandeur of the ordering thought," he said.[20] Like a thunderclap, a revelation, he knew what he wanted to be—a historian of art and the Middle Ages. Each fresco was a representation of order, sheer order. On one side, the medieval hierarchy was arrayed against a background that resembled the cathedral of Florence: pope, emperor, cardinals, kings, rich and poor, St. Dominic guiding from on high; on the other side, Thomas Aquinas on a level above the human sciences personified by beautiful female figures, and at their feet the great thinkers of antiquity—Aristotle, Cicero, Euclid, Ptolemy, and others.

Returning to France, Mâle immediately gave himself over to a serious reading of Dante, and for a time thought he might do a study of the influence of Dante on Italian art. "I followed the sublime poet across three worlds: a magisterial work, a summa of human intelligence, and the imperishable glory of Italy."[21] While teaching—he had taken a position at his old lycée at St.-Étienne—he plunged into careful readings of Eugène Viollet-le-Duc and Adolphe-Napoléon Didron. He was studying, writing, formulating the ideas that he published in article form several years later and in book form more than ten years later. "It was at Monthieux that the plan for my first book came to me, and it was there that my destiny was fixed."[22]

Still, Mâle remained independent of the formally Catholic movements of the era. Such movements came into being to revive the most powerful and successful elements of medieval church life, such as scholastic philosophy, monasticism, and pilgrimage. Individual churchmen, like all others who turned to the Middle Ages, had their own fads and fancies, some of them not far removed from the nationalism of the politicians and the esotericism of some novelists. The renewal of scholastic philosophy brought new attention to Thomas Aquinas, other scholastics, and the church fathers too; several monastic foundations produced historians and manuscript specialists, and the pilgrimage revival brought people to centers of prayer and devotion, some of which—one thinks of Chartres, first of all—were showcases of medieval art.[23]

A revival of medieval scholastic philosophy was in progress at the same time that Mâle was developing his history of medieval religious thought. [24]

But this revival had no observable influence on him. His goal was to show how the "thought" of the Middle Ages was a systematization and synthesis of the thought of the church fathers by way of the ancient Greek and Roman philosophers. Dante was the model here, and Mâle considered him as a possible subject for his École Normale dissertation. At the École Normale, Plato and St. Augustine were the principal philosophical ghosts. Father Alphonse Gratry, a chaplain who left the École by mid-century and was eventually admitted to the Académie française as a philosopher, was more in the tradition of the philosophies of inner experience synthesized in the teaching of St. Augustine, rather than in the Aristotelian Thomistic tradition. Gratry's ideas were preserved in the philosophical teaching of Léon Ollé-Laprune, and we do know that Mâle worked with Ollé-Laprune's recasting of Aristotle.[25]

When Mâle began to read the writings of medieval theologians, a massive collection of medieval and patristic authors was at his disposal. It was his good fortune that an ecclesiastical entrepreneur of a generation earlier, the abbé Jacques-Paul Migne, had published hundreds of volumes of the principal extant writings of Christian thinkers across the centuries. An entrepreneur, Migne was primarily a publisher and not a scholar or leader of any kind of movement. He was not a medievalist or interested in a revival or reestablishment of anything medieval, but he made possible Mâle's work on the Middle Ages. At the right time, he was able to secure the help of the right people.[26] Dom Jean-Baptiste Pitra, the man responsible for the editing of the patrologies, was a monk of the Benedictine-revival monastery at Solesmes and necessarily a disciple and associate of Dom Prosper Guéranger, founder of the restored monastic community.[27] Indirectly, then, Mâle benefitted from the revival of Benedictine monasticism at Solesmes that sustained Dom Pitra: Pitra's motivation as editor of historical editions came from reliving the monasticism of an earlier historical epoch.

The Classical and Romantic Foundations

Before and after his actual course work at the École Normale, Émile Mâle's intellectual temperament was formed by experiences that we can simply but correctly label "classical" and "romantic." He was born in Commentry (Allier) and grew up in the small mining town of Monthieux—long since part of the city of St.-Étienne—where his father had been appointed mining engineer. The first family home in Monthieux was at one end of a large park landscaped in the days of Louis XVI. Since the park was open toward the west, the setting sun had a powerful effect, particularly when it gave the clouds a fringe of gold or purple as it set behind the distant mountains. The cry of peacocks added to an effect Mâle later recalled as Edenesque. Childhood aesthetic pleasures, joy in tradition and continuity, were part of an amalgam of experiences. Reading the *Bucolics* and *Georgics* of Virgil, he combined in his mind's eye the images of the farms of Tityrus or Monalcus and the scenes of his own countryside. Although the farms of his region did not really resemble the old Celtic huts with thatched roofs that he dreamed of as he read, they did have some kind of ancient, even Gallo-Roman quality. Mâle was convinced of it by a verse of Virgil traced on a wall that was part of the property belonging to another great house of Monthieux: "O fortunatos nimium sua bona norint agricolas!" (Happy the people of the land who do not fail to recognize the good things that are theirs.) Later when he visited Italy, the clean lines and bright tiles of Italian houses reminded him of his Monthieux house, and he further reminded himself that the winds of the Mediterranean, the Roman lake, came up the Rhone valley as far as Monthieux.[28]

From Homer through Dante, a variety of ancient and medieval texts nourished and shaped a spirit of order and beauty, and by his third year the beauty of the ancient poetry dominated his sensibilities: "The adorable epithets of Homer, the music of Virgil's verse, opened up for me an enchanted world. There were passages of the Georgics in which I thought I found the beauties of the enclosure of Monthieux. It seemed to me that a sweet ambrosia flowed through my veins, and I can only think with pleasure of this first dazzling experience of beauty, . . . I felt so happy in the company of the ancient and modern poets that the teaching profession appeared to me to be the natural career. Surrounded by mills, mines, and factories, I never for an instant thought of becoming an engineer."[29] He said that he passed his lycée years in a semi-sleep, in the company of Homer and Virgil. He remembered that he stole from evening study time some forbidden moments to read Homer in translation. These joys made his lycée formation a pleasure and the educational system of the Third Republic a native land as connatural to him as the general Bourbonnais culture he grew up in.

The lycées in Émile Mâle's day catered to a very tiny portion of those who were of school age. In 1872, when he entered the lycée at St.-Étienne, the percentage of boys between the ages of eleven and seventeen who went to the state secondary schools was under 2 percent. In fact, until 1925 the number was still under 3 percent. Mâle was a member of a special group of boys who were admitted to lycées and later of the even smaller group that finished. On average, only about 50 percent of students who took the baccalaureate exam passed it. Officials of the Third Republic did make many changes in the lycées; there was more French, more history, and more geography. Students were encouraged to use individual judgment, and there was much formal discussion of the importance of merit and the unimportance of privilege.[30] Gaining virtually all available prizes when he passed his baccalaureate, Mâle moved from the lycée at St.-Étienne to the Lycée Louis-le-Grand at Paris to begin his lengthy preparation for admission to the École Normale. In a letter to his parents, he wrote, "I distribute my time in the manner that seems the most advantageous, so that I do not lose a minute. I work conscientiously at everything, even German." He wandered through the new and used bookstores, once almost exceeding his budget on an old edition of Montaigne, available with an appealing reduction.[31] On Sundays he visited the Louvre and other museums, discovered the Théâtre Français, the Opéra Comique, and concerts in general. For the first time he heard the music of Wagner, of which he wrote, "The melody . . . the dreamlike poetry transported me, and in a lightning flash gave me a glimpse of the Middle Ages.[32]

On an earlier trip to Paris—for the Exposition Universelle in 1878—a visit to Notre-Dame cathedral was the high point: "Since the time when, as a child, I heard my father read evenings the novel of Victor Hugo to my mother, I desired passionately to see the famous cathedral. . . . It left a profound impression on me. When I was asked the most beautiful thing I had seen in Paris, I answered without hesitating Notre-Dame."[33] The same excitement was evident some years later when, with two other students, he represented the student body of the École Normale at Hugo's funeral. As he wrote to his parents in May 1885: "We took almost three hours to go from the Place de l'Étoile to the Pantheon. . . . The Place de la Concorde is indescribable. It is a sea of heads; here and there you see the shining of armor and helmet of the cavalry who rear up their horses to contain the crowd. All the statues, representing the cities of France, that surround this square are veiled in immense black crepe. The gas jets are lit and hung with crepe also—When you turn around you perceive the cortege descending the Champs Elysées, and as far as you can see there are tops of heads. In the distance you see the great catafalque under the Arc de Triomphe."[34]

In his youthful reveries, Mâle sensed a unity between Greco-Roman culture and his land: his home, the trees, winds, gardens, earth smells, and all his surroundings. He brought to his reading of classical authors the intuition, feeling, individual conscience, and experience that are considered to be the essential qualities of French romanticism. And his powers to evoke scenes and images were surely enhanced by an early passion for painting. He continued to paint until about 1892 and carefully noted the development of then-contemporary painting styles: impressionism, naturalism, symbolism. In his free time he would paint for his own amusement, sometimes on canvas, sometimes even on the walls in his father's garden. Although he had a generic attraction for some Italian painting and Dutch landscapes, his own paintings were conscious imitations of impressionist, Nabi, and symbolist painters, and of the individual painters Daubigny, Bastien-Lepage, Sérusier, and Puvis de Chavannes. He was fascinated by the evocation of other times and places, but most of all by the work of Puvis de Chavannes, who had revived the art of wall decoration and "classical" subjects. His art history education was the minimal lycée experience and the reading of Charles Blanc.

Mâle said that he "lived in intimacy" with Romanesque and Gothic art, filling his notebooks with sketches, facts, and ideas.[35] The sketches, some of them made as early as 1872, were small, detailed, and well proportioned. In the beginning he worked with great seriousness because he wanted to be an artist, a career his father finally refused to allow. His sense of perspective was evident and he had already learned to convey movement. Mâle continued to sketch scenes and figures until he became totally involved in his dissertation on the thirteenth century. During his research trips he carried small five-inch by two-inch notebooks with him, wherein he noted both iconography and architectural details. His drawings here, though much more simple, show a trained eye and a steady hand; there are floor plans, arches, pillars, and sculptural details. In these notebooks, always the same size and the same format, are the observations that he later organized into the many journal articles he published, some of which became chapters in his books.[36]

Mâle's appreciation of the classics was intellectualized and strengthened by his formal education at the École Normale, then under the classicizing influences of Désirée Nisard and Georges Perrot. Nisard believed that "admiration of the classics" was the best occupation for an educated person, and that what he called "French commentary" was superior to German philological explanation. The director from 1880 to 1883, Fustel de Coulanges, wanted basically to make the École Normale the best institution of higher learning in the nation.[37] In his curriculum, a literature major was required to study in depth historical and philological disciplines: epigraphy, paleography, historical geography, and political economy. When Mâle entered the École Normale in

1883, Georges Perrot had just taken over the direction of the school. Perrot wrote, "Democracy needs an elite, to represent the only superiority it recognizes, that of the mind. It is up to us to recruit this elite, or, to speak more modestly, to work to furnish some of the elements that will constitute it."[38] He tried without success to make the École Normale a graduate school, admitting only those with the licentiate degree, but he also defended the traditional syllabus. Such elitism brought criticism from those who said the school was not fulfilling its function of giving pedagogic training to secondary teachers. His great book was *Histoire de l'art dans l'antiquité,* and when he learned that Mâle loved Greece and art he took a great interest in the young man.[39] It was to Georges Perrot that Mâle dedicated his major thesis, published as *L'Art Religieux du XIIIe siècle en France.*

Teaching a rhetoric based on classical models at the beginning of his professional career, Mâle spent four years at Toulouse, where he numbered among his colleagues the philosopher Victor Delbos and Jean Jaurès, the future leader of French socialism. Jaurès and two other *normaliens* made a companionable and productive intellectual circle. According to an informal history of the Toulouse law faculty, "They gathered together every day at the café. Jaurès spoke, Rauh philosophized on concept and idea and commented on recent scientific themes. Émile Mâle, who little liked philosophy, tried to divert the conversation to art or history. Hauriou listened to it all passionately; all four of them came finally to the law faculty to assist at Hauriou's course, and there the miracle was produced: the café conversation had become a system; the concepts of Rauh were combined with the prophetism of Jaurès; the historical recollections and Latin quotations furnished by Émile Mâle came to be enshrined in the reasoning process."[40] He was a recognized success as a teacher. A student who had just received a grant for a Paris lycée wrote him in 1892 saying, "You know how to arouse in the minds of all your students the curiosity to know things, to get them to open their intelligence to all the great ideas, to bring out of them their own point of view, which allows them to take an interest in everything and to profit from everything."[41] When he began teaching in Paris, his schedule was arranged to allow him time to work on his thesis, and the cathedral and church visits in the 1890s enabled him to verify his reading of the medieval theologians. Those years before finishing and defending the thesis left little time for socializing, although he took breakfast each day with his friends Victor Delbos and Léon Morand. For Mâle, Paris was the Bibliothèque Nationale, the library of the École Normale, the Louvre, the Musée de Cluny with its collections of medieval sculpture and jewelry,[42] and the Trocadéro with its Musée des Monuments Français. On rare occasions there were concerts and theater performances.

Naturally it was important to him that he continue his research while teaching. In July of 1898, he wrote to the rector of the Paris lycées expressing the desire to remain at the lycée Lakanal because he appreciated the type and quality of secondary school education that he found there: "A class where I could not study texts closely, or where I must forbid myself every erudition would be of no interest to me."[43] Most of all, his students recalled both his insistence on mastery of data and his imaginative evocation of the past. In his course in advanced rhetoric at Louis-le-Grand were Réné Massigli, French ambassador to England in 1944; Louis Massignon, the Islamicist; Augustin Fliche, the church historian; and Marc Bloch, the medievalist. A student wrote him on behalf of the others: "Each day we become ever more Latinists and Hellenists, and at a time when people assault Latin and Greek repeatedly, when they seek to annihilate the language that Demosthenes spoke, and that of which Cicero made such marvelous use."[44] Another student, Georges Huisman, wrote half a century later: "Once a week, he abandoned syntax to teach us the topography of ancient Rome, and it was a wondrous hour. . . . Mute with admiration, we listened to our professor of Latin transform himself into archeologist, historian, and poet, and before our every eyes make the Forum of the Republic or the imperial basilicas rise out of the ground, without having recourse to projections or illustrations."[45]

At Mâle's dissertation defense in 1899, Charles Victor Langlois said to him, "Sir, your Latin thesis is unattackable; as regards your principle thesis, it is remarkable, it is a monument, it will last."[46] In one sense it is surprising that Langlois said this because he later wrote, "The man of today who writes about the past necessarily adds something to the document that he employs: But what? His personal reflections that he imposes upon the reader. Now these reflections are both useless and dangerous. . . . The true role of the historian is to put the people of today in contact with the original documents that are traces left by the people yesterday, without mixing anything of himself in them."[47] In his own writing, Langlois always stayed with analytical monographs, unlike Seignobos and Lavisse. Obviously, he had no problem with Mâle's pedagogically effective rhetoric because of the close connections that Mâle was able to establish at every turn between medieval theological texts and the artistic representations of the religious scenes evoked by these texts. Members of the committee in general were apparently surprised that Mâle took the old church dogmas seriously, that he sustained his position without an overweight footnote apparatus, and, finally, that he wrote in a rich style that any cultivated reader could appreciate. Later George Perrot wrote to him, "From the time of Fustel de Coulanges, nothing has made us better relive the genius of an epoch."[48]

Clearly Mâle integrated classicist and romantic sensibilities, a new version of an old experience. The early postrevolutionary period to 1817 was a phase of romanticism marked by the nationalist and nature orientations (inspired by August Wilhelm and Friedrich Schlegel) of Madame de Staël and Benjamin Constant, with their new favoritism of the medieval and Christian world over the ancient world, the northern European world in contrast to the Mediterranean world, as well as the opposition of the nationalist and modern to classicist doctrines. Chateaubriand's sensibilities represented the center of the movement during this period. A second phase (1818–29) was dominated by the writings of Lamartine, Vigny, Victor Hugo and Alexandre Dumas in their early careers and the paintings of Géricault and Délacroix, and was accompanied by the heightening of opposition to royalism and Catholic power. A third phase beginning in 1830 coincided with the July Monarchy and was a period of creative maturity for the principal romantics. The final phase in the 1840s saw the rise of a new range of writers and artists, such as Musset and Nerval.[49] On the face of it, the romantics favored medieval literature because of its obvious traceable connaturality to nineteenth-century French Christian or post-Christian culture. But it was not so much opposition to the Greco-Roman classics that characterized the French romantics as it was opposition to the neoclassicism of the seventeenth century. And during the monarchy of Louis Philippe, emphasis on Greco-Roman classics predominated over a nostalgic medievalism embodied in Victor Hugo's *Notre-Dame de Paris*. Pierre Moreau says that the exoticism of the past was rejected because "bourgeois reason imposed itself on [the poetry of the past] and bent it to its own ideas and judgments."[50] Acceptance of Greco-Roman classics did not lead to an imitation of them, because this, too, was one of the principal sins of neoclassicism. Rather, there was a new set of forms, described by Sainte-Beuve— writing when the romantic movement itself was mostly spent—as Asian: "With Buffon and Jean-Jacques, the French influence, in spite of its conquests and picturesque acquisitions, still remained in Europe; with . . . Bernadin, Chateaubriand, and Lamartine, by luxury and excess of colors, it is decidedly in Asia."[51] Sainte-Beuve, following Quintilian, was contrasting the "Asiatic" and the "Attic" style, the former characterized by music of the phrase and richness of expression and the latter by neatness and conciseness.

Émile Mâle praised the rich prose of Chateaubriand and other French romantics, adopted their appropriation of Greco-Roman classics, and gave scholarly form to their medieval enthusiasms. When he was in his seventies and living in Rome, a feature writer for a regional journal caught up with him in the church of St.-Louis des Français before the tomb of Pauline de Beaumont, friend of Chateaubriand. At that time Mâle said, "Ah yes, even though I am an unrepentant classicist, I love the great Breton. He gave us our taste for the Middle Ages. Do you recall his pages on the cathedrals?"[52] Unrepentant, indeed, because he was a classicist from his youth. By substituting the classicism of the romantics for the medievalism of the romantics when interpreting medieval art history, Mâle accomplished the consummate transformation of medievalism.

The Study of Medieval Catholic France

Theologians, historians and archaeologists, conservators and restorers took on primary importance for Mâle after his emotional and intellectual encounter with the Florence frescoes.[53] Returning to teach in the lycée at St.-Étienne, his course work finished at the École Normale, he still had not decided on a thesis topic. With the experience at Florence still fresh in his memory, he gave free rein to his suddenly and fully established master passion for the Middle Ages, and he used every minute not taken up by his teaching duties to pursue his studies. In the library of the Palais des Arts he discovered two treasures: Eugène Viollet-le-Duc's magisterial *Dictionnaire raisonné de l'architecture française du XIe au XVIe siècle* and the journal founded by Adolphe-Napoléon Didron, *Annales archéologiques*.[54] As soon as Mâle found his seat on the trolley that he took home from the lycée, he opened whichever volume of the *Dictionnaire* he was working on and began to read. The *Annales archéologiques* made an even stronger impression on him.[55] In the preface to his first book, *L'Art religieux du XIIIe siècle en France,* Mâle acknowledged his debt to all his predecessors but to Didron in particular.[56]

Before the arrival of Viollet-le-Duc, few government officials, collectors, or scholars concerned themselves with the study and conservation of medieval architecture and sculpture, either on location or in the museums.[57] Mâle liked to point out the influence of Chateaubriand on these conservators and collectors: "From *Le Génie du Christianisme* went forth the great musical waves that had stirred up the sensibilities of new generations. Guided by an enchanter they discovered the beauty of Christian art."[58] Inspired mainly by the Norman archeologists, the actual restoration work in France was initiated by Ludovic Vitet, animated by Prosper Mérimée, and effected by Eugène Viollet-le-duc. Mâle said of Vitet, "He distinguished himself by his *Scènes historiques de la Ligue* and by his brilliant articles in the *Globe* on art. He was at the same time a historian and an artist. People knew that he had studied the architecture of the Middle Ages in the books of English and Norman archeologists. He seemed completely prepared for his new functions, and he fulfilled them with rare conscientiousness. His reporting was printed as a model."[59] Ludovic Vitet persuaded Guizot to create the post of inspecteur général des monuments historiques. Appointed to it in 1830, Vitet clarified the essential tasks of inventory and conservation. As he defended the values of medieval art, he had the good sense to analyze vandalism in its various forms in order to counteract it. Mâle most appreciated Vitet's efforts to save the menaced monuments, especially his work to save the St. John Baptistery of Poitiers. Mâle said that Mérimée "gave to the romantics a lesson of simplicity. A professional archeologist has never described the different parts of a church with greater conscientiousness, nor in greater detail"[60] Although Mérimée's conclusions are out-of-date today, they moved the historical discussion forward in their own day. He analyzed the characteristic expressions of Romanesque and Gothic art, abandoning the outmoded hypothesis that tied Gothic architecture to the pointed arch. Mâle later evoked the difficulty of Mérimée's voyages: taking night coaches and sometimes abandoned by the drivers of his rented transports. Mérimée had to persuade civil officials to spare great works of architecture and priests to put aside plans to plaster over medieval interiors. Not for him the simple assumptions of the amateur archeologists nor the romantic dreams of the writers of fiction, though he was both an amateur archeologist and a novelist.

Of course, the name synonymous with nineteenth-century architectural restoration in France was Eugène Viollet-le-Duc himself. Like Émile Mâle years later, Viollet-le-Duc was first attracted to medieval architecture when he was in Italy. From Rome he described his experience of medieval monuments to his father: "They touch me infinitely more than ancient monuments. I love the cathedral of Florence more than the Parthenon. In fact, I have discovered some immense treasures from the Middle Ages."[61] He said that if you could restore Saint-Germain Auxerrois, you would have something worth a thousand times more than the cathedral of Siena. But "you may as well ask a fish to smile. It is the last idea that will even enter the head of a Parisian."[62] Mâle attributed the modern discovery of the Gothic to Viollet-le-Duc, and his own understanding of the rational beauty and proportions of Gothic style derives from him. At St.-Étienne he mastered the architect's voluminous writings and later compared him to Champollion, who first deciphered Egyptian hieroglyphics; each discovered a "world."[63]

Mâle's research and historiography was built, first and foremost, on the writing of Adolphe-Napoléon Didron who, by his own writings and by his editorship of *Annales archéologiques,* most developed the embryonic discipline of iconography: the identification of themes, persons, objects, and motifs that are represented by artistic forms. Utterly devoted to the revival of Gothic architecture and art, he was a journalist, a dealer in devotional objects, a stained-glass window designer. Victor Hugo had been an inspiration to him since the days when he had served on architectural committees with him. In 1845, Didron dedicated his manual of iconography to the great novelist.[64] The journal *Annales archéologiques* brought together the principal research on Gothic architecture, including Viollet-le-Duc's proselytizing: "Our conclusion is quite simply that French thirteenth-century architecture, which was fashioned from our materials and in our climate to suit our character, and which is beautiful, often formally admirable, and not very costly, should be the only form of architecture studied in France."[65] Didron himself wrote that "the beautiful thirteenth-century French style suits all climates, all countries, all nations—as is evident from the cathedrals of Uppsala, Cologne, Canterbury, Amiens, Clermont-Ferrand, and so on."[66] His most important work, *Iconographie chrétienne: Histoire de Dieu* is a study of the representation of individual members of the Trinity in medieval art. Didron provides a long introduction explaining why the sculpture and glass of the Middle Ages was for the people, and how the organization of ideas behind the art followed the pattern of Vincent of Beauvais. Of Vincent's encyclopedia, the *Speculum Majus,* Didron wrote, "This order, at once analytical and chronological, natural and historical, is quite remarkable. I consider it superior to those invented by Bacon, by the Encyclopedists of the eighteenth century, and even by Marie Ampère, whose classification is just about the most recent and preferable to all those that have been attempted up to now. This order is precisely the one in accordance with which are arranged the statues that decorate the exterior of the cathedral of Chartres."[67] In *L'Art religieux du XIIIe siècle en France,* Mâle placed in high relief these two notions of Didron: that the cathedral was for the people, and that it was designed in accordance with the theologians' desire for an encyclopedic representation—with religious interpretation—of all human learning. More important, he used the structure of the *Speculum Majus* as the organizing principal of his own work.

Mâle further developed his methodology under the influence of Charles Cahier and Arthur Martin, two priests whose great monograph on the cathedral of Bourges was an item-by-item study—clear, with historical accuracy the goal and religious sentiment the motivation: "One of us, preaching the Lenten sermons of Bourges in 1839, found himself quite naturally led by his love of Christian monuments, and by the marvelous opportunity of a long stay in the cathedral, so little known, to pass entire days under the vaults of the basilica where he had just preached the word of God. It was at first only a matter of religious diversion, pious relaxation after the meditations and fatigue of the pulpit."[68] Slowly, he says, the religious sightseeing became attentive observation, and almost imperceptibly a study, because finally he discovered that there was nothing to tell him, in full, what those marvels meant. "All those great figures had lost their proper language, and seemed determined not to respond to the curiosity of the late-comer who arrived after so many uncaring generations for information about their thought."[69]

Other studies—popularizations really—of Christian iconography appeared in the twenty-five odd years before the publication of Mâle's *L'Art religieux du XIIIe siècle en France*. One of the series published by the abbé Migne included a *Dictionnaire iconographique* by a Louis-Jean Guénebault. Count Grimouard de Saint-Laurent authored a six-volume *Guide de l'art chrétien,* and the abbé Jules Corblet published a *Vocabulaire des symboles et des attributs employés dans l'iconographie chrétienne,* both works descriptions of persons, objects, and events from Christian history—useful to church decorations, preachers, and the curious though not scholarly works. By 1890 a textbook and syllabus, Xavier Barbier de Montault's *Traité d'iconographie chrétienne,* had been put together for use in seminaries. This brought a certain evolution to term, notes Harry Bober, the editor of the Bollingen edition of Mâle's works: "From its beginnings and early formation in the hands of leading scholars, it [the study of iconography] had filtered down in handbook distillations to elementary academic instruction."[70] The preface to *L'Art religieux du XIIIe siècle en France* is a concise history of religious iconography in France, with emphasis, of course, on medieval iconography.[71] Ultimately Mâle pulled together the haphazard iconographical studies that had appeared since the middle of the century. His powerful syntheses absorbed and developed the conservation and restoration studies of Viollet-le-Duc, the deciphering efforts of Adolphe-Napoléon Didron, and the historical and religious simplicity of Cahier and Martin. In effect, he channeled the passions of Chateaubriand and the romantic novelists, even as he brought to full flower the historical logic of iconography.

As a young professor, Mâle ardently promoted the teaching of art history at the lycée and university levels. He observed that we look for a history of the Middle Ages in the university curricula in vain, in spite of the work of Didron and others. Although there were courses in medieval French literature, the important thinkers, all of whom wrote in Latin, were neglected—Thomas Aquinas, Gulielmus Durandus, Vincent of Beauvais—"And it is in their works only that we will find the secret of these times."[72] Only the art vested religious life and ideas with a perceptible form that was worthy of them: "the cathedral, with its mystical geometry, its thousands of painted or sculpted personages, is, to be precise, theology, liturgy, sacred science clothed in perceptible forms."[73] The written vesture of the ideas was far less beautiful: "When the thought is beautiful, the form is very often mediocre. . . . What the thirteenth century did not know how to say it carved."[74] Naturally, the advantages gained by the study of the Middle Ages are also gained by the study of Renaissance and modern art. Mâle highlighted the specific importance of the study of medieval art for understanding the France of the past, recognizing that students can also learn much about other countries. He did not want his students to "pass with indifference before the works into which their fathers had put so much genius and love"; they should not be strangers in their own country. But he eschewed the quasi-religious qualities of nationalism: "Michelet wanted France to be a religion; let it at least be a subject to be taught."[75] Mâle's use of his own love of France as a means of communicating the value of the medieval religious art patrimony was appropriately in evidence years later when he was appointed to teach at the Sorbonne. No one before him had placed the cultural, historical, and civic importance of art education into such high relief. Six years after the appearance of Mâle's article on the teaching of art history, Georges Perrot published an entire book on the topic of art in secondary education, wherein he lamented that Mâle's admonitions had not been heard. Perrot developed the case, saying that art history added to a student's knowledge and understanding of the past. Sometimes art fills in lacunae in the written tradition; for example, statues can tell of attitudes toward the role of an emperor or of changes in an emperor's personality.[76]

Mâle's *L'Art religieux du XIII* siècle en France* achieved such renown that he was appointed to teach a new course on this history of Christian art in the Middle Ages at the Sorbonne. In his opening lesson on 8 December 1906, he again explained the crucial importance of the study of the Middle Ages for an adequate understanding of the culture of modern France: "The art of the Middle Ages is perhaps the most original creation of France." In other areas there are rivals and masters to the French: the Italian Dante gave the epic poem its perfect form and the English Shakespeare realized the potentialities of poetry and beauty in drama, but "on the other hand, there is nothing in Europe that can be compared to the cathedral of Chartres or the cathedral of Reims."[77] The Romanesque churches of Germany are half-Germanic, half-Italian and really stem from the Holy Roman Empire of Charlemagne; furthermore, Germany has no variety and no novelty compared to the architectural originality of the different regions of France. Reviewing the origins of Gothic art, Mâle wrote, "I do not know if there is a spectacle more beautiful than to see, at the beginning of the thirteenth century, France become the educator of Europe."[78]

This opening lecture contains a refutation of the then popular view that Gothic architecture began in Germany, engendered by the German love of nature with all its exuberance and its intricacy. Although Mâle was pleased to see that few German scholars continue to support this view, the error was of such long standing—Mâle singled out Sulpiz Boisserée, the friend of Goethe, for dishonorable mention—that he must continue to preach the priority and superiority of French Gothic. [79]

He notes the influence of French art on Hungary, Scandinavia, and England. Looking southward, he describes possible influences of Cluny and Cîteaux on the great Spanish cathedrals, pointing out the features that the cathedral of St. James at Compostela had in common with St.-Sernin of Toulouse. In Italy, in spite of the work of Italian artists, many of the great churches show French influence. "We are permitted to conclude, then, that France awakened the genius of Italy, asleep for centuries. The artists of Italy owe as much to our great Gothic masters as Dante and Petrarch to our troubadours."[80] Reviewing the sources of French iconography, he underlines the influence of the mystery plays on post-thirteenth-century art. This, of course, was the principal theme of his study of art at the end of the Middle Ages: "One must conclude that it is France, by the intermediary of the theater, that created the new Christian iconography."[81] Here, he would have to change his mind because, whatever the influence of France on Italy before and during the thirteenth century, Italian artists of the fourteenth and fifteenth centuries very much influenced the French religious art that came after them.[82]

In 1912–13, Mâle gave two lectures under the auspices of *La Revue française politique et littéraire*. These lectures, part of a series called Conférences Chateaubriand, were centered on the forces behind the building of the cathedrals and on the great medieval patron of the arts, the duc de Berry. Of the cathedrals, he says, "To build the cathedrals that so astound us today, much enthusiasm, much genius, and also much money were necessary. I would like to show you in this lecture, that all the lively forces of France collaborated in this great work, and that there are on our soil no monuments that belong more to the nation."[83] Mâle emphasizes the Frenchness of the cathedrals in order to render them personally meaningful to his listeners. His brief history includes the usual citations about the people's participation in the building of the cathedrals, where the money came from, and the achievements and methods of workers and artists. The key role of clergy and theologians in determining the art programs is underscored. He gives his usual elegant description of the monuments, reminding his listeners, virtually all of them French, that the cathedrals represented their heritage. The duc de Berry, who was "something other than a hero," is also commended for his support of the beauties of art and architecture on French soil: "It is thanks to him above all, that great French art did not become a victim of the Hundred Years' War. . . . If, then, we judge that French art is one of the most noble creations of France, we have the right to demand for the duc de Berry, not only indulgence, but gratitude."[84]

Citizen and *Académicien*

As someone who felt the humiliation of the French defeat in the Franco-Prussian War as a child, Émile Mâle had decided that one day he would make up for it in his own way: "That war that I could not yet understand, but the disasters of which I learned as if half dreaming, marked the child that I was with a profound imprint. I felt later that our defeat was connected with my very substance, and I had from then on the secret desire to do something one day that would bring honor, however little it be, to a humiliated France."[85] Mâle as an adult was very private about his politics, having friends on the French Left and the French Right across the years. His great friend, the socialist Lucien Herr, was extremely active in political discussion, writing under an assumed name. His hidden proselytizing was rewarded with success because he numbered among his converts Jean Jaurès and Léon Blum. Mâle himself was fascinated by Herr and very much under the influence of his extraordinary powers of philosophical discourse. Only in the domain for which he is best known, political thought, did Herr have no real influence on Mâle, for the latter was never active in politics and appreciated political ideas more for their shape and subtlety. In other areas of life, Herr's influence was apparent:

Mâle requested Herr to read and comment on his thesis, and Herr introduced the young Mâle to the music of Wagner. Years later, when Lucien Herr became engaged to marry a young woman who had originally come to Paris to study with Mâle, it was to Mâle that he first announced the engagement.[86]

On the other hand, Mâle was a kindly mentor to the art historian Louis Gillet,who was himself sympathetic to the right-wing nationalism of Maurice Barrès. In fact, the calm political stance of Mâle contrasted so much with Gillet's feelings that he interpreted Mâle's calm, reasoned ways as indifference: "This great intellectual led the existence of a calm visionary, knowing nothing here below except those things that are worthy of love, indifferent to the general hubbub, without intrigue, without ambition, skirting the edges of the crowd, taken up only with a few of the great ideas and some of the most precious dreams of the human race—the best efforts of the human imagination— one can say of such a life that it is made of the stuff of dreams."[87] Gillet said that Mâle came out of his political isolation in World War I. In fact, he caricatured Mâle, who voted in all national elections. "For the first time the author became aware that he was dreaming; the clash of arms awakened him."[88] Otherwise, "he always remained on the sidelines, keeping his grievances to himself, and preferring the society of the dead to that of the living. . . . He lived only with the shades."[89] In spite of this strange exaggeration, Gillet on the whole is reverential: "I do not believe that I have ever seen him [Mâle] without going away enriched, refreshed, and having renewed my store of enthusiasm, for such was his empathy and his capacity for admiration."[90] At least his remarks indicate that Mâle was not a standard-bearer for any political party, and they contain one correct notion, that World War I did activate Mâle to impassioned expression.

Events early in the war brought the artistic passion of Mâle to the surface. The German cannonading of Reims cathedral profoundly affronted Mâle's love of beauty and of France. For him, nothing was more valuable, more representative of the highest effort of the human person than Reims cathedral, and nothing could be more representative of human malice than its destruction. It was 1914, and Reims had been hopelessly scarred, blackened by soot and flames, partially destroyed: "When France learned that the cathedral of Reims was in flames, her heart shrank; those who wept for a son, still found tears for the holy church."[91] France is the great unity summed up in the cathedral of Reims; so the cathedral can be compared to a son, a member of the family, to oneself.

Mâle had always considered it virtually proven that German medieval architecture was totally derived from outside sources, above all from France. What had before been a negative judgment about originality of German Gothic now turned to anger.[92] "[They] have turned their cannons on the beautiful statues that have spread peace about them, that speak only of charity, of gentleness, of forgetfulness of self. They have taken aim at the apostles who presented themselves as disarmed as Christianity itself, and who today are as mutilated as soldiers. The entire world has been moved by this crime: everyone feels that a star had paled, and that beauty had been diminished on the earth."[93] He points to his beloved *Divine Comedy* to illustrate the perversity of this destruction. What if some tyrant had destroyed the *Divine Comedy* of Dante, with its beauty of order, richness of thought, and perfection of form, he asks. Mâle recalls the value of Reims for the French, who enter the cathedral to seek, first of all, the place where Joan of Arc, "that angel from heaven," stood during the crowning of her king. Then, for the only time in his life, Mâle uses his intellectual power militantly. Those portal statues with their elegance and fine smiles were the flower of a civilization that could be likened to the Greek civilization. The Germans came to learn from this civilization and have now turned against their old masters: "What a wonderful occasion for Caliban to destroy the work of his master and to say then to the world that it was he who invented Gothic art."[94] Mâle evokes the image of the smoking, crumbling cathedral and dreads the winter when the stones begin to detach themselves and fall, one by one. His only resort is to proclaim the cathedral's virtues, beauty, and perfection. His articles, appearing first in the *Revue de Paris,* were collected toward the end of the war in *L'Art allemand et l'art français du moyen âge,* along with other materials.[95] This was a politics of the defense and promotion of beauty. What Louis Gillet called Mâle's "capacity for admiration" of beauty took precedence over political platforms and party loyalties.[96]

In 1918, with his first two major works behind him, Mâle was elected to the Académie des Inscriptions et Belles-Lettres within the Institut de France.[97] He wrote to Louis Gillet, "The Institut heaps praise upon me right now. The Académie française gives me an award; the Académie des Inscriptions, a chair. I think of the precursors, the founders of the history of French art, who themselves received nothing but abuse. Ideas do finally make their way. The French themselves will end by admiring France."[98] He was designated to succeed Msgr. Louis Duchesne as director of the École Française at Rome in 1923. At the insistence of members of the Académie des Inscriptions and of

Raymond Poincaré, president of the Council of Ministers charged with the confirmation of these appointments, he accepted, though he was reluctant to leave his students at the Sorbonne. As he ended his teaching years there, he appeared this way to Germain Bazin: "Having attained the age of sixty, he offered the paradoxical silhouette of a retired cavalry officer, whose elegant moustache, aquiline nose, and proud bearing he had; his voice a little weak but musical, he communicated to his students the warmth of a teaching that was also a discrete profession of faith; you might believe that a legend was being recounted, but you were still ruled by strict historical disciplines."[99] Friends and colleagues in France pressed for his election to the Académie française while he continued his work in Italy. In 1924, Joseph Bédier wrote to him, "When you present yourself, whatever be the circumstances, I shall vote for you: you know it, and that is why I have not hurried to answer you; you scarcely need to know what I shall do, but what the others will do."[100] At the urging of friends, then, he presented himself for membership in the Académie, and in June 1927, he was elected to the chair recently held by the poet Jean Richepin, and earlier by Montesquieu and Alexandre Dumas, the younger. In his *Discours de réception* of 28 June 1928, Mâle praised his immediate predecessor, Jean Richepin, as was proper to the occasion, adding some thoughts about the value of words and their mystery and about the creative power of a people. But he began with a word of praise for those who had elected him to the Académie: "You wished to say that the cathedrals are worth as much as our most beautiful poems, that France put as much genius in them as in her most profound books, and that those who have spent their lives studying them have not worked in vain. I thank you for believing that when I set myself to the task of deciphering the thought that these old stones express, I was able to do something useful for my country."[101] Mâle himself felt that he had made a contribution to France's self-understanding, and he believed that the Académie had understood the value of his work in the same way as he understood it.

Just the year before, in 1927, a collection of the major journal articles—those not previously integrated into his books—was published: *Art et artistes du moyen âge,* with studies of the influence of Arab art on the churches of central and southern France, Gothic architecture in the south of France, the history of Mont-Saint-Michel, and the importance of the miniaturist Jean Bourdichon. In his preface to *Art et artistes* he told of his joy as a young researcher when he was so much alone in his interest in the art and architecture of medieval France: "I asked myself if there was anyone in France who would be moved by these marvels. . . . My joy was great at Chartres one day when a peasant of the Beauce, a descendant of those who harnessed themselves to the carts to transport the stone of Notre-Dame, came to my side to contemplate the statues of the south porch. 'I never come to Chartres,' he told me, 'without admiring the cathedral.' I had at last met a Frenchman who loved the art of France."[102] Mâle then said that he had exaggerated as a young man. There were people in those early days who studied and loved the French art of the Middle Ages, even though the situation since that time has much improved. He certainly knew, that same year in which he was elected to the Académie française, how his work had served to bring about the change among the well educated.

In a study of the religious art of Gaul, written in his old age, he praised the "genius" of France, the genius of peoples, rather than their formal politics. [103] He recalls the major invasions of French soil, the destruction, and the magnificent rebuilding that went on. These examples console him because they prove that "French genius is indestructible." Then Mâle, the old man, the leading scholar of the past, who has just finished a major study of France's earliest days, calls for a new, lively, and enlightened approach by the architects and urbanists responsible for city planning and rebuilding. Let them create modern houses that are inspired by the "divine proportion" of the Italian Renaissance, known also to the Middle Ages. Let the urban planners open vast perspectives replacing ruins with parks. "Let them bring the country into the city, with air, light, and sun."[104] At the end of his history of the Christian art of Gaul, he writes, "It is to the honor of the great bishops of Gaul that they believed it necessary to maintain, in the world, real beauty."[105]

Influence: The Varieties of Reconciliation

Mâle's influence on his famous students, though genuine, was more on the level of inspiration (the eminent value of medieval iconography and its importance for modern France) and example (respect for data and care in analyzing them) than on the level of data selection and methodology. For his students, his works constituted a historiographical and literary monument that could not be redone. They said that he was "the first to teach that the history of forms is the history of thought" (Henri Focillon), that he made them "understand the soul of the Middle Ages" (Marcel Aubert), that his method was "the only valuable one as far as the Christian art of the Middle Ages is

concerned" (Louis Reau), and that the lessons he taught were "so alive that
the memory of them always enchants" (Germain Bazin).[106] Mâle had no real
disciples, but some scholars followed more directly in his footsteps than others. The work of Marcel Aubert, for example, grew more directly out of
Mâle's projects than did the work of Focillon.

L'Art religieux du XIIIe siècle en France in its first simple edition was respect-
fully received. Georges Perrot, a mentor of Mâle's and director of the École
Normale, had said, "From the time of Fustel de Coulanges, nothing has made
us better relive the genius of an epoch."[107] Louis Réau says that when Mâle was
appointed to teach the history of Christian art at the Sorbonne in 1906 there
were no genuine art courses in the universities and lycées. Ernest Lavisse, a little earlier, had engineered at the Sorbonne a type of adjunct chair of art history that covered everything from the catacombs through impressionism. But
because Mâle had presented and defended his dissertation with such brilliance
that scholars in connected disciplines in the Paris institutions of higher education learned of his achievement, he was invited to teach special courses at the
Sorbonne. Réau wrote that Mâle's talents as a writer enabled him to appeal to
the general public. Yet he managed to avoid the banal generalizations that the
chartists (professors and graduates of the École des Chartes) somewhat con-
temptuously believed to be characteristic of all popular authors.[108]

The four great syntheses written by Mâle were in all libraries and in the
houses of tens of thousands of educated French. They gained for him the post
he occupied in the French university system, as well as election to the
Académie française. According to the office of his publisher, Armand Colin,
each edition of Mâle's four major works, represented about 5,000 copies. This
would mean that between 1900 and, let us say, 1980 only 50,000 copies of
L'Art religieux du XIIIe siècle en France, 30,000 copies of L'Art religieux de la fin
du moyen âge en France, 35,000 copies of L'Art religieux du XIIe siècle en France,
and 15,000 copies of L'Art religieux après le concile de Trente had been sold. But
during this period there were also reprinted editions, paperback editions, the
several editions of some of his shorter works, and the translation of his major
works into English, German, Spanish, and Italian (obviously, the diffusion of
the translations tells us little about Mâle's influence in France). The first
paperback edition of L'Art religieux du XIIe siècle en France numbered about
40,000 copies, and the editions of his study of the churches of early Christian
Gaul, Chartres cathedral, Albi cathedral, the essay collection Arts et artistes du
moyen âge, and a postwar presentation of selections from his major works have
gone into thousands of copies for each edition (publishers are by and large
unable to unearth this information for us).[109]

Of Mâle's acknowledged admirers, the one who eventually achieved great-est fame was Marcel Proust.[110] He came to know Mâle's work when Robert de Billy lent him a copy of the original edition of the 1898 thesis. In 1900, Proust had sent Émile Mâle a copy of his article "Ruskin à Notre-Dame d'Amiens," which had appeared in the *Mercure de France*. In a letter to Mme Catusse in 1905, Proust referred to *L'Art religieux du XIIIe siècle en France* as the "beauti-ful book of Mâle," calling it a "pure masterpiece and the last word in French iconography."[111] Periodically throughout the years, Proust used Mâle as a source for things medieval. In his 16 August 1904 article in *Le Figaro,* "La Mort des cathédrales," Proust quoted him. Although he footnotes Mâle in sketches for *À la recherche du temps perdu,* there were no footnotes in the printed editions. Jean Autret says, "It was Émile Mâle who furnished or sug-gested to Marcel Proust almost all the details on religious art that he intro-duced in *Swann*."[112] Proust scholar Luc Fraisse says that Mâle the scholar and teacher was mirrored in the personality of Elstir, the painter in *À la recherche du temps perdu.* Fraisse points out that "a note in Cahier 54 indicates that [Elstir] owes much to Émile Mâle. Proust evokes there 'the opinion of Elstir (Mâle) on good and bad restorations.'" And when Marcel, the protagonist of the novel argues with his love Albertine—again evoking Elstir—"it is as if in the fictional painter a Claude Monet and an Émile Mâle were coexisting and not coming to any mutual understanding." Elstir evaluating Gothic art and archi-tecture plays a role in the novel corresponding to the role played by Émile Mâle in the life of Proust.[113]

In spite of such appreciation, Mâle's influence on the general public came gradually. As *Mercure de France* reported at the time of his election to the Académie française: "Émile Mâle is not known by the general public. He is not seen at major Parisian events and social gatherings. He does not write for newspapers and he is not sought out for interviews on contemporary issues. But his works are read and admired by the well educated in Europe and out-side of Europe." Mâle's life is easy to sum up, says the author of the article: he had traveled, studied, taught, and written.[114]

Finally, however, even textbooks and tour guides gave increased attention to the beauty and national importance of medieval religious art and architec-ture. Mâle himself had always believed that an examination of texts would aid historians: "I shall share with you an idea that has preoccupied me for a long time. Nothing would be more useful to us, in my opinion, than to gather together the textbooks of national history that, in every country, we place in the hands of grammar school children. These books have received the approval of the authorities and make known the aspirations of a people. There you can learn what to expect of the future generations that you are forming. These little books would certainly bring us more truth than the official pronouncements we hear." A textbook, as Alain Choppin has pointed out, is really a digest of the society that produces it. One should study the content, diffusion, and official promotion of the text to understand more clearly its relation to the producing society.[115]

Although the Catholic school texts placed more emphasis on the civilizing role of the church than did the public school texts, both types placed equal emphasis on the beauty of the art and architecture. In one major textbook, Gauthier and Deschamps (Hachette), a change occurred between the 1904 and 1928 editions that I would attribute to Émile Mâle. In the 1904 edition there is no mention whatsoever of cathedrals or religious art. In the 1928 edition, however, there is a cathedral discussion running several pages with subheadings on "The Construction of Cathedrals," "Notre Dame of Paris," and "The House of the People." The authors say, "There are no structures more beautiful than the great churches called cathedrals, built from the thirteenth century on. Each city in France wanted to have a beautiful cathedral. The poor worked for nothing; the rich donated money; great lords were seen digging up the soil and harnessing themselves to carts loaded with construction material."[116] To be sure, the notion that cathedrals were the work of the people had been placed in relief since the days of Victor Hugo and Viollet-le-Duc, but the privileged place of the cathedrals in the French national patrimony was given most powerful expression in Mâle's first book. Beginning around 1950, the textbooks for the upper primary grades and for the secondary schools gave attention to chronology, techniques of construction, the stages of religious art history, and the relation of the art to the religious teachings of the medieval period. Other textbooks offered selected paragraphs from Mâle's studies of the twelfth and thirteenth centuries: the 1959 Réunion des professeurs (Ligel) and the "accompanying texts" volume of the 1959 Labal (Hachette). By the 1960s, some of the texts for upper grades and lycées were produced by authors competent in religious art history. For example, the 1964 Isaac (Hachette) balances discussions of architecture, sculpture, and glass; there are discussions of the subject matter of the art, and there are references to Italian art. One might also ask whether the 1964 Durif and Labal (Hachette), quoting from "a great French poet" the words, "In the Middle Ages, the human race thought nothing of importance that it did not write in stone,"[117] found the sentence in Victor Hugo's *Notre-Dame de Paris* or found it dramatically presented in the conclusion of Mâle's *L'Art religieux du XIIIe siècle en France*.

The most popular French tourist guides after 1950 included, where appropriate, quotations from and bibliographical references to the works of Mâle
and his great students. In the 1950–51 *Guide vert, Chartres,* Mâle's study of
Chartres is suggested as a study that is "well documented and illustrated," and
the 1952–53 *Guide vert, Environs de Paris,* refers to the writings of Marcel
Aubert. From then on there are references to works of Mâle and his students.[118] Mâle is quoted in the contemporary *Guide bleu, Île de France,* and his
contribution to the general fund of iconographical information is still seen in
Michelin's *Guide vert, Environs de Paris.* Of Chartres cathedral the *Guide bleu*
notes, "From this exceptionally homogeneous building, built essentially in
less than thirty years, emerges the classical type of cathedral, which will be
repeated in the course of the following years at Reims and Amiens, and which
in the celebrated formula of Émile Mâle is called 'the very thought of the
Middle Ages made visible.'" The guide discusses the extraordinary blue color
of the most famous window of the Blessed Virgin, "de la Belle Verrière," "of
which Émile Mâle said that it puts us in contact with the beyond."[119]

Of course, Mâle's work had always been appreciated in church circles.
After his death, there were several articles about him in the church-affiliated
journals *L'Enseignement chrétien* and *Ecclesia.*[120] The authors emphasized the
Christian faith and sentiments expressed in Mâle's writings, one of them erro-
neously suggesting that he was a "pious" (*dévot*) Christian—family and friends
remember him as a sincere and moral Christian, yes, but never "pious."
Churchmen and church organizations adopted Mâle's ideas in somewhat haphazard fashion—and here we are halfway between the cultivated reader and
the general public. His first book received favorable notice in the Jesuit fort-
nightly journal *La Civiltà Cattolica* (17 October 1903). In the Parisian Catholic
daily *La Croix* (21 December 1910) another cleric writing of his second book
noted that it ought to be in all the rectory libraries of France. "It would train
our pastors to respect our artistic tradition; it would teach them the meaning
and value of their churches and the profound significance of the venerable
vestiges of medieval art." In the years following World War I, *L'Ami du clergé*
(18 January 1923), the most widely received journal for French priests,
reported on his work in some detail, and brief selections from his books were
published in *La Voix de Notre-Dame de Chartres,* the official publication of the
cathedral staff. These are a few examples from among many. His years in
Rome, of course, brought him into friendly contact with important members
of the Catholic hierarchy, including the future Pius XII. Catholic intellectuals
had a more rounded and balanced appreciation of Mâle's goals and gifts. Right

after Mâle's death, the Jesuit Paul Doncoeur wrote that his works would be esteemed as long as scholars and readers understood exactly what the historian had set himself to accomplish: not a history of aesthetics or techniques, but rather the history of the relation of the images—the subject matter—to the theological sources. Such an appreciation of Mâle's accomplishments is fundamentally correct.[121]

In sum, as André Grabar wrote in 1962, "The literary and scientific work of Mâle holds a very sure place in the awareness of all of us; he is part of the intellectual and, in part, sentimental baggage of every cultivated man in France, and as such he is both of our own times and ageless." Similar appreciations were offered at the time of Mâle's death in 1954. In *Le Monde,* 8 October 1954, André Chastel wrote that Mâle's oeuvre was a great "structure": the master interpretation of stained glass, miniature, and sculpture that is "nuanced" today: "Everyone remains indebted to him." Pierre Gaxotte, the same day in *Le Figaro,* wrote that Mâle's ideas "belong today to the public domain of teaching and criticism." Élie Lambert, in a journal article written shortly after Mâle's death, made clear that "in its straight simplicity, the life made a single unity with the considerable work of the great professor, master of all our historians of art, who was at the same time a great scholar and a great writer." Henri Daniel-Rops, shortly after Mâle's death, conceived the idea of erecting some kind of memorial to Mâle on the grounds of Chartres cathedral. When a bust of Mâle was unveiled in the garden park behind the cathedral in 1963, Daniel-Rops evoked the moment when, lost in reflection within the cathedral, "The image of the old master imposed itself so much then on the evening pilgrim, that he seemed to appear before him to guide him to La Belle Verrière, or to make him admire the marvelous tracework of the vaults of the transept. And the visitor said to himself that it would be a great day when he would see the poet of the cathedral honored in a fitting way."[122] Mâle showed the way to generations of scholars, who, along with him, taught the reading public to understand and appreciate the beauty and value of a medieval French Catholic culture that had been ignored or disdained for centuries.

EPILOGUE: *Between the Wars, Vichy, and the New Republics*

French men and women have expressed, modified, or renounced their Catholicism in relation to the nation as maintained by a succession of governments, with each government as the official coordinator of heritage, history, patrimony, monuments, and national idea. Catholics would profess loyalty to *France* but not necessarily to a *nation* managed by a secular government. In the revolutionary era, the modification or renouncement of Catholicism by the revolutionary priests insured that identity with nation would be a secular enterprise. From then on, the Catholic attitudes and behaviors posted across the greater part of the nineteenth century were defensive, the antagonism greatest when the coordinating government was a *republic*. But with the turn of the century, in an era of great conflict, with laws expelling church people from the country and with laws separating church and state, there came a renewed idea of the French nation as a political and social unit embracing the values and interests of all its citizens. Government officials were far from unanimous in their acceptance of church influence, but with the coming of war the only solution was a political *union sacrée,* which registered across social and cultural divisions as a détente.

The political and social détente of World War I and the cultural reconciliation before and after the war represented a type of resolution of the Catholic and secular nationalist struggle to possess the minds and hearts of French citizens. It was not really a secure détente, but more a détente of circumstances; a stable compromise between factions rather than a definitive resolution of the old antagonisms. That old nineteenth-century rivalry between official, self-consciously Catholic French and official, self-consciously republican/secular French had played itself out, but new versions of this antagonism were always possible. Clearly, the most dramatic and the most tragic of these was the Vichy government.

In the wake of French defeat by the armies of Hitler in 1940, a collaborationist administration headed by the aged hero of World War I, Marshall Philippe Pétain, installed itself in the famous spa town of Vichy. The political and social agenda were really shaped by Vice-Premier Pierre Laval, an opportunist who had done stints as foreign minister and as premier in the middle 1930s, and who organized the new government along the lines of Maurras-style nationalism, traditional values, and conservative politics. With its "Work, Family, Fatherland" ethos and its support of church conservatives, Vichy managed to attract those who had maintained their distance from the republican nation. Earlier hierarchical reconciliation to the Republic was virtually forgotten when Pétain's government offered the church special status in return for its strong support. There even surfaced again the old cliché about defeat as retribution for French infidelity to Catholicism.

Well before Vichy, in those years after World War I, the old factions would start to have at it again. In the early 1920s, the government—a legislature with a majority of Catholic parliamentarians—accommodated Catholic concerns: old privileges in Alsace, renewed acceptance of the proscribed religious orders, and the reestablishment of diplomatic relations with the Vatican. A radical left was swept back into power after the Poincaré government sent troops from the occupied Rhineland into the Ruhr industrial region in an attempt to scare Germany into adherence to the schedule of reparations payments set up at the Treaty of Versailles. The move was disapproved universally outside France, and it was disapproved in the main by an irritated French electorate. The new premier, Edouard Herriot, could not resist the old anticlerical stance as a means of unifying and stabilizing the left. He tried to go back on the conservative promotion of the Alsatian church-state exception, to reapply carefully the old restrictions on religious orders, and to go back on the restored diplomatic links with the Vatican. Alsatians vociferously objected. The struggles over secularism that marked the turn of the century in France, when Alsace was part of Germany, were outside their ken. The announcement, then, that the official separation of church and state functions, written into French law and maintained across the first part of the century, would be extended to the restored territories of Alsace and Lorraine, met with major opposition. The *cartel des gauches,* the left coalition, bowed out of the Herriot program when the Christians arose en masse. Father Albert Bessières evoked the old folk ditty, "Frère Jacques, dormez-vous" saying, "Monsieur Herriot has played the role of Frère Jacques: he has sounded the alarm." For more centrist republicans, communists were a greater problem than churchmen anyway. One minister of the interior substituted "Communism, there is the enemy" for the old Gambetta epithet.

The condemnation of the *Action française* in 1926 opened the field to a personalist Catholicism, with an ideology—clearly presented by Emmanuel Mounier's journal, *Esprit*—positioned midway between individualist liberalism and the collectivist doctrines of fascism and communism. On the conservative side, the aging Catholic World War I generals Louis Franchet d'Espérey ("desperate Frankie" to the British troops) and Edouard de Castelnau (along with Charles Mangin the most hard-hearted of the attacking generals of Verdun) carried the old standards of antirepublicanism and antifreemasonry. The anticlericals among republican politicians targeted, among other groups, professional organizations of Catholic *institutrices,* even though they existed only for the edification and continuing education of the members.

In the early 1930s, the government was confronted by the international financial crisis that began with the 1929 market crash. It was a charmed life for French enterprises and agriculture across several years because investments were smaller, more localized, and therefore less likely to be affected by the international market malaise. Even so, André Tardieu's government of moderate reform was rejected: radicals were voted in, and the socialists received the largest number of popular votes. Reactions from the right and far right were dramatic and pointed, although the bloody and lethal 1934 riot in the Place de la Concorde, which left fifteen dead and fifteen hundred injured, was not a coup attempt as the left had charged. Conservative movements, sometimes inspired by Italian-German fascism and sometimes independent of it, seldom cultivated church support because they saw the church as a rival. Jacques Doriot's Parti Populaire Français, Henri Dorgerès's league of farmers, and Colonel François de la Rocque's league of veterans, therefore, did not have a clear Catholic connection.

By this time, the secularism that menaced Catholic life was no longer produced by the national government, but rather by an alienated and resentful working class. French priests, concerned by worker alienation, struggled to establish movements of working-class youth, and the Jeunesse Ouvrière Chrétienne (the JOCs) became the principal Catholic organizational response, more successful than any attempts to sponsor labor unions for older workers. Catholic social liberals, tempered by fear of communism (and papal control), supported a strong centrist republican government. Of course, the republican alliance with the left, Léon Blum's Popular Front, created other problems. Awareness of Blum's Jewish ancestry reactivated some of the old prejudices dormant since the Dreyfus Affair of thirty-five years earlier. Blum himself was a brilliant intellectual and a moderate politician, more preoccupied with keeping Mussolini and Hitler at bay and determining an appropriate response to the fascist coup against republican/socialist forces in Spain than in advancing a socialist agenda. His government lasted only two years, preceded and followed by the ascendancy of Pierre Laval, Paul Daladier, and Paul Reynaud, politicians whose experimentation with moderation and compromise prepared them, unfortunately, for the role they would place in structuring the Vichy regime. In the meantime, the progress of practical atheism could be blamed on the progress of socialism (and communism), whether in its Popular Front setting or on its own. Church leaders were more generally comfortable with the Right, and in 1939 the *Action française* was rehabilitated.

And so, Vichy. The great drama of the 1940 German invasion, which knocked France out of the war, was a new challenge to the church, even though, as in World War I, many people returned to active churchgoing. The defeat of the French army, with its 92,000 deaths, has been called "a funny war," "a strange defeat," and "a strange victory" because it did not have the length and spread of a major war. The incompetence of the French premier and then-War Minister Edouard Daladier and General Maurice Gamelin was a surprise, and the German invasion strategy was far from faultless. Lines of panzers cut through the Ardennes, a German advance awaited in vain in World War I, but unexpected at the beginning of this new war. The French forces, failing to take advantage of the overextended, narrow German attack, fell back, and the British, cut off from any possibility of reinforcement, retreated to Dunkirk for evacuation. With Gamelin urging surrender, Daladier's successor as premier, Paul Reynaud, urged the appointment of Marshall Pétain to work out an agreement with Hitler. Not part of the plan was the rebellion of the youngest of the French generals, Charles de Gaulle, his flight to London, and the subsequent set-up of a Free French government in exile.

To begin with, widespread hope (a papal nuncio used the expression "the Pétain miracle") was shared by both left- and right-wing Catholics, and the hierarchy went about the business of rectifying the Marshall's marriage and presiding at the consequent church wedding (although Pétain himself was represented by proxy). The old man, who years earlier had been an egregious womanizer and a virtual secularist (known to have said, however, "a good Mass never did anyone any harm"), finally became a fairly regular churchgoer. French Catholics had not had a practicing Catholic for president or premier since the departure of President MacMahon in 1879. Members of the Catholic hierarchy began their dilemma-laden exercise of authority in the occupied zone and under the Vichy government, where they combined praise of Pétain with the energizing of the old educational and Catholic-action apostolates. In the occupied north of France, a similar loyalty was not possible; only obedience. But archbishops and bishops from north and south united to propose submission to "established authority," thus avoiding all reference to regime legitimacy. The government motto of "Work, Family, and Fatherland" provided élan for such youth movements as the Scouts and the pilgrimage-oriented *Routiers*. Both the instructor roster of the Vichy school for middle management at Uriage and the leadership of major veteran organizations contained serious Catholic personalities.

Although Catholics in the main occupied the lower echelons of the government, the few high-placed Catholic functionaries worked for the maintenance and enhancement of the new church status. Ministers of education Jacques Chevalier and Jérome Carcopino explicitly supported Catholic values and, with a necessary bow to open schools, religious education in the schools. The old conservative Catholic temptations to dominate returned, combined with something far worse: accommodation to the Nazi persecution of the Jews, with Vichy officials supporting German anti-Jewish measures in the occupied zone. Initial restrictions imposed by the set of laws determining the legal status of the Jews, the *Statut des Juifs,* were received with a great deal of "understanding" by the hierarchy. Whereas in the late 1930s, Cardinals Verdier of Paris and Maurin of Lyon promoted discussions and issued documents denouncing "racism," and Maurin's successor, Cardinal Gerlier, had set up a meeting on racism and anti-Semitism, the new status of Catholicism helped numb the hierarchy to the restrictions on Jewish professional and economic maneuverability. Across the Vichy years, the activities and pronouncements of Cardinal Gerlier alternated between alarmed condemnation and simple counsels to legality—and moderation—in the application of anti-Jewish ordinances. Pétain and Xavier Vallat, secretary for Jewish affairs and another "highly placed" Catholic, could take hope from the willingness of Gerlier to dialogue on the regulative value (in terms of limiting the excess economic power and inappropriate social or education influence of Jews) of the legislation. For all their insistence on "justice" and "charity" in the application of the laws, Gerlier and the others did not weigh in on the illegality and evil of the laws themselves. Reports from Rome, delivered by Vichy's ambassador to the Holy See, Bérard, were also consoling: the ambassador said that the Vatican had no fundamental objections to the *Statut des Juifs* but was only concerned about its application. The suspicions of the papal nuncio to Vichy, Bishop Valeri, and his subsequent disagreement with the Bérard report did not reach the general public. It remained, then, for individual bishops and priests to counsel cooperation or resistance according to their own lights.

Vice-Premier Pierre Laval, with the assistance of the secretary for Jewish affairs, conceded more and more to German demands. First, foreign-born Jews were rounded up, then French Jews were registered, and finally the roundup of French Jews began. The sight of men, women, and children being herded into collection centers and then on to trains moved Gerlier and Suhard to strong condemnation. In this they were joined by the old *Sillon* member Archbishop Saliège of Toulouse (though not by Archbishop Liénart of Lille, an early opponent of racism). Even though this pro-Semitism was sporadic and idiosyncratic, the bishops earned the resentment of diehard French fascists and anti-Semites. The only continuing and active support of the Jews was provided by a priestly underground, including men who after the war established reputations as liberal, engaged, Catholic theologians: Gaston Fessard, Henri de Lubac (at the end of his life, a cardinal) and Yves de Montcheuil. One-third of French Jews and two-thirds of foreign Jews perished during those years.

French church leaders were more preoccupied by the use of French forced labor in Germany. Many of the soldiers captured during the "funny war" were imprisoned, and hundreds of thousands of other French citizens were selected for work in Germany. Conservative bishops, however, would venture to speak only for the release of resistance priests or Catholic resisters from official church youth groups. Bishops and priests were diffident, timid, even sycophantic in response to Vichy incongruity: on one hand, government support of the full range of prerogatives claimed by the church since the Revolution, and, on the other hand, neglect of the fundamental Catholic moral imperatives of justice and charity. They promoted, accommodated, or resisted the Petain government—often promoting, most often accommodating, and occasionally resisting. But the pattern and the proportions were almost the same for other cultural and social players on the political scene. In the last analysis, the Vichy regime was not stressed so much by an outbreak of the old

Catholic-secularist antagonism as by the struggle of each side for government recognition. The church hierarchy and church institutions received favorable treatment certainly, but the old republican contingent was also well represented.

During the Vichy years, de Gaulle's London-based government kept contact with Resistance fighters from across the political spectrum—left, center, and right (with Catholics in each). In London de Gaulle had a tension-filled relationship with, but the genuine support of, Winston Churchill. President Roosevelt, however, supported the Vichy government until the beginning of 1943, a choice that considerably hindered the operations of de Gaulle's Free French forces in Africa. When the invasion of France began with the Normandy landing, de Gaulle was informed after it began, and only later were his forces, under the leadership of General Leclerc, allowed to proceed to the liberation of Paris. De Gaulle had to immediately organize national and local political authorities to represent his own center-right political goals, adroitly avoiding alliances with right-wing movements and any real compromise with the left. In the provisional government that followed the German retreat, a third of the ministers (including Georges Bidault and René Plevin), were, like de Gaulle himself, practicing Catholics. When the constitution of the Fourth Republic was finally redacted, de Gaulle, declining what he considered the structurally weak presidential office, went into retirement.

In the Fourth Republic (1946–58), secularism—albeit with a low anticlerical content—was the reigning style. There were Catholic premiers, but Sunday Mass-going was a private, ideally hidden, affair. Officials wanted to ensure the continued coordination of communists, socialists, and Catholics, in place during the Resistance years, and avoid the renewal of Third Republic and Vichy conflicts. The Ministry of the Interior was preserved as a stronghold of secularism, and local administrators—the *corps préfectoral*—were pressured to forego public religious expression. For a long time, the largely but not exclusively Catholic political party, the Mouvement Républicain Populaire (MRP), gained more support from practicing Catholics than did the Gaullist party. It looked as if the MRP, with its avowed aim of reconciling the church to the Republic, would set the style for Catholics in government, but eventually the Gaullist and, indeed, other political parties came to address major Catholic concerns. When de Gaulle and his Fifth Republic took center stage in 1958, the MRP was becoming superfluous. The continuing alienation of the working class, attracted to communism and other movements of the left, alarmed the church hierarchy into support of the budding worker-priest movement. When the priests, transformed into workers, began to occasionally fall under the influence of the communists, the pope refused to let the French church continue the experiment. This was an internal church dispute, but it resulted from engagement with the larger society.

Ten years after World War II, the French government was trapped in the complex politics and violence of North Africa. Algeria by the twentieth century had become for old French settler families a part of France, with a political administration, economic style, and school system that was an extension of the French mainland. The struggle to keep Algeria French in the face of the Arab-Algerian struggle to control the country, and in the face of a post-colonial solution promoted by French politicians, had driven extremists to the edge of rebellion. Demand and support for de Gaulle's return to national life on his own terms brought him out of the earlier, self-imposed retirement. He returned as last premier of the Fourth Republic and the Fifth Republic's first president, an office he designed with Régis Débré to avoid the executive-legislative confusions of the Fourth Republic. When de Gaulle accorded independence to Algeria, a virtual civil war menaced the mainland, with Catholics on both sides of the divide. In French public life there was no longer a homogeneous Catholic position.

The Gaullist republic was, after the passing of the Algerian crisis, politically stable, economically sound, and internationally respected. But the nation's university students, often under the influence of Marxist-oriented writers and intellectuals, began to protest traditional education and what they took to be their very limited future possibilities. Both church and government were the targets of the radical philosophical and social scientific interpretations of Parisian intellectuals. Students in the Paris universities, whipped into action by a few leaders in May of 1968, demonstrated, harangued, and degenerated into throwing stones and torching cars. For weeks, public life in Paris and elsewhere was on the verge of chaos. Workers joined the students. Conservatives of different stripes counterdemonstrated. De Gaulle maintained control, although with difficulty. Then, within the year, the man who had preserved France from chaos in the 1940s and returned it to prosperity in the 1960s, resigned in response to defeat on a minor referendum. With a centrist electorate fearful of leftist intellectuals and their political potential, Georges Pompidou and Valéry Giscard d'Estaing were able to continue the Gaullist political enterprise—and the general's Catholic identification. By that time a new liberal French Catholicism had emerged out of the open discussion and expression evident at the Second Council of the Vatican. Liberal Catholic

Fig. 13. General Charles de Gaulle (shown here with General Philippe Leclerc) in front of Notre-Dame cathedral in the course of the celebration of the liberation of Paris during World War II. (Roger-Viollet/Getty Images)

theologians appeared in public discussion with secular and Marxist intellectuals and subsequently cooperated on joint publication projects.

The way was open for a return to socialism, no longer opposed by a major Catholic bloc. François Mitterrand, a leader of the socialist opposition since the days of the Fourth Republic, was elected president by a small majority in 1981. In his fourteen years as president, the enigmatic Mitterrand expediently passed from moderate socialist to a socialist free spirit and in the end seem to be posting a quasi-de Gaulle image: the glory of France rather than the triumph of the workers. For some, he appeared to be the consummate intellectual, and for others he appeared to be a man without shame.

Socialist politics in general targeted both capitalist and religious independence and isolation. The minister of education, Alain Savary, tried to hold to account the Catholic school system, which under the Gaullists had enjoyed state support and was free to administer its programs pretty much as it wanted. The vast majority of French bishops were ready to work with him, especially as he was open to their suggestions for change in the proposed legislation. The Savary plan was no real threat to in-house Catholic control of the programs themselves, but fear that church schools might be confused with state schools troubled the Catholic parents (even though only a minority of them were regular churchgoers). Playing on this parental fear, conservative political parties used the issue to stage massive demonstrations against the Mitterrand government. When the affair was over, with Savary's resignation and a return to the status quo ante, some journalists believed that Catholics had once again demonstrated their solidarity against a secularizing state. In fact, the whole thing had been political and economic, a solid minority of Catholics going with the Mitterrand government.

With the very Gaullist Jacques Chirac in the presidency by the mid-1990s, the opposites had crossed. On one hand, the funeral of the socialist agnostic, ex-president Mitterrand was a Catholic ceremony. On the other hand, official Catholicism, represented by the archbishop of Paris, born Jewish and a convert in his teens, Jean-Marie (Aaron) Lustiger, embraced the Republic as the real France. Even representatives of the old anti-Catholic *Ligue Française de l'Enseignement* declared, "We have accepted religions as enduring cultural facts out of which France has been made." If anything the leaders of French Catholicism were more accepting of pluralism of commitment and public expression of it. Witness the controversy over the wearing of the veil by Muslim students in the school system, a freedom of expression championed against some resolutely secular members of the government by Lustiger himself: "Is there a republican religion that prohibits one from being a Catholic, a Protestant, a Jew, a Muslim—even a skeptic? The republican ideal of citizenship does not claim to be a substitute for religion." Catholics today accept the secular national ideal, even more than in the early détente decades, and conversely, freethinkers and members of other faiths, in the main, recognize that Catholicism is an integral part of the national heritage.

Appendix: The "Nation" Conundrum

All kinds of human activity go into the making of a nation. John Hutchinson and Anthony Smith point out contrasting interpretations of this activity in the introduction to their anthology, *Nationalism*. "The concept of *nation* has, in fact, been contested on two fronts: . . . there is little agreement about the role of ethnic, as opposed to political, components of the nation; or about the balance between 'subjective' elements like will and memory, and the more 'objective' elements like territory and language." They add, "perhaps only religious attachments have rivaled national loyalties in their scope and fervour"![1] In any case, historians, social scientists, and ordinary citizens have come to see is that both deeds and ideas make a nation. On one hand, armies and politicians, trades people and clergy *do* things. On the other hand, thoughts, interpretations, and goals—freighted with emotion—make sense of, idealize, and carry further the work of nation-making. Geoff Eley and Ronald Suny in their introduction to *Becoming National: A Reader* write, "This need to constitute nations discursively, through processes of imaginative ideological labor—that is, the novelty of national culture, its manufactured or invented character, as opposed to its deep historical rootedness—is probably the most important point to emerge from the more recent literature."[2] A national identity is an amalgam of sentiments and ideologies that both cause and are caused by the formation of the modern nation. The clairvoyantly titled *Imagined Communities* of Benedict Anderson emphasizes this essential element while pointing to the practical importance of newsprint; and John Breuilly, in his *Nationalism and the State,* concretizes nationalism as politics.[3]

The principal modern interpretations of the meaning of nation and nationalism have come from Giuseppe Mazzini (1805–72) in Italy and Ernest Renan (1823–92) in France. Mazzini wanted to line up the elements that went into the make-up of a nation: territory and language as a foundation; then the vote, right to work, and economic participation, leading to a general idea transmitted through education. Renan wanted to indicate the continuing efforts of idealization and commitment that gave a nation its daily reality. The nation is a product and a producer of collective experiences centered and stabilized by religion, high agricultural and industrial activity in the interest of a functioning economy, the consolidation of the structures of government (state), and the gradual insinuation of a unifying idea. As Eugen Weber puts it, expanding on Renan, "Nations come down to common memories and common consent. But memories can be concocted, and consent imposed. So the asserted principles of nationalism turn out to be a kind of programmatic mythology. Like ethnicity or religion, linguistic reference can provide symbols of those 'common collective practices which alone give a palpable reality to otherwise imaginary community.' Nations more often follow States than precede them, either because a State works hard to forge them, or because the existence of that State crystallizes opposition sentiment into nationalism."[4] Concocted memories, imposed consent, programmatic mythology, linguistic reference, the nature of the relation to the state: these are the realities, mental and physical, that readers must look to when studying the history of a nation and its nationalism.[5]

The earliest stage of national development is the ethnic group. Basic components of the postclan, posttribal unities are peasants and artisans, urban elites, priests/monks/scribes who administer beliefs and rites, all in systematic interaction with one another.[6] Here, in particular, religion has often played a major role because of the power of the basic stories, or myths, of the community and the power of the priesthoods responsible for their dissemination: no other factor has been "so crucial as the presence and influence of a communal salvation religion with its rites, liturgies, customs, sacred language and sacred texts, and its organized priesthoods."[7] Priesthoods conserve and edit, as well as disseminate the stories, and they develop official interpretations—in effect, a political theology. In modern times, the intelligentsia fill in the role of the priests of history.

Class loyalties and the common cause of people in agricultural and industry go into the elemental composition of a nation. Liah Greenfeld believes that beginnings of national awareness in medieval Britain came out of class loyalties first and cultural awareness second. In England, Henry VIII's break with Roman religious authority and, later, the "commonwealth" language of a Parliament opposed to Stuart absolutism fostered experience of English identity in some segments of the population. Class and *métier* certainly did go into the composition of ethnicity—or "popular protonationalism." Ernest Gellner, in a telling diagram of the social structure of agrarian societies, distinguishes layers of military, administrative, and commercial classes at the top and under them, lateral/parallel strips representing communities of agricultural producers. But these components do not go together willingly: he believes that "for the ruling stratus as a whole, and for the various sub-strata within [society], there is a great stress on cultural differentiation, rather than homogeneity."[8] In industrialization, in contrast, progress of differentiated but coordinated groups of producers counts the most: "Modern society is not mobile because it is egalitarian; it is egalitarian because it is mobile."[9] In fact, the industrial progress requires a more unified, purposeful, "objective" education. This reduces the divisiveness of those insulated communities of agricultural producers (a divisiveness maintained by the clerks and clergies of these communities). The largely centrical forces of industry and the largely centrifugal forces of agriculture incorporate the dominant and lesser ethnic goals.

Eric Hobsbawm's expression "popular protonationalism" covers all of the sentiments and ideologies that go with ethnic group loyalties.[10] Peter Alter distinguishes (following Friederich Meinecke) *cultural nation* and *political nation*.[11] The cultural nation comes out of common heritage and language, as well as religious and other customs. By constructing a political administration and incorporating other peoples and social strata beyond the limits of the original ethnic group or cultural nation, the political nation or nation-state is formed. It is based on the will of a citizenry with common political goals: "The nation as a community of responsible citizens expressing a common political will through the state is constituted, in theory at least, by individual commitment to the ideas of 1789 and to the *grande patrie*. Here, nation and state are synonymous; the unifying whole is formed by a uniform language, a uniform judicial and administrative system, a central government and shared political ideals."[12] Alter would call the positive, incorporating movement toward nation-state "*risorgimento* nationalism," and the later return of domination and control by a segment of the population "integral nationalism"—of which Fascist Italy and Nazi Germany are the infamous primary examples. A new type of ethnocentrism inspired nation formation in the twentieth century with the collapse of the Russian, Austro-Hungarian, and German empires after World War I and the collapse of the Soviet Union (old Russian empire without dynastic associations) at the beginning of the 1990s. The attempts to construct smaller nations out of these larger imperial/federative units led to a renewed self-expression of the old *ethnie,* called "patriotic groups" by Miroslav Hroch. He studied their social composition in relation to the industrial revolution and emergence of bourgeois capitalism and, accordingly, examined national movements in Bohemia, Finland, Estonia, Slovakia, Lithuania, Bulgaria, Flanders, and Macedonia.[13]

In sum, the nation-state results from various combinations of mobilization, territorialization, and politicization, enhanced by popular memory of participation in the romance and mystery of a historical drama. Religion can serve as foundation, catalyst, antithesis, or parallel force. In France it was a foundation and catalyst under the old regime and has been an antithesis (divorce/defense) or parallel force (détente) ever since.

Notes

INTRODUCTION

1. Erik H. Erikson, *Childhood and Society* (New York, 1950).

2. Charles Taylor, *Sources of the Self: The Making of the Modern Identity* (Cambridge, Mass., 1989), 37.

3. The classic text is George Herbert Meade, *Mind, Self, and Society from the Standpoint of a Social Behaviorist* (Chicago, 1934). For guidance in sorting out the extensive and diverse subsequent literature, I am indebted to Alan Williams, who favors the work of Anthony Giddens, especially his *Modernity and Self-Identity* (Stanford, 1991). In a more recent study of Russian national identity formation, which reviews some major literature on the general subject, Ronald Grigor Suny emphasizes the multiple and fluid qualities of identity. See "Constructing Primordialism: Old Histories for New Nations," *Journal of Modern History* 73 (2001): 862–96. And on multiple, fluid identities in nineteenth-century France, see Roger V. Gould, *Insurgent Identities: Class, Community, and Protest in Paris from 1848 to the Commune* (Chicago, 1995).

4. Pierre Birnbaum, *The Idea of France*, trans. M. B. DeBevoise (New York, 1998), 10–11, 20.

5. Fernand Broulard, Yves-Marie Hilaire, and Gérard Cholvy, eds., *Matériaux pour l'histoire du peuple français,* 3 vols. (Paris, 1982–92), 1:12.

6. Ibid., 13.

7. Ibid., 13, 23.

8. Ibid., 127. In the field of history of religions, scholars work with broad categories, e.g., Ninian Smart's "dimensions" of religion: mythic, ritual, doctrinal, ethical, social, and personal. See *The Religious Experience of Mankind,* 5th ed. (New York, 1996). For our purposes the social (sociological) and personal (psychological) dimensions are understood insofar as they are expressed by perceptible adherence to myth (fundamental story), ritual (worship services), doctrines (theology), and ethics (behavior). I have considered possible uses for these categories in modern French religious history in an article-review of Mona Ozouf, *Festivals of the French Revolution, History and Theory* 28 (1989): 112–25.

9. Pierre Nora, ed., *Les Lieux de mémoire,* 7 vols. (Paris, 1984–92). The initial, single volume entitled *La République;* the second, third, and fourth volumes all bear the title *II La Nation,* each successive volume indicated by one, two, three asterisks; the fifth, sixth, and seventh volumes all bear the title *III Les France,* each successive volume indicated by arabic numerals and subtitles.

10. *Les Lieux de mémoire: La République,* 8.

11. Steven Englund has clearly pointed out the overlap, confusion, and—yes—considerable merits of these volumes. See "The Ghost of Nation Past," review of *La Nation,* by Pierre Nora, *Journal of Modern History* 64 (1992): 316. See also "History in a Late Age: A Review Essay of Pierre Nora, ed., *Les France,*" *French Politics and Society* 14 (1996): 68–79.

12. See appendix, "The *Nation* Conundrum."

13. Possibilities here are outlined in David A. Bell, *The Cult of the Nation in France: Inventing Nationalism, 1680–1800* (Cambridge, Mass., 2001). But after 1789, religion became distinct, and most often separate, from loyal national self-identification.

14. Philip Schlesinger, "On National Identity: Some Conceptions and Misconceptions Criticized," *Social Science Information* 26 (1987): 260−61. See Robert Gildea, *The Past in French History* (New Haven, 1994) for discussion of the interplay of political culture and national memory, where religious faith as such is not what determines a political orientation, but rather individual experiences of specific faith communities. "It will be my contention that what defines a political culture above all is not some sociological factor such as race or class or creed but collective memory, that is the collective construction of the past by a given community" (10). Gildea's topics are Revolution, Bonapartism, Grandeur, Regionalism, Catholicism, and Anarchism.

15. Anne-Marie Thiesse, *La Création des identités nationales: Europe XVIIIe−XXe siècle* (Paris, 1999), 11.

16. Ibid., 14. The "kit" image is taken from Orvar Löfgren, "The Nationalization of Culture," *National Culture as Process,* a re-edition of *Ethnologica Europea* 19 (1989): 5−25.

17. Englund, "Ghost of Nation Past," 316.

18. Major syntheses of French religious history and general French history lay out landmark events and key personalities of the modern era, 1798 to 1918. See Ralph Gibson, *A Social History of French Catholicism* (New York, 1989), François Lebrun, ed., *Histoire des catholiques en France* (Paris, 1980), Adrien Dansette, *Histoire religieuse de la France contemporaine: L'Église catholique dans la mêlée politique et sociale,* rev. ed. (Paris, 1965), Gerard Cholvy and Yves-Marie Hilaire, *Histoire religieuse de la France contemporaine,* 3 vols. (Toulouse, 1985−88), and Jacques LeGoff, René Remond, and Philippe Joutard, eds., *Histoire de la France religieuse: Du roi très Chrétien à la laïcité républicaine, XVIIIe−XIXe siècle,* 1st ed. 1991 (Paris, 2001). Jean-Marie Mayeur et al., *L'Histoire religieuse de la France, 19e−20e siècle: Problèmes et méthodes* (Paris, 1975) is the bibliography.

CHAPTER 1. BETWEEN CHURCH AND NATION

1. The number recorded is 291. The Second Estate, the nobles, had almost the same number of delegates (285), but the Third Estate, the commoners, had about as many delegates (578) as the first two Estates combined.

2. Archival research here is built on earlier important studies of these three clergy choices. The *poseurs,* from the pages of the radical *Feuille villageoise,* have been identified in Melvin Edelstein's study (1977) of that review; the *abdicataires* have been partially analyzed in the research accomplished and championed by Marcel Reinhard (work published in 1964 that has received renewed recognition in the recent Claude Langlois, Timothy Tackett, and Michel Vovelle, eds., *Atlas de la Révolution française,* vol. 9 *Religion* (Paris, 1996). *Rétractés* have been catalogued in the Archives Nationales publication, *La Légation en France du Cardinal Caprara (1801−1808): Répertoire des demandes de réconciliation avec l'Église* (1979). The baseline for the clergy population is found in Timothy Tackett and Claude Langlois, "Ecclesiastical Structures and Clerical Geography on the Eve of the French Revolution," *French Historical Studies* 11 (1980): 715−45. Rodney J. Dean, *L'Église constitutionnelle, Napoléon et le Concordat de 1801* (Paris, 2004), offers both exhaustive treatment and genuine synthesis.

3. I will trace the vagaries of these ideas in a book length-study, now in progress, on revolutionary priests and bishops. But see in particular Catherine Maire, *De la cause de Dieu à la cause de la Nation: Le jansénisme au XVIIIe siècle* (Paris, 1998), and Dale K. Van Kley, *The Religious Origins of the French Revolution: From Calvinism to the Civil Constitution, 1560−1791* (New Haven, 1996). The two magisterial texts for the study of clerical culture and behavior, before and during the Revolution, are John McManners, *Church and Society in Eighteenth-Century France,* 2 vols. (Oxford, 1998), and Timothy Tackett, *Religion, Revolution, and Regional Culture in Eighteenth-Century France: The Ecclesiastical Oath of 1791* (Princeton, 1986). See also Dale K. Van Kley's review of the writings of John McManners and Bernard Plongeron, "Christianity as Casualty and Chrysalis of Modernity: The Problem of Dechristianization in the French Revolution," *American Historical Review* 108 (2003): 1081−104, and Nigel Aston, *Religion and Revolution in France, 1780−1804* (Washington, 2000).

4. Whereas the labels *abdicataires* and *retractés* were current in the revolutionary decade, *poseurs* is simply a dictionary term in both French and English. I have not tried to trace its use during the Revolution. On the changing roles of priests, see Nicole Lemaître, ed., *Histoire des curés* (Paris, 2000).

5. *La Feuille villageoise,* adressée chaque semaine à tous les villages de la France pour les instruire des loix, des événements, des découvertes qui intéressent tout Citoyen: proposée par souscription aux propriétaires, fermiers, pasteurs, habitans et amis des campagnes, I (hereafter *LFV*), title page.

6. *LFV,* Avertissement, 2.

7. See Maurice Pellisson, "Un Jésuite passé à la Révolution: Joachim Cérutti," *Revue politique et parlementaire* (1906): 292–315.

8. Melvin Allen Edelstein, *La Feuille villageoise: Communication et modernisation dans les régions rurales pendant la Révolution* (Paris, 1977), 68–69, 72, 74–75. In his appendix C, Edelstein shows the distribution of letters by department but finds that the specific villages within the departments and the priests who are curés therein are more integral to the understanding of revoluionary activity than simple departmental residency or origins. The partis pris of individual priests dominate in his and my analyses because the number of persons tabulated is not sufficient to establish other kinds of statistical significance. See also the discussion in Serge Bianchi, "Les Curés rouges dans la Révolution française," *Annales historiques de la Révolution française* 54 (1982): 364–92.

9. *LFV* I, no. 4 (21 October 1790), 50.

10. *LFV* I, no. 15 (6 janvier 1791), 269, 274.

11. *LFV* I, no. 20 (10 février 1791), 360.

12. Ibid., 359.

13. *LFV* II, no. 51, (15 septembre 1791), 451.

14. Ibid., 452.

15. *LFV* III, no. 2 (6 octobre 1791), 26.

16. *LFV* III, no. 10 (1 décembre 1791), 223.

17. *LFV* III, no. 7 (10 novembre 1791), 155–56.

18. *LFV* III, no. 18 (26 janvier 1792), 427.

19. Ibid.

20. *LFV* III, no. 10 (10 novembre 1791), 157.

21. *LFV* IV, no. 27 (24 mai 1792), 193–205.

22. *LFV* V, no. 13 (27 décembre 1792), 293–94.

23. *LFV* IV, no. 36 (31 mai 1792), 228.

24. *LFV* IV, no. 27 (29 mars 1792), 9.

25. Ibid., 9–10.

26. *LFV* V, no. 12 (20 décembre 1792), 266. For the language controversy during the Revolution, see Michel de Certeau, Dominique Julia, and Jacques Revel, *Une Politique de la langue: La Révolution française et les patois: L'Enquête de Grégoire* (Paris, 1975).

27. *LFV* IV, no. 50 (13 septembre 1792), 558–60.

28. *LFV* V, no. 16 (17 janvier 1793), 361.

29. *LFV* VI, no. 27 (3 avril 1793), 2.

30. *LFV* VI, no. 29 (18 avril 1793), 49.

31. *LFV* VI, no. 36 (6 juin 1793), 235.

32. *LFV* VI, no. 42 (18 juillet 1793), 367.

33. *LFV* VI, no. 29 (18 avril 1793), 50.

34. *LFV* VI, no. 32 (9 mai 1793), 121–25.

35. *LFV* VI, no. 36 (6 juin 1793), 217–20.

36. *LFV* VI, no. 42 (18 juillet 1793), 373.

37. Ibid.

38. *LFV* V, no. 23 (7 mars 1793), 536–37.

39. *LFV* V, no. 8 (22 novembre 1792), 174.

40. *LFV* VI, no 43 (25 juillet 1793), 377–88.

41. *LFV* VI, no. 44 (1 août 1793), 415.
42. Ibid.
43. Ibid., 416.
44. Ibid., 417.
45. Ibid.
46. Ibid.
47. *LFV* VI, no. 48 (29 août 1793), 511.
48. Ibid., 518.
49. *LFV* VI, no. 50 (12 septembre 1793), 558.
50. Ibid., 561.
51. *LFV* VII, no. 18, (30 janvier 1794), 415.
52. *LFV* VII, no. 27 (Quartidi, 14 Germinal, l'an 2 // 3 avril 1794), 12.
53. Ibid.
54. Ibid.
55. Ibid., 12–13.
56. Ibid., 13.
57. Ibid., 35.
58. Ibid., 35–36.
59. The foundation studies of *abdicataires* appeared in 1964, when Marcel Reinhard presented a research methodology for a quantitative and qualitative analysis of the abdications of 1793–94. Bernard Plongeron, Maurice Bordes, Michel Vovelle, Mlle Rebouillat, and M. L. Fracart presented statistics and analysis for the city of Paris, Provence, and the departments of Gers, Allier, and the Deux-Sèvres, respectively. All based themselves in part on the same series in the Archives Nationales F19 872–93, *Lettres de prêtres classées; démissions données devant diverses administrations,* pairing these cartons with appropriate documentation in departmental and private archives, and I follow their lead. By and large, dossiers of individual priests were collected under their own names by the national government offices, and summaries of abdication activity came in from regional headquarters. These outstanding studies were virtually forgotten when Timothy Tackett published *Religion, Revolution, and Regional Cultures in Eighteenth Century France.* Reinhard, Tackett, and subsequent studies are resumed in Langlois, Tackett, Vovelle, *Atlas de la Révolution française,* vol. 9: *Religion.* See Marcel Reinhard, ed., *Actes du quatre-vingt neuvième congrès national des sociétés savantes,* Lyon 1964, section d'histoire moderne et contemporaine, tome I (Paris, 1964).
60. This would have been about one-sixth of the total number of priests working in France in 1790, one-third of the curés. But by the time the abdications began in 1793, there was a much smaller number of priests officially functioning and the vast majority of these were constitutionals. See Michel Vovelle, *La Révolution contre l'église: De la Raison à l'Être suprême* (Paris, 1988), 101–15. Vovelle's subsequently contested figures have in the main been confirmed in a model study of regional abdications, Kenneth R. Fenster, "The Abdicating Clergy in the Gironde," *Catholic Historical Review* 85 (1999): 541–65.
61. Vovelle, *Révolution contre l'église,* 135.
62. Ibid., 138. For further information on the Caprara delegation, see the section "Retracting the Oath—Patterns of Guilt and Justification."
63. Ibid., 131.
64. Ibid., 63, 67.
65. See Bernard Plongeron, "Abdicataires parisiens" in Reinhard, *Actes,* 47.
66. Vovelle, *Révolution contre l'Église,* 138.
67. Archives Nationales (hereafter AN) F19 889, Pasquer.
68. Ibid.
69. Ibid.
70. Ibid.
71. Ibid.

72. Ibid.

73. Ibid.

74. Ibid.

75. AN F19 873, Beulazet. The Beulazet dossier is discussed in Serge Bianchi, "Les Curés rouges," 382−83.

76. AN F19 873, Bevalet.

77. AN F19 876, Courtonne.

78. AN F19 880, Gillard.

79. AN F19 872, Baudot.

80. AN F19 872, Bedane.

81. AN F19 877, Denis.

82. AN F19 875, Chambon.

83. AN F19 887, Darros.

84. AN F19 891, St.-Didier.

85. Ibid.

86. AN F19 889, Paintandre.

87. AN F 19 876, Courbec.

88. AN F19 889, Paintandre.

89. AN F19 872, Abadie.

90. AN F19 884 Lacombe.

91. AN F19 883, Julien. Here with an asterix he footnoted his text, "I sent a small work to the printer in 1790, which was entitled *Le mariage des prêtres, ou le célibat détruit,* in which I had to rebuke the foolish and exalt the wise."

92. AN F19 883, Julien.

93. Ibid.

94. AN F19 877, Destremour.

95. AN F19 878, Dyvincourt.

96. AN F19 891, Sousciat.

97. AN F19 890, Poncy.

98. AN F19 891, Sousciat.

99. AN F19 891, Surdraud.

100. Ibid.

101. AN F19 878, Douchin.

102. AN F19 878, Duffay.

103. Ibid.

104. AN F19 873, Baudin.

105. AN F19 879, Le Forestier.

106. AN F19 884, Lacouture.

107. AN F19 880, Géruzez.

108. AN F19 880, Génain.

109. AN F19 872, Allaire.

110. AN F19 880, Genet.

111. AN F19 879, Marchand.

112. AN F19 883, Jatz.

113. AN F19 878, Duvivier.

114. AN F19 880, Gibert.

115. AN F19 880, Géruzez.

116. AN F19 876, Coinon.

117. Ibid.

118. Ibid.

119. AN F19 876, Cotillon.

120. Ibid.

121. Ibid.

122. AN F19 889, Petit.

123. Sources used for this study include selected cartons from the AN series F19, AN microfilms of the *dossiers Caprara* (AF IV 1897, 1898, 1899), and the two volumes on the Caprara legation published by the AN, *La Légation en France du Cardinal Caprara (1801–1808)*, and Jeanine Charon-Bordas, *Inventaire des archives de la Légation en France du Cardinal Caprara, 1801–1808* (Paris, 1975). About every tenth petition was in Latin. I have not worked with the Latin petitions because the formality of writing in Latin seemed to preclude significant variation in self-expression.

124. AN F19 1009. *Catéchisme à l'usage des paroissiens de Pleurtuit, en réponse au catéchisme intitulé: "Catéchisme très-simple à l'usage des fidèles de la campagne, dans les circonstances actuelles,"* par Charles-François Hamart, religieux bénédictin & curé de la paroisse de Pleurtuit (Saint-Malô, 1791).

125. AN F19 1009, Lettre du commissaire du Directoire exécutif près le département de la Seine transmettant copie de la rétraction de serment devant la municipalité de Bayeux (Calvados) par Louis François Antoine Michelet, originaire d'Ivry et vicaire de Fauchet, évêque constitutionnel de Calvados, 5e jour complémentaire an IV.

126. AN AF IV 1897, d. 1, *Absolutiones et rehabilitationes juratis, intrusis, ordinatis a constitutionalibus aliisque, a die prima augusti 1802 ad totum decembrem 1802,* pièce 41, Michel Gibal.

127. AN AF IV 1897, d. 5, *Absolutiones et rehabilitationes ecclesiasticorum secundi ordinis traditorum litterarum ordinationis et civiliter conjugatorum, a die prima januarii 1802 usque ad diem 30 julii ejusdem anni,* pièces 62–63, Jacques René Tourteau.

128. AN AF IV 1897, d. 5, Tourteau.

129. AN AF IV 1897, d. 3, pièce 74. Claude-Nicholas-Joseph Collignon.

130. AN AF IV 1897, d. 3, pièce 27. Guillaume Bruzac.

131. AN AF IV 1898, d. 2, pièce 44. Martin Bergès.

132. AN AF IV 1897, d. 4, pièces 114–15. Louis-Alexandre-Pierre Bourdon.

133. AN AF IV 1897, d. 3, pièce 29. Jean-Baptiste-Antoine Mailloc.

134. AN AF IV 1897, d. 1, pièce 36. Hyacinthe Doux.

135. AN AF IV 1897, d. 4, pièces 29–31. François Dusser.

136. AN AF IV 1897, d. 1, pièce 58. Nicholas-Joseph Groult.

137. AN AF IV 1897, d. 3, pièce 53. Pierre Barthélémé Barruel-Labeaume.

138. AN AF IV 1898, d. 2, *Absolutiones ecclesiasticorum qui matrimonium attentaverunt vel ecclesiasticam professionem ejuraverunt, a die prima januarii ad totum aprilem 1803,* pièces 81–82, Pierre Vistorte.

139. AN AF IV 1898, d. 8, pièces 87–88, Jean-Baptiste L'Abbé.

CHAPTER 2. NATIONAL IDEALS AND THEIR FAILURE

1. See *Pratiques religieuses: Mentalités et spiritualités dans l'europe révolutionnaire* (1770–1820), ed. Paule Lerou, Raymond Dartevelle, and Bernard Plongeron (Paris, 1988), and *Les Fêtes de la Révolution: Colloque de Clermont-Ferrand (juin 1974),* ed. Jean Ehrard and Paul Viallaneix (Paris, 1977). On the varying roles of festivals within a culture and the mutations of festival forms, see Michel Vovelle, *Les Métamorphoses de la fête in Provence de 1750 à 1820* (Paris, 1976), and *La Mentalité révolutionnaire: Société et mentalités sous la Révolution française* (Paris, 1985). For the place of revolutionary culture in national life, see Lynn A. Hunt, *Politics, Culture, and Class in the French Revolution,* anniversary edition (Berkeley and Los Angeles, 2004).

2. Mona Ozouf, *La Fête révolutionnaire, 1789–1799* (Paris, 1976). For an appreciation of the considerable merits of the text, see Lynn Hunt, foreword to Mona Ozouf, *Festivals and the French Revolution,* trans. Alan Sheridan (Cambridge, Mass., 1988).

3. The Directory had special commissaires that surveyed the activities of the departmental administrations and then reported back to the Directory. I believe that my evidence and interpretation

counters Ozouf's argument that the government functionaries misunderstood the religious dynamics at play, minimal though they were. It is quite evident that there were no, or only negligible, religious dynamics. Ozouf, *La Fête révolutionnaire*, 261–68.

4. The classical study of festival failure is still Albert Mathiez, *La Théophilanthropie et le culte décadaire, 1796–1801: Essai sur l'histoire religieuse de la Révolution* (Paris, 1903). Whereas Ozouf imagines an occult success, Mathiez traces a manifest failure. For an extended discussion of the psychological and sociological analyses offered by Ozouf in support of her thesis, see my review-essay on *Festivals and the French Revolution,* by Mona Ozouf, trans. by Alan Sheridan, *History and Theory* 28 (1989): 112–25. James Friguglietti, "The Social and Religious Consequences of the Revolutionary Calendar" (Ph.D. dissertation, Harvard University, 1966) is still essential but can be supplemented by Matthew Shaw's "Reactions to the French Republican Calendar," *French History* 15 (2001): 4–25. For a discussion of the festivals in the context of the government education program, see Emmet Kennedy, *A Cultural History of the French Revolution* (New Haven, 1989), chap. 11. A presentation of the earlier, successful festivals is found in Albert Mathiez, *Les Origines des cultes révolutionnaires, 1789–1792* (Paris, 1904), Alphonse Aulard, *Le Culte de la Raison et le culte de l'Être suprême, 1793–1794* (Paris, 1892), and, of course, Mona Ozouf, *La Fête révolutionnaire*.

5. The Anniversary of the Death of the King was regulated by the laws of 23 nivôse an IV (13 January 1796) and 24 nivôse an V (13 January 1797). The festivals of 14 July and 10 August were decreed anew on 10 thermidor an IV (27 July 1796). There was further regulation of the system when the festival of the Sovereignty of the People was decreed for 30 ventôse and an annual commemoration of the coup of 18 fructidor was instituted by the laws of 13 pluviôse an VI (1 February 1798) and 29 thermidor an VI, respectively (16 August 1798). Other one-time-only festivals were occasionally celebrated, such as the funeral celebration of General Hoche and the memorial of the French representatives assassinated after the Congress of Rastadt.

6. See Mathiez, *Théophilanthropie,* 35–36. The bibliography collected in the Alan Sheridan translation of Mona Ozouf's study—*Festivals and the French Revolution*—guided my travels through the André Martin and Gérard Walter *Catalogue de l'histoire de la Révolution française,* 5 vols. (Paris, 1936–55).

7. Pierre-Claude Daunou, *Discours prononcé pour l'anniversaire du 10 août,* 23 thermidor an III (11 August 1795) (Paris, 1795), 1. Interventions in the Convention and Directory sessions were published by the Imprimérie nationale in Paris; several pamphlets were printed by private presses.

8. The basic elements of this presentation of legislators' hopes for the festivals figured at the beginning of "Three Ways of Imagining Sacrality: Promoting, Regulating, and Rejecting the French Revolutionary Festivals," which appeared in a festschrift honoring the Benedictine theologian Dom Ghislain Lafont: *Imaginer la théologie catholique,* ed. Jeremy Driscoll (Rome, 2000): 173–202.

9. François-Xavier Lanthenas, *Développement du projet de loi ou cadre pour l'institution des fêtes décadaires,* 22 nivôse an III (12 January 1795).

10. Pierre-Toussaint Durand de Maillane, *Opinion sur les fêtes décadaires,* an III (1794–95), 2.

11. Charles-Jacques Bailleul, *Motion d'ordre sur la discussion relative à l'instruction publique,* Séance du 13 germinal an VII (3 March 1799), 19.

12. Louis Joubert, *Opinion sur le project de résolution présenté par la commission d'instruction publique sur l'organisation des écoles primaires,* Séance du 28 nivôse an VII (18 January 1799), 10.

13. Joseph Echasseriaux, *Reflexions et projet de décret sur les fêtes decadaires,* an III (1794–95), 3.

14. Antoine-Christophe Merlin de Thionville, *Opinion sur les fêtes nationales,* 9 vendémiaire an III (30 September 1794), 2.

15. Marie-Joseph Chénier, *Rapport sur la fête des Victoires,* 27 vendémiaire an III (18 October 1794), 3.

16. Ibid., 4.

17. Léonard-Honoré Gay-Vernon, *Opinion sur les institutions relatives à l'état civil des citoyens, & le projet de la commission présenté par Leclerc,* 21 frimaire an VI (11 December 1797), 6–7.

18. Jean-Jacques Bosquillon, *Discours prononcé en présentant au Conseil des Anciens un exemplaire de la constitution de l'an 3,* imprimée par le citoyen Bertrand Quinquet, Séance du 23 thermidor an VII (11 August 1799), 3.

19. Louis Dubois-Dubais, *Discours à l'occasion de la fête du 10 août,* an VII (1799), 20.

20. Louis Dubois-Dubais, *Discours à l'occasion de la fête de 9 thermidor,* an VII (28 July 1799), 17.

21. Nicholas-Joseph Parent Réal, *Motion d'ordre tendante à faire consacrer, par la fête du premier vendémiaire, l'accord parfait qui existe dans l'histoire de la révolution française entre l'époque de la fondation de la république et celle de l'acceptation de la constitution,* 18 fructidor an VII (5 September 1799), 11.

22. Joseph-Marie Lequinio, *Des fêtes nationales,* n.d., 6−7.

23. Louis-François-René Portiez de l'Oise, *Rapport et projets de décrets sur la célébation de la fête de la journée du 9 thermidor,* n.d., 4.

24. Michel-Pierre Luminais, *Discours sur la rapport fait par Grelier sur un monument à élever et sur une fête perpétuelle à célebrer en mémoire du 18 fructidor,* 20 fructidor an VI (6 September 1798), 2.

25. Pierre Mortier-Duparc, *Rapport sur la distribution proposée du portrait du général Marceau,* 28 messidor an VI (16 July 1798), 8.

26. Antoine Français, *Opinion sur la fête du 1 vendémiaire,* an VII (22 September 1798), 2.

27. Lequinio, *Des fêtes nationales,* 6.

28. François Antoine Daubermesnil, *Rapport au nom de la commission chargée de présenter les moyens de vivifier l'esprit public,* 7 floréal an IV (25 April 1796), 4.

29. Louis-Marie de La Revelliére-Lépaux, *Réflexions sur le culte, sur les cérémonies civiles et sur les fêtes nationales,* an VI (1797−98), 33.

30. Joseph-Antoine Débry, *Motion d'ordre sur la célébration d'une fête consacrée à la souveraineté du peuple,* an VII (1798−99), 7.

31. Pierre-Jean Audouin, *Motion d'ordre pour la formation d'une commission qui soit chargée de présenter un travail sur les institutions républicaines,* 19 fructidor soir, an V (5 September 1797), 2−3.

32. Raymond de Barennes, *Opinion sur la résolution du 6 thermidor, relative aux fêtes décadaires,* 12 fructidor an VI (29 August 1798), 2.

33. Félix Bonnaire, *Rapport au nom des commissions d'instruction publique et des institution républicaines, réunies. Sur les fêtes décadaires.* Séance du 19 messidor an VI (27 June 1798), 4.

34. François-Louis Sherlock, *Opinion sur le projet de résolution relative au calendrier républicain,* 12 thermidor an VI (30 July 1798), 3.

35. Martin-Noël Brothier, *Rapport sur la résolution du 3 thermidor ayant pour objet de faire observer comme jours de repos décadis et fêtes nationales,* 17 thermidor an VI (4 August 1798), 4.

36. Lequinio, *Des fêtes nationales,* 20.

37. Jean-Marie Collot d'Herbois, *Quelques idées sur les fêtes décadaires qui peuvent être appliquées à tous projets imprimés jusqu'à ce jour,* 30 nivôse an III (20 January 1795), 1−2. Small wonder that resentment against the *fêtes décadaires* transferred easily to the other festivals: the legislators themselves from the beginning confused the annual festivals and the *fêtes décadaires.* See Bernard Plongeron, "La Fête révolutionnaire devant la critique chrétienne (1793−1802)," in *Les Fêtes de la Révolution: Colloque de Clermont-Ferrand,* particularly 537−41.

38. Jean Guinau-Duprès, *Opinion sur la résolution relative aux fêtes décadaires,* 2 fructidor an VI (19 August 1798), 14.

39. Jacques-Antoine Creuzé-Latouche, *Opinion sur le second projet de la commission concernant les fêtes décadaires & la célébration des mariages,* 1 thermidor an VI (19 July 1798).

40. Marie-Joseph Chénier, *Rapport fait à la Convention nationale au nom du comité d'instruction publique.* Séance du premier nivôse an III (21 December 1794), 3.

41. Ibid., 4.

42. Jean-François Barailon, *Opinion sur la résolution du 6 thermidor, relative aux fêtes décadaires.* Séance du 12 fructidor an VI (29 August 1798), 4.

43. Joseph Terral, *Refléxions sur les fêtes décadaires,* an III (1794−95), 9.

44. Ibid.

45. Ibid., 13.

46. On the transmission of ideas from leaders to the population at large during the Revolution, see Albert Soboul, "Classes populaires et Rousseauisme sous la Révolution," *Annales historiques de la*

Révolution française 34 (1962): 421–38. Soboul traces the passage of Rousseauvian ideas across the meetings of the "sociétés populaires" animated by the Jacobins. Even though there was a popular literature, it cannot be said that it effectively propagated political thought. For Roger Chartier, it was not Enlightenment ideas that moved the people, but rather political expediencies that forced them to heed the proposals of the political speakers. See *Les Origines culturelles de la Révolution française* (Paris, 1991). Marc Malherbe blames central planning for the eventual failure: "Les Fêtes nationales à Bordeaux sous le Directoire," *Liber Amicorum: Études offertes à Pierre Jaubert* (1992): 495–517. He writes, "The imaginary of the festival was created at Paris and then pushed from department to department. . . . The gain for unity was a loss in imagination and spontaneity" (504).

47. A presentation of the earlier, successful festivals is found in Albert Mathiez, *Les Origines des cultes révolutionnaires, 1789–1792* (Paris, 1904), A. Aulard, *Le Culte de la Raison et le culte de l'Être suprême, 1793–1794* (Paris, 1892), and, of course, Ozouf, *La Fête révolutionnaire*.

48. *Rédacteur,* 14 vendémiaire an VI (5 October 1797), repr. in Alphonse Aulard, *Paris pendant la réaction thermidorienne et sous le Directoire: Receuil de documents pour L'histoire de l'esprit public à Paris,* 5 vols. (Paris, 1898–1902), 4:363–68.

49. See AN BB3 87, Rapport du Bureau central du 11 vendémiaire an VI (2 October 1797), repr. in Aulard, *Paris pendant la réaction thermidorienne,* 362–63.

50. Bronislaw Baczko argues that the question facing the post-Thermidorian Convention "How to be done with the Terror?" developed into "How to end the Revolution?" See his *Ending the Terror: The French Revolution after Robespierre,* trans. Michel Petheram (New York, 1994).

51. This situation is outlined in Colin Lucas, "The Rules of the Game in Local Politics Under the Directory," *French Historical Studies* 16 (1989): 345–71.

52. See Olwen Hufton, "The Reconstruction of a Church, 1796–1801," *Beyond the Terror: Essays in French Regional and Social History, 1794–1815,* ed. Gwynne Lewis and Colin Lucas (New York, 1983), 345–71.

53. Isser Woloch, "'Republican Institutions,' 1797–1799," in *The French Revolution and the Creation of Modern Political Culture,* vol. 2, *The Political Culture of the French Revolution,* ed. Colin Lucas (New York, 1988), 384. Jean de Viguerie would have readers note, however, that on occasion the *fêtes décadaires* were a success. See his *Christianisme et révolution: Cinq Leçons d'histoire de la Révolution française* (Paris, 1986), esp. 224–25. Mathiez, in *Théophilanthropie,* 474–82, says that the central commissaire of the department of the Seine, Dupin, was able to report, probably with justification, that the *fêtes décadaires* were tolerably well attended in the Paris area (even during the last years of the Directory). Sherri Klassen finds evidence that the Festival of Old Age enjoyed some continued success because of the solidarity of the younger with the older women. See "The Domestic Virtues of Old Age: Gendered Rites in 'La Fête de la Vieillesse,'" *Canadian Journal of History* 32 (1997): 393–405.

54. In the Archives Nationales the relevant series are F1C, Ministère de l'Intérieure: administration général—Esprit public; AFIII, Archives du pouvoir exécutif (1789–1815): Directoire exécutif (an 8-1815). In the various archives départmentales (hereafter AD) data has been drawn from series L, Documents spécialement relatifs aux administration de départment, de district et de canton (1790–1800). The ministers of the interior in the Directory government were the following: Pierre Bénézech, from 3 November 1795 (12 brumaire an IV); Nicholas-Louis François de Neufchâteau from 16 July 1797 (28 messidor an V) to 10 September 1797 (24 fructidor an V), when he was appointed to the Directory, but he filled the position a second time from 17 June 1798 (29 prairial an VI); Letourneaux was interior minister for the interim.

55. AN F1CIII Seine 25.

56. Ibid., L'Administration centrale du département de la Seine au Ministre de l'Intérieur, 2 fructidor an VI (18 August 1797).

57. Ibid., Le commissaire du Directoire exécutif, 10e arrondissement, canton de Paris au ministre de l'Intérieur, 28 thermidor an V (15 August 1797).

58. Ibid., Les administrateurs du département de la Seine au ministre de l'Intérieur, le 28 frimaire an VII (13 December 1798).

59. Ibid., anonymous communication from the corps de musique, garde nationale, inserted in the covering document, Le ministre de l'Intérieur à l'Administration municipale du cinquième arrondissement du canton de Paris, prairial an VII (May-June 1799).

60. AN F1CI 84, Archives du directeur d'instruction publique, projet et esquisse de perspective par Tourment, thermidor an IV (July-August 1796). For a study of festival architecture, see James A. Leith, *Space and Revolution: Projects for Monuments, Squares, and Public Buildings in France, 1789–1799* (Montreal, 1991).

61. AN F1CI 85, Pétition de traiteur au théâtre de l'Estrapade, Cardinaux au citoyen ministre de la Police générale, 6 prairial an VI (25 May 1798).

62. AN F1CI 84, Analyse des travaux du bureau des fêtes nationales, des théâtres, et des monuments [a document reworked and extended in the office of the Ministry of the Interior] depuis le 12 brumaire jusqu'au 30 floréal an V (19 May 1797).

63. Ibid.

64. AN AFIII 109, dossier 503, Transmission des lettres relatives aux difficultés apposées par les ministres de culte par le ministre de l'Intérieur à la commission des institutions républicaines, le 23 messidor an VI (11 July 1798).

65. Ibid., Lettre de l'administration municipale de canton de Creigny (Yonne), 10 prairial an VI (29 May 1798).

66. Ibid., Lettre de l'administration municipale de Toucy (Yonne), 20 prairial an VI (8 July 1798).

67. AN AFIII 109, dossier 503, Lettres et pétitions demandant au corps législatif de fixer les modalités de célébration du décadi et provenant des habitants du canton d'Autun (Saône et Loire), vendémiaire-brumaire an VII (September-November 1798).

68. Ibid., Lettre provenant du juge de paix du canton de Caumont (Calvados), 22 frimaire an VI (12 December 1797).

69. Ibid., Lettre provenant du citoyen Dotar de Paris, 18 messidor an VI (6 July 1798).

70. Ibid., Lettre provenant de l'administration du Lot et Garonne, nivôse-pluviôse an VI (December–February 1797–98).

71. Ibid., Lettre du commissaire du Directoire exécutif près du canton de Cérilly (Allier), le 15 nivôse an VI (4 January 1798).

72. See *Annales de la religion* 8.5:26 (volume 8 is divided into five parts each having its own pagination); the journal was published in eighteen volumes from 1795 to 1803.

73. AN F1CI 86, le Directoire exécutif au Conseil des Cinq Cents, ventôse an VII (February-March 1799).

74. Ibid.

75. Ibid., le commissaire du Directoire exécutif près l'administration centrale du départment des Ardennes au ministre de l'Intérieur, 5 pluviôse an VII (24 January 1799).

76. AN AFIII 109, dossier 503, Pétition pour la célébration du décadi et la mise en place des institutions républicaines, provenant des habitants d'Autun (Saône-et-Loire), 14 pluviôse an V (2 January 1797) [perhaps an VI (1798), because all the other petitions are from an VI].

77. Ibid., Pétition par des habitants de Versailles (Seine et Oise), 27 frimaire an VI (17 December 1797).

78. Ibid., Pétition par Belos, président d'âge du tribunal civil de la Seine, 3 nivôse an VI (23 December 1797).

79. Ibid., Transmission du ministre de l'Intérieur à la commission d'instruction publique de pièces relatives à la résistance des prêtres catholiques à la célébration du décadi: l'administration de Gironde, observations de Fisson-Joubert, 25 frimaire an VI (15 December 1797).

80. AN F1CIII Seine 25, Rapport au Ministre, an VII (1798–99). This summary of reports is accompanied by reports from all the arrondissements. A portion of it is reprinted in Aulard, *Paris pendant la réaction thermidorienne,* 5:196–97. Aulard says that he has not found the material in the AN,

referring instead to A. Schmidt, *Tableaux de la Révolution française,* vol. 3. I have found this material, and so readers should note the archival reference given here.

81. Ibid.

82. Ibid.

83. Documentation from four departments was examined, following the example of Lynn Hunt in *Politics, Culture, and Class,* to see how the festivals were evaluated by administrations in generally republican (left) and antirepublican (right) departments of the Northwest (Seine-Inférieure), Massif Central (Haute-Vienne), Southeast (Isère), and South (Hérault). Differences and similarities between Seine-Inférieure and the Isère are given here, but the results are not conclusive because in left departments there are right cantons and in right departments there are left cantons. The bibliography for Seine-Inférieure is Victor Sanson, *Répertoire bibliographique pour la période dite "Révolutionnaire" 1789–1801 en Seine-Inférieure,* 5 vols. (Rouen, 1911–12). No such bibliography exists for the Isère, though readers may consult Aimé Champollion-Figeac, "L'Esprit public de départment de l'Isère après le 9 thermidor et jusqu'au Directoire," in *Chroniques dauphinoises* III, first published in 1880 (Marseilles, 1973).

84. When a statistical base is available, it is advisable, even necessary, to study a religious belief, practice, or experience in all the departments. See Timothy Tackett, *Religion, Revolution, and Regional Culture in Eighteenth-Century France: The Ecclesiastical Oath of 1791* (Princeton, 1986). On the other hand, sufficient data can be found to reconstruct the religious world of one department and interpret its significance for the rest of France. See Suzanne Desan, *Reclaiming the Sacred: Lay Religion and Popular Politics in Revolutionary France* (Ithaca, 1990).

85. For example, the letter from the police administration in Paris in the departmental records of Seine-Inférieure and the decrees from the central administration of the Isère: AD Seine-Inférieure, L 361, Lettre du ministre de la police générale aux administrations centrales et municipales, aux commissaires du Directoire exécutif près de ces administrations, 26 frimaire an VII (16 December 1798); AD Isère L 255, le Président de l'administration centrale du département de l'Isère, 6 vendémiaire an VII (27 September 1798).

86. AD Seine-Inférieure, L 361, Président de l'administration municipale du canton de Creil au président de l'administration centrale du département de la Seine-Inférieure, 19 brumaire an VII (9 November 1798).

87. Ibid., Le commissaire du Directoire executif près de l'administration municipale du canton du Creil du départment de la Seine-Inférieure à l'administration centrale de ce département, 12 frimaire an VII (2 December 1798).

88. Ibid.

89. Ibid.

90. AD Seine-Inférieure, L 1806, District de Gournay—instruction publique, prospectus du décadaire chantant ou d'un receuil d'hymnes patriotiques pour toutes les fêtes de l'année, n.d.

91. Ibid.

92. AD Isère, L 255, Président de l'administration municipale du canton d' Eybens à l'administration centrale du département de l'Isère, 23 frimaire, an VI (13 December 1797).

93. Ibid., Extrait du procés verbal de l'administration municipale du canton d'Eybens du 20 frimaire an VI (10 December 1797).

94. Ibid., L'Administration municipale du canton urbain de Voiron au président de l'administration centrale du département de l'Isère, 24 frimaire an VII (14 December 1798).

95. Ibid., Rapport du commissaire du Directoire exécutif de Voiron sur la décoration du temple décadaire, 26 fructidor an VI (12 September 1798).

96. Monitoring is clearly evident in police reports preserved in the cartons of the Ministère de Justice, série BB3. These and other relevant materials are reprinted in Aulard, *Paris pendant la réaction thermidorienne et sous le Directoire,* vols. 4 and 5.

97. Merlin de Thionville, *Opinion sur les fêtes nationales,* 4.

98. For a summary of the broad consensus of historians of religion, psychologists, and anthropologists on the roles of myth in human society, see Kees Bolle, "Myth," *The Encyclopedia of Religion* (New York, 1986–87), 10:261–73.

99. For a summary of the broad consensus of scholars on the role of ritual in society, see Evan M. Zuesse, "Ritual," *The Encyclopedia of Religion,* 12:405–22. I am well aware that historians of religion are still elaborating myth and ritual theory. Catherine Bell notes that the discussion has gone through at least two phases, one in which there is a separation of thought and action (assigning thought to myth and action to ritual), and another in which the two are integrated. She warns us that our theories form us as observers of others' rituals, making it difficult to find the participants' own dividing line between thought and action—if, in fact, there is anything of the sort. See chapters 1 and 2 of her *Ritual Theory, Ritual Practice* (New York, 1992).

100. See Eviatar Zerubavel, *The Seven Day Circle: The History and Meaning of the Week* (New York, 1985), chaps. 2 and 3.

101. See J. Laplanche and J.-B. Pontalis, *Language of Psychoanalysis,* trans. Donald Nicholson Smith (New York, 1973): Here, "what is transferred essentially, is psychic reality—that is to say, at the deepest level, unconscious wishes and fantasies associated with them. And further, manifestations of transference are not verbatim repetitions, but symbolic equivalents of what is being transferred" (460).

102. For a presentation of the development of definitions of transference and transference techniques from Freud to the present day, see Merton M. Gill, *Analysis of Transference,* 2 vols. (New York, 1982). James W. Jones reconsiders transference specifically in order to develop a viable psychoanalytic approach to the sacred in *Contemporary Psychoanalysis and Religion: Transference and Transcendence* (New Haven, 1991).

CHAPTER 3. RELIGIOUS AND SECULAR EXTREMES AT THE BEGINNING OF THE NINETEENTH CENTURY

1. For introductions to the Neo-Christians and the Idéologues as ensembles, see George Boas, *French Philosophies of the Romantic Period* (New York, 1964; orig. pub. 1925), chaps. 2 and 3 (it was Boas who promoted the label "Neo-Christian"), and Frederick Copleston, *A History of Philosophy IX: Maine de Biran to Sartre* (London, 1975), chaps. 1 and 2. For basic bibliography on the romantics and the Idéologues, see below, notes 10 and 13, and for a bibliography of individual Neo-Christian intellectuals, note 37.

2. By "intellectual temperament" I mean a disposition of the mind regarding ultimate values—a combination of thoughts and emotions. This is essentially what Gordon Allport calls a "religious sentiment," defined as "a disposition, built up through experience to respond favorably and in certain habitual ways, to conceptual objects and principles that the individual regards as of ultimate importance in his own life, and having to do with what he regards as permanent or central in the nature of things." See his *The Individual and His Religion* (New York, 1950), 65. I am concerned here with delineating individual expression in public life rather than exploring the contours of the "public sphere." On the problems of mapping a public sphere, intellectual or otherwise, see Dena Goodman, "Public Sphere and Private Life: Toward a Synthesis of Current Historiographical Approaches to the Old Regime," *History and Theory* 32 (1992): 1–20.

3. Chateaubriand, *Essai sur les révolutions, Génie du Christianisme,* ed. Maurice Regard (Paris, 1978), 41. Textual citations are to this edition.

4. Chateaubriand, *Mémoires d'outre-tombe,* 2 vols., ed. Maurice Levaillant and George Moutinier (Paris, 1951), 1:398.

5. Chateaubriand to Baudus de Villenove, 5 April 1799, *Correspondance générale,* vol. 1, 1789–1807, ed. Béatrix D'Andlau, Pierre Christophorov, and Pierre Riberette (Paris, 1977), 89.

6. Ibid. On the influence of the French-speaking milieu in England, see Fernand Baldensperger, *Le Mouvement des idées dans l'émigration française (1789–1815),* 2 vols. (Paris, 1924), and on

the influence of English Christianity, see Madeleine Dempsey, *A Contribution to the Study of the Sources of the Génie du Christianisme* (Paris, 1928).

7. *Correspondance générale,* 91.

8. Ibid., 93−96.

9. See M. P. Christophorov, "La Génèse du *Génie du Christianisme,*" *Cahiers de l'Association internationale des études françaises* 3, 5 (1951): 191−201, and Henri Guillemin in *L'Homme des "Mémoires d'outre-tombe"* (Paris, 1964), with reference to the letter from Chateaubriand's uncle Bedée published in *Bulletin* 6 (1937) of the *Société Chateaubriand.* The earlier studies of Chateaubriand's religiosity are A. Viatte, *Le Catholicisme chez les Romantiques* (Paris, 1922), Victor Giraud, *Le Christianisme de Chateaubriand,* 2 vols. (Paris, 1928), and Pierre Moreau, *La Conversion de Chateaubriand* (Paris, 1933). Readers would be better advised to consult Pierre Clarac, "Le Christianisme de Chateaubriand," in his *À la recherche de Chateaubriand* (Paris, 1975), even though Clarac concentrates on Chateaubriand's later years. See Ghislain de Diesbach, *Chateaubriand* (Paris, 1998) for a useful current biography.

10. See D. G. Charlton, "The French Romantic Movement," in *The French Romantics,* 2 vols. (Cambridge, 1984), 1:16−24. For the best attempt to analyze and synthesize the elements of the European romanticisms, see Georges Gusdorf, *Fondements du savoir romantique* (Paris, 1982). On the word itself, see Maurice A. Schroder, "France—Romanesque—Romantique—Romantisme," in Hans Eichner, *"Romantic" and Its Cognates: The European History of a Word* (Toronto, 1972). The Romanticisms were a major influence on the work of historian Émile Mâle (see chapter 7).

11. See Emmanelle Rebardy, "La Révolution contraire: Chateaubriand et *le génie du christianisme,* 1802. Genèse d'une pensée réactionnaire," *Annales historiques de la Révolution française* (1997): 499−501; Bertrand Aureau, "Chateaubriand et l'enthousiasme révolutionnaire," *Bulletin de l'Association Guillaume Budé* (1998): 173; and Jean Dagen, "À partir de *l'Essai sur les révolutions:* De la comparaison à la symbole," *Bulletin de l'Association Guillaume Budé* (1998): 160.

12. My orientations for exploring the data on Chateaubriand's religious experience came from Fred Davis, *Yearning for Yesterday: A Sociology of Nostalgia* (New York, 1979), and from one of Davis's sources, Charles A. Zwingmann, "'Heimweh' vs. 'Nostalgic Reaction': A Conceptual Analysis and Interpretation of a Medico-Psychological Phenomenon" (Ph.D. diss., Stanford University, 1959).

13. Emmet Kennedy, *A "Philosophe" in the Age of Revolution: Destutt de Tracy and the Origins of "Ideology"* (Philadelphia, 1978) is the definitive biography of De Tracy. The classic study of "ideology" and the Idéologues is F. Picavet, *Les Idéologues* (Paris, 1891); recent research on the Idéologues is set in the broadest possible historical context in Georges Gusdorf, *La Conscience révolutionnaire: Les Idéologues* (Paris, 1978). See also Brian W. Head, *Ideology and Social Science: Destutt de Tracy and French Liberalism* (Dordrecht, 1985). For an overview of the intellectual and political setting, see Martin S. Staum, *Minerva's Marriage: Stabilizing the French Revolution* (Montreal, 1996).

14. Tracy, *Analyse raisonnée de l'Origine de tous les cultes, ou religion universelle: Ouvrage publié en l'an III par Dupuis, citoyen français* (Paris, 1804), iii−iv.

15. *Élémens d'idéologie* was published in five separate parts from 1801 through 1815 in Paris; finally, a unified five-volume edition was published, also in Paris, in 1824−26. The first and second parts of *Élémens d'idéologie* have been reprinted (Paris, 1970) with Henri Gouhier as editor. The printed text of the "Mémoire sur la faculté de penser" appears in *Mémoires de l'Institut national des Sciences et des Arts, Sciences morales et politiques* 1 (1798): 283−450. See Kennedy, *"Philosophe" in the Age of Revolution,* 45.

16. See Keith Baker, "Appendix B: A Note on Early Uses of the Term 'Social Science,'" in *Condorcet: From Natural Philosophy to Social Mathematics* (Chicago, 1975), 371−72, 393, and. Head, *Ideology and Social Science,* 128. The continuing philosophical relevance of Tracy is explored in Charles Porset, "Destutt de Tracy et le fondement de la morale," *Les Idéologues: un mouvement philosophique pour l'avenir,* les colloques du cercle parisien de la Ligue française de l'enseignement: Actes du colloque, 1990 (Paris, 1991): 7−19.

17. Tracy, *Analyse,* 160.

18. Tracy to Maine de Biran, 27 prairial an XII (15 June 1804), in Maine de Biran, *Oeuvres complètes,* 14 vols. (Paris, 1930), 6/7:281−82.

19. Tracy, *Quels sonts les moyens de fonder une morale chez un peuple?* (Paris, 1798), 17.

20. Ibid.

21. Tracy, *Analyse,* 95.

22. See the review of *Abrégé de 'l'Origine de tous les cultes' par Dupuis, citoyen français, un volume en 8° à Paris, an VI,* in *Mercure français,* 30 nivôse, 10, 20, 30 pluviose an VII (20, 30 January, 9, 19 February 1799): 257–74, 3–7, 65–76, 129–41.

23. Tracy, *Analyse,* 143, 147, 70.

24. My orientation in exploring the relation of Tracy's work to his personality comes from Ian Mitroff. Rather than isolating a simple psychological experience, such as Chateaubriand's nostalgia, I submit a brief profile of a personality type. For further discussion of the use of diverse but compatible elements of psychological theories in historiography, see my "Suggestions on Writing the History of Psychological Data," *History and Theory* 16 (1977): 297–305. For a summation of Mitroff's work, see John V. Knapp, "Personality and Proof: The Mind of Science," *ReVISION* 7, 2 (1984–85): 4–18, otherwise consult Ian I. Mitroff, *The Subjective Side of Science* (New York, 1974), and *Methodological Approaches to Social Science* (New York, 1978).

25. There is no full study of the *Mercure* during this period. For a survey, see Eugène Hatin, *Bibliographie historique et critique de la presse périodique française* (Paris, 1866), 24–27. For a study of the *Mercure* and its publisher in the generation before, see Suzanne Tucoo-Chala, *Charles-Joseph Panckoucke et la librairie française* (Paris, 1977). The classical study of the Chateaubriand intellectual circles is Charles Sainte-Beuve, *Chateaubriand et son groupe littéraire sous l'Empire,* ed. Maurice Allem, 2 vols. (Paris, 1948). Joanna Kitchin, *Un Journal "philosophique": La Décade (1794–1807),* (Paris, 1965) is the standard reference. For references to Tracy's intellectual circles, see above, note 13.

26. The reference, found in the 1803 edition of *Le Génie du Christianisme,* 3, pt. 3, liv. 1, chap. 3, p. 77, is cited in Kennedy, *"Philosophe" in the Age of Revolution,* 96.

27. See note 25, above.

28. *Mercure de France* 1 (1800): 38.

29. Kitchin, *Journal "philosophique,"* 112.

30. Ibid., 117–21.

31. Ibid., 83–87.

32. Ibid., 174–77.

33. Chateaubriand did finally lay out the discourse in his *Mémoires,* 1:649–59

34. The details of the jury members' deliberations are reported in C. Latreille, "Chateaubriand et les prix décennaux d'après des documents inédits," *Revue d'histoire littéraire de la France* 18 (1911): 767–80.

35. Quoted in Kennedy, *"Philosophe" in the Age of Revolution,* 197. Kennedy found this quote by chance in a barely legible letter.

36. On the Class of Moral and Political Sciences, Tracy's bailiwick in the Institute, see Staum, *Minerva's Message.*

37. For comparisons of personalities within groups or traditions, see Boas, *French Philosophies,* and Copleston, *A History of Philosophy IX.* Joseph de Maistre is the subject of a modern scholarly biography: Richard Lebrun, *Joseph de Maistre: An Intellectual Militant* (Kingston, Ont., 1988). Readers may still use Henri Moulinié, *De Bonald: La vie, la carrière politique, la doctrine* (Paris, 1916) and should consult Jules Gritti, *Bonald, la Révolution française et le réveil religieux* (Paris 1962), while noting Michel Toda, *Louis de Bonald: théoricien de la contre-révolution* (Étampes, 1997). Albert J. George shows that Ballanche's position was a compromise between "ultras" (such as de Maistre and de Bonald) and "liberals" (followers of Rousseau and Condorcet) in *Pierre Simon Ballanche: Precursor of Romanticism* (Syracuse, 1945), as does also Michael Reardon in "Pierre Ballanche as a French Traditionalist," *Catholic Historical Review* 53 (1968): 573–99. Ballanche as Christian and Romantic is studied in Arthur McCalla, *Romantic Historiography: The Philosophy of History of Pierre-Simon Ballanche* (Boston, 1998). Chateaubriand's life and experiences are juxtaposed to those of his intellectual peers, including Ballanche, in Marc Fumaroli, *Chateaubriand: Poésie et terreur* (Paris, 2003).

CHAPTER 4. PIETY AGAINST POLITICS

1. For a summary history of nineteenth-century pilgrimage, see Pierre Pierrard, "La Renaissance des pèlerinages au XIXe siècle," in Jean Chélini, ed., *Les Chemins de Dieu: Histoire des pèlerinages chrétiens des origines à nos jours* (Paris, 1982). On the geography and history of European pilgrimage, see Mary Lee Nolan and Sidney Nolan, *Christian Pilgrimage in Modern Europe* (Chapel Hill, 1989), and on French popular Catholicism of the era, see Thomas A. Kselman, *Miracles and Prophecies in Nineteenth-Century France* (New Brunswick, N.J., 1983).

2. For this information and for statistics on pilgrimages of subsequent decades, with some indication of geographical origins and social class of the pilgrims, see Philippe Boutry and Michel Cinquin, *Deux pèlerinages au XIXe Siècle: Ars et Paray-le-Monial* (Paris, 1980). See also the important work of Raymond A. Jonas, "Monument as Ex-Voto, Monument as Historiosophy: The Basilica of Sacré-Coeur," *French Historical Studies* 18 (1993): 482–502; "Restoring a Sacred Center: Pilgrimage, Politics, and the Sacré Coeur," *Historical Reflections/Réflexions Historiques* 20 (1994): 95–123; and *France and the Cult of the Sacred Heart: An Epic Tale for Modern Times* (Berkeley and Los Angeles, 2000).

3. Ruth Harris *Lourdes: Body and Spirit in the Secular Age* (New York, 1999) supersedes all previous studies of the Lourdes apparitions, shrine development, and pilgrimage organizations. Full documentation is found in René Laurentin's *Lourdes: Histoire authentique des apparitions,* 6 vols. (Paris, 1961–64).

4. The small village of Pontmain in the Sarthe was spared from Prussian invasion and not long before the Prussian menace some small children saw the Virgin; the connection between the two was easy to make. When the Prussians were besieging Paris, two French laymen, H. Rohault de Fleury and L. Legentil began agitating for a National Vow of submission to the Sacred Heart. A committee formed in 1873 succeeded in persuading the French National Assembly to officially support the construction of the Basilica of the Sacré Coeur on the hill of Montmartre. See Boutry and Cinquin, *Deux pèlerinages.*

5. At its beginnings a small weekly in newspaper format, *Le Pèlerin* restricted itself to pilgrimage news. Once involved in broader commentary on religious and national life, it became an increasingly shrill and tasteless critic of Freemasons, Jews, and the national government. Still political after World War I—this time, progovernment—*Le Pèlerin* became a general family review in 1933. See Jacqueline et Philippe Godfrin, *Une centrale de presse catholique: La Maison de la Bonne Presse et ses publications* (Paris, 1965).

6. The article is signed J. Gondry de Jardinet. *Le Pèlerin* 1 (12 juillet 1873), organe du conseil général des pèlerinages [Paris, rédaction et administration, 6 rue François].

7. Ibid., 4

8. Ibid., 7.

9. Other shrines published reviews and bulletins, but I would still maintain that *La Voix de Notre-Dame de Chartres* covered the widest variety of religious, political, and economic news. For the multiple Lourdes reviews/bulletins, see the bibliography in Harris, *Lourdes.* I was introduced to *La Voix* many years ago by the archivist of the diocese of Chartres, Pierre Bizeau, and my first survey of its contents was graciously published by the then-director of the Marian Library of the University of Dayton, Theodore Koehler, S.M., in *Marian Library Studies* of 1978, a volume that appeared several years later.

10. Harris, *Lourdes,* 16.

11. Cited in Chanoine Goussard, *M. l'abbé Ychard: Chanoine Vicaire-général honoraire, supérieur du petit séminaire de Chartres* (Chartres, 1896), 42.

12. Here, and in all future reference to the pages of *La Voix,* the volume, month and page will be given immediately in the text rather than in the notes. Editions of this pious review are difficult to come by. Naturally, there are several sets of it (1857–1969) available in the archives of the diocese of Chartres; the Bibliothèque Nationale possesses copies from only a few decades of the twentieth century. In the United States, the University of Dayton's Marian Library possesses a run from 1857 to 1880 and individual issues of July and August, 1899, and March, April, May, 1901.

13.   This and other information on the founding of the Maîtrise and its connection with *La Voix* can be found in Alexander Clerval, *L'Oeuvre des Clercs de Notre-Dame de Chartres, 1853–1885* (Chartres, 1910). Clerval, whose study of the medieval schools at Chartres was at one time the standard work, served as superior of the choir school at Chartres and professor of church history at the Institut Catholique of Paris. For some background on the origins of Ychard's apostolic interests, Clerval suggested that one look at the maxims and rules of Bartholomew Holzhauer (1613–58), founder of a similar institute (the Bartholomites) in Germany.

14.   Besides Clerval's pious history of the *L'Oeuvre des Clercs* and the modern Maîtrise, cf. also his study of the medieval Maîtrise: *L'ancienne maîtrise de Notre-Dame de Chartres du Ve siècle à la Révolution* (Paris, 1899).

15.   Cited in Clerval, *L'Oeuvre des Clercs,* 117. Note that there is a typographical error, 1861 instead of 1860, on this page in Clerval's book. Ychard's money-raising methods were simple and honest: for comparison, see the study of religious commercialism at Lourdes, Suzanne K. Kaufman, *Consuming Visions: Mass Culture and the Lourdes Shrine* (Ithaca, 2004).

16.   Yves Delaporte, "Chartres," *Dictionnaire d'histoire et de géographie ecclésiastique,* vol. 12 (1953), cols. 549–50. And see Robert Branner, *Chartres Cathedral* (New York, 1969), 71.

17.   See his *Monographie de la cathédrale de Chartres,* 3 vols. (Chartres, 1887–92). Bulteau was revised by the abbé Alexandre Brou (1862–1947) to tone down the rigor with which he opposed some Chartrian legends dear to his fellow clergy; Bulteau notes his agreement to the revision in the preface. His earlier *Description de la cathédrale de Chartres* (Chartres, 1850) is a brief and honest predecessor of the three volume work. Bulteau, leaving behind his antagonists at Chartres, spent the later part of his priestly career in the diocese of Cambrai. The Bulteau story is briefly related in Ernest Sevrin's *Un évêque militant et gallican au XIXe siècle, Mgr. Clausel de Montals,* 2 vols. (Paris, 1955), 2:472–74. Sevrin was archivist of the diocese of Chartres before the current Father Pierre Bizeau.

18.   For a more complete discussion of the dating of the statue, cf. Yves Delaporte, *Les Trois Notre-Dame de la cathédrale de Chartres,* 2nd ed. (Chartres, 1965). On the Delaporte himself, see Pierre Bizeau, "Yves Delaporte, chanoine de Chartres (18 décembre 1879–11 avril 1979)," in *Notre-Dame de Chartres,* September 1979, 18–21.

19.   Churchgoing across the decades in many dioceses of France, with attention to gender and age is recorded in Fernand Broulard, Yves-Marie Hilaire, and Gérard Cholvy, eds., *Matériaux pour l'histoire du peuple français,* 3 vols. (Paris, 1982–92).

20.   Barbara Corrado Pope, "Immaculate and Powerful: The Marian Revival in the Nineteenth Century," in C. W. Atkinson, C. H. Buchanan, and M. R. Miles, *Immaculate and Powerful: The Female in Sacred Image and Social Reality* (Boston, 1985), 195. Sandra L. Zimdars-Swart, *Encountering Mary: From La Salette to Medjugorje* (Princeton, 1991) is a comparative study of apparitions and their shrines.

21.   But in *La Voix* one does find a distinct female vision even so. See below, "Chartres and Lourdes," 106–9.

22.   Corrado Pope, "Immaculate and Powerful," 195.

23.   See J. and P. Godfrin, *Presse Catholique,* and Michel Guy, *Vincent de Paul Bailly, fondateur de "La Croix," cinquante ans de luttes religieuses* (Paris, 1955).

24.   See René Laurentin and A. Durand, *Pontmain, Histoire authentique,* 2 vols. (Paris, 1970).

25.   For a full discussion of this relic, see Otto Von Simson, *The Gothic Cathedral* (New York, 1956), 49ff.

26.   In 1899, the organizers at Lourdes brought off a national pilgrimage for men, in part to offset the idea that most pilgrimages were undertaken by women and children: Corrado Pope, "Immaculate and Powerful," 188. And see Philippe Boutry, "Les structures paroissiales de la périphérie de Paris au lendemain du Concordat," in *La Religion dans la ville,* ed. Philippe Boutry and André Encrevé (Bourdeau, 2003), for a model of parish study.

27.   If this is the "feminization" of religion in the sense of "psychological, social and political impulses," that Jules Michelet, the avid republican historian, isolated in order to "link women's rejection of the Revolution and republican principles to their apparent submission of priests," then it

deserves its own categories. The formulae are those of Harris, *Lourdes,* 212–13, where the author offers a sophisticated rebuttal to overall negative evaluations of the feminization of religion in the nineteenth century.

28. *Dictionnaire de biographie française,* ed. Prevost and Roman d'Amiot (Paris, 1959) 8: col. 97.

29. *Procès-verbaux de la Société archéologique d'Eure-et-Loir,* tome XI (Chartres, 1905).

30. *La Voix de Notre-Dame de Chartres,* 1901, 2 (premier supplément), 559.

31. See the works of Raymond A. Jonas cited in note 2.

32. On the relationship of Edouard Pie and Bishop Clausel de Montals, see Ernest Sevrin, *Un Évêque militant et gallican,* passim. On Pie's theology and politics, see Etienne Catta, *La Doctrine politique et sociale du Cardinal Pie, 1815–1882* (Paris, 1959).

33. Taking two samples from the record books of the Archconfraternity of Notre-Dame de Chartres, a central devotional organization of the cathedral, we find that in 1857 men numbered about one-fifth of the total enrollment of 1,453, and in 1914 men number about one-fifth of the total enrollment of 2,217. These volumes can be accessed by the staff of the archives of the Diocese of Chartres.

34. See Pierre Sorlin, *"La Croix" et les juifs 1880–1899: Contribution à l'histoire de l'antisémitisme contemporain* (Paris, 1967).

35. *Notre-Dame de Chartres* (Chartres, 1891), hereafter cited as *Notre-Dame,* with page references in the text.

36. See J. and P. Godfrin, *Presse Catholique,* 49.

37. The *Dictionnaire d'archéologie chrétienne et de liturgie* was edited by Dom Cabrol, Henri Leclercq, and H. I. Marrou, 15 vols. (Paris, 1907–53). Although criticized for its archeological inaccuracies and certain prejudices, this monumental work is still highly regarded as an invaluable source for the study of Christian antiquity.

38. The Sertillanges-led contingent, and other like groups, were small in number by comparison with the midcentury pilgrimages. In 1968, the year before the termination of *La Voix,* a lengthy serial article on Charles Péguy provided statistics for each year from 1935 through 1963. The most significant increases in numbers began in 1942, when the tally reached 650 while that of the previous year had been only 100; in 1943, the figure rose from 650 to 1,250; in 1945, following a year of no pilgrimage, from 1,250 to 3,000; in 1947, from 3,700 to 5,200; in 1953, from 7,800 to 10,000; in 1957, from 13,000 to 17,000. Finally, in 1963 and the years following, 20,000 students came. Jean Aubonnet, the scholar who as a young man had started this series of pilgrimages, said in 1955, "We dreamed of these crowds. . . . In any case, we prayed much for this intention" (1968, 4, 42). A student chaplain observed in 1956 that a "taste for authenticity attracted the young people to such an enterprise" (1968, 4, 44).

CHAPTER 5. LOCAL LANGUAGES FOR THE DEFENSE OF RELIGION

1. Quoted in Michel de Certeau, Dominique Julia, and Jacques Revel, *Une Politique de la langue: La Révolution française et les patois: L'Enquête de Grégoire* (Paris, 1975), 11.

2. See Caroline C. Ford, "Which Nation? Language, Identity, and Republican Politics in Post-Revolutionary France," *History of European Ideas* 17 (1993): 31–46. For a survey of work on the politics of language since the Revolution, see Philippe Vigier, "Diffusion d'une langue rationale et résistance des patois, en France, au XIXe siècle: Quelques Réflexions sur l'état présent de la recherche historique à ce propos," *Romantisme* 25–31 (1979): 191–208.

3. The statistics for regions where French-related dialects (patois) are spoken do not exhibit the same consistency as the non-French-related dialects. For a brief history of each of the linguistic minorities of France, see Meic Stephens, *Linguistic Minorities in Western Europe* (Dyfed, Wales, 1976), chap. 9.

4. In 1947, Canon Fernand Boulard published a map of strong, lukewarm, and weak religious practice, valid not only for the twentieth century but also for the nineteenth. For a reproduction of the map and an illuminating discussion of its importance, see Ralph Gibson, *A Social History of French Catholicism, 1789–1914* (New York, 1989), 170–80.

5. See Hervé Le Bras and Emmanuel Todd, *L'Invention de la France: Atlas anthropologique et politique* (Paris, 1981), 40–44; Hervé Le Bras, *Les Trois France* (Paris, 1986), chap. 1. On the related issue of secular regional identities in competition with secular national identity in the nineteenth century, see Robert Zaretsky, *Cock & Bull Stories: Folco de Baroncelli and the Invention of the Camargue* (Lincoln, Neb., 2004).

6. I understand "culture" to be, in the words of Clifford Geertz, "a system of inherited conceptions expressed in symbolic forms by means of which men communicate, perpetuate, and develop their knowledge about and attitudes toward life." See Clifford Geertz, "Religion as a Cultural System," in *The Interpretation of Cultures: Selected Essays* (New York, 1973), 89. Accordingly, language is an essential component of this process. "Milieu" is a more generic label for social environment. I use the word in the sense of *poids de milieu:* the weight, the force, the effect of social environment. Here I follow the usage of Philippe Vigier in "Diffusion d'une langue rationale," cited above in reference to the politics of language, but, in fact, a fundamental work on virtually all of the linguistic issues raised in this chapter. For reservations on the labeling value of the term, see Adam Kuper, *Culture: The Anthropoligists' Acccount* (Cambridge, Mass., 1999).

7. See Henry Peyre, *La Royauté et les langues provinciales* (Paris, 1933), chap. 3: "Politique d'Alsace et de Roussillon"; Marie Marquis de Roux, *Louis XIV et les provinces conquises: Artois, Alsace, Flandres, Roussillon, Franche-Comté* (Paris, 1938); Ferdinand Brunot, *Histoire de la langue française: Des origines à 1900,* vol. 7, *La Propagation du français en France jusqu'à la fin de l'ancien régime* (Paris, 1926). The legal basis for Louis XIV's politics was the 1539 decree of Villers-Cotterêts.

8. David Bell, "Recent Works on Early Modern French National Identity," *Journal of Modern History* 68 (1996): 98.

9. See Danielle Trudeau, "L'Ordonnance de Villers-Cotterêts et la langue française: Histoire ou interprétation," *Bibliothèque d'humanisme et Renaissance* 65 (1983): 461–72, cited in Bell, "Recent Works," 98n46, and the recent synthesis of Gilles Boullard, "L'Ordonnance de Villers-Cotterêts: Le Temps de la clarté et la stratégie du temps (1539–1992)," *Revue historique* 101(1999): 45–100.

10. The fundamental reference work, an assembly and analysis of virtually all of the statistics on religious practice collected in the modern era, is Fernand Boulard, Yves-Marie Hilaire, and Gérard Cholvy, *Matériaux pour l'histoire religieuse du peuple français,* 3 vols. (Paris, 1982–92); these volumes will be cited hereafter as *Matériaux* 1, 2, or 3.

11. See Alfred Wahl and Jean-Claude Richez, *L'Alsace entre France et Allemagne, 1850–1950* (Paris, 1994), esp. 241–57.

12. This may be an even better indication of church loyalty than simple churchgoing, according to Ralph Gibson in *Social History of French Catholicism,* 159: "Of the acceptance—grudging or otherwise—of clerical authority, and of sacramental and individual religion, the taking of Easter communion was a fair indicator." For a study of the church-state confrontation on the language question beginning in 1890, see Joan L. Coffey, "Of Catechisms and Sermons: Church-State Relations in France, 1890–1905," *Church History* 66 (1997): 54–66.

13. See Fernand Boulard and Jean Rémy, *Pratique religieuse urbaine et régions culturelles* (Paris, 1968), chap. 8.

14. See *Matériaux* 2:552–54, and Archives départementales (hereafter AD) Bas-Rhin IV 494. Fonds de l'Evêché, registres: Schiltigheim; Enquête sur la situation de la paroisse de Schiltigheim suite d'une plainte contre le curé, 1874.

15. *Matériaux* 3:197.

16. *Matériaux* 2:183, 552–53.

17. Pierre Zind, *L'Enseignement religieux dans l'instruction primaire publique en France de 1850 à 1873* (Lyon, 1971), 248. Sarah A. Curtis, *Educating the Faithful: Religion, Schooling, and Society in Nineteenth-Century France* (DeKalb, 2000) explains the qualities and goals of Catholic education during this period. See esp. chap. 4.

18. Paul Lévy, *Histoire linguistique d'Alsace et de Lorraine,* vol. 2, *De la Revolution française à 1918* (Paris, 1929), 509, and 240–41; Frédéric Moffet, *Psychanalyse de l'Alsace* (Colmar, 1951), 71.

19. On Victor Duruy, see Sandra Horvath-Peterson, *Victor Duruy and French Education: Liberal Reform in the Second Empire* (Baton Rouge, 1984), chap. 4. On the politics of education during the Second Empire, see Jean Maurain, *La Politique ecclésiastique du Second Empire, de 1852 à 1869* (Paris, 1930), esp. 580−99, 676−85, 748−80. See also the surveys of education during this period: Antoine Prost, *Histoire de l'enseignement en France, 1800−1967* (Paris, 1968), 155−87; Louis-Henri Parias, ed., *Histoire générale de l'education en France,* vol. 3, *De la Révolution à l'Ecole républicaine* (Paris, 1981), esp. 325−47.

20. This vitally important survey is reproduced in Eugen Weber, *Peasants into Frenchmen: The Modernization of Rural France, 1970−1914* (Stanford, 1976), 498−501.

21. Horvath-Peterson, *Duruy,* 106.

22. Cited in Horvath-Peterson, *Duruy,* 105.

23. E. Frenay, *L'École primaire dans les Pyrénées-Orientales, 1833−1914* (Perpignan: Archives départementales des Pyrénées-Orientales, Service éducatif, 1983), no. 9. According to this record, 188 schools were private and 185 were public, information from the same sources reproduced in Weber, *Peasants* (see note 20, above).

24. Gérard Cholvy, "Régionalisme et clergé catholique au XIXe siècle," in *Régions et régionalisme du XVIIe siècle à nos jours,* ed. Christian Gras and Georges Livet (Paris, 1977).

25. John E. Craig, *Scholarship and Nation Building: The Universities of Strasbourg and Alsatian Society, 1870−1939* (Chicago, 1984), 23−28. See also Dan P. Silverman, *Reluctant Union: Alsace-Lorraine and Imperial Germany, 1871−1918* (University Park, Penn., 1972), chap. 1.

26. Gérard Cholvy, "Enseignement religieux et langues maternelles en France au XIXe siècle," *Revue des langues romanes* 82 (1976): 40−41.

27. Alfred Wahl, *Confession et comportement dans les campagnes d'Alsace et de Bade, 1871−1939,* 2 vols. (Strasbourg, 1980).

28. Gérard Cholvy, *Géographie religieuse de l'Hérault contemporain* (Paris, 1968).

29. Wahl, *Confession,* 890.

30. Ibid., 1252.

31. Cholvy, *Géographie,* 421−23.

32. Paul Leuilliot, *L'Alsace au début du XIXe siècle: Essais d'histoire politique, économique et religieuse, 1815−1830,* 3 vols. (Paris, 1960), 3:318.

33. Ibid., 319−20.

34. Archives Nationales (hereafter AN) F17 10794. This carton is part of a series running from F17 10757 through F17 10798: Mémoires, classés par académies sur "les besoins de l'instruction publique dans une commune, au triple point de vue de l'Ecole, des Elèves, et du maître," presentés par les instituteurs au concours ouvert entre eux par arrêté du 12 décembre 1860.

35. See Anthony J. Steinhoff, "Protestants in Strasbourg, 1870−1914: Religion and Society in Late Nineteenth Century Europe" (Ph.D. diss., University of Chicago, 1996), chap. 7.

36. All of these more extended references to language and religion were from essays eliminated early on in the competition. In the dossier, *à conserver,* there was no mention of religion and German at all.

37. See René Epp, *Mgr Raess, Évêque de Strasbourg, 1842−1887* (Griesheim-sur-Souffel, 1979); also, René Epp, "De la Révolution à l'annexion," in *Le Diocèse de Strasbourg,* ed. Francis Rapp (Paris, 1982), 171−250.

38. Epp, *Raess,* 170. Ernest Hauviller wrote a veritable indictment of Raess's germanophile maneuvers under French rule in "Mgr Raess, Evêque de Strasbourg: Un Prélat germanisateur dans l'Alsace française," *Revue Historique* 189 (1937): 98−121.

39. AN F17 9147, dossier 1. Inspecteur de l'académie de Strasbourg au recteur, Strasbourg, 28 October 1863.

40. Ibid. Lettre de M. Boucault, officier d'Academie, October-November 1866.

41. Archives de l'Evêché de Strasbourg (hereafter AES): Registres du conseil épiscopal, reg. 131, p. 94. Séance du 14 octobre 1861. Pétition à Monseigneur de la part des délégués du canton de Souffelsweyersheim.

42. AN F17 9147. Lettre de l'abbé Bretz, aumônier du Chateau Impérial de Strasbourg, a M. Heinrich, Inspecteur des écoles primaires en résidence à Colmar, Strasbourg le 30 Octobre 1863.

43. See Gaston May, *La Lutte pour le français en Lorraine avant 1870: Étude sur la propagation de la langue française dans les départements de la Meurthe et de la Moselle* (Nancy, 1912); and Louis Maggiolo, *Rapport présenté au Conseil départemental de la Meurthe sur la situation de l'instruction primaire pendant l'année 1861/62* (Nancy, n.d.).

44. J. Wirth, *La Langue française dans les départements de l'Est, ou des moyens et des méthodes à employer pour propager la langue rationale dans les parties de l'Alsace et de la Lorraine où l'idiome allemande est encore en usage* (Paris, 1867), 108.

45. See AN F17 9147, dossier 1. Lettre de M. Lasaule de l'Ecole normale primaire de la Moselle au Ministre de l'Instruction publique, 11 August 1869.

46. See Louis Cazeaux, *Essai sur la conservation de la langue allemande en Alsace* (Strasbourg, 1867). For a study of Cazeaux's ministry without, however, reference to his linguistic concerns, see Claude Muller, "Louis Cazeaux, curé de Saint-Jean Strasbourg, 1859–1870," *Annuaire de la Société des Amis du Vieux Strasbourg* 15 (1985): 33–38. On the *Revue,* see Claude Muller's exhaustive archival study of the diocese of Strasbourg, *Dieu est catholique et alsacien: La Vitalité du diocèse de Strasbourg, au XIXe siècle, 1802–1914* (Strasbourg, n.d.), 1024–26. My introduction to these issues was Paul Lévy, *Histoire linguistique.*

47. Cazeaux, *La langue allemande,* 30.

48. Ibid., 31.

49. Ibid., 32.

50. Ibid., 36.

51. Ibid., 37.

52. Ibid., 37.

53. Ibid., 38.

54. Ibid., 41.

55. Ibid., 42.

56. P. Mury, "Chronique: La Langue allemande et le catéchisme diocésain," *Revue catholique d'Alsace* 1 (1859): 83.

57. The *Nécrologie* published by the diocese of Strasbourg states that Ignace Waltzer was born in 1808 and died in 1895. He served in a variety of pastoral appointments and was made an honorary canon of the cathedral in 1883.

58. Ignace Waltzer, "La Langue allemande en Alsace," *Revue catholique d'Alsace* 1 (1859): 153.

59. Ibid.

60. Ibid., 155.

61. Ibid., 156.

62. Ibid., 157.

63. There appears to be only one reference before 1871 (when Cazeau and Waltzer were in full swing). It cited a petition to the bishops to "prevent the German language from being proscribed in the primary schools, as appears to be happening now." In fact, this is a reference to the Souffelsweyersheim clergy. Their petition is found in AD Bas-Rhin 1V504: Fonds de l'Évêché, régistre: Souffelsweyersheim. No mention is made of any response to the petition. See AES Registres du conseil episcopal, reg. 131, p. 94. Séance du 14 octobre 1861: Pétition à Monseigneur de la part des délégués du canton de Souffelweyersheim.

64. AES Correspondance avec le préfet du Haut-Rhin, reg. 117, p. 242, 6 February 1886.

65. Ibid., 252.

66. See Claude Muller, "Politique, religion et langue dans la Moselle allemande, d'après un rapport de Mgr Fleck au Pape (1887)," *Archives de l'Église d'Alsace,* 10/49 (1990–91): 190–96.

67. Stephen L. Harp, *Learning to be Loyal: Primary Schooling as Nation-Building in Alsace and Lorraine, 1850–1940* (Dekalb, 1998), chaps. 3 and 4.

68. See Marquis de Roux, *Provinces conquises,* 251–64. The term "Roussillon" in the old regime could refer to the adjoining regions of Capcir, Cerdagne, Conflent, Vallespir, les Fenouillèdes, and Roussillon proper. This territory has comprised the department of Pyrénées-Orientales since the Revolution.

69. Poeydavant, "Mémoire sur la province de Roussillon," *Bulletin de la Société agricole, scientifique et littéraire du département des Pyrénées-Orientales* 51 (1910): 1340, cited in Peter Sahlins, *Boundaries: The Making of France and Spain in the Pyrénées* (Berkeley and Los Angeles, 1989), 123.

70. See Domenec Bernardo and Bernat Dieu, "Conflict linguistique et redédications culturelles en Catalogne-Nord," *Les Temps moderns,* nos. 324—26 (1973): 305—6.

71. I prefer the label "local religion" to "popular religion" for all those expressions of religious thought and sentiment that are not at the same time expressions of institutional Catholicism. The label comes from William A. Christian, *Local Religion in Sixteenth Century Spain* (Princeton, 1981), but see the essays on and bibliographies of French local religion in Bernard Plongeron, ed., *La Religion populaire: Approches historiques* (Paris, 1976); and Bernard Plongeron and Paule Lerou, eds., *La Piété populaire en France: Répertoire bibliographique,* 4 vols. (Paris, 1984–). The expressions "great tradition" and "little traditions" have been used by the anthropologist Milton Singer in *When a Great Tradition Modernizes: An Anthropological Approach to Indian Civilization* (Chicago, 1972). "Local religion" was the subject of substantial scholarly argument a generation ago when these books were published. I believe that historians today are more willing to choose a label and list the data to which they want it applied—hence my simple list in the text.

72. Sahlins, *Boundaries,* 124.

73. See Timothy Tackett, *Religion, Revolution, and Regional Culture in Eighteenth Century France: The Ecclesiastical Oath of 1791* (Princeton, 1986), 350–51; Dominique Varry and Claude Muller, *Hommes de Dieu et Révolution en Alsace* (Turnhout, Belgium, 1993); and Philippe Torreilles, *Histoire du clergé dans le département des Pyrénées-Orientales pendant la Révolution française* (Perpignan, 1890).

74. Peter McPhee, "Counter-Revolution in the Pyrenees: Spirituality, Class, and Ethnicity in the Haut-Vallespir, 1793–1794," *French History* 7 (1993): 324.

75. Ibid., 325.

76. Ibid., 326.

77. Ibid., 328.

78. Ibid., 326.

79. Michel Brunet, *Le Roussillon: Une Société contre l'État, 1780–1820* (Toulouse, 1986), 460.

80. Ibid., 466.

81. Ibid., 468.

82. AN F17 9147, dossier 1. Lettre du Recteur de l'Academie de Montpellier au Ministre de l'Instruction publique, 31 December 1866.

83. Citations in this and the previous paragraph are found in AN F17 19782, Montpellier, Hérault, Lozère. See note 34, above, on the series to which this carton belongs. Essays from Pyrénées-Orientales are included in this carton, though there is no mention of the department in the AN inventory or on the carton label.

84. AN F17 10782, Montpellier, Hérault, Lozère. Pierre Imbert, instituteur d'Estagel, Canton de Latour, arrondissement de Perpignan, 31 January 1861. The document is printed in Frenay, *L'Ecole primaire,* no. 33.

85. AD Pyrénées-Orientales 1V7. Letter du Monseigneur l'Évêque de Perpignan au Préfet et au maire de Perpignan, 9 May 1872.

86. *Matériaux* 3:42.

87. AD Pyrénées-Orientales 1V8. Lettre de Préfet au Ministre de la Justice et des cultes, 21 July 1888.

88. AD Pyrénées-Orientales 1V13, Mandements, lettres pastorales, circulaires de Mgr Ramadié. Lettre Pastorale de Monseigneur l'Evêque de Perpignan à l'occasion de son entrée dans son diocèse (Paris, 1865), 5.

89. AD Pyrénées-Orientales 1V13. Lettre Pastorale et Mandement de Monseigneur l'Evêque de Perpignan à l'occasion de la publication d'un nouveau catechisme à l'usage de son diocèse (Perpignan, 1868), 13–14.

90. AD Pyrénées-Orientales 1V13. Lettre pastorale de Monseigneur l'Evêque de Perpignan au clergé de son diocèse, 9 March 1872, 6.

91. AD Pyrénées-Orientales 1V15. Mandements, lettres pastorales, circulaires de Mgr Goussail. Lettre pastorale de Monseigneur l'Evêque de Perpignan au clergé et aux fidèles de son diocèse sur l'oeuvre des séminaires (Perpignan, 1890), 11.

92. Lettre circulaire de Mgr l'Evêque de Perpignan, no. 42, 1898, cited in Eugène Cortade, "La Langue catalane et l'église dans le diocèse d'Elne-Perpignan," *Tramontane* 491–92 (1965): 211–16.

93. Cited in Jean Sagnes, *Le Pays catalan* (*Capcir-Cerdagne-Conflent-Roussillon-Vallespir-et le Fenouillèdes*) (Pau, 1985), 1:732.

94. See Mathias Delcor, "Les Prêtres érudits du Roussillon," *Revue d'histoire de l'Eglise de France* 71 (1985): 25–46.

95. For a discussion of this, see Bernardo and Rieu, "Conflit linguistique," 318–19.

96. Henri Baudrillart, *Populations agricoles de la France* (Paris, 1893), 3:333, cited in Sahlins, *Boundaries*, 264.

97. Sagnes, *Le Pays catalan,* 1:730.

98. Ibid., 733–34.

99. Frenay, *L'École primaire,* no. 9.

100. See Cholvy, *Confession et comportement,* 421–23.

101. William Brustein, *The Social Origins of Political Regionalism: France, 1849–1981* (Berkeley and Los Angeles, 1988), chaps. 7 and 8; see Sagnes, *Le Pays catalan,* 1:732.

CHAPTER 6. THE LIMITS OF PERSONAL RECONCILIATION

1. On the origin and use of the expression *union sacrée,* see Jean-Jacques Becker, "Union sacrée et idéologies bourgeoises," *Revue historique* 264 (1980): 65–66. On religious and secular tensions in the period, see Maurice Larkin, *Religion, Politics, and Preferment in France since 1890* (New York, 1996). For a chronologically broader perspective, see Charles Tilly, *The Contentious French* (Cambridge, Mass., 1986).

2. Maurice Barrès, *Les Diverses Familles spirituelles de la France* (Paris, 1917), 1–2.

3. "The Nationalist Revival before 1914," in *My France: Politics, Culture, Myth* (Cambridge, Mass., 1991), 195. The entire chapter is a clear profile of the nationalisms that developed in the era preceding World War I. For a negative interpretation of Barrès in particular, see Robert Soucy, *Fascism in France: The Case of Maurice Barrès* (Berkeley and Los Angeles, 1972).

4. Barrès, *Familles spirituelles,* 3–4, 267–68. Numerous testimonies by and about priests are given in chap. 3, "Catholiques"; testimonies by and about *instituteurs,* in chap. 6, "Socialistes."

5. For scholarly studies of religion in military and national life during the World War I era, see Jacques Fontana, *Les Catholiques français pendant la grande guerre* (Paris, 1990); Nadine-Josette Chaline, ed., *Chrétiens dans la Premiére guerre mondiale* (Paris, 1993); and Annette Becker, *La Guerre et la foi: De la mort à la mémoire, 1914–1930* (Paris, 1994). For a study of the influence of the war on intellectual life, see Martha Hanna, *The Mobilization of Intellect: French Scholars and Writers during the Great War* (Cambridge, Mass., 1996). For *instituteurs* in particular, see Jacques Ozouf and Mona Ozouf, *La République des instituteurs* (Paris, 1992). Xavier Boniface, *L'Aumônerie militaire française, 1914–1962* (Paris, 2001) is a study of priests in World War I and subsequent conflicts, but is limited to chaplains.

6. Cited in Fontana, *Catholiques français,* 126.

7. Becker, "Union sacrée et idéologies bourgeoises," 70.

8. Fontana, *Catholiques français,* 131.

9. Jean-Jacques Becker, "Union sacrée, l'exception qui confirme la règle," *Vingtième Siècle* 5 (1985): 116.

10. Robert Tombs, introduction to *Nationhood and Nationalism in France: From Boulangism to the Great War, 1889–1918,* ed. Robert Tombs (New York, 1991), 3. A classic psychological study of the distinction—in the realm of religious identity—between sentiment and more explicit intentions and ideologies is Gordon Allport, *The Individual and His Religion* (New York, 1950), chaps. 1 and 6.

11. Jean-Jacques Becker, 1914: *Comment les français sont entrés à la guerre* (Paris, 1977), 30–52. On the singular value of Becker's work, see Jay Winter, preface to Jean-Jacques Becker, *The Great War and the French People,* trans. Arnold Pomerans (New York, 1985), 1–2.

12. Stéphane Audouin-Rouzeau, "The National Sentiment of Soldiers During the Great War," in Tombs, *Nationhood,* 94. This article summarizes Audouin-Rouzeau's book-length study of trench newspapers, *Les Combattants des tranchées: À travers leurs journaux: 14–18* (Paris, 1986).

13. This library began as a private collection, the Bibliothèque et musée de la guerre. After World War I, it was transferred to the Nanterre campus of the University of Paris. See Daniel J. Sherman, "Objects of Memory: History and Narrative in French War Museums," *French Historical Studies* 19 (1995): 49–74.

14. For a brief description of the history and the role of *La Revue pédagogique* in French education, see Pénélope Caspard-Karydis and André Chambon, *La Presse d'éducation et d'enseignement, XVIIe siècle–1940,* 4 vols. (Paris, 1980–91), 3:478–81. The education office of each French department published a *Bulletin d'enseignement.* I declined to use these bulletins as a complement to my analysis of *La Revue pédagogique* after sampling the wartime issues from several departments: they were often made up of material originally published elsewhere.

15. Fontana, *Catholiques français,* 271.

16. Brugerette has separate sections on combatants, stretcher-bearers, and medics [*infirmiers*]. Joseph Brugerette, *Sous le régime de la Séparation, la reconstitution catholique, 1908–1936,* vol. 3 of *Le Prêtre français et la société contemporaine* (Paris, 1938), 349–427. For a comparison of French clerical nationalism with those of other countries, see A. J. Hoover, *God, Germany, and Britain in the Great War: A Study in Clerical Nationalism* (New York, 1989).

17. *La Preuve du sang: Livre d'or du clergé et des congrégations, 1914–1922,* 2 vols. (Paris, 1925), 1:xxiv. The Secrétariat de la documentation catholique assembled the information by sending questionnaires to the secretariats of bishops and religious congregations.

18. For a discussion of canon law, see Fontana, *Catholiques français,* 277–80.

19. Henry Bordeaux, introduction to *Preuve du sang,* 1:xxiv, xxvi.

20. *Prêtre aux armées:* Bulletin bimensuel des prêtres et des religieux mobilisés, 1 May 1915, 84.

21. Ibid., 1 July 1915, 169.

22. Ibid., 15 June 1917, 910.

23. Ibid., 15 August 1916, 583.

24. Ibid., 1 November 1916, 665.

25. Ibid., 15 November 1916, 687.

26. Ibid., 1 July 1918, 1304.

27. A. Ménétrier, *Moine et soldat: Le R.P. Edouard de Massat, 1860–1915* (Toulouse, 1918), 226, 332, 327–28, 335.

28. L. G., *L'Abbé Jean Audouin, clerc minoré, sergent au 135e d'infanterie* (Angers, 1917), 24.

29. P. L. Guinchard, *Un Jeune* (Paris, 1918), 54, 58.

30. M. Grivelet, *Mémoires d'un curé: Fantassin, aviateur, résistant* (Is-sur-Tille, 1970), 24–25, 28–29.

31. Mgr. Hector-Raphaël Quilliet, *Un Officier prêtre: L'Abbé Joseph-Eugène-Marie Arlet—Allocution prononcée en l'église de Saint-Michel-de-Lions* (Limoges, 1918), 7, 5.

32. Chanoine Max Caron, *Un Lys brisé* (Paris, 1918), 152, 283, 180, 156–57.

33. *Vaillant Apôtre et vaillant capitaine: Le Père Pierre Durouchoux, prêtre de la Compagnie de Jésus, capitaine au 274e d'infanterie* (Toulouse, 1918), 25, 24.

34. André de Font-Reaulx, S.J., *René de la Perraudière, novice de la Compagnie de Jésus, sergent d'infanterie française* (Toulouse, 1918), 85, 37, 43, 42, 44.

35. André de la Barre de Carroy, *Une Ame droite: André de la Barre de Carroy, aumônier militaire au 102e de ligne* (Paris, 1923), 115.

36. *Une Fleur de saint abandon: Le P. Jean-Louis Dabo de la Congrégation de Jésus et Marie* (Besançon, n.d.), 25.

37. Paul Vigue, *Le Sergent Pierre Babouard du 125e d'infanterie* (Paris, 1917), 214.

38. Lud. Loiseau, *Un Bon Prêtre et un bon Français: L'Abbé Georges Sevin, curé d'Yèvre-la-Ville* (Pithiviers, 1921), 112–13.

39. The Jesuit review *Études* published regular reports of battlefield experiences; these were collected in Léonce de Grandmaison, ed., *Impressions de guerre de prêtres soldats: Batailles et champs de bataille; Avec les Allemands; L'Année religieuse au front; Episodes* (Paris, 1916). Here the causes of God and France were united, the rosary was praised, the horrors of war were occasionally evoked, and edifying stories were repeated—such as "The Little Trooper" [*patriouilleur*], a lad of nonreligious upbringing who was a simple warrior of honest faith.

40. Albert Valensin, *Lucien Chabord: La vie mystique dans les tranchées* (Paris, 1918), 38, 37.

41. Ibid., 61, 47.

42. Ibid., 74, 40.

43. Jean Nourisson, *Lettres de Jean Nourisson, aspirant au 153e régiment d'infanterie* (Paris, 1919), 147, 151, 118, 120.

44. See Pierre Mayoux, *Paul Doncœur, aumônier militaire* (Paris, 1966), 37. See also the recent study by Dominique Avon, *Paul Doncoeur, SJ (1880–1961): Un croisé dans le siècle* (Paris, 2001).

45. Pierre Lelièvre, *Le Fléau de Dieu: Notes et impressions de guerre* (Paris, n.d.).

46. Jean Norton Cru, *Témoins: Essai d'analyse et de critique des souvenirs de combattant édités en français de 1915 à 1928* (1929; repr. Nancy, 1993), 172–75.

47. Lelièvre, *Fléau de Dieu,* 76–77, 79.

48. Ibid., 87–88.

49. Among the clergy testimonies that have only been published in recent years are Jean Julien Weber, *Sur les pentes du Golgotha: Un prêtre dans les tranchées* (Strasbourg, 2001), Adelphe Pousse, *Une soutane sous la mitraille: Carnets de la Grande Guerre d'un curé de campagne* (Jaignes, 2000).

50. Becker, *Great War,* 151.

51. See Becker's report on teachers in Doubs in *Great War,* chap. 5, and the extended archival work on teachers in the Isère by P. J. Flood. Teachers were required to report on "attitudes in and organization of local village *communes* throughout the war" (P. J. Flood, *France, 1914–1918: Public Opinion and the War Effort* [NewYork, 1990], ix). For a discussion of the problem of writing World War I history for children's textbooks, thus incorporating it into a teachable national identity, see Anne-Louise Shapiro, "Fixing History: Narratives of World War I in France," *History and Theory* 36 (1997): 111–30.

52. Ozouf and Ozouf, *La République,* 351.

53. Of the sons of tradespeople and artisans, 38 percent declared themselves Catholic; of the sons of farmers, 43 percent; of the sons of *instituteurs,* 47 percent. See ibid., 183.

54. For these and other responses not included in Ozouf and Ozouf, *La République,* I have consulted the responses to Jacques Ozouf's questionnaire preserved in the Musée National d'Éducation at Mont-Saint-Aignan, Rouen. These responses (hereafter MNE, Fonds Ozouf) are sorted according to the department, identification number, and sex of individual. My sampling comes from two clericalized departments: the Nord, occupied during the war, and the Vendée.

55. Ozouf and Ozouf, *La République,* 188.

56. *La Revue pédagogique,* n.s., 65 (July-December 1914): 202, 217–18, 215–17.

57. Ibid., 221.

58. *La Revue pédagogique,* n.s., 66 (January-June 1915): 1–3.

59. See Paul Lapié, *L'Instituteur et la guerre* (Paris, 1915), 76.

60. *La Revue pédagogique,* n.s., 66 (January-June 1915): 245, 251–52.

61. Ibid., 457–59.

62. *La Revue pédagogique,* n.s., 67 (July-December 1915): 182–83, 181.

63. Ibid., 297, 380.

64. Ibid., 460, 463–64.

65. *La Revue pédagogique,* n.s., 68 (January-June 1916): 68–69, 527–41.

66. Maurice Masson, *Lettres de guerre: Août 1914-avril 1916* (Paris, 1917).

67. *La Revue pédagogique*, n.s., 71 (July-December 1917): 277.

68. *La Revue pédagogique*, n.s., 72 (January-June 1918): 377.

69. Ibid., 311.

70. *La Revue pédagogique*, n.s., 73 (July-September 1918): 130, 127.

71. Ibid., 130–31.

72. *La Revue pédagogique*, n.s., 72 (January-June 1918): 199.

73. Joseph Pascal, *Mémoires d'un instituteur* (Paris, 1974), 88–89.

74. Paul Cazin, *L'Humaniste à la guerre: Hauts de Meuse, 1915* (Paris, 1920), 1–2, 168–69.

75. A study analogous to, though different in focus from, the present one is Margaret H. Darrow, "French Volunteer Nursing and the Myth of War Experience in World War I," *American Historical Review* 101 (1996): 80–106, in which the author analyzes the gamut of roles *attributed* to nurses more than the roles they themselves *assumed*.

76. Albert Bessières, *Âmes nouvelles-instituteurs-soldats: Une "Promotion de l'espérance"* (Paris, 1917), 120, 289.

77. Ozouf and Ozouf, *La République*, 216.

78. MNE, Fonds Ozouf, Nord, Gaston Jean.

79. Ibid., Nord, Gustave Taine.

80. Ibid., Vendée, Paul Bouté.

81. Ibid., Vendée, Eugène Fonteneau.

82. Ibid., Vendée, Roger Clot.

83. Ibid., Nord, André Canivez.

CHAPTER 7. RECONCILIATION OF CULTURES IN THE THIRD REPUBLIC

1. "Culture" has been defined by the anthropologist Clifford Geertz as a "historically transmitted pattern of meanings embodied in symbols, a system of inherited conceptions expressed in symbolic forms by means of which men communicate, perpetuate, and develop their knowledge about and attitudes toward life." See Clifford Geertz, "Religion as a Cultural System," The *Interpretation of Cultures: Selected Essays* (New York, 1973), 89. In the decades since the appearance of this essay, the concept of culture has become highly politicized.

2. All these volumes were published in Paris by Armand Colin.

3. John Van Engen argues that a choice does not have to be made between a Catholic golden age and an Indo-European religious folk culture: there is an interaction, in that the mentalities of the lower classes influenced the theological ideas of the elite, and the preaching of the theologians and clergy was absorbed by the common people. See "The Christian Middle Ages as a Historiographical Problem," *American Historical Review* 91 (1986): 537–38. Michel Lauwers prefers to speak of "milieux" within "culture" in "'Religion populaire,' culture folklorique, mentalités: Note pour une anthropologie culturelle du moyen âge," *Revue d'histoire ecclésiastique* 82 (1987): 221–58.

4. For a brief explanation of this discipline, see Louis Réau, *Iconographie de l'art chrétien*, vol. 1 (Paris, 1955), 1–11. The value of Mâle's work, specifically as synthesis, is explained in Léon Pressouyre, "Émile Mâle, le moyen âge et nous," interview in *Préfaces*, no. 2 (1987), 130. The validity of Mâle's basic theses is indirectly supported by the synthesis article of Herbert L. Kessler, "On the State of Medieval Art History," *Art Bulletin* 72 (1988): 166–89. Examining a decade's worth of monographs, Kessler draws together broad conclusions on periodization, the medieval art object, and production from scholarly writing that "has focused on single works or on small groups of related monuments" (186).

5. See in particular the articles on Mérimée and Viollet-le-Duc in Pierre Nora, ed., *Les Lieux de mémoire: II Nation***** (Paris, 1984–92). Otherwise consult *Le "Gothique" retrouvé avant Viollet-le-Duc: Exposition à l'Hôtel de Sully, 31 octobre 1979–17 février 1980* (Paris, 1979). Earlier attempts to recuperate

and collect medieval *objets* are studied in Stephen Bann, *The Clothing of Cleo: A Study of the Representation of History in Nineteenth-Century Britain and France* (Cambridge, 1984), chap. 3: "Poetics of the Museum: Lenoir and Du Sommerard."

6. André Chastel glosses the term "patrimony" as "an artistic and architectural (monumental) heritage in which one can recognize oneself." See "Le Patrimoine," in Nora, ed., *Les Lieux de mémoire: II La Nation**, 420.

7. These Catholic intellectuals and their spiritual experiences are examined in Frédéric Gugelot, *La Conversion des intellectuels au catholicisme en France, 1885−1935* (Paris, 1998). See also the study of Maritain, his wife Raissa, and their contemporaries in Richard D. E. Burton, *Holy Tears, Holy Blood: Women, Catholicism, and the Culture of Suffering in France, 1840−1970* (Ithaca, 2004), introduction and chap. 4. Burton presents Claudel and Huysmans in his *Blood in the City: Violence and Revelation in Paris, 1789−1945* (Ithaca, 2001), chaps. 8 and 9.

8. Jean-Marie Mayeur and Madeleine Rebérioux, *The Third Republic from Its Origins to the Great War, 1871−1914,* trans. J. R. Foster (New York, 1984). Ideological intensity could not have characterized the country as a whole. Mayeur and Rebérioux say, "The real cement which kept the republican party together was . . . the common desire to secularize the state and social life" (84). By the 1880s, peasants and members of the middle class found their own interests best represented by the republicans. That year the republican government received more than 50 percent of the vote in all but six departments. See the maps charting "the conquest of the Republic by the Republicans," ibid., 32−35. Maurice Agulhon's broad and balanced interpretation of the secular and religious antagonisms in government should also be consulted; see *The French Republic, 1879−1992,* trans. Antonia Nevill (Cambridge, Mass., 1992), chap. 1, "Ten Founding Years, 1879−1889."

9. There were, still and all, some first moves toward dialogue. Robert J. Smith cites the texts of Ernest Lavisse ("little marvels of reconciliation"), who taught at the École Normale from 1876 to 1880 but whose influence on the École and the Sorbonne continued for over thirty years. Lavisse, in fact, never declared himself during the Boulanger or Dreyfus affairs, remaining "more of a nationalist than a partisan politician." Joseph Bédier, a good friend of Mâle, emphasized the close textual analysis that he and his mentor Gaston Paris had learned in Germany. But he was also a free spirit: "A free-thinker, a Dreyfusard, and a friend of Lucien Herr and Jean Jaurès, Bédier was nevertheless not a socialist." See Robert J. Smith, *The École Normale Supérieure and the Third Republic* (Albany, 1982), 61, 62, 65.

10. Émile Mâle, *Souvenirs et correspondance de jeunesse: Bourbonnais-Forez-École Normale Supérieure* (Nonette, 2001), 125.

11. To his parents, 5 November 1883, Papers of Émile Mâle (hereafter PEM), Bibliothèque de l'Institut de France, MS 7657. The PEM contain photocopies only of Mâle's letters to his parents. The originals have been donated to the town of Commentry (Allier), Mâle's birthplace.

12. Ibid.

13. The coursework notes, along with some sketch notebooks that formed part of Mâle's iconographical research, are in the possession of the family, pending donation to a library or museum.

14. To his parents, 21 July 1884, PEM, MS 7657.

15. Mâle, *Souvenirs,* 53.

16. *Discours de distribution des prix du lycée de Toulouse* [31 juillet 1891] (Toulouse, 1891), 10.

17. Mâle, *Souvenirs,* 152.

18. Ibid., 73, 87.

19. Ibid., 152. There was, in fact, a varied and active group of Catholics at the École Normale in the first decades of the twentieth century. See Paul Cohen, "Les Élèves Catholiques de l'École Normale Supérieure, 1906−1914," *Cahiers d'Histoire* 29 (1984): 33−46. Formal religious practice was not widespread, although some of the *normaliens* were practicing Catholics and even members of the St. Vincent de Paul Society. See also the author's more broadly based study, *Piety and Politics: Catholic Revival and the Generation of 1905−1914 in France* (New York, 1987).

20. "Vocation italienne," *L'Amour de l'art,* 46−48 (1950): 3. See also Mâle, *Souvenirs,* 173.

21. "Vocation italienne," 3.

22. "Hommage à M. Émile Mâle de l'Académie française," *Mémorial de la Loire et de la Haute Loire*, 28 July 1928, and Mâle, *Souvenirs*, 94–97.

23. On nineteenth-century French enthusiasm for shrines and apparitions, see Thomas A. Kselman, *Miracles and Prophecies in Nineteenth-Century France* (New Brunswick, N.J., 1983).

24. For a classical and brief general history of the Thomist revival, see Etienne Gilson, "In the Spirit of Scholasticism," chap. 12 of Etienne Gilson, Thomas Langon, and Armand Maurer, *Recent Philosophy: Hegel to the Present* (New York, 1962). The writings of Vincenzo Buzzetti, professor at the seminary of Piacenza, represented the transition from the technique of overlaying, dear to the previous centuries, to the ways of the modern neo-Thomists: "They had to rediscover the true doctrine of Thomas Aquinas hidden beneath the layers of alluvia deposited on it by the past five centuries" (331). Equally important in the Thomist revival was Joseph Pecci, professor at the seminary of Perugia, and Giovanni Cornoldi, professor at the seminary of Padua. Pecci was the brother of Pope Leo XIII, who brought neo-Thomism into the center of Catholic intellectual life in 1897. Pecci (by then a cardinal), Cornoldi, and Pope Leo XIII founded the Roman Academy of St. Thomas Aquinas. This effort was paired with the publication of Leo's encyclical letter promoting a return to scholastic philosophy in general and Thomas's philosophy in particular, *Aeterni Patris* of 4 August 1879. Ultimately the best studies of neo-Thomism produced in France—and Belgium—came after Mâle's work on the thirteenth century had been published. An outstanding school of Thomism was established in Belgium at the University of Louvain. French Dominicans began the publication of the *Revue Thomiste* in 1893, and their leading intellectuals, A. D. Sertillanges and Pierre Mandonnet, did their major work in the twentieth century. For a contemporary summary, see Gerald A. McCool, *The Neo-Thomists* (Milwaukee, 1994).

25. The archives of the École Normale contain the library loan records of the Mâle years. Bibliothèque (Registre des emprunts)/Élèves/1885–86, lists the books Mâle checked out (thirty-three titles on the philosophy of Greece and Rome, literature, mythology, and religion), including Ollé-Laprune's *Essai sur la morale d'Aristote*. See also Smith, *École Normale*, chap. 4. Ollé-Laprune was an influence on Maurice Blondel, like Ollé-Laprune a committed Catholic. On Gratry, see *Le Père Gratry, 1805–1872: L'homme et l'oeuvre d'après des documents inédits* (Paris, 1901).

26. For a summary of earlier studies of Migne, see R. Howard Bloch, *God's Plagiarist: Being an Account of the Fabulous Industry and Irregular Commerce of the abbé Migne* (Chicago, 1994).

27. See Fernand Cabrol, *Histoire du Cardinal Pitra* (Paris, 1893). At first Pitra wanted to do substantial editorial work, but soon time constraints forced him to reproduce existing editions. He contented himself with brief indications of editions chosen and the addition of minimal commentaries, notes, and charts. Working day and night, he moved with great speed and was ultimately responsible for both patrologies—though other scholars did collaborate in minor ways. By the time the two patrologies were issued, Pitra was a cardinal and encouraging Migne to do an edition of the General Councils in time to benefit scholars at the First Vatican Council. See 107–8.

28. For the information on these childhood and school years, see Mâle, *Souvenirs*, 67–73.

29. "Hommage à M. Émile Mâle de l'Académie française," and Mâle, *Souvenirs*, 94–97.

30. See V. Isambert-Jamati, *Crises de la société, crises de l'enseignement: Sociologie de l'enseignement secondaire français* (Paris, 1970), especially the statistics in the appendix.

31. To his parents, 4 July 1881, 24 January 1881, PEM, MS 7657.

32. Mâle, *Souvenirs*, 118.

33. Ibid., 105–6.

34. To his parents, 8 June 1885, PEM, MS 7657.

35. Mâle, *Souvenirs*, 122.

36. Many of Mâle's sketches are reproduced in the *Souvenirs*.

37. See the study and collected texts of François Hartog, *Le XIXe siècle et l'histoire: Le cas Fustel de Coutanges* (Paris, 1988).

38. *Le Centénaire de l'Ecole Normale, 1795–1895*, cited in Theodore Zeldin, *France, 1848–1945*, vol. 2: *Intellect, Taste, and Anxiety* (Oxford, 1977), 339.

39. *Emile Mâle, le symbolisme chrètien,* catalogue of the Exposition Emile Mâle (hereafter *Exposition*), edited and arranged by Monique Kuntz, head librarian of the Bibliothéque Municipale de Vichy, for the exhibition of 28 May–20 June 1983, at Vichy (Allier), France, 2.

40. Paul Ourliac, *Annales de la Faculté de droit,* tome 16, fasc. 2 (Toulouse, 1968).

41. Georges Chemineaux to Emile Mâle, 22 September 1892, PEM, MS 7587.

42. On the building of these collections see *Le Gothique retrouvé, avant Viollet-le-Duc,* Exposition at the Hôtel de Sully, 31 October 1979–17 February 1980 (Paris, 1979).

43. To the Rector of Paris, 8 July 1898, Archives Nationales F 17 24519.

44. A student at the Lycée Louis-le-Grand representing his class, to Emile Mâle, 31 December 1901, PEM, MS 7587.

45. Georges Huisman, "Emile Mâle, déchiffreur des cathédrales," *Arts,* 13–19 October 1954. Huisman was appointed director of fine arts for the French government in 1934.

46. *Exposition,* 4. The president of the committee was Georges Perrot; the members: Henri Lemonnier, professor of art history; Auguste Bouche-Leclercq, historian of the ancient world; Charles Langlois, professor of paleography and history of the Middle Ages; Petit de Julleville, professor of language and literature of the Middle Ages; and Emile Gebhard, professor of Provençal literature.

47. Cited in William R. Keylor, *Academy and Community: The Foundation of the French Historical Profession* (Cambridge, 1975), 178. See also Martin Siegel, "Clio at the Ecole Normale Supérieure: Historical Studies at an Elite Institution in France, 1970–1904," *History of Historiography* 8 (1985): 37–49.

48. Further considerations of the historians of this period and their ambiance can be found in Daniel Moulinet, "L'art religieux du XIIIe siècle en France: Genèse d'un grand livre," *Transversalités: Revue de l'Institut catholique de Paris,* no. 70 (April-June 1999): 187–208.

49. See D. G. Charlton, "The French Romantic Movement" in the collection he edited, *The French Romantics,* vol. 1 (Cambridge, 1984), 1–34. James Smith Allen, *Popular French Romanticism: Authors, Readers, and Books in the Nineteenth Century* (Syracuse, 1981) is a study of the varieties of Romanticism in their social and political context.

50. Pierre Moreau, *Le Classicisme des romantiques* (Paris, 1952), 239–40.

51. Cited in ibid., 448.

52. *L'Ouest-Éclair,* 12 May 1931.

53. The two most important studies of nineteenth-century archaeologists, conservers, and restorers are Paul Léon, *La Vie de monuments français: Destruction, restauration* (Paris, 1951), and Jean Mallion, *Victor Hugo et l'art architectural* (Paris, 1962). For a recent, concise history, see Jean-Michel Léniaud, *Jean-Baptiste Lassus (1807–1857) ou le temps retrouvé des cathédrales* (Paris, 1980), chap. 2: "À la recherche d'une nouvelle culture, l'art médiéval." On the cathedral and the Gothic revival, see Alain Erlande-Brandenburg, *The Cathedral: The Social and Architectural Dynamics of Construction,* trans. Martin Thom (New York, 1994), introduction.

54. "Hommage à M. Émile Mâle de l'Académie française," and Mâle, *Souvenirs,* 174–75.

55. Cited in Mâle, *Souvenirs,* 174–75.

56. In the introduction to his *Iconographie chrétienne,* Didron argued that the medieval sculpture and stained glass were designed for the faithful in general and that the organization of ideas embodied in the art followed the division of Vincent of Beauvais's *Speculum majus.* These two notions were placed in high relief in Mâle's study of thirteenth-century religious art. See Adolphe-Napoléon Didron, *Iconographie chrétienne: Histoire de Dieu* (Paris, 1843).

57. For studies of this period, see Paul Léon, *La Vie de monuments français: Destruction, restauration* (Paris, 1951); Jean Mallion, *Victor Hugo et l'art architectural* (Paris, 1962); Jean-Michel Léniaud, *Jean-Baptiste Lassus (1807–1857) ou le temps retrouvé des cathédrales* (Paris, 1980), chap. 2: "À la recherche d'une nouvelle culture, l'art médiévale"; *Le Gothique retrouvé, avant Viollet-le-Duc,* Exposition at the Hôtel de Sully, 31 October1979—17 February 1980 (Paris, 1979); Erlande-Brandenburg, *Cathedral.*

58. Émile Mâle, "L'Académie et la défense des monuments de la France," in *Trois siècles de l'Académie française (1635–1935),* par les Quarante (Paris, 1935), 423.

59. Mâle, "L'Académie," 425. See Christopher M. Greene, "Romanticism, Cultural Nationalism and Politics in the July Monarchy: The Contribution of Ludovic Vitet," *French History* 4 (1990): 487–509, and Françoise Bercé, *Les Premiers travaux de la Commission de monuments historiques, 1837–1848* (Paris, 1979).

60. Mâle, "L'Académie," 428. See Paul Léon, *Mérimée et son temps* (Paris, 1962).

61. Cited in Léon, *La Vie des monuments français*, 204. On Viollet-le-Duc, see Bruno Foucart, "Viollet-le-Duc et la Restauration," in *Les Lieux de mémoire II, La Nation*, ed. Pierre Nora (Paris, 1986); Pierre-Marie Auzas, *Eugène Viollet-le-Duc, 1814–1879* (Paris, 1979), and Kevin D. Murphy, *Memory and Modernity: Viollet-le-Duc at Vézeley* (University Park, Penn., 2000). Specific features of Viollet-le-Duc's career are analyzed in Hubert Damisch, introduction to Eugène Viollet-le-Duc, *L'Architecture raisonnée, extraits de "Dictionnaire de l'architecture française,"* ed. Hubert Damisch (Paris, 1978), and Jean Michel Leniaud, *Viollet-le-Duc ou les délires du système* (Paris, 1994).

62. Léon, *La Vie des monuments*, 204.

63. "Hommage à M. Emile Mâle de l'Académie française," and Mâle, *Souvenirs*, 94–97.

64. Adolphe-Napoléon Didron, *Manuel d'iconographie chrétienne, grecque et latine* (Paris, 1845), iv.

65. *Annales archéologiques* 4 (1846): 267, cited in Georg Germann, *Gothic Revival in Europe and Britain: Sources, Influences, and Ideas*, trans. Gerald Onn (Cambridge, Mass., 1973), 140.

66. *Annales archéologiques* 4 (1846): 129, cited in Germann, *Gothic Revival*, 143.

67. Adolphe-Napoléon Didron, *Iconographie chrétienne*, xiii.

68. Charles Cahier and Arthur Martin, *Vitraux peints de Saint-Etienne de Bourges* (Paris, 1842), i.

69. Ibid., ii.

70. See Harry Bober, editor's foreword in Emile Mâle, *Religious Art in France: The Twelfth Century*, trans. Marthiel Matthews (Princeton, 1978).

71. In addition to the books that preceded his own efforts, Mâle cites historical reviews: *Annales archéologiques*, of course; *Le Bulletin monumental*, founded by Arcisse de Caumont; the *Revue de l'art chrétien*, founded by the abbé Corblet; the *Bibliothèque de l'Ecole de Chartes; La Revue archéologique; La Gazette archéologique;* and the *Bulletins* and *Mémoires* of the individual French departments. See Louis Réau, *Iconographie de l'art chrétien*, vol. 1 (Paris, 1955), 12–19, for a recent outline of the history of iconography that includes presentations of studies in hagiography and the history of liturgy. In Jan Bialostocki's entry "Iconography," in the *Dictionary of the History of Ideas*, vol. 2 (New York, 1973), Mâle is given only passing mention.

72. "L'Enseignement de l'histoire de l'art," *Revue universitaire* 1 (15 January 1894): 14.

73. Ibid., 14–15.

74. Ibid., 15.

75. Ibid., 17. On nationalism in modern France, see Robert Tombs, ed., *Nations and Nationalism in France: From Boulangism to the Great War* (New York, 1991).

76. See Georges Perrot, *L'Histoire de l'art dans l'enseignement secondaire* (Paris, 1900), 34n1, 16ff.

77. "'L'Art chrétien au moyen âge': Leçon d'ouverture faite à la Sorbonne le 8 décembre 1906," *Revue bleue* 7 (1907): 138.

78. Ibid., 139.

79. Boisserée was among those instrumental in the neo-Gothic continuation of the building of Cologne cathedral, begun in the Middle Ages but left incomplete until the nineteenth century. In 1833, he published his principal study of medieval architecture. See W. D. Robson-Scott, *The Literary Background of the Gothic Revival in Germany* (Oxford, 1965), 282ff.

80. "'L'Art chrétien au moyen âge,'" 173.

81. Ibid.

82. This change is reflected in the second edition (1922) of *L'Art religieux de la fin du moyen âge en France*.

83. "L'Art gothique: Les collaborateurs de le cathédrals," *La Revue française politique et littéraire*, 28 January 1912, 487.

84. "Le Moyen âge; Le duc de Berry—protecteur des arts," *La Revue française politique et littéraire*, 6 July 1913, 381.

85. Mâle, *Souvenirs,* 86.

86. Lucien Herr to Émile Mâle, 13 October 1911, PEM, MS 7655. on the life and work of Herr, see Charles Andler, *Vie de Lucien Herr, 1864–1926* (Paris, 1932); Daniel Lindenberg and Pierre-André Meyer, *Lucien Herr, le socialisme et son destin* (Paris, 1977), and the *Correspondance entre Charles Andler et Lucien Herr, 1891–1926,* ed. Antoinette Blum (Paris, 1992).

87. Louis Gillet, *Amitiés littéraires* (Paris, 1928), 126.

88. Ibid., 127.

89. Ibid.

90. Ibid., 125.

91. "La Cathédrale de Reims," *Revue de Paris,* 15 December 1914, 294.

92. To appreciate the profound anti-German antagonism of Mâle and other French scholars during this war, we should review the larger context: in the nineteenth century, many French intellectuals expected Germany to liberate France from some of its ordinariness in literature and philosophy because they idealized German intellectual life. See Claude Digeon, *La Crise allemande de la pensée française, 1870–1914* (Paris, 1959). In the face of German invasion, academics indebted to German thought—to wit, Charles Seignobos and Lucien Herr following a line of thought earlier developed by Fustel de Coulanges and Émile Durkheim—were perfectly ready to denounce the Germans as barbarians and hypocrites.

93. "La Cathédrale de Reims," 294.

94. Ibid., 295.

95. *L'Art allemand et l'art français du moyen âge* (Paris, 1917).

96. The German occupation of northern France in 1940 and the creation of the collaborationist Vichy regime found Mâle in his native Bourbonnais. Seventy-six years old and retired, he did not attempt major essays on this new German invasion. But in *Rome et ses vieilles églises,* published in 1942, he pointedly reflects on the barbarian attacks on Rome. For French readers, the allusion to the Nazi presence would have been clear. See *Rome et ses vieilles églises* (Paris, 1942). I am indebted to Francis-Noël Thomas for pointing out the reference to the barbarian invasions.

97. The Académie brought together scholars in the archaeology, philology, and history of Greco-Roman, Egyptian, Near Eastern, Islamic, and Oriental cultures.

98. To Louis Gillet, 15 December 1918, *Exposition,* #184.

99. Germain Bazin, "Le Souvenir d'Émile Mâle," *Le Figaro littéraire,* 16 October 1954.

100. Joseph Bédier to Émile Mâle, 12 September 1924, PEM, MS 7580.

101. "Discours de réception de Émile Mâle â l'Académie française," *Institut de France,* no. 98 (Paris, 1928), 6.

102. Émile Mâle, *Arts et artistes du moyen âge* (Paris, 1927), v–vi.

103. Émile Mâle, *La Fin du paganisme en Gaule et les plus anciennes basiliques chrétiennes* (Paris, 1950).

104. Ibid., 6–7.

105. Ibid., 327.

106. The citation from Henri Focillon is found in the copy of *Vie de formes* (Paris, 1934) that the author inscribed "À mon maître, Monsieur Mâle, qui nous enseigna le premier qu'histoire des formes est histoire de l'esprit. Hommage et respectueuse amitié." Marcel Aubert to Émile Mâle, 21 September 1948, PEM,MS 7653. See also Louis Réau, "À Émile Mâle: In Memoriam," *Académie d'architecture: Bulletin* (4e trimestre, 1954), 7, and Bazin, "Le Souvenir." Guy Thuillier and Jean Tulard, in *Les Écoles historiques* (Paris, 1990), 43, offer a "Tableau des attaches intellectuelles de Lucien Febvre," where Émile Mâle is placed with Louis Courajod on the "mes auteurs" side of the graph (the other side is "Mes pères et mes compagnons").

107. Rapport sur la thèse d'Émile Mâle. F17 24519, Archives Nationales; cited in *Exposition,* #105.

108. Réau, "À Émile Mâle," 6.

109. I am grateful to Anne Nesteroff of the publishing house of Armand Colin for information on the editions of Mâle's work and general difficulties of estimating the number of copies published. In the past fifteen years entirely new editions of Mâle's major works have been published.

110. Mâle's letters are classified in relation to his publications and the events in his life. They are found, then, throughout the cartons of the PEM.

111. Quoted in Richard Bales, *Proust and the Middle Ages* (Geneva, 1975), 28.

112. Jean Autret, "La Dette de Marcel Proust envers Émile Mâle," *Gazette des Beaux-Arts,* VIe période, vol. 51 (1958-1er semestre): 59.

113. See Luc Fraisse, *L'Oeuvre cathédrale: Proust et l'architecture médiévale* (Paris, 1990), 103, 256. There is a large collection of correspondence from persons of all walks of life in the PEM.

114. See Lucien de Sainte-Croix, "Émile Mâle: Un grand historien de l'art au Moyen Age," *Mercure de France,* 15 September 1927, 7.

115. See *Les Nouvelles littéraires,* 17 October 1949, 6. On textbooks, see Alain Choppin, "L'Histoire des manuels scolaires une approche globale," *L'Histoire de l'éducation,* 9 (December 1980): 1 −25. For a study of the influence of Lavisse, see Pierre Nora, "Ernest Lavisse: Sôn role dans la formation du sentiment national," *Revue historique* 228 (1962): 73 −106. See also the surveys of Jacqueline Freyssinet-Dominjon, *Les Manuels d'histoire de l'école libre, 1882−1959, de la loi Ferry à la loi Debré* (Paris, 1969), and Dominique Maingueneau, *Les Livres d'école de la République (discours et idéologie)* (Paris, 1979).

116. See page 50.

117. See page 211.

118. But there are no references to his four major studies because the team of editors would provide references only to readily available, single-subject works (pertaining to an individual monument or region). For help in the study and interpretation of tourist guides, I wish to thank Yves Petot and Alain Arnaud of editorial staff of the Guides Michelin. For a full history of the Michelin guides, see Stephen L. Harp, *Marketing Michelin: Advertizing and Cultural Identity in Twentieth-Century France* (Baltimore, 2001).

119. *Guide bleu, Île de France* (Paris, 1976), 239, 246; *Guide vert, Environs de Paris* (Paris, 1962). Until very recently each volume of the *Guides bleus* was the work of an individual author or editor, who would decide what references to base a presentation on and where quotes from important authors would be appropriate. For this information, I wish to thank Georges Anthoinette, archivist for the publisher Hachette.

120. Joseph Tranchant, "Émile Mâle (1862−1954): Historien de l'art religieux," *L'Enseignement chrétien* (January 1958): 196−211; Madeleine Ochsé, "Un grand humaniste chrétien: Émile Mâle," *Ecclesia* (August 1962): 75−84.

121. Paul Doncoeur, "L'Oeuvre religieuse d'Émile Mâle," *Études,* 283 (1954): 257−58.

122. "Notice sur la vie et les travaux de M. Émile Mâle," *Institut de France, Académie des inscriptions et belles-lettres* (Paris, 1962), 4. See Élie Lambert, "La Vie et l'oeuvre d'Émile Mâle," *Revue universitaire* 64 (January-February, 1955), and Henri Daniel-Rops, "Discours [pour l'inauguration de buste d'Émile Mâle]" (édité par la Ville de Chartres et le Syndicat d'Initiative, 1963), 19. All these articles and press notices are found in PEM, MS 7661.

APPENDIX. THE "NATION" CONUNDRUM

1. John Hutchinson and Anthony D. Smith, eds., *Nationalism,* Oxford Readers (New York, 1994), 5.

2. Geoff Eley and Ronald Grigor Suny, eds., *Becoming National: A Reader* (New York, 1996), 8.

3. See Benedict Anderson, *Imagined Communities: Reflections on the Origin and Spread of Nationalism* (London, 1983), and John Breuilly, *Nationalism and the State* (New York, 1982).

4. *Times Literary Supplement,* 26 October−1 November 1990, 1149.

5. This study is now supported by a number of reviews such as *The Journal of Nationalism, National Identities,* and *Totalitarian Movements and Political Religions.*

6. Anthony Smith, *The Ethnic Origins of Nations* (New York, 1986), 42.

7. Ibid., 124.

8. Ernest Gellner, *Nations and Nationalism* (Ithaca, 1983), 10.

9. Ibid., 25.

10. E. J. Hobsbawm, *Nations and Nationalism Since 1780: Programme, Myth, Reality* (New York, 1990).

11. Peter Alter, *Nationalism* (London, 1989), 8–12. A brilliant study of the vicissitudes of proto-national (ethnic) loyalties in the building of a modern nation is Anastasia Karakasidou, *Fields of Wheat, Hills of Blood: Passages to Nationhood in Greek Macedonia, 1870–1940* (Chicago, 1997). In the author's words, "The national consciousness of the Greek nation had been overwritten upon localized memories of personal experience" (235) as the Bulgarian village of Guvezna was gradually transformed into the Greek village of Assiros.

12. Ibid., 9.

13. Miroslav Hroch, *Social Preconditions of National Revival in Europe: A Comparative Analysis of the Social Composition of Patriotic Groups Among the Smaller European Nations,* trans. Ben Folkes (New York, 1985), 22–30.

Further Reading

Readers can find all archival and primary source references, as well as appropriate basic bibliography, in the endnotes. That basic bibliography is here annotated and expanded, with special attention to the works that support the introductions to Parts 1, 2, and 3.

INTRODUCTION

Pierre Birnbaum, *The Idea of France,* trans. M. B. DeBevoise (New York, 1998) is a helpful introduction to questions of national and religious identity, even though he identifies the leading Protestant of the bourgeois monarchy, François Guizot, as a Catholic. But there is no text for modern France that has the coverage and clarity of David A. Bell on old-regime France, *Cult of the Nation in France: Inventing Nationalism, 1680–1800* (Cambridge, Mass., 2001). For years, the standard textbook for modern French history has been Gordon Wright, *France in Modern Times,* now in its fifth edition (New York, 1995), but for special insights into the interrelationships of church, state, and social experience, see the classic by Theodore Zeldin, *France, 1848–1945* (Oxford, 1977), especially vol. 2: *Intellect, Taste and Anxiety.* Pierre Nora, ed., *Rethinking the French Past,* trans. Arthur Goldhammer, 3 vols. (New York, 1996–98), is a vast collection of essays that explore every aspect of French cultural life, including religion, nationalism, and both religion and nationalism together; all my citations in the present text are from the French edition.

Ralph Gibson, *A Social History of French Catholicism* (New York, 1989) is still unsurpassed as a masterful synthesis and social interpretation of issues national and religious. In fact, both general and scholarly appreciation of the book's clear presentation of complex issues and statistics has increased over the past decade and a half.

There are two authors whose work on the varieties of French religious experiences as social and political dramas combines case history and narrative. The writings of James F. McMillan are all basic here, but the essays that readers should see in conjunction with the histories supplied in this book are the following:

"French Catholics: *Rumeurs infames* and the *Union Sacrée, 1914–1918,*" in *Authority, Identity, and the Social History of the Great War,* ed. Frans Coetzee and Marilyn Shevin-Coetzee (Providence, R.I., 1995).

"Religion and Gender in Modern France: Some Reflections," in *Religion, Society and Politics in France since 1789,* ed. Frank Tallett and Nicholas Atkin (Rio Grande, Ohio, 1991).

"Religion and Politics in Nineteenth-Century France: Further Reflections on Why Catholics and Republicans Couldn't Stand Each Other," in *The Politics of Religion in an Age of Revival: Studies in Nineteenth-Century Europe and Latin America*, ed. Austen Ivereigh (London, 2000).

"'Priest Hits Girl': On the Front Line in the 'War of the Two Frances,'" in *Culture Wars: Secular-Catholic Conflict in Nineteenth-Century Europe*, ed. Christopher Clark and Wolfram Kaiser (Cambridge, 2003), 77–101.

As this book goes to press, these studies are still not collected under one cover. Such is not the case for the stimulating essays of Richard D. E. Burton. Individual chapters in *Holy Tears, Holy Blood: Women, Catholicism, and the Culture of Suffering in France, 1840–1970* (Ithaca, 2004) and *Blood in the City: Violence and Revelation in Paris, 1789–1945* (Ithaca, 2001) explore psychological and social determinants of religious and national experience using a case history approach. Religion is a minor feature in Herman Lebovics, *True France: The Wars over Cultural Identity, 1900–1945* (Ithaca, 1992), but crucial, separate developments of twentieth-century cultural identity are placed in high relief.

Major syntheses of French religious history and general French history lay out landmark events and key personalities of the modern era, 1798 to 1918. Adrien Dansette, *Religious History of Modern France* (New York, 1961) is the most accessible single history of French Catholicism in English, although the better version is the last edition of the original French, *Histoire religieuse de la France contemporaine: L'Église catholique dans la mêlée politique et sociale*, rev. ed. (Paris, 1965). François Lebrun, ed., *Histoire des catholiques en France* (Paris, 1980) is much more usable that any of the others, although many historians appreciate the attempt to cover all levels of society and areas of cultural life in Gérard Cholvy and Yves-Marie Hilaire, *Histoire religieuse de la France contemporaine*, 3 vols. (Toulouse, 1985–88). Jacques LeGoff, René Remond and Philippe Joutard, eds., *Histoire de la France religieuse: Du roi très Chrétien à la laïcité républicaine, XVIIIe-XIXe siècle*, 1st ed. 1991 (Paris, 2001) slightly privileges thematic over chronological ordering. These last two works are not really syntheses, as the titles might suggest, but more collections of related essays that cover their respective time periods. Jean-Marie Mayeur et al., *L'Histoire religieuse de la France, 19e-20e siècle: Problèmes et méthodes* (Paris, 1975) is an exhaustive guide to the relevant historiography.

PART I: DIVORCE

John McManners, *The French Revolution and the Church* (New York, 1969) is a brief and original synthesis for the general reader, but even scholars have benefited from the author's ideas for further research in the field. Both general readers and scholars will find his *Church and Society in Eighteenth-Century France*, 2 vols. (Oxford, 1998) to be an indispensable study that offers the results of Herculean archival work in a fascinating narrative essential to the understanding of the century. Nigel Aston, *Religion and Revolution in France, 1780–1804* (Washington, 2000) is a survey containing a rich variety of examples. Owen Chadwick, *The Popes and European Revolution* (New York, 1981) has a broad European focus, especially appropriate in the Napoleonic era, and a lively narrative that is founded on an exemplary choice of sources.

In the task of sorting out religious, intellectual, and high and low cultural experiencs, Emmet Kennedy, *A Cultural History of the French Revolution* (New Haven, 1989) is the place to start. John Markoff, *The Abolition of Feudalism: Peasants, Lords, and Legislators in the French Revolution* (University Park, Penn., 1996) pairs the *cahiers de doléances* with revolutionary activities that at times involved or implied religious motivation. The high political context for all of this can be clearly followed in the two recent works of Michael P. Fitzsimmons: *The Night the Old Regime Ended* (University Park, Penn., 2003) and *The Remaking of France: The National Assembly and the Constitution of 1791* (Cambridge, 1994).

Hugh Gough, *The Terror in the French Revolution* (New York, 1998), can serve as general introduction and as a first step for those who want to attempt Patrice Guennifey, *La Politique de la Terreur: Essai sur la violence révolutionnaire, 1789–1794* (Paris, 2000), a vital work that traces the origins of the Terror in earlier votes and decisions that would otherwise appear anodine enough. David Jordan, *The King's Trial: Louis XVI vs. the French Revolution* (Berkeley and Los Angeles, 1979) is a clear narrative of the beginning of it all.

General guides and histories of the Revolution are familiar to all readers, but I favor a work, eminently useful to both general readers and students that mysteriously and quickly went out of print in the United States: Colin Jones, *The Longman Companion to the French Revolution* (1989). Otherwise, François Furet and Mona Ozouf, eds., *A Critical Dictionary of the French Revolution,* trans. Arthur Goldhammer (Cambridge, Mass., 1989) is a standard reference. William Doyle, *The Oxford History of the French Revolution* (New York, 1989) is surprisingly rich is detail for an introductory work. Owen Connelly, *The French Revolution and the Napoleonic Era,* 3rd ed. (Belmont, Calif., 1999) ranges widely across the Empire and comes up with the concrete statistics, military and otherwise, precisely where they are needed. The title of Martyn Lyons, *Napoleon Bonaparte and the Legacy of the French Revolution* (New York, 1994) is perfect for this balanced and readable account.

CHAPTER I

For the effects of the Enlightenment on Catholicism and the effects of the divisions within Catholicism on church-state relations, see Dale K. Van Kley's review of the writings of John McManners and Bernard Plongeron, "Christianity as Casualty and Chrysalis of Modernity: The Problem of Dechristianization in the French Revolution," *American Historical Review* 108 (2003): 1081–104, a work that presages a book, which one can only assume will be a vital as *The Religious Origins of the French Revolution: From Calvinism to the Civil Constitution, 1560–1791* (New Haven, 1996). Here readers can find dramas and controversies that had direct bearing on the religious tensions of the Revolution, especially those that would have agitated the clergy— Jansenism front and center. The book should lead some readers to the masterpiece of

Catherine Maire, *De la cause de Dieu à la cause de la Nation: Le Jansénisme au XVIIIe siècle* (Paris, 1998).

The vital final years of the old-regime church can be followed out in the wise and foolish maneuvers of its leaders, presented in Nigel Aston, *The End of an Elite: The French Bishops and the Coming of the Revolution, 1786–1790* (Oxford, 1992). But the book that has grounded studies of revolutionary priests and bishops for almost a generation now is Timothy Tackett, *Religion, Revolution, and Regional Culture in Eighteenth-Century France: The Ecclesiastical Oath of 1791* (Princeton, 1986), to be complemented (introduced, if possible) by Paul Christophe, *1789: Les prêtres dans la Révolution* (Paris, 1986). These texts make it clear that much more than theological partis pris went into the behavior and choices of the clergy as they became revolutionary or counterrevolutionary. And for statistics on the priests who rejected their status with greater and lesser degrees of radicality and violence, the essential source is Michel Vovelle, *The Revolution Against the Church: From Reason to the Supreme Being,* trans. Alan José (Cambridge, 1991).

Henri Grégoire, greatest of the revolutionaries among the priests and greatest of the priests (and bishops) among the revolutionaries, is the subject of two remarkably developed interpretations: Alyssa Goldstein Sepinwall, *The Abbé Grégoire and the French Revolution: The Making of a Modern Universalism* (Berkeley and Los Angeles, 2005), to be complemented by Rita Hermon-Belot, *L'abbé Grégoire: La politique et la vérité* (Paris, 2000).

Rodney J. Dean, *L'Église constitutionnelle, Napoléon et le Concordat de 1801* (Paris, 2004), written in French by an Englishman, is the first full study of the constitutional church, eminently useful both in its introductory presentation and in its focus on the Napoleonic period.

CHAPTER 2

Lynn Hunt, *Politics, Culture, and Class in the French Revolution,* anniversary edition (Berkeley and Los Angeles, 2004) combines fundamental social statistics with a clarity of interpretation that has established this text as a vital and necessary prerequisite to understanding culture imagery in relation to political behavior. For Roger Chartier, it was not Enlightenment ideas that moved the people, but rather political expediencies that forced them to heed the proposals of the political speakers: see *The Cultural Origins of the French Revolution,* trans. Lydia G. Cochrane (Raleigh-Durham, 1991).

The basic study of the formation and fortunes of the calendar—and consequently the festivals—across the entire revolutionary decade is James Friguglietti, "The Social and Religious Consequences of the Revolutionary Calendar" (Ph.D. diss., Harvard University, 1966): two generations of historians have wondered why the author never saw fit to publish this text. Of course, the book that has stood as the point of reference, fortunately because of its comprehensiveness and originality, and unfortunately because its theses are seldom contested, is Mona Ozouf, *Festivals and the French Revolution,* trans. Alan Sheridan (Cambridge, Mass., 1988). Readers who attempt Michel

Vovelle, *Les Métamorphoses de la fête en Provence de 1750 à 1820* (Paris, 1976) and *La Mentalité révolutionnaire: Société et mentalités sous la Révolution française* (Paris, 1985) will find an alternate presentation of the dynamics of the festivals. For a discussion of the festivals in the context of the government education program, see the already cited Emmet Kennedy, *A Cultural History of the French Revolution,* chap. 11.

As a guide to the religious sentiments of, and problems faced by, the population at large, the genuinely groundbreaking study of Suzanne Desan, *Reclaiming the Sacred: Lay Religion and Popular Politics in Revolutionary France* (Ithaca, 1990) remains in a class by itself. James A. Leith, *Space and Revolution: Projects for Monuments, Squares, and Public Buildings in France, 1789–1799* (Montreal, 1991) studies the architecture and some of the mechanics of the festival celebrations

The French government from 1795 through 1799, the Directory that presided over the failure of the festivals, becomes a stage in a more long-term development in Isser Woloch, *The New Regime: Transformations of the French Civic Order, 1789–1820s* (New York, 1994). It was immediately preceded by the post-Thermidorian (post-Robespierre) Convention, for which the question, "How to be done with the Terror?" developed into "How to end the Revolution?" according to Bronislaw Baczko, *Ending the Terror: The French Revolution after Robespierre,* trans. Michel Petheram (New York, 1994).

For the sake of comparison, see Sudhir Hazareesingh's study of festivals under the Second Empire, *The Saint Napoleon: Celebrations of Sovereignty in Nineteenth-Century France* (Cambridge, Mass., 2004).

CHAPTER 3

On the lives of Chateaubriand and Destutt de Tracy: Ghislain de Diesbach, *Chateaubriand: Poésie et terreur* (Paris, 1999) has written a valuable modern study, although readers may also consult George Painter, *Chateaubriand: A Biography* (London, 1977), whereas Emmet Kennedy, *A "Philosophe" in the Age of Revolution: Destutt de Tracy and the Origins of "Ideology"* (Philadelphia, 1978), even if it were not the only major study of Destutt de Tracy, would still be a likely candidate for the definitive biography.

Of course, for the study of the romanticisms in literature, several major bibliographies and journals provide keys to the extensive material. Those reading French intellectual history may benefit most from D. G. Charlton, "The French Romantic Movement," in *The French Romantics,* 2 vols. (Cambridge, 1984), 1:16–24, but those concerned more with social history should begin with James Smith Allen, *Popular French Romanticism: Authors, Readers, and Books in the Nineteenth Century* (Syracuse, 1981).

On the Idéologues, Martin S. Staum, *Minerva's Message: Stabilizing the French Revolution* (Montreal, 1996) offers full background on the Class of Moral and Political Sciences, Tracy's bailiwick, in the Institut de France. Brian W. Head, *Ideology and Social Science: Destutt de Tracy and French Liberalism* (Dordrecht, 1985) is more specific.

Intellectual and religious challenges to Napoleon's government, and to the emperor himself can be explored in a text that is the best popular "read, " as well as the best orientation to the scholarship on the Empire, of recent decades: Steven L. Englund, *Napoleon: A Political Life* (New York, 2003). Jacques-Olivier Boudon, *Histoire du Consulat et de l'Empire* (Paris, 2000) and any studies written or edited by Jean Tulard represent the best in Napoleonic scolarship in France.

PART II: DEFENSE

Guillaume de Bertier de Sauvigny, *The Bourbon Restoration,* trans. Lynn M. Case (Philadelphia, 1966) is the classic account, by a professor (and priest) whose aristocratic ancestor was one of the most famous early martyrs of the Revolution. Bertier de Sauvigny's other studies of the period are also vital, but readers will find that Geoffrey Cubitt, *The Jesuit Myth: Conspiracy Theory and Politics in Nineteenth-Century France* (Oxford, 1993) is as broad as its subtitle implies. That the historical foundation of "conspiracy" was more antagonism and self-defense (at times self-service) makes this work a crucial study of antagonisms growing deeper with each passing decade. See Robert Gildea, *The Past in French History* (New Haven, 1994), chap. 5, for the variety of Catholic memories of revolutionary persecution.

Any move toward openness on the part of French prelates was opposed by a conservative papacy and the quickly growing body of French bishops and priests who believed that they would benefit more from a Roman power base. Austin Gough, *Paris and Rome: The Gallican Church and the Ultramontane Campaign, 1848–1853* (Oxford, 1986) offers a detailed account of the tensions that could only be alleviated by a clerical united front against secular politics. Pope Pius IX inspired a fortress mentality that he had first defaulted into amidst the political and military crises of his reign. E. E. Y. Hales, *Pio Nono: A Study in European Politics and Religion in the Nineteenth Century* (New York, 1954) has become a classic study, and Maurice Agulhon, *The Republican Experiment, 1848–1852,* trans. Janet Lloyd (Cambridge, Mass., 1983), is a very helpful introduction to the dramatic central years of the nineteenth century.

For the subtleties of religious and political loyalties among Catholics—and others—during the reign of Napoleon III, see Sudhir Hazareesingh, *From Subject to Citizen: The Second Empire and the Emergence of Modern French Democracy* (Princeton, 1998). Jacques-Olivier Boudon, *Paris, capital religieuse sous le Second Empire* (Paris, 2001) studies the central church administration and its relation to Rome during this period

John McManners, *Church and State in France, 1870–1914* (New York, 1972) is a surprisingly close analysis of the events and personalities involved in that long period of alternating stress and dialogue, which finally evolved into détente with the coming of the war. Joseph Brugerette chronicled the principal instances of clerical opposition to governmental lèse-majesté in matters of religion in *Le Prêtre français et la société contemporaine,* 3 vols. (Paris, 1933–38), especially vols. 1 (*La Restauration catholique, 1815–1871*) and 2 (*Vers la Séparation, 1872–1905*). His study, *Le comte de Montlosier et son temps (1755–1838)* (Aurillac, 1931), portrays the leading anticlerical aristocrat of the preceding era, who was willing to erode his own power base in attacking the Jesuits.

Karen Offen, "French Women's History: Retrospect (1789–1940) and Prospect," *French Historical Studies* 26 (2003): 727–67 is an important review of historiographical problems and recent studies. On the increased role of women in nineteenth-century French Catholicism, see Claude Langlois, "Feminisation du catholicisme," in Jacques Le Goff, René Rémond, and Philippe Joutard, eds., *Histoire de la France religieuse,* vol. 3: *Du roi Très Chrétien à la laïcité républicaine.* The first section of Maurice Larkin, *Religion, Politics and Preferment in France since 1890: La Belle Epoque and Its Legacy* (New York, 1995) covers the last decade of "defense." Jan Goldstein, *Console and Classify: The French Psychiatric Profession in the Nineteenth Century* (New York, 1987) displays the turf disputes between secular psychologists and religious teachers and counselors.

For the place and role of Protestantism and Judaism in the Third Republic, see Philip Nord, *The Republican Moment: Struggles for Democracy in Nineteenth-Century France* (Cambridge, Mass., 1995), and for fresh and subtle look at the ideological divide that separated the two Frances, see Sudhir Hazareesingh, *Intellectual Founders of the Republic: Five Studies in Nineteenth-Century French Political Thought* (New York, 2001). But to give the defensive right the last word, check René Rémond, *The Right in France from 1815 to De Gaulle,* trans. James M. Laux (Philadelphia, 1969), a useful book by an esteemed and senior scholar.

CHAPTER 4

Thomas A. Kselman, *Miracles and Prophecies in Nineteenth-Century France* (New Brunswick, N.J., 1983) sets pilgrimage alongside other manifestations of intense religious experience and highlights the relation of all these phenomena to social and political life across the century. Of all the books in this bibliography, this is the one to read after, or in conjunction with, Ralph Gibson. For pilgrimage only, Mary Lee Nolan and Sidney Nolan, *Christian Pilgrimage in Modern Europe* (Chapel Hill, 1989) is a broad and basic introduction to the topic in English. For the commonalities and specifics on devotion to Mary the mother of Christ, see Sandra Zimdars-Swartz, *Encountering Mary: From La Salette to Medjugorje* (Princeton, 1991), and Barbara Corrado Pope, "Immaculate and Powerful: The Marian Revival in the Nineteenth Century," in C. W. Atkinson, C. H. Buchanan, and M. R. Miles, eds., *Immaculate and Powerful: The Female in Sacred Image and Social Reality* (Boston, 1985). Those who want to understand the rampant commercialism that surrounds the apparition shrines must read Suzanne K. Kaufman, *Consuming Visions: Mass Culture and the Lourdes Shrine* (Ithaca, 2004).

There are no current and useful historical studies of nineteenth-century pilgrimage or devotional life at Chartres, but the best guide to the art and architecture of the medieval cathedral is Émile Mâle, *Chartres,* trans. Sarah Wilson (New York, 1983). John James, *Chartres: The Masons Who Built a Legend* (Boston, 1982) is an introduction to the author's work on the specifics of construction.

Two recent studies of pilgrimage and devotion present church-state issues, theology, and a genuine but graceful interpretation of religious experience. Raymond A.

Jonas, *France and the Cult of the Sacred Heart: An Epic Tale for Modern Times* (Berkeley and Los Angeles, 2000), and Ruth Harris, *Lourdes: Body and Spirit in the Secular Age* (New York, 1999) offer sympathetic historical interpretations of the saints and sinners who believed themselves to be in contact with Christ and Mary. On the apparition of Mary at La Salette, most problematic of "apparitions" because of the personal ordinariness, if not mediocrity, of the visionaries, consult chap. 1 in the aforementioned Richard D. E. Burton, *Blood in the City.* David Blackbourn, *Marpingen: Apparitions of the Virgin Mary in Nineteenth-Century Germany* (New York, 1994) is a model study of the social, cultural, and especially political conditions that produced, and were subsequently affected by, visionaries and their supporters.

CHAPTER 5

Eugen Weber, *Peasants into Frenchmen: The Modernization of Rural France, 1970–1914* (Stanford, 1976) discusses the dynamics of language and religion in relation to national identity in several key chapters. I have already explained my debt to this foundation text. Caroline Ford, *Creating the Nation in Provincial France: Religion and Political Identity in Brittany* (Princeton, 1993) offers an alternative explanation—the church enabling local people to experience and express national loyalties.

The fundamental study of language as a tool of both church and state in France is Michel de Certeau, Dominique Julia, and Jacques Revel, *Une Politique de la langue: La Révolution française et les patois: L'Enquête de Grégoire* (Paris, 1975). Inasmuch as the catechizing of children in their own language was of vital church and educational interest, studies of religious and public education show some of the anxieties and goals of all involved. Sandra Horvath-Peterson, *Victor Duruy and French Education: Liberal Reform in the Second Empire* (Baton Rouge, 1984) is fundamental for understanding the national education programs that clergy were reacting to. Joan L. Coffey, "Of Catechisms and Sermons: Church-State Relations in France, 1890–1905," *Church History* 66 (1997): 54–66, is a model study that should be collected along with the author's studies of related church-state issues.

Both language and religion come into major play in two studies of social and economic development in the Roussillon, two studies of social and economic development in Alsace. For the prerevolutionary era in the Roussillon, there is Peter Sahlins, *Boundaries: The Making of France and Spain in the Pyrenees* (Berkeley and Los Angeles, 1989), and for the revolutionary era there is Peter McPhee, "Counter-Revolution in the Pyrenees: Spirituality, Class, and Ethnicity in the Haut-Vallespir, 1793–1794," *French History* 7 (1993). McPhee deals with these issues and surrounding regions in some of his book-length studies. For the nineteenth century in Alsace, see Stephen L. Harp, *Learning to be Loyal: Primary Schooling as Nation-Building in Alsace and Lorraine, 1850–1940* (Dekalb, 1998), and Anthony J. Steinhoff, "Protestants in Strasbourg, 1870–1914: Religion and Society in Late Nineteenth Century Europe" (Ph.D. diss., University of Chicago, 1996). Both Harp and Steinhoff have little to say about specifically Catholic identity, of course.

William Brustein, *The Social Origins of Political Regionalism: France, 1849–1981* (Berkeley and Los Angeles, 1988) will be helpful in sorting out the complex array of tensions that complicate linguistic loyalties.

PART III: DÉTENTE

Maurice Larkin, *Church and State After the Dreyfus Affair: The Separation Issue in France* (New York, 1974) is a clear report on the hostility that led to the formal separation of church and state. Surely the fullest account of the bizarre treason trial of a Jewish army officer that so agitated Catholic and secular France is Jean-Denis Bredin, *The Affair: The Case of Alfred Dreyfus*, trans. Jeffrey Mehlman (New York, 1986). The period is also brilliantly covered by John McManners in the second half of his *Church and State in France*. And see Larkin's *Religion, Politics, and Preferment in France Since 1890* for more on the preseparation era and a full report on later developments in the twentieth century.

A useful current biography of Cardinal Lavigerie, the pope's messenger of reconciliation with the Third Republic, is François Renault, *Cardinal Lavigerie: Churchman, Prophet, and Missionary, 1825–1892*, trans. John O. Donohue (Atlantic Heights, N.J., 1994). The text of Lavigerie's formal call to *ralliement* to the Republic and related documents can be found in Xavier de Montclos, *Le Toast d'Alger: Documents, 1890–1891* (Paris, 1966). For a full summary of the papal politics, alternately helpful and detrimental to détente, see Owen Chadwick, *History of the Popes, 1830–1914* (New York, 2003).

CHAPTER 6

Jean-Jacques Becker, *The Great War and the French People*, trans. Arnold Pomerans (New York, 1985) is the text that fundamentally altered our later twentieth-century perceptions of what World War I meant to the people of France. The essential texts on the specifically Catholic experience of war are obviously Jacques Fontana, *Les Catholiques français pendant la grande guerre* (Paris, 1990), and Annette Becker, *La Guerre et la foi: De la mort à la mémoire, 1914–1930* (Paris, 1994). Both await a translator at this writing.

Stéphane Audoin-Rouzeau, *Men at War, 1914–1918: National Sentiment and Trench Journalism in France During the First World War*, trans. Helen McPhail (New York, 1992) is an invaluable study, not only because it provides authentic soldier testimony, but because it offers the most useful set of models for sorting out the combatant identities as soldiers and citizens. Martha Hanna, *The Mobilization of Intellect: French Scholars and Writers During the Great War* (Cambridge, Mass., 1996) displays an array of cogent interpretations and subtle sensibilities, both those of combatants and those of noncombatants.

On the experience of being an *instituteur* across the last part of the defense and the entire détente era, see Jacques Ozouf and Mona Ozouf, *La République des instituteurs* (Paris, 1992). The Ozoufs have created a classic that offers statistics, experiences, and a virtually unassailable analysis of teachers caught between the two Frances in the Third Republic and between France and Germany in World War I.

CHAPTER 7

This chapter itself is the only study of Émile Mâle available in English and probably will remain such. Mâle's three great studies of medieval religious art have been published in beautiful Bollingen Series editions by Princeton University Press, *Religious Art in France, the Twelfth Century: A Study of the Origins of Medieval Iconography,* trans. Marthiel Matthews (1976), *Religious Art in France, the Thirteenth Century: A Study of Medieval Iconography and Its Sources,* trans. Marthiel Matthews (1984), and *Religious Art in France, the Late Middle Ages: A Study of Medieval Iconography and Its Sources,* trans. Marthiel Matthews (1986). Émile Mâle, *Souvenirs et correspondance de jeunesse: Bourbonnais-Forez-École Normale Supérieure* (Nonette, 2001), though done up by a small publisher in the provinces, is a sumptuous book of informal memoirs, letters, and images— official and family photos, Mâle's own early artistic efforts, and a full repertoire of illustrations of his travels in France and Italy.

The École Normale, France's greatest institution of higher learning of the period, prepared Mâle for his role of reconciler. Robert J. Smith, *The École Normale Supérieure and the Third Republic* (Albany, 1982) is clear and brief. Mâle was by profession a historian, and William R. Keylor, *Academy and Community: The Foundation of the French Historical Profession* (Cambridge, Mass., 1975) explains this professional setting. Mâle's first inspiration for the study of medieval art (architecture) was Eugène Viollet-le-Duc, presented in Kevin D. Murphy, *Memory and Modernity: Viollet-le-Duc at Vézeley* (University Park, Penn., 2000), a text complemented by a study of the medieval cathedral architecture in its own right, Alain Erlande-Brandenburg, *The Cathedral: The Social and Architectural Dynamics of Construction,* trans. Martin Thom (New York, 1994). Mâle's exhaustive readings in medieval Latin religious literature were made possible by the massive publication project of the abbé Jacques-Paul Migne, presented in the entertaining R. Howard Bloch, *God's Plagiarist: Being an Account of the Fabulous Industry and Irregular Commerce of the Abbé Migne* (Chicago, 1994). In *Piety and Politics: Catholic Revival and the Generation of 1950–1914* (New York, 1987), Paul M. Cohen discusses religious practice at the École Normale and other institutions in the decade before World War I.

There were other approaches to medieval life and literature that paralleled Mâle's, but these were motivated by different goals. Gerald A. McCool, *The Neo-Thomists* (Milwaukee, 1994) is an accessible study of the revival of medieval philosophy as part of Catholic seminary renewal, and Janine R. Dakyns, *The Middle Ages in French Literature, 1851–1900* (Oxford, 1973) presents the "use" made of the Middle Ages for literary and artistic effect in modern French literature.

Finally, for a full look at the tensions created by France's republican governments, see Maurice Agulhon, *The French Republic, 1879–1992,* trans. Antonia Nevill (Cambridge, Mass., 1992), and Jean-Marie Mayeur and Madeleine Rebérioux, *The Third Republic from Its Origins to the Great War, 1871–1914,* trans. J. R. Foster (New York, 1984).

EPILOGUE

W. D. Halls, *Politics, Society and Christianity in Vichy France* (Providence, R. I., 1995) is the primary guide to the political and religious drama of the Vichy years. on the roles of Catholic politician and administrators, the previously cited Maurice Larkin, *Religion, Politics and Preferment in France Since 1890* is invaluable. The dean of Vichy studies is Robert O. Paxton, and his *Vichy France, 1949–1944: Old Guard and New Order* (New York, 1972) is required reading for all of us. Julian Jackson, *France: The Dark Years, 1940–1944* (New York, 2001) is the great recent study of the era, to be complemented by a remarkable re-creation of the banality and beauty of ordinary French lives at that time: Robert Gildea, *Marianne in Chains: Daily Life in the Heart of France During the German Occupation* (New York, 2002). The leading French scholar on Vichy is Jean-Pierre Azéma, and readers may begin with *From Munich to the Liberation, 1938–1944,* trans. Janet Lloyd (Cambridge, 1984).

Given the extent to which religious identity is a function of protofascist or socialist/communist partis pris, the politics of the twenties and thirties are vital subjects here. It is important, then, to consult, Eugene Weber, *The Hollow Years: France in the 1930s* (New York, 1994), which presents both left and right as part of the larger story, and then Robert Soucy, *French Fascism: The First Wave, 1924–1933* (New Haven, 1986) for a look at the surprising, earlier rise of the right. A classic biography of a central political figure of the twenties and thirties is Joel Colton, *Léon Blum: Humanist in Politics* (New York, 1966), but the more radical postwar return to Marxism among French university types is presented in the lively and graceful Tony Judt, *Past Imperfect: French Intellectuals, 1944–1956* (Berkeley and Los Angeles, 1992).

Finally, although ranging over four centuries and not just four generations, Norman Ravitch, *The Catholic Church and the French Nation, 1589–1989* (New York, 1990) is a historical essay that with honesty and erudition evaluates the role of the Catholic church—on its own terms—in French dynastic and national life.

Index

Page references in *italics* indicate illustrations and photographs.